MW01259593

"With extensive research, Rimi Xhemajli provides important insight into one of the most fascinating and underserved topics in the history of Methodism and the period of the Second Great Awakening. This study, which provides valuable background for issues still alive in today's church, will be of great interest for students of both US religious history and modern religious experience."
　　—CRAIG S. KEENER, Asbury Theological Seminary

"Although historians have long known about Methodist 'enthusiasm,' Rimi Xhemajli has gone well beyond earlier work in documenting the centrality of supernatural phenomena among Methodist circuit riders in the United States' early history. With thorough research in the works of the circuit riders themselves, this book shows the utterly pervasive presence of dreams, visions, angelic appearances, healings, exorcisms, power encounters with evil powers, extraordinary appearances of fire, wind, and light, slayings in the Spirit, and more. The book offers a needed historical corrective, but also a challenge for contemporary churches to learn from what has gone before."
　　—MARK NOLL, author of *The Rise of Evangelicalism*

"How does one explain the growth of Methodism in America to the point where it became the largest Protestant denomination in America by the mid-1800s? The Methodist theology of grace? The preaching ability of the circuit riders? Their targeting the poor and lower classes? Their organizational ability and class meetings? In his thorough research, Dr. Xhemajli shows that the American Methodist circuit riders themselves did not attribute that explosive growth to any of these factors . . . but to the supernatural power of God—the power of God that the circuit riders experienced in their personal lives and the power of God that broke out in their public ministries. When manifestations of the Spirit's power show up among Methodists today, often the accusation is made that such phenomena are Pentecostal, not Methodist. But Dr. Xhemajli shows these phenomena were Methodist 150 years before there were any Pentecostals!"
　　—FRANK H. BILLMAN, author of *The Supernatural Thread
　　in Methodism*

"One hundred fifty years of religious and cultural ascendency have led many to believe Methodism to be among the 'safest' of religious traditions, about as exciting as a four-door family sedan or the overabundance of green bean casseroles at a church potluck. Thanks to Rimi Xhemajli we can see this is a gross misconception. By highlighting the interest in the supernatural among early Methodist preachers, Xhemajli shows how spiritually dynamic—and effective—this tradition's roots are. Among religious traditions, early Methodism was closer to a souped-up sports car or a red hot chili pepper."

—LESTER RUTH, Duke Divinity School

"Through examining the accounts of the circuit riders themselves, Xhemajli shows that the presence and power of the Holy Spirit pervaded their ministries. He persuasively argues that the supernatural was not incidental to their work but essential, raising serious questions for contemporary Methodism in America. I hope this book will be widely read and deeply pondered."

—HENRY H. KNIGHT III, Saint Paul School of Theology,
Leawood, Kansas

THE SUPERNATURAL
AND THE CIRCUIT RIDERS

The SUPERNATURAL *and the* CIRCUIT RIDERS

The Rise of Early American Methodism

Rimi Xhemajli

FOREWORD BY
Allan H. Anderson

☞PICKWICK *Publications* • Eugene, Oregon

THE SUPERNATURAL AND THE CIRCUIT RIDERS
The Rise of Early American Methodism

Pickwick Publications
An Imprint of Wipf and Stock Publishers
199 W. 8th Ave., Suite 3
Eugene, OR 97401

www.wipfandstock.com

PAPERBACK ISBN: 978-1-7252-6921-7
HARDCOVER ISBN: 978-1-7252-6920-0
EBOOK ISBN: 978-1-7252-6922-4

Cataloguing-in-Publication data:

Names: Xhemajli, Rimi, author. | Anderson, Allan H., foreword.

Title: The supernatural and the circuit riders : the rise of early American Methodism / Rimi Xhemajli ; with a foreword by Allan H. Anderson.

Description: Eugene, OR : Pickwick Publications, 2021 | Includes bibliographical references and index.

Identifiers: ISBN 978-1-7252-6921-7 (paperback) | ISBN 978-1-7252-6920-0 (hardcover) | ISBN 978-1-7252-6922-4 (ebook)

Subjects: LCSH: Methodism. | United States. | Methodist Church. | Supernatural.

Classification: BX8236 .X44 2021 (print) | BX8236 .X44 (ebook)

Dedication

For Rachel, Anna, and Peter

Table of Contents

Foreword

IT WAS MY PRIVILEGE to supervise Adhurim (Rimi) Xhemajli's doctoral research at the University of Birmingham, completed in 2019, and on which he has based this book. This study is important, not least because Xhemajli is the first to investigate specifically the role and impact of the supernatural in the ministry of the early American Methodist preachers in the late eighteenth and early nineteenth centuries. These preachers, known as "circuit riders," operated in the years following the American colonies' break with Britain in 1776, and for this and other reasons followed a quite different trajectory from that of the British Methodists. It could be said that early Methodism in the United States was much more revivalist, and that while British Methodism was establishing itself organisationally and undergoing a time of routinization, American Methodism was expanding in areas untouched by Christianity and using methods uniquely suited to these frontier areas. The result was rapid growth. The circuit-riders' task was to evangelize the American western frontier, and they did this by following what they saw as essential to Wesleyan Methodism, a keen experiential sense of the miraculous, or what the author terms the "supernatural." The Holy Spirit was the source of this new experiential religion, one exceptionally suited to the ravages and hardships of people eking out an existence on the frontier.

This book introduces us to these remarkable preachers and their lifelong mission. It is an in-depth investigation of how the circuit riders identified with a supernatural ministry and understood this to be a manifestation of the power and presence of the Spirit of God. Xhemajli has spent many years researching the stories of these preachers, especially through meticulously examining their own accounts in journals and letters, and those of their contemporaries. As a result, he is able to write with authoritative precision from these archives and auto/biographies. He demonstrates how as a result of the supernatural displays of God's power, Methodism rapidly expanded to become the largest denomination in the United States by the mid-nineteenth century.

From my perspective as a scholar of Pentecostalism, this study is also significant because of early Methodism's role in the Protestant revival movements from which modern Pentecostalism emerged, specifically in the nineteenth-century Holiness movement. The Pietist movement in seventeenth- and eighteenth-century Lutheranism stressed the importance of a personal, supernatural experience of God through the Holy Spirit, sometimes called "new birth," over and above what they saw as mere head knowledge of Christianity. Pietism, which also drew inspiration from Catholic mysticism, gave emphasis to the importance of emotion in Christian experience and encouraged a personal relationship with God. It encouraged the working of the Spirit to bring about a changed, morally ascetic Christian life separated from "the world." The Moravian movement of Count Nicolaus von Zinzendorf (1700–1760) and his community at Herrnhut was a Pietist movement, and had a profound effect upon John Wesley and the early Methodist revival. Wesley's contact in the British colony of Georgia with Moravian missionaries who challenged him about his personal experience of Christ during his return voyage to England, led him to his Aldersgate conversion experience in 1738 when he felt his "heart strangely warmed."

There were many similarities between German Pietism and early Methodism, which indeed we could describe as both "pietist" and "evangelical." The author shows how there were unusual manifestations of the Spirit in the ministries of the American circuit riders. Wesley himself had said that the gifts of the Spirit had been withdrawn when dry, formal men had begun to ridicule them, and that these gifts had returned to some of his fellow Methodists. Xhemajli confirms how Wesley himself believed in the supernatural and experienced this in his ministry, which influenced the American circuit riders, perhaps above all their most well-known leader, Francis Asbury. Wesley's doctrine of entire sanctification and the possibility of spiritual experiences subsequent to conversion undoubtedly influenced these early American preachers, as the author of this book shows. These also ignited the Holiness movement and its later offspring Pentecostalism. As too often happens with revival movements, schism follows, but most of this occurs after the period discussed in this book. Eventually a polarization arose within Methodism between those who believed fervently in Wesley's experiential religion with its "Christian perfection" teaching and those who did not. The former subsequently formed the Holiness movement, which eventually seceded from mainstream Methodism, while the latter remained in it.

Evangelical Protestantism, especially of the Methodist variety, became the dominant subculture in the USA in the nineteenth century and still exerts a profound influence on American life and culture. American Methodism was the frontier religion par excellence. It stressed personal freedom and allowed the emotional and "supernatural" element of popular religion, and extended its offer of religious power and autonomy to marginalised women, to African American slaves, and to the poor and dispossessed as a whole. Central chapters in this book explore how the concept of the supernatural permeated both the private and the public experiences of the circuit riding preachers. The supernatural governed every aspect of their lives: their religious conversions, their calling to the ministry, their evangelistic strategies, and even the hardships and opposition they encountered. There was also a public manifestation of supernatural activity in their revival meetings and other forms of pastoral and public ministry. These manifestations were all considered evidence of the immediate power and presence of God's Spirit.

In investigating the significance of the supernatural in the circuit riders' ministry, Xhemajli constructs a theology of the "supernatural" by discerning specific patterns in the circuit riders' use of this and similar terms to describe their experiences. He not only investigates the impact of these supernatural experiences on the preachers themselves, but also the impact on their audiences. As a result, the author presents a fresh historical perspective on how the supernatural experiences of the circuit riders and their audiences contributed to the sudden expansion of early American Methodism. The closing chapters of the book argue for a direct link between the supernatural and this expansion, especially through an analysis of Methodist camp-meetings and other revival meetings. Clearly, both the circuit riders themselves believed that the presence of supernatural acts contributed to the growth of American Methodism, and the author makes a convincing argument in support.

There have been many other studies on early American Methodism, but what is distinctive about this one is its focus on the phenomenon and role of the supernatural in this movement. To my knowledge, this has not been done before, and yet it is so important for us to understand the context of Methodist revivalism. As a result, the reader will have a much fuller picture of what is one of America's most influential religious movements, and the precursor of what we usually understand as "Evan-gelicalism" and "Pentecostalism" today. I commend this fascinating study to you wholeheartedly, in the belief that it will open up untold informa-tion and perspectives on one of the greatest Christian revival movements of the modern age. The implied conviction of the author of this book is that for Methodism to halt its serious decline, it needs to return to its roots and once again demonstrate the power of God in a ministry of the supernatural.

Allan H. Anderson

Acknowledgments

THIS PROJECT WAS CERTAINLY a labor of love, and I will always be grateful for the educational, theological, and personal paths it took me down. The road had some bumps (long nights and serious headaches), and every time, there were some remarkable people there to get me through. For that, I will always be grateful.

That being said, I want to first and foremost acknowledge my wife Rachel—my friend, my partner, and the love of my life. I could not achieve this work (or any other work) without your daily support and insight. So, from the bottom of my heart: thank you. I want to also acknowledge my two wonderful children. Anna and Peter, may I always be a godly and faithful example to you; I love you both with all that I am. Finally, to the rest of my family, especially my parents (both sets!): thank you for being there for me and believing in me.

I want to thank Dr. Allan Anderson for his invaluable supervision, encouragement, and friendship. Allan, in so many ways, this project needed you to become a reality. Also, to Prof. Bill Burtness: thank you for always following Christ and leading others to do the same. It all began with you.

I want to thank the many Methodist and Wesleyan historians, colleagues, and friends who have supported and encouraged me throughout this investigation. Serving with all of you has been a privilege. And a heart-felt thank you to my many Pentecostal and Charismatic brothers and sisters (especially at the Assemblies of God and YWAM); your input in this undertaking has been eye opening.

Lastly, though most importantly, I want to acknowledge and honor the One who makes all things possible . . . *Soli Deo Gloria.*

Introduction

UNTIL THE END OF 2019, for a period of five years, I served in the United Methodist Church (UMC) and was a member of the UMC clergy. During that time, I became heavily engaged in discovering the legacy, history, and spiritual formation of Methodism as well as what made the movement so extensive. Even long before this, especially during my graduate education (MA, MDiv, and later PhD), I became specifically acquainted with the celebrated success and historical significance of the circuit rider ministry. I also began to discover the significance of the supernatural, at least as the ministry understood it, and the role it appeared to play in Methodist revivals. I was surprised to learn that very little past research had been conducted on the subject.

Truly, it is extraordinary that the supernatural has not been researched in detail as its prevalence and significance, upon reading circuit rider journals, is undeniable. It is my understanding that the reason why very little research (academic or public) has been conducted on this matter is because most historians and scholars have interpreted the supernaturalism present in early Methodism as insignificant.[1] In other words, there seems to have been an apparent sidestepping or historical bias against the nature of supernaturalism in these ministries. To quote the scholar Ann Taves, "Methodist historians [want] to downplay the role of these [manifestations] in the Methodist ministry . . . but in fact [the

1. I later found support for my theory in turning to Methodist scholar Frank Billman's book. In response to this dilemma, Billman explained that when he took graduate Methodist history classes, he also wondered why he did not learn "anything about the supernatural manifestations of the power of God that took place in Wesley's ministry and the ministry of many other early American Methodists." The answer, he claimed, was "bias by the historian." If the historian did not believe in the supernatural or believed that Wesley and the early Methodists were merely superstitious in that regard, then these facts would be omitted from their histories. For more information, see Billman, *Supernatural Thread in Methodism*, 33–34.

phenomena] continued for decades," especially between the 1770s and 1830s.[2]

In light of this, one of the primary goals of my work has been to factually reintroduce the circuit rider ministry and its supernaturalism by demonstrating the clearly significant effect that it had on the movement and its expansion.[3] The circuit riders themselves expressed that the supernatural was a critical component in early Methodism and played a large part in propelling it. By focusing on primary sources and juxtaposing them with secondary sources (especially in regard to supernatural interpretations and Methodist expansion), this book has sought to accurately rediscover and draw attention to the circuit riders and their ministry's corresponding supernatural acts derived from "the power and presence of God."[4] While the ministerial dedication of the circuit riders in evangelism has long been discussed and admired by historians and theologians (who commonly cite this dedication, along with their countercultural positions and evangelistic strategies, as the cause of their booming ministry),[5] it is my desire for both the academic and public world to obtain a fuller and clearer picture of the history and theology behind the circuit rider ministry, which is largely regarded as one of America's most influential Christian phenomena.[6]

Another major motivation in undertaking this research stems from my personal exposure to supernatural phenomena. Growing up in Kosovo, many locals, including my own parents, practiced various rituals and spells in order to manipulate the spirit world and experience a supernatural result or desired benefit. Following the devastation

2. Taves, *Fits, Trances, and Visions*, 57.

3. See Wakeley and Boehm, *Patriarch of One Hundred Years*, 21.

4. Finley, *Sketches of Western Methodism*, 60.

5. For instance, see Watson, *Class Meeting*, 19–30; Turner, "Redeeming the Time," 148, 224–25; Richey, *Methodism in the American Forest*, 6–7, 26–27, 63–64; Ruth, *Early Methodist Life and Spirituality*, 7, 161–89; *Little Heaven Below*, 186–88, 209–22; Hempton, *Methodism*, 5, 30–33, 41–47, 140, 201; O'Byrne, "How Methodists Were Made," 8–11, 213–50; Sargant, *Battle for the Mind*, xx, 106–7, 220–21, 225; Hatch, *Democratization of American Christianity*, 40, 89, 140; Billman, *Supernatural Thread in Methodism*, 43–44; Wigger, "Fighting Bees," 93–95, 105–7; *Taking Heaven by Storm*, 4–20.

6. See Wakeley, *Heroes of Methodism*, iii–iv; Powell, "Methodist Circuit Riders in America," 30; Findling and Thackeray, *Eighteenth Century*, 8; Hardman, *Seasons of Refreshing*, 122; Bainbridge, *Sociology of Religious Movements*, 72; Bloesch, *Reform of the Church*, 107; Billman, *Supernatural Thread in Methodism*, 33–34.

of war and death in my country (and family), I left the Muslim faith I was raised under and became an atheist. A divine encounter with Jesus Christ then led me to both my Christian conversion and ministry. So, as supernatural events were familiar to me, it was unsurprising to learn of the supernatural events found within the circuit rider ministry; however, what was surprising to me was the fact that the truth regarding the ministry (and its supernatural component) appeared to be disregarded by historians who did not consider or understand it.

I would also like to point out that early Methodism, with its supernatural component, played a major role in sparking and maintaining the Second Great Awakening (dating roughly from the 1790s to 1840s) that rocked America to its core, redefining religious expression and its place in society. So, when you are reading about the nature and effect of the supernatural in early Methodism, you are also largely reading about the nature and effect of the supernatural in the Second Great Awakening as, again, the circuit rider ministry was a massive engine behind this Awakening. As such, while this book peels away the layers of early Methodism, it peels away the layers of the Second Great Awakening, in turn.

In addition to early Methodism being a pivotal part of the Second Great Awakening, it was through early Methodism that the Holiness movement emerged, which gave birth to several new denominations such as the Wesleyan Church and the Nazarene Church. Beyond this, American Pentecostalism also initially "emerged from the Wesleyan [or early Methodism] tradition" and resulted in the creation of a number of Pentecostal and Charismatic denominations, such as the Assemblies of God.[7] Chapter 8 further explores and verifies the idea that "Pentecostalism is primitive [or early] Methodism's extended incarnation."[8] This realization, then, throws quite a light on the importance of understanding and studying the theology and practices of the circuit rider ministry and the impact that it had on American Christianity.

Indeed, it is my belief that conclusions reached concerning the correlation between the supernatural and the circuit rider ministry will benefit historians and theologians as well as the modern Christian church because this research unearths a lost and vital facet of the circuit rider ministry and challenges the public to consider the relevance of

7. Synan, *Holiness-Pentecostal Tradition*, 358.

8. Bruner, *Theology of the Holy Spirit*, 37.

supernatural acts in the church today. It also powerfully illustrates the effects of believing and participating in the supernatural power of God and the way in which revivals can be achieved locally and nationwide through such belief and participation. Armed with this new knowledge, it is my hope that, just as the circuit riders fanned the flame of the Second Great Awakening, so our generation, in reviving the circuit rider legacy, can witness the rise of yet another Great Awakening.

Synopsis

This book contains two parts. Part One consists of chapters 1–3; it provides a comprehensive definition and explanation of the supernatural as well as historical background and information on Methodism's humble beginnings. Part Two consists of chapters 4–8; it is the heart of the book and investigates (first) the role of the supernatural in the lives of the circuit riders and their ministry and (second) the part that the supernatural ultimately played in the rise of early American Methodism. Each chapter ends with a wrap up in order to cut a clear path through the material. In chapters 1–3, this comes in the form of a brief summary. In chapters 4–7, this comes in the form of concluding comments that, in addition to providing a brief summary, provide an in-depth analysis of the chapter's material. A further breakdown of the book is as follows:

- Chapter 1 defines the term *supernatural* (compared to *natural*) and explores it in both a historical and modern context. The chapter also provides an in-depth investigation of the circuit riders' identification and understanding of the term, specifically regarding its relationship to the *power and presence* of God's Spirit.

- Chapter 2 features Wesley, the founder of Methodism and the first English circuit rider.[9] It emphasizes his belief in and practice of the supernatural, which he passed on to the American circuit rider ministry.

- Chapter 3 is devoted to describing the early historical development of the circuit rider ministry in America. It also includes (in-text or footnoted) biographical introductions to the circuit riders featured in this work (including Asbury).

9. See also Woodburn, *Indiana Magazine of History*, 124.

- Chapter 4 focuses on researching the supernatural within the private lives of the circuit riders and unearthing the role that the supernatural held in their personal religious conversions as well as their ministerial callings, evangelistic strategies, and ministerial hardships; it also researches spiritual warfare and the affect it had on the circuit riders' lives.

- Chapter 5 is dedicated to analyzing public supernaturalism. It features documented public manifestations of the power and presence of God, followed by a comprehensive investigation of the circuit riders' understanding of and response to their ministry's commonly experienced supernatural phenomena (being slain in the Spirit, enthusiastic emotional expressions, dreams, visions, trances, exorcisms, healings, the raising of the dead, and divine weather shifts).[10]

- Chapter 6 is designated to further investigating public criticism of the ministry's supernatural manifestations (often dubbed *religious enthusiasm* by the public) as well as the circuit riders' own thoughts on the controversial topic of religious enthusiasm.[11]

- Chapter 7 investigates the correlation between the supernatural and the growth of Methodism in America.[12] This investigation is primarily conducted through the analysis of Methodist camp meetings and other revivals, which often included supernatural events; the characteristics of Methodist revivals (and their connection with the Second Great Awakening) are also discussed at length. Ultimately, this chapter demonstrates the impact that the supernatural had on the ministry's growth and answers the question of whether the circuit riders believed that the presence of supernatural acts contributed to Methodist expansion.[13]

- Chapter 8 concludes the (above) outlined investigation and its corresponding research while also reconnecting it with the relevance of this investigation.

10. See also Jackson, *Lives of Early Methodist Preachers*, 6:169.

11. See also Lyles, *Methodism Mocked*, 33; Swift, *Religion and the American Experience*, 48; Lawrence, *One Family Under God*, 101–2.

12. See also Kirby et al., *Methodists*, 177.

13. See also Whedon, "Methodism in the Cities of the United States," 497; Hempton, *Methodism*, 183.

Part I

The Definition of the Supernatural and the Beginnings of Early American Methodism

Chapter 1

The Supernatural: Laying the Framework

THE CIRCUIT RIDERS WERE ministers who traveled tirelessly on horseback throughout their circuits and districts with the goal of evangelizing the American frontier. They were part of the mission strategy of Wesleyan Methodism (founded by evangelist John Wesley), called and commissioned to spread the gospel. Beginning in the early 1770s with only ten official preachers, the number of circuit riders increased so rapidly that, in 1784, the circuit riders became the key figures in forming their own American denomination, the Methodist Episcopal Church (MEC).[1] This increase continued to the point that, by the 1830s, the MEC had become the largest American denomination.[2]

According to Wigger, a prominent scholar of early American Methodism, Francis Asbury, "the real founder of American Methodism,"[3] attributed the "lifeblood of the [Methodist or circuit rider] movement"[4] to the presence of the supernatural. Bearing that in mind, this book has been written in order to uncover the clear significance—the role and impact—of the supernatural in the early American Methodist circuit rider ministry (from the 1770s through the 1830s), specifically

---

1. Tigert, *Constitutional History of American Episcopal Methodism*, 516. For more information regarding this matter, see chapter 3.

2. Garnett and Matthew, *Revival and Religion Since 1700*, 127; Kirby et al., *Methodists*, 177.

3. Duren, *Francis Asbury*, 164.

4. Wigger, *Taking Heaven by Storm*, 112.

its significance within the lives of the individual circuit riders and their audience members as well as, ultimately, their ministry's growth.[5]

In order to investigate the role of the supernatural, it is important to first investigate the definition of the supernatural and to discuss the circuit riders' viewpoint along with their understanding of supernatural incidents. This chapter is devoted to such an investigation. Attention is also placed on the circuit riders' distinction between *supernatural* and *natural*.

To begin, according to the *Oxford English Dictionary*, the term *supernatural* is defined as "a manifestation or event attributed to some force beyond scientific understanding or the laws of nature."[6] Similarly, the *Cambridge Dictionary* defines *supernatural* as a "force or event" that "cannot be explained by science."[7] In general, for the circuit riders, this "force" that brought about unexplainable events was identified as the Triune Christian God (consisting of the Father, Son, and Holy Spirit), whom the circuit riders served and proclaimed.[8] Specifically, acts that were believed to originate from "the operations of the Holy Spirit"[9] (or, at times, demonic beings) were, for the circuit riders, considered to be supernatural.[10] O'Byrne confirmed that, similar to the modern understanding of the term *supernatural*, the circuit riders understood that supernatural incidents generated events that were otherwise considered "physically impossible."[11] Circuit rider Dow declared that these events could not be explained because a "supernatural" event is a performance or manifestation of God, the "eternal being that is everywhere present," and is, thus, beyond the seen and explainable world.[12] Furthermore, the specific phrase *power and presence* of God was often used throughout

5. While the circuit rider ministry continued to a lesser degree up to the 1860s, this study focuses on the height of their ministry (up to the 1830s).

6. "Supernatural" (*OED*).

7. "Supernatural" (*CED*).

8. For more information regarding Methodist beliefs of the Trinity, see Willimon, *United Methodist Beliefs*, 5–6.

9. Asbury, *Journal of the Rev. Francis Asbury*, 1:232.

10. For instance, see Asbury, *Journal of the Rev. Francis Asbury*, 2:53, 180; Billman, *Supernatural Thread in Methodism*, 53–56, 62–67, 78; Doles, *Miracles & Manifestations*, 197, 218; Frank, "Methodism's Polity," 314. Some supernatural occurrences were attributed to witchcraft and demons. For more information, see chapters 4–5.

11. O'Byrne, "How Methodists Were Made," 76.

12. Dow, *History of Cosmopolite*, 351. See also Dougherty, *Logic of Religion*, 76. At the same time, the Bible explains in John 4:24 that "God is spirit."

circuit rider documents and was employed by the circuit riders to communicate the idea that God's Spirit was in their midst and in the process of performing a supernatural act;[13] a comprehensive study of the phrase is featured later in this chapter.

The Supernatural: Laying the Framework

Before directly investigating the definition and concept of the *supernatural* from a circuit rider perspective, the term should first be considered more broadly; therefore, this section features an in-depth word analysis, followed by a breakdown of both the historical and modern usage as well as statistics surrounding the term.

The Supernatural: An In-Depth Definition

The term *supernatural* derived from medieval scholars of the fifteenth century. During that time, the Latin word *supernaturalis* was used to refer to forces or entities outside of physical nature that could suspend, alter, or bypass physical/natural forces.[14] In other words, the term *supernatural* can be understood as an event or force that surpasses all of the known logical, natural laws.[15] Because it surpasses the natural, along with its physical laws and reason, it is called *super*-natural—superior to the natural.[16] Hence, supernatural phenomena have no limit and are not controlled by the laws of nature. These phenomena can be manifested as invisible or visible.[17] When they occur, they have the power to change things in the natural that normally would not be possible.[18]

13. Lee, *Short History of the Methodists*, 285; Jackson, *Lives of Early Methodist Preachers*, 6:169.

14. Stark, *Exploring the Religious Life*, 10.

15. Kapic and McCormack, *Mapping Modern Theology*, 158.

16. Newman et al., *Tracts for the Times*, 14; Grant and Godwin, *Rescue of Faith*, 87; Alcott, *Words of Power*, 32–33; *Zion's Home Monthly*, 138; Ruickbie, *Brief Guide to the Supernatural*, 107–58; Hayes, *Miracles*; Stinson, "Finite Supernatural," 328; Wesley, *Explanatory Notes upon the New Testament*, 433–35; "Nature" (*OED*); Warkulwiz, *Compendium of the Doctrines of Genesis 1–11*, 82.

17. For more information, see Platt, *Philosophy of the Supernatural*, 13–19.

18. For similar and slightly different interpretations, see Newman et al., *Tracts for the Times*, 14; Grant and Godwin, *Rescue of Faith*, 87; Alcott, *Words of Power*, 32–33; *Zion's Home Monthly*, 138; Ruickbie, *Brief Guide to the Supernatural*, 107–58; Hayes, *Miracles*.

Supernatural power comes from a spiritual, unseen realm (such as is found in the realm of God, angels, and demons).[19] It is believed that everything natural has been created through "a supernatural intelligent" realm;[20] therefore, the natural realm does not have the power or the means to make any changes in the supernatural realm.[21] Supernatural power is only displayed in the natural realm by the will of a supernatural being, such as the will of God or other spiritual beings (angels, demons, etc.).

However, the supernatural can also merge with the natural through human agency such as in times of prayer[22] and intercession.[23] For example, circuit rider Abbott recorded a testimony in which "people on the circuit fell like dead men. [He] preached, and [they] had a powerful time, many were cut to the heart, some fell to the floor."[24] Abbott testified that, during his circuit preaching, he became an agent or intermediary of God's supernatural presence flowing into his audience. God's supernatural presence caused the natural realm to be altered, and some of Abbott's audience members were so emotionally and physically influenced by the divine presence that they fell to the ground "and lay as if they were [dead people]."[25] Thus, the natural force (Abbott and the audience) was subject (and receptive) to a supernatural force (God).

The Supernatural: A Brief History

Since a large part of the current world's population is working to glean and advance scientific, natural, and mathematic explanations for reality, the supernatural perspective is widely alienated, often disputed or deemed

19. Lindbeck, *Elijah and the Rabbis*, 15–17.

20. Sober, "Intelligent Design," 445. Colossians 1:16 states: "For through him God created everything in the heavenly realms and on earth. He made the things we can see and the things we can't see—such as thrones, kingdoms, rulers, and authorities in the unseen world. Everything was created through him and for him." Hebrews 11:3 states: "By faith we understand that the universe was formed at God's command, so that what is seen was not made out of what was visible."

21. Matthews, *International Handbook of Research in History*, 1812.

22. For a brief introduction to the meaning of prayer, see "Prayer" (*EBO*).

23. For a brief introduction to prayer as intercession, see Plater, *Intercession*, 29–46.

24. Abbott and Ffirth, *Experience and Gospel Labours*, 95.

25. Abbott and Ffirth, *Experience and Gospel Labours of the Rev. Benjamin*, 209. For more information regarding the phenomenon of falling down or being slain in the Spirit, see chapter 5.

irrelevant.[26] In fact, taking suspicion of the supernatural one step further, A. Newton argued in his dissertation that religious supernaturalism is used to control people.[27]

As further discussed in chapter 2, this skepticism of the supernatural principally dates back to the Age of Enlightenment (predominantly eighteenth century). Prior to the Age of Enlightenment, within Christendom, people were much more receptive to the belief in and practice of the supernatural.[28] In general, thinkers and philosophers of the Age of Enlightenment, however, considered belief in supernatural acts to be primitive and superstitious and, therefore, useless to the world.[29] The hope of this worldview was (and still is) that, one day, all of the supposed supernatural activities would be explained by reason or science.[30] This skepticism of supernatural acts was also reflected in the Early American Republic's newspapers, such as *The Universalist Watchman*; for example, in 1812 this newspaper echoed popular belief by stating that the "enlightened age [had] pronounced all supernatural appearances to be nothing more than vagaries of the imagination."[31] Furthermore, some, such as Weatherly, tried to encourage and teach the public "to look to natural causation as the origin of supernatural seemings" through the use of logical arguments and scientific facts.[32]

During the late seventeenth and eighteenth centuries, the Christian church began to be affected by the Enlightenment's rationalism, slowly adopting the view that Christian supernaturalism was simply "superstitious material and [instead chose to] focus purely on 'natural religion.'"[33] For example, Tillotson (1630–1694), the Archbishop of Canterbury from 1691 to 1694, explored the Bible through the use of reason and the

26. Coon et al., *That Gentle Strength*, 300; Escobar, *New Global Mission*, 72–74; Escultura, *Scientific Natural Philosophy*, 7–8.

27. Taylor, "Is Religion 'Just' Supernatural Agency," ii–iii.

28. See also Birx, *Twenty-First-Century Anthropology*, 1:465.

29. See "Supernaturalism" (*EBO*). Due to the importance of the Age of Enlightenment in relation to early Methodism (Wesley and the American circuit riders), it is further discussed in chapter 2.

30. Visala, *Naturalism, Theism and the Cognitive Study of Religion*, 168.

31. Ballou, "Marvelous Story," 1.

32. Weatherly and Maskelyne, *Supernatural*, 8. See also Beville, *Preaching Christ in a Postmodern Culture*, 23.

33. Hodges, *Securing America's Covenant with God*, 82–83.

senses in order to extract its "perfect . . . moral and natural laws."[34] Toland (1670–1722), in his controversial books *Christianity Not Mysterious* and *Tetradymus*, disputed the supernatural origins of biblical "miracles" and endeavored to explain them through rational arguments; he further declared that the authors of the Bible "intended" their readers to understand that these miracles were not supernatural but, rather, natural phenomena.[35] Tindal (1657–1733), the son of a minister, became famous following his book *Christianity as Old as the Creation*, which aimed to completely remove supernaturalism from Christianity and focused on "pure religion" that was free from primitive "priestcraft and superstition."[36]

During the nineteenth century, due to the lingering effects of the Enlightenment throughout Europe, rationalism shaped and brought about a new theological perspective of anti-supernaturalism. This anti-supernatural view began to have its effects on Protestantism (beginning in Europe and spreading to America). Prominent Presbyterian theologian Warfield (1851–1921) was largely influential in expanding this theological perspective. Warfield's book *Counterfeit Miracles* was written in order to advocate the notion that the gifts of the Spirit and the occurrences of supernatural wonders or "charismata ceased with the Apostolic age." Warfield was also known for his criticism of supernatural occurrences in various nineteenth-century revivals (including Methodist revivals).[37]

This rationalistic attack on Christian supernaturalism further extended into the twentieth century, largely through the work of Bultmann (1884–1976), a German theologian who many consider to be highly influential.[38] His signature work on theological criticism was presented in his book *History of the Synoptic Tradition*.[39] Bultmann saw Christian or biblical supernatural activities as unfit for the modern world; instead, these activities were, according to Bultmann, generally "mythological" in nature (derived, primarily, from ancient Hellenistic myths).[40] Bultmann

---

34. Tillotson, *Works of the Most Reverend Dr. John Tillotson*, 239.

35. Toland, *Tetradymus*, 5. See also Toland, *Christianity Not Mysterious*, 49.

36. Tindal, *Christianity as Old as the Creation*, 1:281.

37. Warfield, *Counterfeit Miracles*, 6, 131–39, 182.

38. O'Keefe, *International Handbook of Catholic Education*, 151; Labron, *Bultmann Unlocked*, 4.

39. For a brief introduction to Bultmann's theology, see Wildman, "Rudolf Bultmann."

40. Bultmann, *Interpreting Faith for the Modern Era*, 291–92.

aimed to "demythologize"[41] Christianity by removing its supernatural aspects and writing about a new purely rational Christianity that would be better understood by a modern, rational individual.[42]

Many scholars, such as the sociologist Berger, found it difficult to accept Bultmann's theological perspective due to it containing little empirical evidence.[43] Another reason for theologians' resistance to Bultmann's view was its potential contradiction to the Bible. For instance, contrary to Bultmann's efforts to transform Christian belief into a natural and rational understanding, the apostle Paul explained that natural people (those relying solely on rational understanding) can neither accept nor understand supernatural phenomena; he stated that "the natural person does not accept the things of the Spirit of God, for they are folly to him, and he is not able to understand them because they are spiritually discerned" (1 Cor 2:14).

Another school of Christian thought, pioneered by modern theologian Hollenweger (1927–2016), claimed that there was no clear-cut distinction between the supernatural and natural, and attempting to forge one was scientifically and theologically outdated.[44] In considering the spiritual gifts listed in 1 Corinthians 12, Hollenweger declared that because the seemingly supernatural gifts (e.g., healing and speaking in tongues) were placed alongside the seemingly ordinary or natural gifts (e.g., knowledge and faith), they fell under the same theological umbrella. He felt that, for the Christian, all spiritual gifts should be utilized and, therefore, considered a common part of "God's creation and the realm of his reign." Hollenweger believed that people consider the more extraordinary gifts to be supernatural until they experience and practice them; after doing so, they realize that these gifts are simply "natural gifts."[45] He supported his theory using a cross-cultural comparison of so-called supernatural and natural activities. Thus, for Hollenweger, the concept of supernaturalism was scientifically and biblically unsound.

41. González, *Story of Christianity*, 2:468.

42. Olson, *Journey of Modern Theology*, 332.

43. See Berger, *Questions of Faith*, 62–63.

44. Thiselton, *Holy Spirit*, 103.

45. Hollenweger, *Pentecostalism*, 224–26. See also Warrington, *Pentecostal Theology*, 75; Thiselton, *Shorter Guide to the Holy Spirit*, 162–63; Hollenweger "Introduction to Pentecostalisms," 125–37.

The Supernatural: Modern Beliefs and Statistics

Despite all of these skeptical arguments and debates surrounding supernatural activity, it should be noted that the majority of Pentecostal and Charismatic Christians (along with many evangelical Christians) believe in the supernatural "gifts of the Spirit"; this Christian perspective is growing, and by 2050, it is predicted that one-fourth of all Christians and one-tenth of the world's population will be affiliated with a form of Pentecostal and Charismatic Christianity.[46]

Recently, the majority of the world's population was reported to believe in a supernatural entity. A 2015 research study conducted by Pawlikowski concluded that, "in modern Western societies," approximately 70 percent of the general population (including many physicians) believed in the existence of supernatural phenomena; millions made pilgrimages all around the world hoping that, in turn, they would receive supernatural healing. Furthermore, Pawlikowski claimed that belief in supernatural phenomena, such as healing, was "stronger among women, African-Americans, Evangelical Protestants, the poorer, sicker, and less educated and the majority of respondents [understood] that God acts through the hands of the physicians."[47]

Within America, in 2017, 87 percent of the population stated that they believed in the existence of a spiritual God,[48] and in 2014, 68 percent of Americans claimed that they did not see a contradiction between science and the belief in a spiritual God.[49] In 2017, approximately 42 percent of the American population indicated that they had previously had a supernatural Christian experience or spiritual awakening.[50] Moreover, "nearly half of Americans report[ed] having at least two supernatural encounters" in their lifetime.[51]

In addition to the individuals who claim to believe in a supernatural God and the supernatural experiences that flow from God, there are also many in the world who consider every form of spirituality or every

46. Johnstone, *Future of the Global Church*, 125.

47. Pawlikowski et al., "Beliefs in Miraculous Healings," 1113–24.

48. "Religion," para. 14. For statistics regarding belief in God, heaven, hell, and other supernaturalism, see Wuthnow, *Experimentation in American Religion*, 6.

49. Masci and Smith, "Is God Dead?," para. 7–8.

50. "Religion," para. 8. An example of spiritual rebirth is portrayed in John 3:3: "Very truly I tell you, no one can see the kingdom of God unless they are born again."

51. Vu, "Survey."

inexplicable experience to be a supernatural reality apart from the presence of a supreme divine being.[52] According to the Pew Research Center, "Nearly three-in-ten Americans say they have felt in touch with someone who has already died, almost one-in-five say they have seen or been in the presence of ghosts, and 15 percent have consulted a fortuneteller or a psychic."[53] Traditionally, it is believed that in certain parts of the world (often places that are classified as developing countries), individuals are heavily inclined to believe in a supernatural reality; a number of these individuals even go so far as to identify various natural causes as a product of this supernatural or spiritual reality.[54]

Thus, as demonstrated by statistics, even for twenty-first-century individuals, belief in supernatural experiences, in general, appears to be rather accepted as a means of attempting to understand life on earth.[55] Indeed, individuals seem to be familiar with and, to a degree, open to the idea of a supernatural reality.[56]

The Supernatural According to the Circuit Riders

Since the circuit rider ministry was a Christian movement, this work investigates supernatural activities of a religious nature. In the circuit rider ministry, the Triune God was generally considered the author and source of such activities.[57] This section presents the definition and purpose of the supernatural according to the circuit riders.

---

52. See Edson, *Mysticism and Alchemy*, 71–72; Denison, *Christ's Idea of the Supernatural*, 213–15.

53. Lugo, "Many Americans Mix Multiple Faiths," para. 5.

54. Duncan, *To Reign as Kings*, 33.

55. For various supernatural testimonies, see Eke, *Book of Great Testimonies*; Hebert, *Saints Who Raised the Dead*; Imhof, *Supernatural Testimonies*; Yeager, *God Still Heals*; Bryan, *Serpent and the Savior*; Bannister, "Exploring Narratives in Supernatural Healing"; Brown, *He Came to Set the Captives Free*; Baker and Baker, *Expecting Miracles*; Billman, *Supernatural Thread in Methodism*; "Testimonies."

56. Noel, *Pentecostal and Postmodern Hermeneutics*, 97.

57. Evans, "Most Distinctive Contribution of Methodists," 1500.

The Supernatural in a Christian Context

Traditionally in Christian circles, the terms *miracle* or *signs and wonders*[58] have often been used to explain a supernatural act.[59] According to the theologian Geisler, "A miracle is a divine interference into the regular course of events. Hence, it is not a natural occurrence but is truly a supernatural event."[60] These supernatural events can occur in various forms, such as: emotional or physical healings, involuntarily falling down (commonly known as "being slain in the Spirit"), exorcisms, the raising of the dead, dreams, visions, trances, prophecies, encounters with God's presence (which can include spontaneously feeling God's love, peace, joy, etc.), hearing God's voice, miraculous changes in the weather, and seeing angelic (or demonic) beings.[61]

A supernatural occurrence can also be considered a spiritual attack or an act of warfare originating from demonic beings. Christians believe that demonic beings, ruled by the devil, are rebellious angels fallen from their original state of goodness.[62] Their desire and mission is to afflict the good creations of God, such as humanity. In John 10:10, Jesus referred to the demonic beings and the devil as thieves, stating that "the thief comes only to steal and kill and destroy; I [Jesus] have come that they may have life, and have it to the full."[63]

Regarding supernatural acts within the Bible, there are numerous accounts that are considered to be unexplainable and transcend natural laws. Indeed, from the first chapter of the Bible, supernatural events are

58. For more information, see also Perrin and Bielo, *Bible Reading of Young Evangelicals*, 110–13.

59. There are scholars, such as Clarke, who argued against this traditional view. He suggested that the "definition of the miraculous should not refer to the supernatural, but should refer to the non-natural." Although Clarke made a good point, this study holds to the more traditional and popular notion that miracles are, in a sense, supernatural activities performed by a supernatural agent (predominately God). For more information on his argument, see Clarke, "Supernatural and the Miraculous," 277–85.

60. Geisler, *Signs and Wonders*, 24.

61. Billman wrote that David Hogan, a minister in Mexico, by the power of Jesus Christ, has raised more than three hundred from the dead; Sithole, a minister in Mozambique, has raised more than four hundred from the dead. See Billman, *Supernatural Thread in Methodism*, 132–33.

62. For more information regarding this phenomenon, see chapters 4–5.

63. For a more meticulous study on the supernatural attacks of demonic forces in Christian life (and partially non-Christian lives), see Unger, *What Demons Can Do to Saints*.

evident. In Genesis 1, God created the natural realm and its inhabitants through his supernatural power; in other words, God supernaturally "gave birth" to creation through his Spirit (Gen 2:7). Some other supernatural Old Testament encounters include: the birth of Isaac (Gen 21:1–7), Moses before the burning bush (Exod 3:3), the ten plagues of Egypt (Exod 7:20–28, 9, 10, 11, 12:30), the Red Sea divided and Israel passing through it (Exod 14:21–31), forty years of manna from heaven (Exod 16:14–35), the sun and moon standing still (Josh 10:12–14), fire devouring Elijah's altar (1 Kgs 18:19–39), and the Shunammite woman's son being raised from the dead (2 Kgs 4:32–37).

Similarly, the New Testament begins with a supernatural event: God was incarnated or born as a man (John 1). Thus, unsurprisingly, Jesus's ministry was full of supernatural encounters. In the time of Jesus's ministry, the mindset of the Jews and surrounding nations was very open to supernatural events, such as the casting out of demons which, during that age, was often practiced through spells and "witchcraft" or "magic." However, even in the midst of a culture quite accepting of spiritual phenomena, Jesus's supernatural acts were shocking and unbelievable— superior to those of other popular religions or mystical practices.[64] It is recorded in John 21:25 that Jesus performed so many supernatural acts that "if every one of them were written down, I suppose that even the whole world would not have room for the books that would be written." A few of Jesus's more well-known phenomena that are recorded in the New Testament are as follows: the calming of the storm (Matt 8:23–27; Mark 4:37–41; Luke 8:22–25), the feeding of the five thousand (Matt 14:14–21; Mark 6:30–44; Luke 9:10–17; John 6:1–14), the healing of two blind men (Matt 9:27–31), the exorcism of the Gerasene demoniac (Mark 5:1–17), the healing of ten men with leprosy (Luke 17:11–19), and the raising of Lazarus from the dead (John 11:1–44).

Jesus also gave authority to his future followers to perform supernatural phenomena (Matt 10:1). In fact, Jesus stated that his followers "will also do the works that I [Jesus] do; and greater works than these will [they] do, because I am going to the Father" (John 14:12). Following his death and ascension, Jesus's disciples considered these words, and after they were filled with the Holy Spirit (Acts 1), the disciples continued to live the same lifestyle that Jesus demonstrated,

64. Keener, *IVP Bible Background Commentary*, 138. See also Grudem, *Systematic Theology*, 418.

performing many supernatural acts.[65] Various forms of these acts (or miracles) were a part of their daily ministry; the disciples became so renowned that sick people would lie down in their shadows to be healed (Acts 5:12–16). Largely through these incidents, the number of Christian converts increased from eleven to thousands (Acts 2:42–47). One of the most well-known converts of the time was the apostle Paul who, in one of his letters, explained that he conducted his entire ministry through the supernatural power flowing from the Spirit of God (1 Cor 2:4).

Documentation of such supernatural phenomena is also found within the circuit rider ministry and can be readily referenced in circuit rider journals, autobiographies, and letters. The circuit riders desired to imitate the lifestyle of Jesus and the first apostles; thus, as Asbury declared, "The signs of their mission were miracles [performed by God], and the signs that followed their ministry [were] convictions and conversions."[66] A few specific examples of the supernatural, described in circuit rider literature and attributed to the hand of the Holy Spirit, are as follows: circuit rider Abbott was known to cause audience members to fall like "dead men"[67] and experience temporary unconsciousness while he preached; circuit rider Garrettson was believed to be a healer and once witnessed new skin form on a burn victim after prayer;[68] and circuit rider Easter was remembered for altering the weather and stopping the rain.[69]

The Purpose of the Supernatural

According to the *Encyclopaedia Britannica*, "the significance of a miraculous event is frequently held to reside not in the event as such but in the reality to which it points (e.g., the presence or activity of a divine power)."[70] Members of Christian circles believe that supernatural incidents occur for a number of reasons.[71] Christians largely hold that a

65. Rosal, *Handbook of Miracles*, 59.

66. Asbury, *Journal of the Rev. Francis Asbury*, 2:266.

67. Abbott and Ffirth, *Experience and Gospel Labours*, 85.

68. Garrettson, *Experience and Travels*, 177–78.

69. Paine, *Life and Times*, 1:55–56. For more information regarding public supernatural occurrences, see chapter 5.

70. "Miracle" (*EBO*).

71. This book does not attempt to outline all of the possibilities as to why supernatural acts happen; rather, it attempts to outline the most commonly identified reasons behind supernatural occurrences.

primary reason why they occur is in order for God to be authenticated within the world;[72] they believe that these events provide the audience with a sign or a wonder that will factually prove and convince the audience of the reality of God. This, in turn, opens doors for further evangelism.[73] Christians also believe that God performs various supernatural manifestations through his people as an act of love and a way of exhibiting his compassion for broken humanity.[74] Another reason why Christians believe that supernatural phenomena are displayed is to demonstrate that God is the world's creator and that he surpasses all other spiritual or natural beings.[75]

The circuit riders, as Christians, held these same beliefs regarding the purpose of the supernatural. Like the apostles before them, their aim was to spread the gospel of Jesus Christ.[76] More specifically, the purpose of the supernatural in their ministry was as follows: it demonstrated to their audiences the authority of God; it authenticated the message of the gospel;[77] it validated the calling of circuit rider ministers;[78] it led to convictions, conversions, and served as an evangelistic tool;[79] it displayed God's love toward humanity;[80] and it highlighted the necessity of living a holy lifestyle.[81] To summarize, the circuit riders largely considered supernatural phenomena to be the seal of their divine work.

72. Deere, *Surprised by the Power of the Spirit*, 103.

73. Pawlikowski et al., "Beliefs in Miraculous Healings," 1115. Also, in John 20:24, Jesus said: "But if I do his work, believe in the evidence of the miraculous works I have done, even if you don't believe me. Then you will know and understand that the Father is in me, and I am in the Father." See also Deere, *Surprised by the Power of the Spirit*, 222.

74. First John 4:10 states: "This is real love—not that we loved God, but that he loved us and sent his Son as a sacrifice to take away our sins." Also, Matthew 14:14 records, "When Jesus landed and saw a large crowd, he had compassion on them and healed their sick."

75. Matthew 4:23–24 records: "Jesus went throughout Galilee, teaching in their synagogues, proclaiming the good news of the kingdom, and healing every disease and sickness among the people. News about him spread all over Syria, and people brought to him all who were ill with various diseases, those suffering severe pain, the demon–possessed, those having seizures, and the paralyzed; and he healed them."

76. Bower, *From Saddlebags to Satellites*, xiii.

77. Harrington, *First Comes Faith*, 4.

78. Sweet, *Circuit-Rider Days in Indiana*, 107.

79. See "Religious," 437.

80. Exman, *Get Ready—Get Set—Grow*, 27–28.

81. For more information on this topic, see chapter 4.

Supernatural versus Natural

As noted earlier, for the circuit riders, a supernatural phenomenon most often originated from the Holy Spirit, although at times it originated from demonic beings. Thus, circuit riders understood that supernatural manifestations arose from the spiritual realm or "a divine power"[82] and not the physical realm;[83] moreover, they understood that "when a supernatural being or power operate[d] in nature . . . [it was] supernatural."[84]

Conversely, they understood that a natural act derived exclusively from an individual's five senses, thoughts, emotions, or circumstances;[85] also, a natural phenomenon was an event that could easily be explained scientifically or with a rational mind or natural reason, demonstrating that, in essence, the event was produced by an earthly being or by the earth surrounding that being.[86] In the words of Asbury, "natural causes produce natural effects," which should be naturally discerned.[87]

Indeed, according to early Methodist understanding, natural phenomena were not "the manifest intervention and direction of a superhuman agency"; rather, they were simply of natural origin.[88] In contrast, acts that came from the outside world (the spiritual realm) and affected the individual's being (body, soul, or spirit) or "natural" world were identified as supernatural, whether manifested in grand, staggering ways or quiet, personal ways.[89]

According to circuit rider Young, as the circuit riders were known to be "filled with the Holy Ghost," they knew that because the natural mind did not have the capacity to comprehend supernatural phenomena, such phenomena could often be judged or misinterpreted.[90] As Asbury

82. Scudder and Cummings, *American Methodism*, 339.

83. Cartwright, *Backwoods Preacher*, 315; Scudder and Cummings, *American Methodism*, 49; Ireson, *Methodist Preacher*, 69.

84. McCosh, *Supernatural in Relation to the Natural*, 101–2.

85. Scudder and Cummings, *American Methodism*, 339; Wesley et al., *Letters of John Wesley*, 222; Wesley, *Explanatory Notes upon the New Testament*, 434.

86. Ireson, *Methodist Preacher*, 69; Wesley, *Journal*, 1:48; Novenson, *Grammar of Messianism*, 192.

87. Asbury, *Journal of the Rev. Francis Asbury*, 1:104.

88. Scudder and Cummings, *American Methodism*, 26.

89. Goetz, "Naturally Understanding Naturalism," 80. See also Wakeley and Boehm, *Patriarch of One Hundred Years*, 159; Finley, *Sketches of Western Methodism*, 84; Asbury, *Journal of the Rev. Francis Asbury*, 3:271.

90. Young, *Autobiography of a Pioneer*, 52.

stated, supernatural phenomena "appear to be foolishness to [natural-minded people]; and that [they] cannot know them, by the strength of [their] natural or acquired abilities."[91] As Methodist preacher and eye-witness eighteenth-century historian Scudder observed, early Method-ists knew that the natural mind "denies the supernatural, and refers all phenomena in human history to natural causes; [thus] the belief in a divine power attending the [circuit rider] ministry . . . appear[s] only a speculation." Supernatural realties were, for the rational mind, seen as "fable, and unworthy the belief of any but the ignorant, the credulous, or the superstitious."[92] Wesley concluded that rationalists were "so far from understanding" supernatural phenomena that they "utterly despise[d]" them. He determined that a rationalist cannot comprehend these mani-festations as one "has not the will, so neither [one] has the Power; because [supernatural matters] are spiritually discerned." Thus, Wesley believed that the "only" way for one to discern and comprehend these matters was "by the Aid of that Spirit, and by those spiritual Senses which he has not."[93]

Even when "natural men" attempted to discern or explain "super-natural things," they did so through "mere natural causes" because they could not comprehend spiritual causes.[94] Consequently, as Wesley stated, "a natural man has no more faith [in the experiential or spiritual gospel] than a Devil, if so much."[95] According to early Methodist understand-ing, "the natural man" was considered to be "alive unto the world, and dead unto God, and . . . he [would] not readily be persuaded to receive . . . the truth of God."[96] Furthermore, supernatural phenomena to the natural mind was "foolishness unto . . . him [who] was never yet [spiri-tually] awakened . . . [because of this fact] he must reject [the spiritual phenomena] as idle fancies of men, what are [in reality] both the wisdom and the power of God."[97] The circuit riders believed that in "this infidel age all these supernatural interpositions are scoffed at as below the

91. Asbury, *Journal of the Rev. Francis Asbury*, 1:52.

92. Scudder and Cummings, *American Methodism*, 339, 527.

93. Wesley, *Explanatory Notes upon the New Testament*, 434. See also Wesley, *Far-ther Appeal to Men: Parts 1–3*, 73–76; Russie, *Essential Works*, 125–31.

94. Wesley, *Explanatory Notes upon the New Testament*, 292.

95. Wesley, *Journal*, 1:393.

96. Wesley, *Sermons on Several Occasions* [Emory], 167.

97. Wesley, *Sermons on Several Occasions* [Emory], 166–67.

wisdom, but, in fact, [they are] above the folly, of human philosophy."[98] The supernatural set up "at defiance all attempts to account for" these occurrences "by any of the common laws of human experience"[99] because the supernatural "was a power to be exercised [and comprehended] by those endued with the Spirit of God"[100] and not natural-minded people. Hence, it can be concluded that, for Methodists, "supernatural origin[s]"[101] were seen as "superior"[102] to natural acts.

The Term Supernatural in the Circuit Rider Ministry

In the circuit rider ministry, the term *supernatural*, in describing a divine event or encounter, was not often used. While there were a number of occasions in which early Methodists, including the circuit riders, used the term *supernatural* to express or communicate a divine spiritual encounter, this was not the norm.[103] While the term *power and presence* referred to divine supernatural activity and was often featured within circuit rider writings,[104] it seems that the circuit riders generally did not find it necessary to specifically label supernatural activities as such because of their inherent belief that all divine, miraculous activities were supernatural in nature.[105] Thus, they recorded specific supernatural activities in detail but did not typically describe them as "supernatural." For example, circuit rider Peck recorded a supernatural event that originated from the

98. Holmes et al., *Methodist Preacher*, 318. Early Methodists even discouraged natural love for one another, instead preferring the superior spiritual love that derived from the Spirit.

99. Scudder and Cummings, *American Methodism*, 255.

100. Gatch, *Sketch of Rev. Philip Gatch*, 72.

101. Beet, "Creation of Man," 9.

102. Asbury, *Journal of the Rev. Francis Asbury*, 1:166. See also Asbury, *Journal of the Rev. Francis Asbury*, 2:96; 3:278.

103. Following are some Methodists, including circuit riders, who employed the term *supernatural* in their respective documents: Peck, *Early Methodism*, 51, 186; Andrews, *Sisters of the Spirit*, 20, 53, 107, 178; Grant and Godwin, *Rescue of Faith*, 72, 73, 79, 80, 87; Moore and Smith, *Life of the Rev. H. Moore*, 32; Pickard, *Autobiography of a Pioneer*, xx, 54.

104. Occasionally, supernatural experiences, as demonstrated in the following chapters (especially chapters 5–6) were also described using the terms *experiential religion, enthusiastic experience,* and *divine display/experience.*

105. Scholars such as Billman attributed the Methodists' supernatural events to divine acts performed by God. See Billman, *Supernatural Thread in Methodism*, xiii–1.

Holy Spirit, though he did not necessarily classify the event in supernatural terms: "The Spirit was poured out from on high upon multitudes, and men and women, old and young, dreamed dreams, saw visions, and were filled with the spirit of prophecy."[106] In this example, the Holy Spirit was the spiritual agent in the event that was clearly supernatural or apart from the natural.

This practice of not explicitly labeling divine spiritual encounters as "supernatural" while still understanding them to be supernatural in origin was prevalent within many Christian circles and also within the biblical text. Indeed, the term *supernatural* was never used in the Bible to describe any divine activity (though the sister term *miracle* was used).[107] However, supernatural events recorded in the Bible, such as Jesus healing a blind man (John 9), were understood by the original audience and Christian readers to indicate a supernatural healing.[108] In John 10:38, Jesus asked his audience to do the following: "Believe in the evidence of the miraculous works I have done. Even if you don't believe in me." Though Jesus did not use the term *supernatural*, his audience comprehended that his divine or spiritual works were miraculous and, therefore, supernatural.[109] Also, because these were supernatural works, the audience understood that such events were rare; consequently, for those present (and for those reading and believing in the biblical text), these works served as an indicator of Jesus's divinity.[110]

Similarly, aside from the less common encounters with demonic beings, it appears that the circuit riders recorded their supernatural encounters in journals, autobiographies, or letters knowing that their Christian audience would understand these encounters to be both divine and supernatural.[111] Due to the fact that they were Christians and had substantial knowledge of the Bible, circuit riders described a supernatural phenomenon using the same language found in the biblical text. The circuit riders anticipated that any future readers of their documents would be predominantly Christian, would understand their recorded manifestations to be supernatural, and would believe that the manifestations

106. Peck, *Early Methodism*, 187.

107. For more information, see Stinson, "Finite Supernatural," 325–26.

108. Lockyer, *All the Miracles of the Bible*, 220.

109. Keener, *IVP Bible Background Commentary*, 138.

110. For a brief commentary concerning this verse, see "Commentaries: John 10:38" lines 1–3.

111. See also Peirce, *Ecclesiastical Principles and Polity*, 332.

originated "through Jesus Christ"[112] and the "agency of the Holy Spirit of God,"[113] whom they served.[114]

For example, circuit rider Hibbard shared one of his testimonies regarding a woman named Rachel who was proclaimed dead and then supernaturally raised again: "She gave the first symptom of returning life, and in about twenty minutes she [spoke] and said, 'O why have I come back again?'"[115] When Hibbard wrote concerning this testimony of raising Rachel from the dead, even though it was not recorded as a supernatural event, the event was understood by the audience to be clearly supernatural, performed divinely by God.[116]

Circuit rider Giles described the circuit riders' supernaturalism by declaring that they were ministers who performed "miracles."[117] It can then be concluded that, in the circuit rider ministry, it was common knowledge that various miraculous or divine manifestations were considered to fall under the umbrella term *supernatural*. Examples of such manifestations are as follows: being slain in the Spirit (i.e., falling down under God's power),[118] enthusiastic emotional expressions (often identified as *religious enthusiasm*),[119] dreams,[120] visions,[121] trances,[122] spiritual warfare with demonic forces,[123] divine healings,[124] the raising of the dead,[125] divine weather shifts,[126] spiritual ecstasy,[127] love,[128] peace,[129]

112. Asbury, *Journal of the Rev. Francis Asbury*, 1:91.

113. Cartwright, *Backwoods Preacher*, 118.

114. See also Lee, *Short History of the Methodists*, iii.

115. Hibbard, *Memoirs*, 164. Because of the theological nature of this testimony, it is also included in chapter 5.

116. For more information regarding the supernatural phenomena of raising the dead, see chapter 5.

117. Giles, *Pioneer*, 62.

118. Cartwright, *Backwoods Preacher*, 9.

119. Ware, *Sketches*, 62.

120. Abbott and Ffirth, *Experience and Gospel Labours*, 7–8.

121. Peck, *Early Methodism*, 187.

122. Garrettson, *Experience and Travels*, 156–57.

123. Asbury, *Journal of the Rev. Francis Asbury*, 1:90.

124. Asbury, *Journal of the Rev. Francis Asbury*, 1:125, 312.

125. Garrettson, *Experience and Travels*, 19–21.

126. Wakeley and Boehm, *Patriarch of One Hundred Years*, 158.

127. Finley, *Sketches of Western Methodism*, 26.

128. Garrettson, *Experience and Travels*, 156–57.

129. Asbury, *Journal of the Rev. Francis Asbury*, 1:157

joy,[130] convictions,[131] and conversions.[132] Consequently, in the following chapters, for the purpose of communicating to twenty-first-century readers a more accurate picture of the spiritual experiences recorded by circuit riders, the term *supernatural* is, at times, added to some textual passages in order to aid in interpretation.

It should also be noted that one of the reasons why the term *supernatural* has been selected for the purpose of this study is because it covers a greater scope of paranormal activity than the word *miracle*. Indeed, the term *miracle* (or *signs and wonders*) is used in the biblical text and, largely, in the Christian world to describe a benevolent or beneficial supernatural event that flows from the loving Spirit of God. The term *supernatural*, however, also encompasses a greater spiritual reality, such as paranormal acts that originate from a belligerent or destructive being (typically, the devil or similar demonic forces), which the circuit riders also came in contact with and journaled about throughout their ministry.[133] At the same time, the term *supernatural* is very frequently used in modern American Christianity, especially in churches affiliated with a form of Pentecostal and/or Charismatic Christianity; in this context, the term describes divine or spiritual encounters. Also, due to its spiritual inclusiveness and mysterious nature (mostly in the context of paranormal activity), the usage of the term *supernatural* is gradually increasing in American popular culture.[134]

Private and Public Supernaturalism

While all phenomena in the circuit rider ministry that derived from the spiritual realm were technically considered to be supernatural, not all supernatural phenomena had the same far-reaching effects on circuit rider audiences. That being said, for the purpose of understanding the supernatural in the circuit rider ministry, the more personal supernatural phenomena that were experienced in the private lives of circuit riders are

130. Finley, *Autobiography*, 186.

131. Finley, *Autobiography*, 232.

132. Holmes, *Methodist Preacher*, 318.

133. For more information regarding spiritual warfare in the circuit rider ministry, see chapter 4.

134. Mazur and McCarthy, *God in the Details*, 59; Bartholomew and Nickell, *American Hauntings*, xii–xv. For instance, there is a popular American television show called *Supernatural*, which, as of 2019, is in its fifteenth season.

identified in this book as *private supernaturalism*. On the other hand, supernatural phenomena that were experienced by circuit rider audiences (and were considered extraordinary and influential) are identified as *public supernaturalism*.

Private supernatural phenomena in the personal lives of the circuit riders occurred very frequently (almost on a daily basis).[135] Initially, private supernaturalism served as the main factor in receiving personal convictions and conversions (which were typically followed by ministerial callings).[136] For instance, during his conversion, circuit rider Gatch recalled how he "felt the power of God affect [his] body and soul."[137] Also, circuit rider Travis described part of his conversion story in which he experienced spiritual "joy [that] sprang up [in his] soul . . . [and] enabled [him] to hope in [his] blessed Redeemer."[138] Hence, circuit riders, such as Abbott,[139] Garretson,[140] Finley,[141] and Cartwright,[142] were typically converted directly through experiences of private supernaturalism.[143]

Private supernaturalism also encompassed individual circuit rider spiritual experiences or infillings, such as divine "grace, mercy . . . peace"[144] or "strength, joy, and power, [which were considered to be] supernatural."[145] For instance, Cartwright declared, "My soul was filled with the love of God." This spiritual infilling of God's love was understood to be supernatural because the source of this infilling did not originate from Cartwright but from God himself. This phenomenon of spiritual infilling is also presented in the biblical text of Ephesians 3:19 in which spiritual love is deemed supernatural because it "surpasses [rational] knowledge." Hence, private supernatural phenomena were instrumental in receiving personal conversions and were beneficial to the circuit

---

135. See also Asbury, *Journal of the Rev. Francis Asbury*, 1:38.

136. For more information regarding this matter, see chapter 4.

137. Gatch, *Sketch of Rev. Philip Gatch*, 12.

138. Travis, *Autobiography*, 27–28.

139. Abbott and Ffirth, *Experience and Gospel Labours*, 11–19.

140. Garrettson, *Experience and Travels*, 11–12.

141. Finley, *Autobiography*, 167–69.

142. Cartwright, *Backwoods Preacher*, 13.

143. For more information regarding the conversions of some of the more prominent circuit riders, see chapter 4.

144. Asbury, *Journal of the Rev. Francis Asbury*, 3:160.

145. Ireson, *Methodist Preacher*, 69.

riders' personal lives as these experiences enabled them to better perform their ministries and to "exhort with . . . power."[146]

While private supernaturalism was greatly influential within the personal lives of the circuit riders, it was not typically influential to their audiences (because these personal encounters did not affect the public directly). Conversely, the circuit rider audiences were directly influenced by public supernatural phenomena. For instance, Cartwright observed an enthusiastic outpouring of God's power wherein people "cried aloud" and "hundreds" fell under the power of God "as men slain in battle."[147] Interestingly, however, as seen in the following chapters, these acts performed through the ministry of the circuit riders were many times not considered to be personally influential to the circuit riders themselves; rather, these acts were considered to be influential to their audiences.[148] In other words, public supernatural phenomena were vital to the public in terms of conversions and the growth of the movement because it served as "the best evidence that . . . God" was present and working through the circuit rider ministry.[149]

In the lives and ministries of the early American Methodist circuit riders, both private and public supernatural phenomena (derived from the Holy Spirit) played a crucial role; in fact, they were codependent as one would not work without the other. For instance, if Asbury did not experience the "peace"[150] of God or had not "felt the power of [the] divine" in certain periods of his life, he would admittedly not have been fully prepared for his ministerial labors.[151] As such, private supernaturalism was vital to the circuit riders' lifestyles, and it also prepared the circuit riders to become agents of public supernaturalism (in evangelistic meetings).[152]

146. Cartwright, *Backwoods Preacher*, 25. See also Asbury, *Journal of the Rev. Francis Asbury*, 1:22.

147. Cartwright, *Backwoods Preacher*, 9, 42, 104.

148. For instance, see Asbury, *Journal of the Rev. Francis Asbury*, 1:165; Young, *Autobiography of a Pioneer*, 54; Smith and Dailey, *Experience and Ministerial Labors*, 29–30; Garrettson, *Experience and Travels,* 91–92.

149. Asbury, *Journal of the Rev. Francis Asbury*, 2:58.

150. Asbury, *Journal of the Rev. Francis Asbury*, 3:137.

151. Asbury, *Journal of the Rev. Francis Asbury*, 1:204. See also Boehm, *Reminiscences*, 441.

152. See also Jackson, *Lives of Early Methodist Preachers*, 5:154.

In investigating the role of the supernatural in the circuit rider ministry, both private and public supernaturalism are explored throughout
this book; however, the majority of research revolves around public supernaturalism, which spurred conversions, revivals, and, consequently,
growth. Hence, chapter 4 is predominately devoted to occurrences of
private supernaturalism while chapters 5, 6, and 7 are predominately
devoted to occurrences of public supernaturalism.

The Significance of the Power
and Presence in the Circuit Rider Ministry

The circuit riders exhibited a ministry full of spiritual "life and fire"[153]
from the Holy Spirit because the "power [and presence] of God constantly
attend[ed their] word."[154] In other words, the circuit riders believed that
the *power and presence* was the active, apparent display of the Triune
God; it was the physical manifestation of heaven touching earth. Within
circuit rider writings, there are overwhelming instances that emphasize
the visible reality of supernatural acts coming from the outpourings
of the power and presence of God; it appears that these outpourings
were considered common encounters within the circuit rider ministry.
Therefore, to better understand the role of the supernatural in the circuit
rider ministry, the role of the power and presence of God, as presented by
the circuit riders, should be explored in depth.

The two terms *power* and *presence* of God, used by circuit riders
throughout their writings, are Christian synonyms commonly found
in the biblical text.[155] Concerning the *power* of God, the book of Acts
provides a wealth of insight. Acts 1:8 states: "But you will receive power
when the Holy Spirit comes on you; and you will be my witnesses in
Jerusalem, and all Judea and Samaria, and to the ends of the earth." Jesus
instructed his disciples to wait for the supernatural power that would
come from the outpouring of the Holy Spirit. Also, the apostle Paul witnessed the power of God that followed his ministry. In 1 Corinthians
2:4, he explained: "And my speech and my message were not in plau-
sible words of wisdom, but in demonstration of the Spirit and of power."
The Greek word δύναμις (noun, "power") sounds like the English word

---

153. Wesley, *Journal*, 2:743.

154. Stevens, *History of the Methodist Episcopal Church*, 1:141.

155. Lee, *Short History of the Methodists*, 285.

dynamite (which is derived from the Greek); as the name suggests, the word indicates a powerful, explosive event. With dynamite, one can cause an environmental change within the natural realm that normally cannot be changed. Biblical dynamite enables a powerful change of the physical realm through supernatural intervention that restores or transforms the physical realm (including people).[156] According to Wesleyan theology, this power enables people to be Jesus's witnesses in the world by performing signs and wonders as "signs and wonders are even now wrought by [God's] holy child Jesus."[157] Early Methodist theology conveyed that, through Christ, Christians have the power of God on earth.[158] In other words, the circuit riders (and Christians at large), through this spiritual dynamite, were able to witness and perform the same wonder-works that Jesus did.[159]

Moreover, in the circuit rider ministry, when the term *power of God* was used, it was highlighting the fact that something supernatural and unpredictable was about to happen.[160] For example, at times, it was as Abbott recorded that "the power of God fell on [him] in such a manner, that it instantly removed from [him] the fear of man."[161] At other times, it was as Finley frequently recorded: during circuit rider meetings "many hardened sinners [and converts fell down], before the power of God, like those slain in battle." Furthermore, often the "demonstration of the power of God [caused] irresistible conviction."[162]

As it pertains to the *presence* of the Spirit of God, this is identified in the Bible as the Greek word παρουσία (noun, "presence") and, occasionally, πρόσωπον (noun, "face") and σκηνόω (verb, "dwell"). The presence of God was understood to describe the fact that God was appearing at a certain place to a certain person or group; thus, God's relational presence was dwelling among people.[163] Moreover, theologically speaking, for the

156. Hellerman, *Philippians*, 190.

157. Wesley, *Works*, 1:187. See also Wesley, *Explanatory Notes Upon the New Testament*, 291–93.

158. Quayle, *Dynamite of God*, 22–23.

159. This was also one of Jesus's promises to his followers in John 14:12: "Truly, truly, I say to you, whoever believes in me will also do the works that I do; and greater works than these will he do, because I am going to the Father."

160. Asbury, *Journal of the Rev. Francis Asbury*, 1:6; 2:15.

161. Abbott and Ffirth, *Experience and Gospel Labours*, 31.

162. Finley, *Autobiography*, 232, 240.

163. Hovey, *American Commentary on the New Testament*, 45.

circuit riders, "the supreme Divinity of Jesus Christ,"[164] God incarnated, was the most visible expression of the presence of God on earth.[165] In brief, the circuit riders' theology of the presence of God indicated the following: that God was present in the meeting, therefore (similar to the power of God), the supernatural would follow.

For the circuit riders, though the terms *power* and *presence* of God were sometimes used separately, from a practical standpoint, the terms are nearly synonymous.[166] For instance, Boehm declared that "the power of the Lord came down" to perform supernatural miracles; Abbott declared that, due to the power of God, about "twelve were converted and many awakened."[167] On the other hand, Lee witnessed times when the "the presence of God" descended and gave birth to signs and wonders;[168] Gatch recalled stories wherein, due to the "presence" of God, souls received conversion.[169]

What appeared to be more common in circuit rider writings was the usage of the two words simultaneously; this usage conveyed a unity wherein the function and role of both, the power and presence of God, were joined together as one word to express the following: God was near and intending to do, or was already doing, something supernatural. For instance, Coke longed for his audience to experience and witness "the power and presence of God assuredly in the midst of [them]."[170] Shadford recalled times when there was "a remarkable manifestation of the power and presence of God [that was felt]," which led large numbers of Virginians to receive conversion.[171] Lee also recalled various manifestations of "the presence and power of God" that brought forth signs and wonders; Lee further testified that, in circuit rider meetings, there were numerous outpourings "of the power and presence of God."[172] Watters recorded testimonies in which "the glorious presence and power

---

164. Cartwright, *Backwoods Preacher*, 124.

165. Rowland and Morray-Jones, *Mystery of God*, 125–26.

166. See also Sproul, *Discovering the God Who Is*, 28–29.

167. Abbott and Ffirth, *Experience and Gospel Labours*, 48.

168. Lee, *Short History of the Methodists*, 55.

169. Gatch, *Sketch of Rev. Philip Gatch*, 86.

170. Coke, *Extracts of the Journals* [1793], 169.

171. Jackson, *Lives of Early Methodist Preachers*, 6:169.

172. Lee, *Short History of the Methodists*, 10, 285.

of God, rested upon" him and his circuit rider meetings.[173] Moreover, Finley once concluded that the circuit rider "meetings were all attended with the presence and power of God."[174]

Therefore, within circuit rider writings, it is difficult to generate a specific formula in distinguishing between the terms *power* and *presence* of God. While one can argue that perhaps the circuit riders knew of these differences, the reality is that these differences are not evident in their writings. Hence, the *power* and *presence* of God, used singularly or joined together, were perceived by the circuit riders as mysterious divine incidents in which both terms worked to produce supernatural manifestations.

However, in an effort to be precise regarding the theological differences between the two terms (although, again, in circuit rider documents, these differences are difficult to distinguish), one might speculate that there were some theological differences in the minds of the circuit riders because there are slight differences presented in the biblical text.

The word *power* in Hebrew is identified as the prime feminine noun יָד that generally means "hand"; in the context of this study, it means "the hand or active work of God." For instance, it is used in Exodus 14:31, which states that "Israel saw the great power that the Lord used against the Egyptians." This indicates that Israel was a witness of the supernatural works that were performed by God's power (or hand) to punish Egyptian oppression.

The word *presence* in Hebrew is identified as the masculine noun פָּנִים that means "face, appearance, or presence." For instance, the usage of the presence is clearly seen in Exodus 33:14, which states: "My Presence will go with you, and I will give you rest." Many times in the Old Testament, after the Israelites spiritually sought God, God revealed himself through his presence, which was perceived as a reflection of his glory (and majestic power).[175] At times, the presence of God in the Old Testament was visibly thick, like a dense mist or cloud.[176]

173. Watters, *Short Account of the Christian Experience*, 64.

174. Finley, *Autobiography*, 289.

175. Raichur, *Presence of God*, 1–5.

176. This is demonstrated in Exodus 40:34, which states: "Then the cloud covered the tent of meeting, and the glory of the Lord filled the tabernacle." Also, 1 Kings 8:11 states: "So that the priests could not stand to minister because of the cloud, for the glory of the Lord filled the house of the Lord."

Therefore, when the power of God was used biblically, it indicated that a supernatural event was currently and actively being performed (as God's hand was in motion). The presence of God, however, was categorized as a less active form that reflected God's majestic glory or a sensation of a "comfort[ing] . . . Divine [nearness]"[177] combined with a "deep solemnity and awe."[178] Flowing from this theological perspective, the presence of God indicated that God was already there, and the power of God indicated that God was actively doing something. In brief, the presence of God indicated an action button about to be activated, and the power of God indicated an action button that had already been activated. Through this logic, it can be argued that the power of God comes after the presence of God. In other words, one can speculate (as this information cannot be proven through circuit rider writings) that since the circuit riders lived a lifestyle in accordance with the Bible, then, for them, the biblical synonyms of the *power* and *presence* of God, while both identifying something supernatural in nature, were intuitively understood and expressed with slight nuances.

To conclude this section, according to circuit rider writings and biblical theology, it can be stated that both the power and the presence of God are considered supernatural in nature.[179] While, at times, these terms (through a strict biblical analysis) can be considered distinct, in reality, for the circuit riders, it is likely that they expressed a single meaning: that the manifestation of divine omnipotence was present in their meetings and supernatural acts were about to (or had already begun to) occur.[180]

Brief Summary

This chapter was dedicated to examining the term *supernatural* and its definition within the modern world, Christianity, and the circuit rider ministry, specifically. It was demonstrated that, while supernatural phenomena were often historically challenged and criticized (especially post-Enlightenment), recent studies have revealed that supernatural acts are something that more than half of the twenty-first-century population believe in or encounter. Thus, it appears that many individuals today

177. Lee, *Memoir*, 13.
178. Phoebus, *Memoirs of the Rev. Richard Whatcoat*, 96.
179. See also Garrettson, *Experience and Travels*, 102–3.
180. Watters, *Short Account of the Christian Experience*, 64.

(especially Christians affiliated with Pentecostal and Charismatic Christianity) welcome various divine encounters or manifestations.

It was also established that circuit riders identified the *supernatural* as acts that derived from the unseen spiritual realm (most commonly, acts attributed to the Holy Spirit) that defied natural laws. Through experience, the circuit riders discovered that it was vital to seek and encounter these supernatural acts because, as they surpassed the natural realm and its governing laws, they served as the greatest and swiftest means of convicting and converting the public.

Regarding the specific source or origin of supernatural activity in their ministry, it was demonstrated that the circuit riders believed that divine supernatural acts were a direct result of an outpouring of the power and presence of God's Spirit. These two biblical terms, the *power* (dynamite, hand) and *presence* (appearance, face) indicated that something supernatural was about to occur or had begun to occur (in the lives of the circuit riders and/or their audiences). Displays of the power and presence of God were something that circuit riders sought after and relied on because, as further presented in the following chapters, these displays greatly contributed to the ministry's growth.

Additionally, it was noted that in order to better understand the supernatural in the lives and ministries of the circuit riders, supernaturalism was divided into two separate categories within this book: private supernaturalism (which occurred within the circuit riders' personal lives) and public supernaturalism (which occurred within the circuit riders' audiences). These categories are utilized throughout chapter 4 (private supernaturalism) and chapters 5, 6, and 7 (public supernaturalism).

Chapter 2

Wesley and the Supernatural

BEFORE THIS STUDY GOES directly into investigating the supernatural in the American circuit rider ministry and its resulting revivals, it is important to first discuss Wesley because he was both the founder of Methodism and "the first circuit rider";[1] thus, he was the model on which global Methodism and the American circuit rider ministry was built and developed.[2] Attention is placed on investigating the role of the supernatural in the life, theology, and ministry of Wesley. The cultural challenges and religious criticism (influenced by the Age of Enlightenment's skepticism) that Wesley and the early English Methodists (from the 1730s to the 1790s) encountered are also discussed along with their success in spreading evangelistic revival and corresponding supernatural occurrences.[3] While Wesley's experiences largely took place in England, it is through exploring these experiences that a clearer picture of the significance of the supernatural in the American circuit rider ministry (from the 1770s through the 1830s) can be gleaned.[4]

1. Woodburn, *Indiana Magazine of History*, 124.

2. See also Clarke, *Memoirs of the Wesley Family*, 23–24; Evans, "Most Distinctive Contribution of Methodists," 1500; Lee, *Reaching Spiritual Maturity*, 92.

3. Charles and Smith, *Scepticism in the Eighteenth Century*, 337.

4. See Watson, *Pursuing Social Holiness*, 7; Andersen and Taylor, *Sociology*, 606.

The Age of Enlightenment and the Supernatural

Prior to discussing Wesley, however, the cultural climate of his day should be introduced, especially as it pertains to the supernatural; this further explains Wesley's (and, subsequently, other Methodist leaders') treatment of the supernatural within the walls of the church and beyond it.[5] During the time of early Methodism, the influence of Age of Enlightenment thinking[6] was continuously increasing and developing.[7] Many have argued that the Enlightenment (also known as the Age of Reason) produced the era of *modernity*, which was "associated with individual subjectivity, scientific explanation and rationalization, [and] a decline in emphasis on religious worldviews."[8] As indicated in chapter 1, the Enlightenment produced naturalism and skepticism toward Christianity.[9] In contrast, Methodism rose up to promote spiritual renewal and biblical Christianity.[10] While both of these positions were expanding, both in England and America, they also clashed with each other. The early Methodists, including those within the American circuit rider ministry, advocated returning to an authentic gospel lifestyle, taking the supernatural component, which featured the "gifts of the Spirit"[11] literally.[12] Conversely, the Enlightenment advocated sole reliance on human reason and scientific methodology, consequently moving the culture away from centuries of religious thought.[13] Thus, early Methodist

5. See Webster, *Methodism and the Miraculous*, 9; Lawson, *Notes on Wesley's Forty-Four Sermons*, 26.

6. The Enlightenment can roughly be placed between 1685 and 1815.

7. See also Hempton, *Methodism*, 21.

8. "Modernity" (*EBO*).

9. Spielvogel, *Western Civilization*, 1:504.

10. Heitzenrater, *Wesley and the People Called Methodists*, 83.

11. Wesley, *Letter to the Right Reverend the Lord Bishop of Gloucester*, 55. For the complete list of the gifts of the Spirit, see Rom 12:6–8; 1 Cor 12:8–10, 28; Eph 4:11; 1 Pet 4:11.

12. Snethen, *Snethen on Lay Representation*, 122.

13. Kant, *Answer to the Question*, 3–4, 6, 9–10, 20–23. See also Botzet, *Heart for God's Glory*, 121–22.

theology, in England and America, can be considered a "reaction"[14] against the Enlightenment's perspectives and aims.[15]

The developing influence of the Age of Enlightenment was largely a product of a chaotic religious system ruling over Europe, fed by the religious wars (Catholics vs. Protestants and Protestants vs. Protestants) and their spiritual dryness.[16] As people began to agree that the meaning of life, truth, and freedom could no longer be found in the church, they pursued other perceived forms of truth and freedom, replacing their hope in Christianity with a hope in natural reasoning and knowledge.[17] Thus, the Enlightenment was born.

There were a number of prominent Enlightenment thinkers who greatly influenced modern thought, such as René Descartes (1596–1650) who was known as the "father of modern philosophy."[18] Primarily through analytical, rational methods of testing the truth, Descartes declared that when one arrived at clear understanding, that was the truth (a form of rational relativism).[19] John Locke (1632–1704), considered to be a prominent thinker in the Age of Reason, argued that God operated "all his faculties in the natural state," meaning that if God revealed anything, it would not be supernatural in nature; instead, his revelation would be considered naturally reasonable to humanity.[20] Hence, supernatural revelation was judged by natural reason, making humanity's reason the

14. Gauvreau, *Evangelical Century*, 48. In addition to the Methodists, the Roman Catholic Church and Lutheran pietism also reacted against Enlightenment modernity. At first, the Catholic Church was unsure how to respond to the secularizing tendencies of Enlightenment thinkers, but it later decided that the best defense against modernity was to become "ultraconservative" in its approach to the world. Thus, the Catholic Church made new changes that were implemented during this period, and the church's anti-Enlightenment reaction remained in place until the end of World War II when it decided to better engage the modern world. The Lutheran pietist movement also opposed modernity, reacting not only against Enlightenment intellectualism but also against the church of the day. Lutheran pietism promoted experiential Christianity, heartfelt experience, spiritual rebirth, inner regeneration, and revival.

15. Ridgeon, *Major World Religions*, 203; Faggioli, *Council for the Global Church*, 75; MacCulloch, *History of Christianity*, 817–19; Mcgrath and Marks, *Blackwell Companion to Protestantism*, 136; Webber, *Divine Embrace*, 69–70.

16. Campbell, *Christian Confessions*, 127; Osudibia, *Religion and the Global Resurgence of Violence*, 216–21.

17. Schmookler, *Parable of the Tribes*, 197.

18. Mark, *Spiritual Intelligence and the Neuroplastic Brain*, 61.

19. Descartes, *Meditations*, 33. See also Stumpf, *Filozofia*, 235.

20. Locke, *Essay Concerning Human Understanding*, 456.

most important human element.[21] David Hume (1711–1776), who could also be identified as a prominent thinker in the Age of Reason, regarded the supernatural world through his analytical arguments and stated that "mere reason [was] insufficient to convince us of [the] veracity [of miracles]."[22] Charles Darwin (1809–1882) came to the conclusion that all humans (and all species) were and are evolving (although, breathed into existence by the Creator) by "natural selection" from "a common ancestor" as opposed to supernaturally being spoken into existence.[23] A few other thinkers considered important to the shaping of modernity were: Francis Bacon (1561–1626), Thomas Hobbes (1588–1679), Baruch Spinoza (1632–1677), Isaac Newton (1642–1727), Montesquieu (1689–1755), Voltaire (1694–1778), Jean-Jacques Rousseau (1712–1778), Denis Diderot (1713–1784), Immanuel Kant (1724–1804), Georg Wilhelm Friedrich Hegel (1770–1831), John Stuart Mill (1806–1873), and Bertrand Russell (1872–1970).[24]

While the Enlightenment predominantly sought to promote living through natural reason, later thinkers sidestepped the stage of examining supernatural activities through reason and pursued secularism, instead. Echoing Taves, the difference between natural and secular reason is as follows: while natural reason aims to explain the physical world through logical reason, secular reason aims to use the facts of the physical world to disprove religion (with or without a supernatural component).[25] One of the most prominent thinkers of secularism was Karl Marx (1818–1883) who declared that religion was "the opium of the people."[26] Marx claimed that humans, as thinkers of the modern age, needed to rid themselves of religion as it trapped people with superstition and fear. Later on, Friedrich Nietzsche (1844–1900) famously declared that God was dead and that modern society had "killed him," thus, humanity needed to become its own god and create both new rules and a new morality of the order of Übermensch or *the Superman*.[27] Sigmund Freud (1856–

21. Lynch, *Handbook of Organizational Theory and Management*, 130.

22. Hume, *Philosophical Essays*, 203. See also McKay et al., *From the Age of Exploration to the Present*, 503.

23. Darwin, *Origin of Species*, 133, 136, 529.

24. See also Kenny, *Ancient Philosophy*, 5.

25. Taves, *Fits, Trances, and Visions*, 15–16; Zucca, *Secular Europe*, 179.

26. Rühle, *Karl Marx*, 57. See also Marx et al., *Marxism, Socialism and Religion*, 8.

27. Hollingdale, *Nietzsche*, 139–40.

1939) called religion "a fairy tale"[28] and deemed religious teachings useless to humanity (although he appreciated the apostle Paul).[29] The more modern philosopher Jean-Paul Sartre (1905–1980), prior to his philosophical career, claimed to have stood in front of his mirror and "cursed God . . . [then] felt a sense of relief."[30] As a result, he concluded that "God does not exist."[31] It was largely through these thinkers that secularism developed.[32]

It was also during the Enlightenment that thinkers, on a larger scale, began to question the Bible and aimed to explain and examine the Bible from a natural perspective.[33] As such, scholars found the best solution was to simply reject all of the supernatural origins in the biblical text.[34] For example, this naturalistic view was adopted by the American founding father, Thomas Jefferson (1743–1826). He was motivated by Enlightenment thinking but still wanted to remain a Christian; this resulted in him publishing a Bible that did not record any supernatural events (such as those present in Jesus's ministry).[35] Other thinkers tried to research the meaning of the Bible through methods introduced by Descartes, by doubting everything and attempting to answer questions about God through mathematical, scientific, or logical enterprises.[36] This means of approaching God became popular during the Age of Reason and was called *deism*, which is the belief in "a creator who does not intervene in the universe."[37] Deism was also commonly referred to as "natural religion."[38] Even among Christian laymen, this new Enlightenment mindset caused a decrease in supernatural belief and supernatural explanations; at the same time, it caused an increase in

28. Freud, *Future of an Illusion*, 29.

29. Nicholi, *Question of God*, 36, 38.

30. Palau and Sanford, *God Is Relevant*, xii.

31. Sartre, *Existentialism Is a Humanism*, 29.

32. For brief information regarding secular beliefs, see Stokes, *Changing World Religions*, 363.

33. Sheehan, *Enlightenment Bible*, 91–92.

34. Martindale, *Nature and Types of Sociological Theory*, 30.

35. See Jefferson, *Jefferson Bible*; Clark, *Language of Liberty*, 347.

36. Descartes, *Discourse on Method and Meditations*, 14, 23–24, 27, 71, 112–21. Rudolf Karl Bultmann, the German theologian referenced in chapter 1, can be placed in this category.

37. "Deism" (*OED*).

38. "Deism" (*EBO*).

doubt and the growth of nominal Christianity.[39] Hence, many thinkers of the Enlightenment sought to "separate" themselves from religion, or at least the supernatural aspect of it.[40]

In the face of wide-spread Enlightenment thinking, Methodism, initially led by Wesley, implored individuals to return to a Christian perspective that included support of supernatural phenomena, principally in England and then in America. As mentioned earlier, these two conflicting positions of Enlightenment and early Methodism were continuously spreading and developing and, at times, battling one another.[41] Ultimately, it can be said that both movements prevailed, in their own way.

The Supernatural in Wesley's Life, Theology, and Ministry

The upcoming sections are dedicated to establishing an understanding of the supernatural in Wesley's life, theology, and ministry. These sections begin by introducing Wesley's early life, education, and personal conversion; this is followed by a delineation of his theology regarding the supernatural, spiritual holiness (sanctification), the Holy Spirit, and spiritual gifts. The last two sections are dedicated to Wesley's life as a circuit rider and, consequently, the development of his evangelistic strategies (which relied heavily on the supernatural).

Brief Introduction to Wesley's Early Life

Aside from being the main founder of Methodism, John Wesley (1703–1791) is considered to be one of the eighteenth century's most prominent figures in evangelical revivals, along with his brother Charles Wesley (1707–1788) and his friend George Whitefield (1714–1770).[42] While

39. Lane, *Age of Doubt*, 97; Lints, *Fabric of Theology*, 207–8.

40. Wokler, *Rousseau*, 29. For other advocates of natural religion, see Spinoza, *Spinoza's Short Treatise on God*, xxiv, 4–7, 74–77; Voltaire, *Voltaire in His Letters*, 222–23; Locke, *Works of John Locke*, 2:230–31; *Works of John Locke* [6th ed.], 624; Newton, *Mathematical Principles*, 311–13.

41. Glover, *Hymnal 1982 Companion*, 1:386; = Landry, *Marx and the Postmodernism Debates*, 18.

42. Outler, *John Wesley*, iii; Pak, *Christian Spirituality in Africa*, 77.

there is much to explore on Wesley, this study's research focuses on the aspects of Wesley's life, theology, and ministry that most directly pertain to the supernatural.

Wesley was the fifteenth of nineteen children born to Rev. Samuel Wesley, rector of Epworth, and his wife Susanna, who homeschooled her children, including Wesley. When he was a child, Wesley escaped a fire that was in his house; the fire became a revelation for Wesley as he saw it as a glimpse of hell. In the future, he would use this image to develop and express the theology of escaping fiery wrath.[43] Also during his early life, Wesley was exposed to a number of supernatural activities, including a demonic visitation combined with an exorcism performed by his father, Rev. Samuel Wesley.[44] Wesley later became an Oxford scholar where he developed much of his critical thinking and rhetorical skills.[45] During his time in Oxford, Wesley led a Christian association with members including his brother Charles and his friend Whitefield. Due to the association's strict Christian methods (establishing daily timeslots for a number of religious activities, such as Bible study, prayer, and fellowship meetings), they became known, disparagingly, as the "Methodists" and their club, mockingly, as the "Holy Club."[46]

Wesley's Supernatural Experience in Receiving the Assurance of Faith

Through the methods observed in the Holy Club, Wesley grew greatly in his religious knowledge and rhetoric; however, he felt that he never experienced "the full assurance of faith."[47] In Wesleyan and early Methodist theology, *assurance of faith* was often identified as the indicator of a full spiritual conversion (including the receiving of Christian salvation) and was derived from a personal "testimony [with] the Spirit of God."[48] In

43. Sargent, *Oxford Methodist*, 19–24.

44. For more information concerning paranormal testimonies and exorcisms in the Wesley family, see Bruce, *Historic Ghosts and Ghost Hunters*, 36–55.

45. Stormont, *Smith Wigglesworth*, 35; Wood, *Meaning of Pentecost in Early Methodism*, 11.

46. Beiler, *Worker and His Church*, 20. See also Porter, *Rediscovering Worship*, 211; "News from Republic of Letters," 1.

47. Wesley, *Works* [AM], 3:174.

48. Wesley, *Works* [AM], 5:174. See also Wesley, *Works* [AM], 7:278; "Letter to Arthur Bedford."

other words, the assurance of faith confirmed to an individual that they were, indeed, spiritually converted and, thus, held salvation and a place with God in the afterlife. This process was also occasionally identified as *evangelical conversion*.[49]

During his early life, Wesley, as a practicing Christian, understood this process of spiritual conversion, but practically, he felt that he lacked it, and this fact always haunted him; Wesley expressed, "I could not find that all this [practiced Christianity] gave me any comfort, or any assurance of acceptance with God."[50] In other words, though Wesley persistently endeavored to be "doing . . . [any] good [he] could," he desired personal assurance of his Christian salvation.[51]

On October 14, 1735, Wesley decided to embark on a missionary trip to the American colony of Georgia. His mission trip there was labeled by many as "unsuccessful."[52] However, it led to a critical revelation. While on the ship to Georgia, there was a great storm that "split the main-sail in pieces, covered the ship, and poured in between the decks, as if the great deep had already swallowed [the passengers] up." Wesley, fearing death, came to the realization that, despite his education and Methodist "methods" of becoming holy, he was as terrified of the storm as the other Englishmen aboard.[53] However, on the ship with him, there was also a group of German Moravians (who practiced holiness and emphasized the importance of experiencing the Holy Spirit).[54] In the midst of the storm, these Moravians calmly sang hymns. Wesley was astonished by this and, as modern scholar Collins explained, he used the incident to "test . . . his own religious experience" and Christian maturity.[55] Wesley realized that whatever assurance the Moravians had, he did not have. Hence, Wesley classified that day as "the most glorious day which [he] had] hitherto seen."[56]

On March 4, 1738, Wesley returned to England from his trip to Georgia and sought friendship with the Moravians living in England.

---

49. Wesley et al., *Letters of John Wesley*, 33.

50. Wesley, *Journal* [AM], 1:98.

51. Wesley, *Journal*, 1:94.

52. Walker, *History of the Christian Church*, 512.

53. Wesley, *Journal*, 1:20.

54. Watson, *Pursuing Social Holiness*, 72.

55. Collins, *John Wesley*, 58–62.

56. Wesley, *Journal*, 1:20.

Through his relationship with them, Wesley admittedly developed a fuller understanding of both the experiential gospel and Christian life. On May 24, 1738, on Aldersgate Street, London, Wesley attended a Moravian meeting, and while listening to a teaching on the book of Romans, encountered the following supernatural experience: "About a quarter before nine, while [the preacher] was describing the change which God works in the heart through faith in Christ, I felt my heart strangely warmed. I felt I did trust in Christ, Christ alone, for salvation; and an assurance was given me, that he had taken away my sins, even mine, and saved me from the law of sin and death."[57] This was the moment when Wesley firmly realized that he had experienced personally, and in a supernatural manner, spiritual conversion.[58] The morning after his supernatural experience, despite the fact that "the enemy injected a fear" in him and he had "temptations," Wesley felt that God empowered him with fresh spiritual "strength."[59] After this phenomenon, Wesley's life and "missionary work"[60] changed forever.[61]

Wesley and the Theology of Supernatural Experience

Upon receiving the experience of his heart strangely warmed, Wesley's theological perspective on the supernatural dramatically developed as, after his spiritual encounter, one of Wesley's main objectives became proclaiming the need to know God "both in theory and experience."[62] Through this, as O'Byrne noted, supernatural or divine spiritual

57. Wesley, *Journal*, 1:97–98.

58. Fewier, "Appeal of the Twentieth Century," 89.

59. Wesley, *Journal*, 1:93, 98–99.

60. Battin, *Ethics of Suicide*, 403.

61. Some scholars, such as Maddox, supported the notion that there were at least three times in Wesley's life in which he experienced significant changes or transitions (the first one being his conversion); however, this study concludes that Wesley had only one major transition that changed him forever (the heart strangely warmed experience) and all of his future transitions were only further developments of his Christian theology and ministry (which were also shaped by the circumstances of his life). For more information, see Maddox, *Responsible Grace*, 20–23. See also Knight, *Presence of God in the Christian Life*, 11–15; Wesley, *Journal*, 1:97–98.

62. Wesley, *Works*, 1:i. See also Wesley, *Sermons on Several Occasions* [Emory], 15–16, 103, 164–66; *Journal*, 1:125.

experiences became one of the cornerstones of early Methodist theology in England and America.[63]

In early Methodism (as well as in modern Christian circles), the experience of spiritual conversion was called *new birth*, *rebirth*, or being *born again*.[64] Wesley declared that conversion was "absolutely necessary, in order to obtain eternal salvation."[65] When individuals were converted or reborn (through the Spirit of God), they were "assured that they [were] in a state of grace, and [could] persevere therein unto salvation, by the Holy Spirit . . . bearing witness with their spirits that they [were] the children of God."[66] This experience was a "supernatural work" and was brought into existence, according to Wesley, by the "supernatural assistance of [God's] Spirit."[67] Indeed, this phenomenon played an inseparable role in early Methodism because, without experiencing Christianity supernaturally, especially in the process of conversion, it could be argued (as Wesley did, followed by the American circuit riders) that one was not an authentic Christian.[68] When Christianity was experienced in a supernatural way (as through an encounter with the Spirit), this often sparked in one a need for a spiritual lifestyle, and with the spiritual presence of God in one's life, Wesley concluded that "all things are possible . . . to him that believeth,"[69] emphasizing the supernatural potential in Christianity.[70]

Because supernatural experience played such a central role in Wesley's life, Methodist theology concerning spiritual experience was later integrated into the Wesleyan Quadrilateral. The term *Wesleyan Quadrilateral* was coined by the twentieth-century Methodist scholar Outler and was based on the four factors (Scripture, tradition, reason, and experience) that Wesley believed comprised the core of Christian

63. O'Byrne, "How Methodists Were Made," 186–87. See also Gauvreau, *Evangelical Century*, 46–47.

64. For more information concerning the process of rebirth, see John 3.

65. Wesley, *Sermons on Several Occasions* [Emory], 208.

66. Wesley, "Letter to Arthur Bedford." See also Wesley, *Sermons on Several Occasions* [Emory], 19, 93; *Works* [AM], 5:434.

67. Wesley, *Sermons on Several Occasions* [Emory], 38, 168.

68. Wesley, *Works* [AM], 5:434. See also Wesley, *Sermons on Several Occasions* [Emory], 209; *Works* [AM], 5:689; Jennings, *Supernatural Occurrences of John Wesley*, 189–95. For more information regarding the role of the supernatural in the American circuit rider ministry, please see chapter 5.

69. Wesley, *Sermons on Several Occasions* [Emory], 22.

70. See also Wesley, *Sermons on Several Occasions* [Emory], 23; McEndree and McEndree, *Body Temple*, 86; Cunningham, *John Wesley's Pneumatology*, 84–86.

thought.[71] In Methodism, spiritual experience was considered to be, after Scripture, "the strongest proof, of Christianity."[72] Thus, the supernatural was an integral part of the life, theology, and ministry of Wesley and also early Methodism in England and then in America.[73]

However, this Methodist theological concept of experiencing "new birth" sounded too unusual and foreign to many people in England and was criticized by many; this disapproval was also seen in English newspapers of the day, such as *The Ipswich Journal*, which advertised a sermon on the "pretensions of the Methodists" and their "religious delusion," warning the public to exercise "caution . . . on the [Methodist concept of] new birth."[74]

The Significance of the Supernatural in Wesleyan Sanctification

Wesley believed that the church, especially the clergy of the Anglican Church (i.e., the Church of England, which was, at the time, the only fully recognized Christian church in England), was spiritually corrupt and, as a result, the entire Anglican Church needed to be sanctified/become holy.[75] Wesley's scriptural beliefs were clear that, echoing Hebrews 12:14, without holiness, "no man shall see the Lord."[76] Thus, the concept of sanctification was vital to early Methodism in England and America.[77]

According to Wesley, when one was spiritually born again, then sanctification, or the process of "inward and outward holiness," began.[78] Wesley's missional goal (along with the goal of the American circuit rider ministry) became "to reform the nation, particularly the Church; and to spread scriptural holiness over the land."[79] Furthermore, humanity had a part to play in its sanctification; not only did one need to receive Christian "justification," but also, one needed to constantly pursue God

71. For more information, see Outler, "Wesleyan Quadrilateral."

72. Spence-Jones et al., *Christian Evidences*, 134.

73. See also Snyder, *Radical Wesley*, 71.

74. Stebbing, "This Day: Public," 4.

75. Wesley, *Journal*, 1:343, 468.

76. Wesley, *Sermons on Several Occasions* [Emory], 208.

77. Harris, *Holy Spirit, Holy Living*, 69.

78. Wesley, *Sermons on Several Occasions* [Emory], 211. See also Wesley, *Journal*, 1:82; *Works* [AM], 5:805; Hervey and Wesley, *Theron and Aspasio*, 294; Taves, *Fits, Trances, and Visions*, 63.

79. Wesley, *Works* [AM], 5:212.

in order to be sanctified. Ultimately, Wesley believed that it was through the supernatural power of God that one was able to become sanctified; without divine intervention, sanctification could not be achieved. The pivotal role that the divine played in the act of sanctification was emphasized in Wesley's following biblical statement (quoting 1 Thess 5:23): "The God of peace shall sanctify thee wholly." Indeed, people could be sanctified or "inwardly renewed by the power of God."[80] However, as Wesley stated, one also had to actively "choose holiness" because this was "the only way, to everlasting Life."[81] Although, without God's "Spirit, [or] his supernatural work [working] in the souls of men,"[82] the process of sanctification was not possible through human choice alone.[83] As Wesley testified, both were needed (the supernatural and the individual will) for one to become holy.[84] Wesley's theology of sanctification became a crucial part of the American circuit rider ministry, as well.[85]

Wesley's Views Regarding the Holy Spirit

Wesley heavily emphasized the supernatural power, presence, and experience of the Holy Spirit, whom Wesley often referred to as "the Holy Ghost," as was common in his day.[86] Prior to Wesley's empowerment by the Spirit of God (the heart strangely warmed experience), even though he was baptized as a child and was considered to be a converted and practicing Christian, he lived what he called a form of "powerless" Christianity.[87] As Wesley pointed out: "I was about ten years old . . . was given in baptism, having been strictly educated and carefully taught . . . [in] keeping all the commandments of God . . . in the meaning of which I was diligent . . . But all that was said to me of inward obedience or holiness I

---

80. Wesley, *Sermons on Several Occasions* [Emory], 44, 78, 214.

81. Wesley, *Journal*, 1:285.

82. Wesley, *Sermons on Several Occasions* [Emory], 39.

83. Wesley, *Works*, 4:20.

84. For more information regarding the supernatural power of the Holy Spirit within the Wesleyan process of sanctification, see Arnett, "Role of the Holy Spirit," 5–23.

85. For more information regarding the sanctification theology of the American circuit riders, see chapter 4.

86. Wesley, *Works* [*AM*], 5:73.

87. Williams, "Wesleys and Peter Bohler," 93.

neither understood nor remembered."[88] He then came to believe that the supernatural presence and acts of the Holy Spirit brought about authentic Christianity; as perceived by contemporary theologian Olson, "for Wesley, authentic Christianity [was] experiential Christianity."[89] Wesley, at one point in a sermon, rhetorically asked: "Do you know what religion is?" He then answered: it is "for a Christian [to be] . . . anointed with the Holy Ghost, and with power."[90]

Wesley also stated that "the Spirit of God . . . is promised, and, upon performance of the covenant which God hath made with us, will certainly . . . be received."[91] Without the supernaturalism of the Holy Spirit, Wesley knew that neither he, nor even the early apostles, could effectively live or understand a Christian life. Moreover, regarding the apostles themselves, Wesley pointed out that, prior to their Pentecost event, "[they] had not, in the full sense, 'new hearts' . . . [because] they [had not] received 'the gift of the Holy Ghost.'"[92] Wesley understood that if the early apostles "were all filled with the Holy Ghost"[93] then, likewise, Wesley and the church at large needed to be filled with the same Spirit.[94] Furthermore, according to Wesley, by "deny[ing] . . . this receiving [of] the Holy Ghost . . . [or the] feeling [of] being moved by the Spirit, or filled with it . . . [one denied] to have any place in sound religion" because whoever denied the divine power and presence of the Spirit denied "the whole Scriptures, the whole truth, and promise, and testimony of God."[95]

Wesley further testified that the supernatural not only worked inwardly but also outwardly.[96] The power of the Holy Spirit, according to Wesley, was at work during his ministry, especially in his preaching. He acknowledged that his preaching would have been ineffectual if it were not for the Holy Spirit. He declared that his and other Methodist preaching was in "vain, unless it [was] attended with the power of that Spirit." Wesley attributed the success of his preaching to the power and

---

88. Wesley, *Works*, 1:98.

89. Olson, *Westminster Handbook to Evangelical Theology*, 21.

90. Wesley, *Sermons on Several Occasions* [Emory], 21.

91. Wesley, *Works* [AM], 5:73.

92. Wesley, *Works*, 1:117–18. Pentecost was a historic event in which the apostles were filled with the power and presence of the Holy Spirit. For more information, see Acts 2.

93. Wesley, *Sermons on Several Occasions* [Emory], 27.

94. Wesley, *Sermons on Several Occasions* [Emory], 314, 388–89.

95. Wesley, *Sermons on Several Occasions* [Emory], 23–24.

96. Wesley, *Sermons on Several Occasions* [Emory], 26–27.

presence of the Holy Spirit who "alone pierces the heart." A sermon or belief standing only "in the wisdom of men, but [not] in the power of God" was considered useless, so Wesley emphasized that the "power [of the Spirit should] be present" in all Methodist meetings, enabling people to "heal [their] soul, and to give [them] a [genuine] faith."[97] In other words, Wesley believed that it was the Spirit who caused him to preach a successful message; it was the Spirit who prompted his audiences to experience conviction and accept the salvation of the gospel.[98] Thus, Wesley placed strong emphasis on the supernatural experience of the Holy Spirit in the early Methodist movement; as presented in the following chapters, this also extended to the American circuit rider ministry.

Wesley and the Gifts of the Holy Spirit

Regarding the supernatural or "extraordinary gifts of the Holy Ghost,"[99] Wesley believed that they were available to the church in his day, as well.[100] Some of the most important supernatural gifts in Methodism were considered to be healing,[101] the casting out of demons,[102] "the word of wisdom . . . the word of knowledge . . . [the] working of miracles . . . prophecy . . . [and] the discerning of spirits." Indeed, through these gifts, Wesley witnessed "so many interpositions of Divine power" that could not be accounted for "in a natural way" because "they were . . . supernatural."[103]

During Wesley's time, however, the gifts of the Holy Spirit were considered by many to have ceased (likely a product of Enlightenment thinking). In response, Wesley argued that he did "not recollect any scripture . . . either in the Old Testament or the New" that "taught, that miracles were to be confined within the limits either of the Apostolic or the Cyprianic [early church] age." In fact, Wesley did not believe that supernatural

97. Wesley, *Works* [*AM*], 5:65.

98. For instance, see Wesley, *Works*, 4:36; *Experience of Several Eminent Methodist Preachers*, 192; Lawson, *Notes on Wesley's Forty-Four Sermons*, 26; Forsyth, "Christianity and Society," 18; Dixon, *Methodism in Its Origin*, 105.

99. Wesley, *Sermons on Several Occasions* [Emory], 25–28.

100. UMC, "Guidelines."

101. In one of his letters, Wesley argued that the miraculous gifts of healing were available in the eighteenth century. See Wesley, *Works* [*AM*], 5:733–34.

102. Wesley acknowledged having personal experiences with demonic oppression, such as spiritual attacks of fear. See Wesley, *Journal*, 1:98.

103. Wesley, *Works* [*AM*], 5:465, 469, 470. See also Throness, *Protestant Purgatory*, 10.

gifts had ceased to exist in "any period of time."[104] However, according to Wesley, the reason why the supernatural gifts of the Spirit were no longer common or, at least, not as common as during the Apostolic Age or the age of the early church was because Christians were no longer interested in wholeheartedly following the gospel and executing God's mission.[105] Wesley argued that the interest of many Christians had become the pursuit of "riches, and power, and [honor]."[106]

Wesley stated that after the Apostolic and early church age ended, many Christians could be considered "nominal Christians." These "so called" Christians "waxed cold" toward living a gospel-oriented lifestyle and "had no more of the Spirit of Christ than the other Heathens" who knew little to nothing of the gospel; according to Wesley, this meant that they had adopted "only a dead form" of Christianity. Wesley identified nominal Christianity as "the real cause why the extraordinary gifts of the Holy Ghost" had ceased to exist in the church of his day; nevertheless, Wesley firmly believed that God willed the gifts of the Spirit to be evident in the church.[107]

Additionally, Wesley argued that because Christians lost their authentic "faith and holiness," in turn, these "dry, formal" believers began to "ridicule whatever gifts they had not themselves, and to decry them all, as either madness or imposture."[108] Because, according to Wesley, the majority of religious people at that time lived lifestyles similar to that of non-Christians, they were not able to personally experience or comprehend the supernatural phenomena that flowed from the gifts of the Spirit, and for this reason, they opposed them.[109] Wesley pointed out that Christians developed a "hardness of [their] hearts," and they were "unready to receive anything [spiritual] unless [they could] see it with [their]

---

104. Wesley, *Works* [*AM*], 5:328.

105. It is generally accepted that the Apostolic Age began roughly around 33 AD (on the Day of Pentecost) and lasted until sometime in the late 90s AD (ending with the death of the last of the twelve disciples, the apostle John). It is generally accepted that the time of the early church began after the apostle John's death (during the late 90s AD) and lasted until Constantine legalized Christianity (through the Edict of Milan) in the Roman Empire in the year 330 AD. See also Pamphilus, *Ecclesiastical History of Eusebius Pamphilus*, xxviii–xxxiii; Baird, *Days That Are Past*, 9–73.

106. Wesley, *Works*, 7:75.

107. Wesley, *Works* [*AM*], 7:75. See also Webber, *Divine Embrace*, 31–32.

108. Whitehead, *Life of the Rev. John Wesley*, 1:430.

109. Aginasare, *Power Demonstration*, 70.

eyes and hear it with [their] ears."[110] The inexperience of spiritual events caused some Christians to protest supernatural phenomena, making it further scarce and the "grand reason why the miraculous gifts were so soon withdrawn."[111]

However, Wesley believed that if individuals instead chose to live a spiritual and scriptural lifestyle, then the gifts of the Holy Ghost would be manifested among them as during the Apostolic Age or the early church.[112] Thus, Wesley believed in the existence and practice of the gifts of the Spirit, and he believed that, through them, God would orchestrate various supernatural phenomena.[113] As demonstrated in upcoming chapters, the American circuit riders continued Wesley's legacy of believing in and practicing the gifts of the Spirit throughout their lives and ministries.[114]

Wesley as the First Circuit Rider

Mostly due to the early Methodists' spiritual "nonsense,"[115] the Anglican Church prohibited Wesley, who was an ordained Anglican priest, from preaching inside the established churches.[116] However, Whitefield offered Wesley a new opportunity to preach, and Wesley, with mixed feelings, accepted it. Wesley later stated: "Being thus excluded from the churches, and not daring to be silent, it remained only to preach in the open air; which I did at first, not out of choice, but necessity." However, this new approach of open-air preaching turned out to be favored as the Spirit made "a way for myriads of people, who never troubled any church, nor were likely so to do, to hear that word which they soon found to be the power of God unto salvation."[117] Wesley began to preach outdoors anywhere he could because, according to him, the world had become his

110. Wesley, *Works* [*AM*], 3:134.

111. Whitehead, *Life of the Rev. John Wesley*, 1:430.

112. Wesley, *Works* [*AM*], 5:465, 474; *Sermons on Several Occasions* [Emory], 207–8; Billman, *Supernatural Thread in Methodism*, 28; Rack, *Reasonable Enthusiast*, 187.

113. For more information about Wesley defending the existence of supernatural spiritual gifts in the modern age, see Wesley, *Works* [*AM*], 5:465–76.

114. For a brief summary of the gifts of the Spirit in the American circuit rider ministry, see Towns, *Ten Most Influential Churches*, 25.

115. Spielvogel, *Western Civilization*, 2:527.

116. Trickler, *Layman's Guide*, 162. See also "London: January 28," 2.

117. Wesley, *Works*, 13:291–92.

congregation.[118] He sought to make Christian services available for all, although his special interest was in those who had been "marginalized"[119] or neglected by the Anglican Church of the day, particularly the working class and the poor.[120]

Wesley, who was seen by the American circuit riders as their mentor and inspiration, was also known to be the pioneer of the circuit rider ministry.[121] During his lifetime, Wesley traveled throughout different circuits (predominately in England) on horseback, covering approximately 250,000 miles and preaching more than 40,000 sermons.[122] His mission was, as it would be for future circuit riders, "to save as many souls as [he could]; to bring as many sinners as [he] possibly [could] to repentance, and with all [his] power to build them up."[123]

Wesley's preaching occurred in diverse outdoor settings, such as fields, barns, and the streets; he simply "preached anywhere"[124] he could.[125] Due to the increase of revivals, followed by the need for more preachers (Wesley could not do it all), he began to appoint other Methodists as preachers in different circuits or locations in order to teach the gospel and aid in revivals.[126] Wesley placed himself in charge of these appointments, stating: "Above all, you are to preach when and where I appoint."[127] Wesley also began to appoint preachers to America, as well, such as: Boardman, Pilmore, Williams, and later on, Rankin, Coke, and Asbury. The upcoming chapter discusses these appointments as well as the early formation of the American circuit rider ministry, in depth.

118. Wesley, *Sermons on Several Occasions* [Emory], 44.

119. Warner, "Towards a Wesleyan Evangelism," 223.

120. Kim, *Rise of the Global South*, 211.

121. Powell, "Methodist Circuit Riders in America," 2–3.

122. Tomkins, *John Wesley*, 199.

123. Wesley, *Works* [AM], 5:219.

124. *Christian Work and the Evangelist*, 719.

125. Later in his ministry, before Wesley preached in any area, he ensured that local Methodist classes were available for new converts.

126. Richey, *Methodism in the American*, 13–14.

127. Wesley, *Works*, 4:521.

Wesley and the Supernatural in Evangelism

Because Wesley saw the world as his congregation, his zeal was for every-one to supernaturally experience God's conversion or rebirth.[128] Wesley exclaimed: "Suffer me now to tell you my principles in this matter. I look upon all the world as my parish; thus far I mean, that, in whatever part of it I am, I judge it meet, right, and my bounden duty, to declare unto all that are willing to hear, the glad tidings of salvation."[129] Especially after his own (spiritual) conversion, Wesley felt a divine prompting to evange-lize to anyone who had not yet experienced Christian salvation.[130]

He also emphasized free and open salvation that was "manifested [to] all [who would] believe" because God "seeks and saves [all who are] lost."[131] This passion to evangelize to the world was combined with his clear Arminian theology;[132] Wesley was so much against Calvinist pre-destination theology (in which only the "elect" were appointed by God to receive salvation) that he claimed it "represents the most holy God as worse than the devil."[133] Wesley often expressed that the power and the grace of God caused people to desire Christian salvation;[134] however, he also believed that it was everyone's duty and responsibility to choose God as seen in the concept of Wesleyan prevenient grace.[135] In brief, *pre-venient grace* is God's "grace [that] stirs the conscience and makes the sinner hunger for God."[136] Wesley believed that, for humanity, the "choice is plain: either [one] must take up [their] cross, or [they] must turn aside from the way of God."[137] Thus, Wesley believed that everyone is responsi-ble for responding to God's grace of their own accord and will.[138] As such,

128. Wesley, *Sermons on Several Occasions* [Emory], 178–79; Snyder, *Radical Wes-ley*, 64.

129. Wesley, *Works*, 1:201.

130. See Wesley, *Works* [AM], 7:8; 5:482.

131. Wesley, *Sermons on Several Occasions* [Emory], 4, 44.

132. Olson, *Arminian Theology*, 108; Webster, *Methodism and the Miraculous*, 14.

133. Wesley, *Sermons on Several Occasions* [Emory], 586.

134. Wesley, *Sermons on Several Occasions* [Emory], 1–2.

135. Ewbank, *John Wesley, Natural Man, and the "Isms"*, 11–12.

136. Schmidt, *God Seekers*, 226.

137. Wesley, *Sermons on Several Occasions* [Emory], 543.

138. A key interpreter of Wesleyan theology concerning free will and predestina-tion was John William Fletcher (1729–1785). For more information, see Fletcher, *First Check to Antinomianism*.

empowered by the grace of God, Wesley chose to preach this responsive gospel to all who would hear as, echoing Hebrews 7:25, God "is able to save to the uttermost all them that come unto . . . him."[139]

As specified earlier, Wesley felt that the main aim of these circuit sermons was to witness and proclaim ways in which people would have an opportunity to "experience inward religion."[140] For instance, at one point, Wesley witnessed a meeting when the power of God's Spirit descended "so mightily among [them], that one, and another, and another, fell down as thunderstruck" (intended by Wesley to mean literally struck to the ground as if by a violent storm, also known as being *slain in the Spirit*). While some were falling, others "were in deep anguish of spirit, [and] were all filled with peace and joy." At least "ten persons . . . found such a change, that sin had no more dominion over them."[141] Wesley became joyful because of the fact that a supernatural touch was evident, and there was great ministerial success. Wesley also witnessed various supernatural encounters within the human heart as sinners repented; while, in the past, these individuals were purportedly afflicted by fear, after these encounters, love and joy were present in them.

In another meeting, Wesley stated that he was "insensibly led" to boldly declare to his audience the scripture knowledge that "God willeth 'all men to be' thus 'saved.'" Wesley then found himself praying that God "would bear witness to his word." Immediately, as he encountered previously, "one, and another, and another, sunk to the earth: they dropped on every side as thunderstruck." Hence, during Wesley's preaching and prayer, God visited the place with "the sword of the Spirit,"[142] causing many to be struck down to the earth and experience conversion. On a similar occasion, Wesley witnessed that, as a result of their spiritual encounters, "many drunkards, many unjust and profane men . . . began to live, and continue so to do, a sober, righteous, and godly life." Wesley expressed that these extraordinary conversions could not have been "owing to novelty, or to any principle but the power of God."[143]

However, Wesley "understood that many were offended at the cries of those on whom the power of God came." For instance, during one

139. Whitehead, *Life of the Rev. John Wesley*, 1:457.

140. Wesley, *Works* [AM], 5:144.

141. Wesley, *Miscellaneous*, 608. For more information on the act of being slain in the Spirit, see chapter 5.

142. Wesley, *Works* [AM], 3:129.

143. Wesley, *Works*, 12:90. See also Wesley, *Works*, 4:721.

meeting, there was a man present who "was a physician" and suspected that Methodist spirituality was "fraud or imposture in the case." However, there was also a female present at the meeting "whom [the physician] had known many years"; she was touched by God and, as a result, "broke out 'into strong cries and tears.'" When the physician saw this, his skepticism began to shake, and he "could hardly believe his own eyes and ears." The physician came near her and "observed every symptom till great drops of sweat ran down her face, and all her bones shook." Witnessing this matter, the physician was shocked and ardently convinced that this "was not fraud, nor yet any natural disorder." Finally, while the physician was further observing her, the Spirit of God touched "both her soul and body [and she was] healed in a moment." Consequently, the physician believed and "acknowledged [that] the finger of God" was truly behind Methodism.[144]

Wesley was also aware that there were those who witnessed supernatural phenomena or "signs and wonders" and still chose to "not believe." When faced with supernatural acts, these individuals would "explain them away" and reason that supernatural occurrences "were purely natural effects; [for instance,] the people fainted away only because of the heat and closeness of the rooms." Others were certain that these phenomena were "all a cheat . . . Else why were these things only in their private societies: why were they not done in the face of the sun?" However, even in these cases, Wesley defended himself and Methodism by reminding these skeptics that God was working with "his arm, not in a close room, neither in private, but in the open air, and before more than two thousand witnesses." Indeed, when the Spirit of God descended, it often caused "one, and another, and another [to be] struck to the earth; exceedingly trembling at the presence of his power." Others would cry "with a loud and bitter cry," and some would engage in "rejoicing, and singing, and with all their might giv[e] thanks to the God of their salvation."[145]

Regardless of public opinion, supernatural occurrences continued and were such common features in Wesley's ministry that there were times when, as modern scholar Knox observed, people "were much scandalized by [them]."[146] In addition to being slain in the Spirit, healings

144. Wesley, *Works* [*AM*], 3:130.

145. Wesley, *Works* [*AM*], 3:134.

146. Knox, *Enthusiasm*, 529. For extensive research conducted on various supernatural encounters in Wesley's life and ministry, see Jennings, *Supernatural Occurrences of John Wesley*.

were prominent. For example, Wesley recorded that doctors told a man, Mr. Meyrick, that he would not live to see the morning; however, after "a few of [them] immediately joined in prayer . . . his sense and his speech returned. Wesley attributed this healing to "the power of God."[147] Wesley witnessed the healing of a case of breast cancer in which, after prayers, Mr. Bell expressed the following: "It was gone; and from that hour I have had no pain, no soreness, no lumps, or swelling; but both my breasts were perfectly well, and have been so ever since."[148] Wesley described a woman who had entirely lost sight in her right eye. One night, she dreamed that the "Savior appeared to [her]; [she] fell at his feet, and [Jesus] laid his hand upon [her] right eye. Immediately [she woke up], and from that moment [she was able to see] as well with that eye as with the other."[149] Wesley recalled "a cripple that could hardly move with crutches . . . [and after prayer] was in a moment made whole."[150]

Within his ministry, Wesley was also involved in many incidents of spiritual warfare and exorcism.[151] For instance, Wesley described one demonically influenced girl who experienced continuous physical pains, fits (of rage), inappropriate language, and compulsions to strip naked (reportedly contrary to her will). However, after many prayers "all these symptoms ceased; and she [continued to live] in health both of soul and body." During one of Wesley's sermons, he encountered a demonically influenced girl who displayed furious gnashing of her teeth and many roaring noises (sometimes it took four people to hold her down for prayers). After many continuous prayers, "God . . . heard the prayer. All her pangs ceased in a moment: she was filled with peace, and knew that the [demon] was departed from her." During another one of his sermons, Wesley encountered a case with a woman who habitually stuck her tongue out of her mouth and distorted her face. Allegedly, the devil then took hold of her mind and threatened to kill her if Wesley attempted to pray over her. "However, [Wesley] prayed on . . . [and] immediately after it was writhed into all kind of postures, the same horrid yell continuing still.

---

147. Wesley, *Works* [*AM*], 3:275.

148. Wesley, *Journal*, 2:112. See also Jennings, *Supernatural*, 56.

149. Wesley, *Journal* [*1773–1790*], 270.

150. Wesley, *Explanatory Notes Upon the New Testament*, 138. See also Maddox, *Responsible Grace*, 147.

151. Jennings, *Supernatural*, 4–47. For more information regarding spiritual warfare in the circuit rider ministry, see chapters 4–5.

But [they] left her not till all the symptoms ceased." After these prayers, the woman was made well, and she rejoiced and praised God.[152]

These incidents are a sample of Wesley's general circuit meetings and highlight the significance of the supernatural within them. Beyond the common occurrences of being slain in the Spirit, healings, and spiritual warfare, Wesley recorded other phenomena that occurred within his ministry, such as: angelic visitations,[153] prophecies,[154] divine dreams,[155] visions,[156] and divine weather changes.[157] Indeed, according to Wesley, various forms of supernatural phenomena persisted throughout his ministry as "the power of God continue[d] to work with almost irresistible force; and there is good reason to hope it will not be withdrawn, till every soul is converted to God."[158]

To conclude, Wesley did his part, faithfully preparing his sermons in the proper manner;[159] however, according to Wesley, all of his efforts would have been in vain had it not been for the Spirit's supernatural presence. According to Wesley, the success of the Methodist revivals (which were historically considered to be successful throughout England) relied heavily on supernatural intervention.[160] Hence, Wesley argued that a "miracle [is a] work of omnipotence, wrought by the supernatural power of God. Now . . . [manifested in Methodist revivals by] the conversion of sinners."[161]

Wesley and Religious Enthusiasm

As demonstrated, many supernatural manifestations followed Wesley's ministry, and consequently, the early Methodist movement in England

152. Wesley, *Works* [*AM*], 3:162, 278, 532, 556.

153. For instance, see Wesley, *Works* [*AM*], 3:22.

154. For instance, see Wesley, *Works* [*AM*], 3:199, 370; Jennings, *Supernatural*, 110–11.

155. For instance, see Wesley, *Works* [*AM*], 3:134, 376, 418, 639; Wesley, *Miscellaneous*, 566.

156. For instance, see Wesley, *Works* [*AM*], 3:115, 437.

157. For instance, see Wesley, *Works* [*AM*], 3:494.

158. Wesley, *Works*, 4:26, 48, 276–77, 427.

159. Meredith, *Real John Wesley*, 192–93.

160. Brown, *Church and State in Modern Britain*, 118.

161. Wesley, *Works*, 12:99.

and America, as well.[162] The early English Methodists (and, later, the American circuit riders) zealously sought revivals, which were largely reached through demonstrations of the power and presence of God. As discussed previously, this often resulted in the early Methodist mission and mindset being considered a threat to the common social, political, and religious order.[163] Initially, Wesley and Whitefield were the main targets of this criticism, reputed to be spreading unbiblical Christianity throughout England.[164] As a result, modern historian Umphrey Lee explained that early Methodism in England and America was often identified using the term *religious enthusiasm*.[165]

This term was largely derogatory, even implying a form of witchcraft or madness.[166] For instance, in 1739, Trapp, who was considered to be an early opponent of Methodism, wrote the following regarding religious enthusiasm: "By Enthusiasm is meant a Person's having a strong, but false Persuasion, that he is divinely inspired; or at least, that he has the Spirit of God some way or other; and This made known to him in a particular and extraordinary Manner."[167] Furthermore, Trapp stated that religious enthusiasts "talk of Dreams, Visions, and Revelations . . . [that are] supported by no Evidence, and consequently [are] false."[168]

The newspapers of those days regularly criticized the Methodists in England, especially because of their religious enthusiasm or enthusiastic expressions. For instance, *The Derby Mercury* accused Methodism of proselytizing and recruiting circuit riders through the use of "enthusiastic preaching"; the paper reported that one young tradesman "of very good substance" had been "seduced" into believing that "God had [spiritually] revealed himself to him," calling him to become an English Methodist circuit rider.[169] The *Caledonian Mercury* warned people in Edinburgh to

---

162. Davies, *Witchcraft, Magic and Culture*, 14.

163. Lee, "Historical Backgrounds," 115.

164. For more information regarding criticism of Wesley and Methodism, see Nockles, "Reactions to Robert Southey," 61–80.

165. Lee, *Historical Backgrounds of Early Methodist Enthusiasm*, 120–21. See also Evans, *History of Modern Enthusiasm*, 119; Hogarth, *Anecdotes of William Hogarth*, 143, 262–64.

166. Billman, *Supernatural Thread in Methodism*, 30; Lyerly, *Methodism and the Southern Mind*, 157.

167. Trapp, *Nature, Folly, Sin, and Danger*, 39. See also Lyles, *Methodism Mocked*, 33; New and Reedy, *Theology and Literature*, 233–34.

168. Trapp, *Nature, Folly, Sin, and Danger*, 40.

169. "Monday's Post," 2.

"consider the danger they [ran] of utterly ruining themselves and their families" by attending Methodist meetings and being exposed to their enthusiastic "doctrine of devils."[170] *The Ipswich Journal* declared that the enthusiastic Methodists operated under a "spirit of confusion and disorder, not of peace" and not of God's Spirit.[171]

Thus, because the participation in and accusation of enthusiasm so greatly shaped Methodism, the remainder of this chapter is dedicated to Wesley's understanding of the concept. Additionally, chapter 6 is further dedicated to illuminating the controversial concept of religious enthusiasm in the American circuit rider ministry.

Categorizing Religious Enthusiasm According to Wesley

The word *enthusiasm* is derived from the Greek word ἐνθουσιασμός, which refers to one being taken by a higher power; a more literal meaning is "possessed by god"[172] or, according to Umphrey Lee, "a divine spirit" violently entering into "the human body."[173] In the time of the circuit riders, the term *enthusiasm* generally carried a degree of supernatural implication within society and was also defined as being an "ill regulated religious emotion or speculation."[174] Furthermore, it was believed that, during a moment of religious enthusiasm, "the individual [left] an ordinary state and enter[ed] one that [was] determined from without and strange, to being no longer 'him or herself.'"[175] The enthusiasts believed that one did not necessary need intellect to communicate with God; instead, emphasis was placed on using emotions or some form of spirituality for divine communication.[176] A more modern Christian understanding (especially among those affiliated with Pentecostal and Charismatic circles) of the word *enthusiasm* is an intense feeling or act that is connected "with the inspiration of the Holy Spirit";[177] thus, it is the Holy Spirit who inspires religious enthusiastic expressions, and consequently, the origin of these expressions is considered to be divine.

170. Ruddi, "Edinburgh," 3–4. See also White, "Infortunate," 3.

171. "Extract of a Letter in the Weekly Miscellany," 2.

172. "Enthusiasm" (*OED*).

173. Lee, *Historical Backgrounds of Early Methodist Enthusiasm*, 13–17.

174. Walker, *Ecology of the Soul*, 76. See also During, *Modern Enchantments*, 52.

175. "Enthousiasmos."

176. Walker, *Ecology of the Soul*, 75–78.

177. Lyles, *Methodism Mocked*, 33.

Wesley was criticized by both the Anglican clergy and the majority of the public for his religious enthusiasm.[178] These parties were often offended in hearing of supernatural events such as the following: "This morning consisted of about one thousand persons . . . [and] the Lord was . . . present . . . [as a person was for] two hours . . . in the visions of God; then the joy, though not the peace, abated."[179] This resulted in the Church of England and the public participating in severe criticism (and, at times, even persecution) of the Methodists; occasionally, as the newspaper *Newcastle Weekly Courant* reported, they were attacked physically and interrupted by "mobs."[180]

This criticism was largely fueled by the cultural move toward rationalism, a product of the Enlightenment. As a result, religious enthusiasts were considered to be a danger to the new reasonable order of society.[181] Philosopher Locke stated that enthusiasm was "founded neither on reason nor divine revelation, but [rose] from the conceits of a warmed or overweening brain."[182] Also, philosopher Kant stated that a religious enthusiast was "properly a deranged person with presumed immediate inspiration and a great familiarity with the powers of the heavens. Human nature knows no more dangerous illusion."[183] Like Locke and Kant, many scholars of the day argued that religious enthusiasm was purely a human delusion or mental disorder. The general public often found enthusiastic acts to be untrustworthy activities and absent, as theologian Laborie asserted, of any "divine origin."[184] Even the Christian community, such as the established clergy in England, found supernatural enthusiasm to be outside of Scripture and human reason. Whether in England or America, these supernatural expressions of enthusiasm were seen, at times, as a sizable threat to the well-established religious traditions.[185]

178. Wesley, *Works* [*AM*], 5:474; 3:134.

179. Wesley, *Works*, 4:39.

180. "London: January 28," 1. See also Wesley, *Journal*, 1:413; Quantin, *Church of England and Christian Antiquity*, 308.

181. Stock, "Enthusiasm," 233.

182. Locke, *Essay Concerning Human Understanding*, 458. See also Hutton, *British Philosophy in the Seventeenth Century*, 185.

183. Kant, "Essay on the Maladies of the Head," 72–73. See also Kant, *Observations on the Feeling of the Beautiful*, 213; Hutton, *British Philosophy in the Seventeenth Century*, 185.

184. Laborie, *Enlightening Enthusiasm*, 139.

185. Lovejoy, *Religious Enthusiasm in the New World*, 216.

Due to the fact that Wesley was quite loyal to the established Anglican Church and the traditional religious order, his goal was never to create a separate denomination but to simply bring reformation or spiritual revival to the Anglican Church.[186] Again, according to the Wesleyan Quadrilateral, Wesley considered religious "tradition" to be a crucial theological component.[187] However, the Church of England, along with the public, continued to criticize Methodism because of the enthusiastic (or supernatural) character of its revivals.[188] Hence, as much as Wesley respected the Anglican Church, he knew that the Holy Spirit was causing these revivals and could not belittle them.[189] Nevertheless, his desire was to be at peace with the church and public. As a result, Wesley had to discover a theological position that would appease those who criticized him and the movement while still allowing an unhindered supernatural flow of the power of God throughout the Methodist movement, including the circuit rider ministry.[190] Since Wesley believed this flow to have originated from God, then it was scriptural and should not cause any offence or division.[191] At this point, Wesley's acquired logical and rhetorical skills would serve as a mediator, defending the supernatural while sidestepping the negative implications of the term *enthusiasm*.[192]

Wesley and His Defense of the Supernatural Component of Methodism

Likely as a result of his education, Wesley deliberately employed reason to express and articulate a thought or idea.[193] Wesley, wanting to defend the Methodists' spirituality while rejecting association with the tarnished term *religious enthusiasm*, chose to refer to enthusiasm as "religious delusion,"[194] consequently assuring the public that the Methodists were

---

186. Compton, *Rekindling the Mainline*, 73; Going et al., *Christian Library*, 3:30; Collins, *John Wesley*, 163–64.

187. See also Thorsen, *Wesleyan Quadrilateral*, 93–106.

188. Oliverio, *Theological Hermeneutics*, 312.

189. Wesley, *Works*, 4:376, 486.

190. Webster, *Methodism and the Miraculous*, 39.

191. Wesley, *Sermons on Several Occasions* [Emory], 616.

192. Eayrs, *Christian Philosopher and Church Founder*, 176.

193. Bullen, *Man Of One Book?*, 134.

194. Wesley, *Journal*, 1:207.

not a form of mentally unsound radicals but, rather, simply Christians who were "born of the Spirit"[195] and exhibited "outward duties, performed in a decent, regular manner."[196] Moreover, to further excuse and defend himself and the Methodist movement, Wesley argued that religious enthusiasm was not derived from God's supernatural presence but, instead, it was "undoubtedly, a disorder of the mind; and such a disorder, as greatly hinders the exercise of reason."[197]

At the same time, Wesley also acknowledged that God spoke through these various spiritual expressions (such as dreams, visions, and trances);[198] thus, Wesley "encourage[d] them,"[199] stating that God gives "remission of sins, and the gift of the Holy Ghost . . . and often in dreams or in the visions of God."[200] Wesley argued that "outcries, convulsions, visions, trances . . . were essential to the inward work, so that [the ministry] could not go on without them." In fact, "perhaps the danger [was], to regard them too little; to condemn them altogether; to imagine they had nothing of God in them." Consequently, Wesley determined that these supernatural phenomena occurred "to strengthen and encourage them that believed, and to make his work more apparent . . . [as God favored some] with divine dreams; others with trances or visions."[201] Wesley also believed that salvation or "saving faith is often" obtained through supernatural "dreams or visions of the night."[202] Hence, even though it appeared, as Taves pointed out, that Wesley criticized and dissociated Methodism with religious enthusiasm, he also "painted himself with it."[203]

Indeed, because Wesley supported the importance of supernatural phenomena in Methodism, he made a point to not exclude them from Methodist theology and practice. On the other hand, in protecting the Methodist church from the scorn of society, Wesley made the decision to remove supernatural acts from under the umbrella term *religious enthusiasm* and instead placed such acts under the category of *religion*

195. Wesley, *Sermons on Several Occasions* [Emory], 203.

196. Wesley, *Sermons on Several Occasions* [Drew], 408.

197. Wesley, *Works*, 5:392. See also Wesley, *Works*, 1:85, 97, 294; Wesley, *Sermons on Several Occasions* [Drew], 408–18.

198. Wesley, *Sermons on Several Occasions* [Jackson], 714.

199. Wesley, *Works* [AM], 5:200.

200. Wesley, *Works* [AM], 3:134.

201. Wesley, *Works* [AM], 7:375.

202. Wesley, *Works* [AM], 5:200.

203. Taves, *Fits, Trances, and Visions*, 16.

of the heart (used to mean experiential, Spirit-led Christianity), which appeared to appease the English social structures of Wesley's day.[204] In this way, Wesley could fully support the supernatural move of the Spirit throughout Methodist ministry while appeasing the rational and suspicious public.[205]

While Wesley categorized supernatural acts using a different name (swapping *religious enthusiasm* with *religion of the heart*), the Methodist experiences of the religion of the heart were largely identical to the experiences encountered by the religious enthusiasts, commonly featuring extraordinary acts, such as shrieking, wailing, and "[falling] to the ground."[206] Thus, Methodist enthusiasm (redefined by Wesley for the benefit of the Anglican clergy of the day, the thinkers of the Enlightenment, and the public) featured manifestations of the experiential religion of the heart and operated according to both Scripture and Christian tradition.[207] Wesley believed that Methodist revivals were experiencing the same supernatural phenomena as "both the prophets of old, and the apostles, [who] were proper enthusiasts . . . [and were] so filled with the Spirit, and so influenced by him who dwelt in their hearts . . . [that] they were wholly actuated by the power of God, and [spoke] only as they were moved by the Holy Ghost."[208]

In employing the term *religion of the heart*, Wesley implied that a Christian operated under both the guidance of Scripture and the stirring of the heart by the Spirit of God.[209] Wesley declared that "the religion of the heart [proclaimed] that God is a Spirit, and they who worship him, must worship him in spirit." According to Wesleyan theology, Christians should be "the true witness[es] of the Spirit . . . by [their] fruit—love, peace, joy; not indeed preceding, but following it."[210] Consequently, Wesley defended Methodism through his reason by presenting it to the

204. Harper, *Way to Heaven*, 119–20; Wesley, *Sermons on Several Occasions* [Jackson], 408.

205. Wesley, *Sermons on Several Occasions* [Emory], 153; *Sermons on Several Occasions* [Jackson], 68.

206. Wesley, *Works*, 4:36.

207. Lee, "Historical Backgrounds," 120; Langford, *Methodist Theology*, 57; Wesley, *Sermons on Several Occasions* [Emory], 353.

208. Wesley, *Sermons on Several Occasions* [Emory], 410.

209. See also Knight, *Presence of God in the Christian Life*, 34–35; Clapper, *John Wesley on Religious Affections*, 101, 112–13, 132–33.

210. Wesley, *Sermons on Several Occasions* [Emory], 108, 153–54, 207–8.

public as not only a supernatural enterprise but also as springing from the fruit of the Spirit or scriptural "holiness,"[211] which enabled one to be a true "witness of his Spirit."[212] Thus, Wesley reasonably combated those who criticized him and the early Methodists by removing attention from supernatural incidents, which were a visible part of the revivals, and instead focusing on presenting the main goal of Methodism, which was the evangelistic spread of the religion of the heart.[213]

Brief Summary

As the founder of Methodism and the first circuit rider, Wesley's theology and work were instrumental in sculpting the American circuit rider ministry (including its supernatural component). As such, this chapter was dedicated to researching the role of the supernatural in Wesley's life, theology, and ministry. The chapter began by introducing the cultural climate of Wesley's time and the ways in which the Age of Enlightenment affected supernatural ministry. It also discussed how the rise of Methodism's experiential religion could be considered a sort of reaction against the rationalism of that time.

The majority of this chapter was dedicated to examining the role of the supernatural in Wesley's life, theology, and ministry, beginning from his own spiritual conversion. It was established that Wesley frequently experienced and depended on the supernatural in both his personal life and ministry. However, Wesley knew that no matter what kind of experience one had, it would "be nothing, unless as it was directed toward inward holiness," which laid the foundation for a supernatural lifestyle.[214] As a result, Wesleyan theology proclaimed that all should pursue scriptural holiness so that they might be spiritually "inwardly moved by the Holy Ghost, to take upon . . . this ministration, for the promoting of his glory, and the edifying of his people."[215] Thus, Wesley encouraged all Methodists (especially preachers) to grow in holiness so that they could move

---

211. Maddox, "Reconnecting the Means to the End," 31.

212. Wesley, *Journal*, 1:120. See also Webster, *Methodism and the Miraculous*, 147.

213. See also Wesley, *Sermons on Several Occasions* [Jackson], 37.

214. Wesley, *Works*, 1:100.

215. Wesley, *Sermons on Several Occasions* [Emory], 37–38. See also Wesley, *Works* [AM], 5:212.

toward and become familiar with supernatural phenomena in their lives and ministries.

Due to its crucial place within his ministry, even while under cultural attack, Wesley defended Methodist supernaturalism, albeit indirectly; he managed to uphold and advocate the value of spiritual experience while identifying it as part of the *religion of the heart* as opposed to the more stigmatized *religious enthusiasm*, though the two terms were considered to be essentially synonymous. As a result, theologian Rack identified him as "a reasonable enthusiast."[216] As a reasonable enthusiast, Wesley remained true to the theology he developed after his supernatural conversion: that is, he viewed Christian spiritual experience as second in importance to Scripture.[217]

Also, as the term *religion of the heart* can be interchanged with the term *religious enthusiasm*, the modern understanding of the term *supernatural* can be interchanged with the term *religious enthusiasm* (especially in the American circuit rider ministry), which was used in the seventeenth and eighteenth centuries.[218] For instance, as demonstrated in chapters 5 and 6, audience members in the American circuit rider ministry often experienced forms of religious enthusiasm, such as shrieking, barking, and physical jerking.[219] The American circuit riders widely encouraged and relied on these experiences of religious enthusiasm, which were reportedly common in their revivals.[220] For example: "The presence of God really filled the place . . . [people] cried or fell . . . [some] occasioned a mixture of various sounds; some shrieking, some roaring aloud . . . Great numbers wept without any noise; others fell down as dead; some sinking in silence; some with extreme noise and violent agitation."[221] These manifestations were labeled as a form of religious enthusiasm and were generally believed, especially by the American circuit riders, to be supernatural

216. Rack, *Reasonable Enthusiast*, 553.

217. Forsaith et al., *Ashgate Research Companion on World Methodism*, 230.

218. Laborie, *Enlightening Enthusiasm*, 140. In his analysis of English society (1500s and 1800s), MacDonald identified *supernatural* as a term that was, at that time, interchangeable with *religious enthusiasm*. See MacDonald, *Sleepless Souls*, 6.

219. Lyerly, *Methodism and the Southern Mind*, 157; Abbott and Ffirth, *Experience and Gospel Labours*, 9; Wigger, *Taking Heaven by Storm*, 276.

220. Billman, *Supernatural Thread in Methodism*, 43. For a brief introduction to American circuit rider revivals and camp meetings, see Beougher, "Camp Meetings and Circuit Riders."

221. Wesley, *Works*, 4:25.

or divine encounters.[222] Supernatural acts, along with those categorized as religious enthusiasm, were proudly seen as the "lifeblood"[223] of the Methodist movement in America.[224] Moreover, some scholars such as Lovejoy argued that, in a sense, the entire American Protestant church during the end of the eighteenth century was touched by the influence of supernatural enthusiasm, which was "a principle of energy that changed the [American] colonists."[225] As aforementioned, chapter 6 explores this matter in detail.

Furthermore, Wesley's personal convictions and practices (including those surrounding the supernatural) were later modeled by the circuit riders. Consequently, the circuit riders understood that, since Methodism sought the experiential religion of the heart, theologically this left room for, and even encouraged, Christians to experience the gospel and live in "namely, the grace of God, the power of his Holy Spirit, which alone [works] in us [and] all that is acceptable in his sight."[226] Wesley asserted that "supernatural power was available to the individual believer"[227] and, thus, believed that the phenomena present in Methodism "were chiefly supernatural, springing from the gracious influences of the Spirit of God which accompanied his word."[228] As modern scholar Kent observed, even though these experiences were intentionally not categorized by Wesley as religious enthusiasm, they were part of the traditional, biblical Christian experience of the religion of the heart through which "examples of healing, prophecy, personal protection, special providences and [spiritual] ecstasy occurred in the Wesleyan societies for a long time."[229]

Indeed, Wesley practiced and theologically advocated the role of the supernatural in Christianity. He especially encouraged it among the Methodist ministers, imploring that they demonstrate a balanced biblical

222. Lyerly, *Methodism and the Southern Mind*, 158.

223. Wigger, *Taking Heaven by Storm*, 112.

224. Peck praised the Methodist movement because of its supernatural component. For more information, see Grow, *From the Outside Looking In*, 18.

225. Lovejoy, *Religious Enthusiasm in the New World*, 215–16. For a unique interpretation regarding enthusiasm, see E. M., "On the Genius of Dr. Johnson," 430.

226. Wesley, *Sermons on Several Occasions* [Emory], 494. See also Cracknell and White, *Introduction to World Methodism*, 148; Webster, *Methodism and the Miraculous*, 12.

227. Kent, *Wesley and the Wesleyans*, 24.

228. Wesley, *Works* [AM], 7:502.

229. Kent, *Wesley and the Wesleyans*, 31.

and spiritual approach and remain "open"[230] to acts of the Holy Spirit.[231] In the end, Wesley's reasoning and perseverance resulted in cultural acceptance. Newspapers, such as *The Morning Chronicle*, reported that Wesley's (and the Methodists') ministerial contributions were perceived to be in "the best interests of mankind."[232] Eventually, Wesley became known as "the best loved man in England and Ireland."[233]

230. Wesley, *Sermons on Several Occasions* [Emory], 406. See also Kent, *Wesley and the Wesleyans*, 8.

231. Taves, *Fits, Trances, and Visions*, 75; Webster, *Methodism and the Miraculous*, 27–30.

232. Mills, "Office of the Commissions," 1.

233. Dobrée, *John Wesley*, 78.

Chapter 3

The History of the
American Circuit Rider Ministry

IN THIS RESEARCH, IT is essential to delineate the history of the structural development of the American circuit rider ministry, and so it is discussed here along with a list of the circuit riders, including Asbury, featured in this work (brief biographical introductions are footnoted or included in the text). As explained in the previous chapter, the design of the circuits was initially laid out by Wesley (in England), which Asbury then implemented (though he further defined the circuits according to American needs) along with the American circuit riders.[1]

Methodist Class Meetings and Societies

Because early Methodism in England quickly spread through revivals, there were many new Wesleyan followers.[2] In order for the new followers to be spiritually nurtured and have regular Methodist fellowship, Wesley organized meetings of various parachurch societies, the primary meetings being the *class meetings*.[3] Initially, the class meetings were comprised of

---

1. Burnett, *In the Shadow of Aldersgate*, 55; Vickers, *Cambridge Companion*, 166; Kuiper, *Church in History*, 356. As further discussed in this chapter, both Francis Asbury and Thomas Coke were the main figures in the founding of American Methodism.

2. Newman and Halvorson, *Atlas of American Religion*, 76; Ditchfield, *Evangelical Revival*, 79.

3. Watson, *Early Methodist Class Meeting*, 95–96.

twelve members, one of whom would serve as a leader of the class.[4] These class meetings featured mandatory weekly meetings and played a tremendous role in strengthening early Methodism through engaging in fellowship, discipleship, reading and studying the Bible, praying, holding each other accountable, and giving to charities.[5] In early Methodism (especially in its early stages in England and then in America), it was considered mandatory for a new convert to participle in these weekly class meetings before becoming a "member-in-good-standing of [a local Methodist] society."[6] In this way, early Methodists could ensure that, before converts immediately joined their society, they were committed to Christianity and had an opportunity to mature spiritually by learning to apply Scripture to their daily lives.[7] Thus, the class meetings were open to all—those new and those experienced in their faith. Wesley's goal for class meetings was to enforce the following: "Do all the good you can, by all the means you can, in all the ways you can, in all the places you can, at all the times you can, to all the people you can, as long as ever you can."[8] As Methodists attended class meetings, it was understood that "to be a Methodist meant to be a member of a class."[9]

Upon faithful attendance of class meetings, attendees presented a ticket from their class leader that enabled them to participate in, and ultimately become members of, their local Methodist society (a local parachurch in which members gathered to worship).[10] Members of any Methodist society, including the circuit riders, did not administer or participate in Holy Communion within their societies.[11] Instead, Methodists received Holy Communion in their local Anglican churches. This was the case in both England and America until American Methodism separated from English Methodism in 1784.[12] Because of the evident importance of Methodist societies and their role in spiritual

4. *One Hundred Thirty-One Christians*, 181–84.

5. Wesley, *Works [AM]*, 5:229; Wright, *Stop the Church's Revolving Door*, 41–43. Also, men and women had separate class meetings.

6. Tyra, *Defeating Pharisaism*, 225.

7. For the general rules of early Methodist societies, see McGee, *March of Methodism*, 30–33.

8. Wesley and Birrell, *Letters of John Wesley*, 423–24.

9. Richey et al., *American Methodism*, 14.

10. Macchia, *Crafting a Rule of Life*, 156.

11. Andrews, *Methodists and Revolutionary America*, 63–68.

12. This is discussed further in the following sections of this chapter.

growth in England, societies were also emphasized from the onset of the American circuit rider ministry.[13] It should be noted that even within these Methodist society meetings (and class meetings), supernatural phenomena were frequently experienced.[14]

The Historical Formation
of the Circuits and Circuit Riders

Due to the rapid growth of Methodist societies in England, Wesley designed and organized Methodist circuits in order to successfully oversee the Methodist societies.[15] Depending on the size of various societies, Wesley arranged one Methodist circuit for each fifteen to twenty (on average) Methodist societies.[16]

As noted in chapter 2, since it was impossible for Wesley to oversee all Methodist circuits and revivals by himself, he recruited various "lay preachers."[17] These lay preachers were appointed to preach and oversee the circuits, and they eventually became known as itinerant preachers.[18] An *itinerant preacher* was a traveling minister appointed to various designated locations (a selected circuit) who was responsible for overseeing and cultivating scriptural holiness and evangelical revivals (with their supernatural component) within that circuit.[19] Depending on the needs of a particular circuit, there were around two to four assigned ministers per circuit. In the early stages of Methodism, one of the appointed circuit ministers was a direct assistant to Wesley (thus, identified as an "assistant") and the other ministers were helpers in the circuits (thus, identified as "helpers").[20]

13. Richey et al., *Methodist Experience in America*, 2:63–64.

14. Abbott and Ffirth, *Experience and Gospel Labours*, 88–89; Finley, *Autobiography*, 197; Cartwright, *Backwoods Preacher*, 306–7; Atkinson, *Centennial History of American Methodism*, 221–22; Peck, *Early Methodism*, 84; Billman, *Supernatural Thread in Methodism*, 58–59.

15. Burnett, *In the Shadow of Aldersgate*, 55; Vickers, "British Methodism," 57; Emery, *Methodist Church on the Prairies*, 37.

16. See also Benson, *Apology for the People Called Methodists*, 200–203.

17. Corn, "Methodism," 297.

18. Mann, *Census of Great Britain, 1851*, 28.

19. Norris, *Financing of John Wesley's Methodism*, 21–22; Heitzenrater, *Wesley and the People Called Methodists*, 167.

20. See also Wesley, *Works [AM]*, 5:229.

In those days, the easiest and fastest way to travel was on horseback.[21] Since, inside an assigned circuit, there were some locations that required covering a great geographical distance, it was necessary for the itinerant preachers to travel via horseback.[22] Thus, the term *circuit rider* was formed. Occasionally, because the circuit riders filled their saddlebags with their possessions, they were also called *saddlebag preachers*.[23] However, these ministers were largely identified as *circuit riders*, specifically in America. It should be noted that the term *circuit rider* was rarely used in England as it appears that the term *itinerant preacher* was used instead.[24]

In America, the circuit riders were selected and appointed during each Methodist Annual Conference.[25] An *Annual Conference* was a meeting of the circuit riders of a particular region; during the meeting, the works of the Methodists within that region were discussed.[26] After numerous outbreaks of Methodist revivals in America, many more Methodist Annual Conferences were established, such as in: New York, Philadelphia, Baltimore, North Carolina, Virginia, and Illinois. Each conference was given a presiding Methodist elder (later, "bishop") who was in charge of appointing, at times, hundreds of preachers to various circuits within that conference.[27] Also, each conference was divided into districts, and within these districts, there was further subdivision into circuits. In each circuit, there were many Methodist societies.[28] Additionally, in each circuit, there was a main circuit rider who met with the other circuit riders quarterly (called *quarterly conferences*) and

21. For more information regarding this matter, see Schivelbusch, *Railway Journey*, 94.

22. Scherck, *Pen Pictures*, 59–60.

23. Tribble, *Colossal Hoax*, 46.

24. See also Smith, *American Spirit*, 314.

25. Later, especially in America, itinerant preachers were responsible for appointing lay preachers (who remained local) to lead and preach at a designed society (at times, more than one society) within a circuit. After the separation of American Methodism from English Methodism in 1784, itinerant preachers became ordained ministers (who could administer Holy Communion). Local lay preachers, on the other hand, remained in the same position, continuing with the responsibility of preaching sermons and leading their society/congregation in worship (though they could not administer Holy Communion). See also McGee, *March of Methodism*, 33–35.

26. Frank, *Polity, Practice, and the Mission*, 131.

27. This system is also known as an episcopal appointment system.

28. Powell, "Methodist Circuit Riders in America," 32–36.

oversaw the entire circuit.[29] The whole American Methodist body met once every four years for the *General Conference*, the purpose of which was to oversee Methodist work and, later, to also select bishops.[30]

Character Qualifications of the Circuit Riders

Those who were being considered for appointment as circuit riders were required to demonstrate commitment to the gospel and knowledge of Methodist ways.[31] A circuit rider candidate was also required to have personally experienced a spiritual conversion (at one point in his life), to have been faithful to the gospel, and to have been called and gifted in proclaiming the gospel.[32] In addition, circuit riders were required to abide under Wesley's authority (again, until 1784 when American Methodism separated from English Methodism) and support his theology (including evangelism and the supernatural component that was discussed in chapter 2).[33] Moreover, aside from intimate knowledge of the Bible, the circuit riders also needed to be familiar with Wesley's writings (such as his Bible study notes and whichever of Wesley's publications were available at the time, such as his *Journals* and written *Sermons*).[34]

Typically, appointed circuit riders were young in age and were known to be very "energetic preachers."[35] Before an individual was even considered for an appointment (according to Wesley and further emphasized by Asbury), that individual needed to know that God had planted a firm desire in him to preach the gospel.[36] Thus, an important criterion in selecting circuit rider candidates was to determine whether the candidate was certain that they were "moved by the Holy Ghost to preach."[37]

---

29. Sandford, "Discourse," 247–48.

30. Teasdale, *Methodist Evangelism*, 16.

31. See also Marshall et al., *From Sea to Shining Sea*, 76.

32. Powell, "Methodist Circuit Riders in America," 37.

33. MEC, *Minutes of the Annual Conferences*, 1:5.

34. Scott, "Review of the Christian Spectator's Strictures," 235–36; Kirk, "Religion, Theology, and Biblical Literature," 142–44.

35. Frank, *American Revolution*, 159.

36. Asbury, *Journal of the Rev. Francis Asbury*, 1:54; Owen, *Sacred Flame of Love*, 75.

37. Wesley, *Works* [AM], 5:230.

After the candidate knew that he was supposed to preach, then Wesley (and, later, the American circuit riders) made other various inquiries to test the quality of the candidate. A prominent question was as follows: "Do they know God as a pardoning God?"[38] As noted, since Wesley had experienced a divine spiritual conversion, he wanted to ensure that all Methodist preachers had encountered a similar experience or conversion (which he viewed as vital to ministry). Therefore, one needed to be personally affiliated with a supernatural encounter of new birth that solidified their full assurance of faith.[39]

Another important question was: "[Do] they [have] the love of God abiding in them?" According to Wesley, Methodist preachers needed to experience the love of God that was "shed abroad in hearts" through the Holy Spirit.[40] "Experience[ing] his precious love" resulted in being internally strengthened.[41] Moreover, by spiritually experiencing God's love, one could "love his brother."[42] Wesley, followed by Asbury in America, further believed that the love of God, reflected in believers, served as an example of the gospel to the world.[43]

Another major question asked of circuit rider candidates was: "[Do] they [have the necessary spiritual] gifts (as well as grace) for the work [of the gospel]?" As discussed in chapter 3, the early Methodists not only believed that "the extraordinary gifts of the Holy Ghost"[44] (such as those described in Rom 12:6–8; 1 Cor 12:8–10) were still active and available, but also, circuit riders were expected to use them.[45] Wesley believed that the divine gifts of the Spirit were given to Christians "from the free grace of God" and were "given to each [Christian] for the profit of the whole body."[46] Thus, Wesley ensured that the Methodist preachers, who were

38. Wesley, Works [AM], 5:230.

39. Heitzenrater, Wesley and the People Called Methodists, 231; Porterfield, Conceived in Doubt, 133.

40. Wesley, Sermons on Several Occasions [Emory], 36.

41. Garrettson, Experience and Travels, 167.

42. Wesley, Sermons on Several Occasions [Emory], 29.

43. Asbury also recalled times in which the love of God refreshed him for his circuit rider sermons. For instance, see Asbury, Journal of the Rev. Francis Asbury, 1:62. See also Wesley, Sermons on Several Occasions [Emory], 92.

44. Wesley, Works, 2:266.

45. Kimbrough, Orthodox and Wesleyan Ecclesiology, 32. For more information on the gifts of the Spirit, see Rom 12:6–8; 1 Cor 12:8–10, 28; Eph 4:11; 1 Peter 4:11.

46. Wesley, Explanatory Notes Upon the New Testament, 457.

about to be appointed to various circuits (even in America), had clearly established their necessary spiritual gifts for ministry.[47]

Another major area in which a potential circuit rider needed to display evidence was the "fruit" of the Spirit.[48] Circuit riders needed to practice (and constantly experience growth in) spiritual fruit.[49] According to Wesleyan theology, the fruit of the Spirit was imparted by God, and through the process of sanctification, humans needed to cultivate it.[50] Methodist circuit riders were urged to be in continuous pursuit of holiness and the cultivation of the fruit of the Spirit.[51]

During the increase of circuit riders in America, all of these above requirements were, at times, summarized into four questions that were asked about the candidates: "Is this man truly converted? Does he know and keep [Methodist] rules? Can he preach acceptably? . . . Has he a horse?"[52] Regarding horses, these animals were instrumental to the ministry of the circuit riders due to the fact that, in those days, this was by far the most efficient way of traveling and fulfilling ministerial duties.[53]

These were just a few of the common questions (those that most pertain to this study) that circuit rider candidates were asked during the candidacy process.[54] Asbury argued that American circuit rider candidates should be examined in order to show themselves as worthy "candidates for the ministry."[55] Furthermore, Asbury declared that circuit riders should preach "with energy. And [circuit rider] ministers must be sent [to preach]; and to be qualified for this mission, they must, like [the

---

47. Kimbrough, "Orthodox and Wesleyan Ecclesiology," 123. See also Wesley, *Works* [AM], 5:734; *Sermons on Several Occasions* [Emory], 25–28; Asbury, *Journal of the Rev. Francis Asbury*, 1:145, 266; Kurian, *Encyclopedia of Christianity*, 1315; Snethen, *Snethen on Lay Representation*, 122.

48. Wesley, *Works* [AM], 5:230.

49. For the complete list of the characteristics of the fruit of the Spirit, see Galatians 5:22–23.

50. MEC, *Doctrines and Discipline*, 127–29; Wesley, *Sermons on Several Occasions* [Emory], 530.

51. Wesley, *Sermons on Several Occasions* [Emory], 214–15.

52. Daniels and Harris, *Illustrated History of Methodism*, 518. See also Beougher, "Camp Meetings and Circuit Riders."

53. Asbury, *Journal of the Rev. Francis Asbury*, 1:13, 23, 33, 84.

54. For information regarding Wesley's requirements for ministry, see Wesley, *Works* [AM], 5:129–31.

55. Asbury, *Journal of the Rev. Francis Asbury*, 2:119.

apostle] Paul, be convinced, convicted, and converted, and sanctified."[56] Also, it was decided that Methodist appointments should be conducted annually in order to keep the circuit riders accountable; in this way, a "minister [would not become] a notoriously wicked man."[57]

To summarize this section, Wesley and Asbury emphasized that all appointed circuit riders needed to perpetually exemplify a healthy inner Christian life, full of dedication and sanctification, and then be gifted in sharing that life with others.[58] Prominent circuit rider Cartwright offered a picture of a typical circuit rider's lifestyle and level of commitment to the ministry:

> When [a circuit rider] felt that God had called him to preach, instead of hunting up a college or biblical institute, [he] hunted up a hardy pony of a horse, and some travelling apparatus, and with his library always at hand, namely, Bible, Hymn Book, and Discipline, he started, and, with a text that never wore out nor grew stale, he cried, "Behold the Lamb of God, that taketh away the sin of the world!" In this way he went through storms of wind, hail, snow, and rain; climbed hills and mountains, traversed valleys, plunged through swamps, swam swollen streams, lay out all night, wet, weary, and hungry, held his horse by the bridle all night, or tied him to a limb, slept with his saddle-blanket for a bed, his saddle or saddle-bags for his pillow, and his old big coat or blanket, if he had any, for a covering. Often he slept in dirty cabins, on earthen floors, before the fire; ate roasting ears for bread, drank butter-milk for coffee, or sage tea for imperial; took, with a hearty zest, deer or bear meat, or wild turkey, for breakfast, dinner, and supper, if he could get it.

The Early Circuit Rider Ministry in America

Initially, Wesley hesitated to appoint Methodist preachers in America.[59] It is believed that the first person to implore Wesley to send Methodist preachers to America was Whitefield.[60] Whitefield, who was already

56. Asbury, *Journal of the Rev. Francis Asbury*, 3:395.

57. Wesley, *Works* [*AM*], 5:228.

58. Castelo, *Embodying Wesley's Catholic Spirit*, 26; Asbury, *Journal of the Rev. Francis Asbury*, 2:119.

59. Lenton, *John Wesley's Preachers*, 266–67. See also Baker, *From Wesley to Asbury*, 26.

60. Richey et al., *American Methodism*, 3.

preaching in many places in America at that time, wrote to Wesley, explaining that America had "room for a hundred itinerants. Lord Jesus, send by whom [you would] send."[61] Wesley was also contacted by Captain Webb, a Methodist who was stationed as a soldier in America, and by Taylor, a Methodist immigrant in America.[62] After much hesitation, Wesley finally welcomed the opportunity to see scriptural holiness and the Methodist ways be introduced in America.

Wesley recorded: "On Thursday I mentioned the case of our brethren at New York . . . [who] were in great want . . . [of] preachers. Two of our preachers, Richard Boardman and Joseph Pilmore, willingly offered themselves for the service."[63] Hence, the first officially appointed (by Wesley) circuit riders in America were Richard Boardman (1738–1782)[64] and Joseph Pilmore (1739–1825).[65] This appointment made them the first "regular Methodist Preachers on the continent"[66] and official "missionaries to the American colonies."[67] Boardman and Pilmore[68] arrived in New Jersey in 1769 and ministered in America until 1774.[69] In the same year (1769), Wesley also appointed Robert Williams (1745–1775) to serve as the third circuit rider in America.[70] Later, Wesley officially

61. Whitefield, "Letter CCL," 439.

62. See also Kinghorn, "Richard Boardman," 18–19.

63. Wesley, *Journal*, 2:312.

64. Boardman was born in Gilmore, England, and started serving as a circuit rider at the age of twenty-five. Wesley found Boardman to be a loving, peaceful man and placed him in various circuits. For more information, see Lockwood, *Western Pioneers*, 35; Kinghorn, "Richard Boardman," 35; Wesley, *Letters of the Rev. John Wesley*, 6:276.

65. Pilmore was born in Yorkshire, England, and became a Methodist through Wesley's teachings. Initially, he served as a circuit rider in Wells and Cornwall.

66. MEC, *Doctrines and Discipline*, 4.

67. Sweet, *Men of Zeal*, 84.

68. The last name Pilmore (of Joseph Pilmore) is often found in different forms, such as Pilmoor, Pillmore, Pilmoore, Pilmoure. However, Pilmore is the most commonly used spelling.

69. Initially, both men preached together in Philadelphia and New York. However, in 1772, Pilmore began riding a Georgia circuit. For more information, see Pilmore, *Journal of Joseph Pilmore*, 57, 186; Atkinson, *History of the Origin*, 172, 187; Lee, *Memoir*, 264.

70. As a circuit rider, Williams's main geographical areas were in Virginia and North Carolina. Williams became a spiritual father to other notable circuit riders, such as Lee and Waters, both of whom played a significant role in the American circuit rider ministry. For more information, see Crook, *Ireland and the Centenary of American Methodism*, 135–39; Lockwood, *Western Pioneers*, 29; Bergland, *Journeys of Robert Williams*, 15.

appointed other Methodist preachers to the American colonies, such as Williams, Shadford, Asbury, and the first superintendent of the early American circuit rider ministry, Rankin.[71]

However, it is important to note that before Wesley sent his first appointments, news arrived that Methodist societies had already been formed in America without Wesley's knowledge.[72] Hence, the first unofficial Methodist preachers were: Robert Strawbridge (1732–1781), a self-ordained Methodist who formed the First Society of Methodists in America and was the "founder of Methodism in Maryland";[73] Philip Embury (1729–1775), who started his first Methodist society in New York and led Methodist classes along with his cousin, the mother of American Methodism, Barbara Heck (1734–1804);[74] and Captain Thomas Webb (1724–1796), the first Methodist "apostle" in America.[75]

Thomas Rankin, Thomas Coke, and Francis Asbury

Before exploring a few important events in the establishment of the American circuit rider ministry, it is important to briefly introduce some of the main figures who played a great role in the creation and development of American Methodism, such as Rankin, Coke, and Asbury. Because Asbury played a greater role (than Rankin and Coke) in developing

71. Frank, *American Revolution*, 151.

72. Andrews, *Methodists and Revolutionary America*, 8.

73. Strawbridge was an Irish-man who had a conversion at the age of twenty-eight. In 1760, he arrived in America and began his circuit rider preaching by forming Methodist societies. For more information, see Maser, "Robert Strawbridge," 3–6; Asbury, *Heart of Asbury's Journal*, 712; Lednum, *History of the Rise of Methodism*, 18; Sweet, *Men of Zeal*, 48–49; Bergland, *Journeys of Robert Williams*, 73; Hurst, *History of Methodism*, 4:31.

74. Embury was converted in 1752. In 1760, Embury and his family immigrated to New York. Embury's cousin Heck also immigrated to New York and convinced Embury to begin preaching to the people there; from then, his ministry was born. For more information, see Hall, *American Religious Leaders*, 163; Hunt, *Religious Bodies*, 431; Andrews, *Methodists and Revolutionary America*, 32; Withrow, *Barbara Heck*, 29–32.

75. Captain Webb's ministry began while he was co-laboring with Embury; Webb also served in various circuits. A great achievement of his was creating the first Methodist society in Philadelphia. For more information, see Withrow, *Barbara Heck*, 32; Powell, "Methodist Circuit Riders in America," 2; Kitchin, "Thomas Webb," 542; Maffitt et al., *Memorial of Philip Embury*, 10; Stevens, *History of the Methodist Episcopal Church*, 1:141.

the American circuit rider ministry, his biographical introduction is followed by a brief description of the role of the supernatural in his life and ministry.

Thomas Rankin

Thomas Rankin (1736–1810) was born in Dunbar, Scotland; during his youth, he was converted through Methodist teachings.[76] Initially, he served as a circuit rider in various places in England. Rankin became Wesley's close assistant and, because he was known to be a "skilled [Methodist] administrator," in 1773, Wesley appointed him as the superintendent, responsible for overseeing American Methodist work.[77] However, in his fifth year of this mission (in 1778), Rankin returned to England where he later was ordained for a "special charge [in] London."[78]

Thomas Coke

Thomas Coke (1747–1814), "the father of Methodist missions," was born in Brecon, South Wales, and was known to be gifted in administration and evangelism;[79] like Wesley, he began to preach in open fields and wherever he could.[80] Coke, who also became one of Wesley's close assistants, was ordained by Wesley in 1784.[81] In the same year, he was appointed co-superintendent (and, later, a bishop) in overseeing American Methodism (together with Asbury).[82] He also ordained Asbury. Although he (and Asbury) played an important role in establishing the independence of American Methodism, Coke was mainly known for his

76. Jackson, *Lives of Early Methodist Preachers*, 5:136, 215; for Rankin's official journals, see 135–217.

77. Bose, *Francis Asbury*, 63.

78. Stevenson, *Methodist Worthies*, 1:26. See also Sherman, *History of the Revisions*, 18.

79. Thomas, "Coke, Thomas."

80. Coke became an ordained minister in the Church of England, as well. After he was introduced to Methodism, he aligned himself with Methodist doctrine. This resulted in severe disapproval from the Anglican Church; in 1777, Coke was dismissed from his position in the Anglican Church. See also Philips, "Coke, Thomas," 780; Young, *Origin and History of Methodism*, 136; Turnbull, *Reviving the Heart*, 157.

81. DePuy, *Methodist Year-Book*, 336.

82. Alvord, *Mississippi Valley Historical Review*, 4:114.

Methodist missionary efforts, especially in the East Indies and Africa.[83] During his visits and leadership in America, he witnessed "God's power" displayed in many areas throughout the country. While Coke was happy with this outcome, he further hoped and believed that God's Spirit would "soon run through the whole" of America.[84]

Francis Asbury

Francis Asbury (1745–1816), who held a catalytic role in forming, developing, and spreading American Methodism (through the ministry of the circuit riders), was born in Staffordshire, England.[85] Throughout his childhood, Asbury's mother read the Bible and sang hymns to him. When he was a teenager, he struggled (like Wesley) with the fact that he had not personally experienced an assurance of faith or spiritual conversion. In search of his spiritual conversion, Asbury attended many Methodist meetings. Although he heard many extraordinary Methodist messages, his question of assurance remained unanswered because he was spiritually "unmoved." One night, when he was fifteen, God made "deep impressions on [his] heart, which brought [him] to Jesus Christ, who graciously justified [his] guilty soul through faith in his precious blood." In this way, Asbury's spiritual conversion was made real to him, and he was finally assured of his Christian salvation.[86]

The following year, when Asbury was sixteen, he encountered another supernatural experience that he identified as a "marvelous display of the grace of God"; this incident sparked in Asbury a deep desire to continue down the path to "full sanctification . . . [and he] was indeed very happy." When he was seventeen, Asbury described in his journals the various Christian meetings that he held. Then, from the ages of eighteen to twenty-one, Asbury served as a circuit rider in England.[87]

After "half a year [of] strong [spiritual] intimations in [Asbury's] mind that [he] should visit America," upon hearing from Wesley about

---

83. Hall, *American Religious Leaders*, 76; Kalas, *Being United Methodist*, 103.

84. Coke, *Letters of Dr. Thomas Coke*, 121.

85. Towers, "African Union Methodism," 44; Dondzila, "Asbury, Francis," 100–101; Sprague, *Annals of the American Pulpit*, 7:13.

86. Asbury, *Journal of the Rev. Francis Asbury*, 1:87–90.

87. Asbury, *Journal of the Rev. Francis Asbury*, 1:88–89. See also Wigger, *American Saint*, 29.

the need for Methodist preachers there, he heartily volunteered as a circuit rider. He was appointed by Wesley to preach in America, and on September 3, 1771, he embarked on his journey. Asbury recorded the reason why he volunteered to come to America by asking: "Whither am I going? To the new world. What to do? To gain honour? No, if I know my own heart. To get money? No, I am going to live to God, and to bring others so to do." Thus, Asbury's heart was to come to America "to reform the continent and spread scriptural holiness over these lands."[88]

As noted previously, Asbury later became the main leader of the entire American circuit rider ministry; using his "planning ahead and resolving disputes"[89] technique, he led Methodism to remarkably quickly become one of the largest denominations of that time.[90] Similar to Wesley's leadership influence and authority in England, Asbury held unparalleled leadership influence and authority in America.[91] However, Asbury led the circuit riders by predominately following and implementing Wesley's theological and spiritual legacy.[92]

Asbury, who identified himself as being filled with the "spiritual baptism . . . of the Spirit,"[93] not only directed the American circuit rider ministry (which was the centerpiece of American Methodism), but he was also one of the most well-known American circuit riders.[94] During his life, he traveled on horseback approximately 270,000 miles and preached over 16,000 sermons.[95] Also, under Asbury's leadership, the MEC membership grew from 1,200 to 214,000, and he was involved in ordaining 700 circuit riders.[96]

Asbury preached and advocated "piety and perseverance, rooted in a classically evangelical conversion experience."[97] During his life, he

88. Merritt, "Letters on Methodism," 447.

89. Wigger, American Saint, 320. See also M'Caine, Letters, 202.

90. M'Caine, Letters, 32–37.

91. Atkinson, Centennial History of American Methodism, 65.

92. For more information about Wesley's legacy, see Lamport, "John Wesley," 2453–55.

93. Asbury, Journal of the Rev. Francis Asbury, 3:84. See also Graham, Secret of Happiness, 152.

94. Powell, "Methodist Circuit Riders in America," 34.

95. Simpson, "Circuit Riders," para. 3.

96. See also Noll, Rise of Evangelicalism, 215; Helland and Hjalmarson, Missional Spirituality, 85.

97. Wigger, American Saint, 5.

sought to go deeper in spiritual encounters in order to, as he stated, "experience close communion with God."[98] Because he constantly desired new spiritual experiences, Asbury was identified as, in the words of circuit rider Boehm, one with "no tedious sameness, no repeating old, stale truths."[99]

Asbury was known to be a strategic and diplomatic leader who loved God and had a heart to see all of America filled with religious experiential revival.[100] He was not only a leader to preachers, but also, because he dedicated his life to sharing the gospel in every part of the (thirteen) states of America, he was an exemplary Methodist preacher himself.[101] Asbury was further known to lead the American circuit rider ministry by preaching an active gospel about an active God with enthusiasm and assertiveness.[102] Later in his life, Asbury was celebrated as one of the most famous American preachers; he also preached to the House of Representatives in Washington, DC.[103]

Introduction to Asbury and the Supernatural

In maintaining a biblically-oriented Christian life both personally and publicly, Asbury relied strongly on the power and presence of God's Spirit. Through prayer, he continuously sought to be "filled with [God's] Spirit"[104] so that he could witness and present a gospel that demonstrated the fact that God was alive in word and deed.[105] Asbury longed to experience the presence of God and share these enthusiastic experiences with other fellow Americans so that they could have a better life.

---

98. Asbury, *Journal of the Rev. Francis Asbury*, 3:88. See also Wigger, *American Saint*, 43.

99. Atkinson, *Centennial History of American Methodism*, 293.

100. Drew, *Life of the Rev. Thomas Coke*, 62; Atkinson, *Centennial History of American Methodism*, 246.

101. Noll, *Work We Have to Do*, 52.

102. See also Kinghorn, "Richard Boardman," 29; Boles, *Religion in Antebellum Kentucky*, 109.

103. Duewel, *Heroes of the Holy Life*, 20.

104. Asbury, *Journal of the Rev. Francis Asbury*, 3:158.

105. Asbury, *Journal of the Rev. Francis Asbury*, 1:48, 222. See also Graham, *Secret of Happiness*, 152.

As was recorded in Asbury's journals, a successful circuit for him was when a "frequent and obvious demonstration of the power of God"[106] was manifested through his sermons. He knew that by preaching the gospel in natural words, he was not able to change any heart. According to Asbury, a true conversion occurred when God was manifested and people willingly "experience[d] the same work of grace which [the circuit riders] preach[ed]." Consequently, Asbury urged the rest of the American circuit rider ministry to apply a similar style of preaching in their circuits.[107]

Furthermore, Boehm declared that Asbury "often felt the power" manifest in his life and ministry, transforming him into "a kind of moral Samson." Contrarily, when Asbury did not sense any supernatural power overshadowing him, "he was like Samson shorn of his strength."[108] Thus, Asbury held that "the power . . . and presence" of "the Spirit of the Lord [who] ha[d] been with [him] in power"[109] was an integral part of the success of his preaching as well as an integral part of the success of the American circuit rider ministry.[110]

As further discussed in chapter 6, even though Methodism was occasionally criticized for the nature of its religious enthusiastic expressions, Asbury, unlike Wesley, was a strong advocate of religious enthusiasm becoming an accepted experiential norm in all Methodist revivals.[111] Asbury believed that religious enthusiasm was divinely initiated and, therefore, was fully in agreement with the Bible and the experiences of the Apostolic Age.[112] As such, no matter how the supernatural was displayed, Asbury suggested that the American circuit riders be partakers in it and not reject or condemn it.[113] Hence, Asbury sought after and shared the full gospel, including all the shapes and forms of its supernatural component, which included religious enthusiasm.[114] Upcoming chapters

---

106. Asbury, *Journal of the Rev. Francis Asbury*, 3:114.

107. Asbury, *Journal of the Rev. Francis Asbury*, 1:7, 23, 79.

108. Boehm, *Reminiscences*, 441. See also Atkinson, *Centennial History of American Methodism*, 293; Wigger, *American Saint*, 285.

109. Asbury, *Journal of the Rev. Francis Asbury*, 1:74, 213, 234.

110. Levington, *Power with God and with Men*, 20.

111. See also Barlow, *Profiles in Evangelism*, 19.

112. See also Asbury, *Journal of the Rev. Francis Asbury*, 2:87.

113. Ware, *Sketches*, 253; Couvares et al., *Interpretations of American History*, 1:318.

114. Asbury, *Journal of the Rev. Francis Asbury*, 2:100.

describe numerous and diverse supernatural occurrences in Asbury's life and ministry and expound on his theology of the supernatural.

The First Annual Conference of 1773 and the Birth of the American Circuit Rider Order

The following section outlines a few crucial events that led to the formation of the official American circuit rider ministry. Apparently, Wesley was not fully satisfied with the overall progress of the initially appointed (aforementioned) circuit rider preachers in America. It was for this reason that he sent Rankin to be his primary assistant or superintendent in America.[115]

Because Wesley felt that American Methodism was withdrawing from his influence, Rankin's main mission was to reform it and make it, once again, fully accountable to the authority and theology of Wesley.[116] Wesley knew that, due to his "uncompromising" nature, Rankin was the most qualified choice for this assignment.[117] Upon his arrival in Philadelphia in July of 1773, Rankin gathered all the American circuit rider preachers for the first Methodist Annual Conference in America.[118]

During this conference, which was officially recorded in the MEC's *Minutes*, the circuit riders had the right to vote on proposed reforms. In the conference, one of the main discussions was whether the American circuit riders were still willing to remain under Wesley's authority and theology (including the supernatural component). The American circuit riders voted unanimously to remain under Wesley's umbrella. Also, during this conference, it was once again established that all American circuit riders had to "strictly avoid administering the ordinances of baptism and the Lord's supper." Any of the circuit riders who disregarded these reinforced rules faced the possibility of being rejected by the Methodist "fellowship . . . [until] they change[d] their conduct."[119]

---

115. Lee, *Dictionary of National Biography*, 47:290.

116. Russell, *American Methodism*, 13.

117. Lee, *Dictionary of National Biography*, 47:290.

118. MEC, *Minutes of the Annual Conferences*, 1:5; Powell, "Methodist Circuit Riders in America," 6.

119. MEC, *Minutes of the Annual Conferences*, 1:5–6.

As noted previously, the Annual Conferences appointed circuit riders to various circuits yearly.[120] In this Annual Conference (1773), Asbury was appointed to the Baltimore circuits, Williams to the Petersburg circuits, King to the New York circuits, etc.[121] At this point, in 1773, there were only ten official preachers serving in America.[122] Nevertheless, it was decided during this conference that the main duty of the circuit riders would remain the same: to spread scriptural holiness and to work toward bringing experiential revivals.[123]

Since Rankin left America in 1778, from 1777 to 1783, American Methodism was left with "no regular [or official] account."[124] However, during the American Revolutionary War (1775–1783), the American circuit rider ministry considered Asbury to be the main leader.[125] At the same time, during these years, the ministry still tried to remain under the terms agreed upon in the Annual Conference (1773).

Also, during this period, American Methodism grew tremendously in membership.[126] A small portion of this growth was thought by some to be a result of Anglican presence in America dwindling during the war. Considering that Methodism was so closely related to Anglicanism, in the earliest stages of Methodist expansion (largely prior to 1780), because "about 75 percent of the [American] Church of England congregations lost their clergymen"[127] due to mounting social pressures and political affiliations, Methodism received some transfer members from the "Church of England . . . [who] early united [themselves] with Methodist societies."[128] However, Methodist leaders and circuit riders claimed that the vast majority of their growth during that period occurred because "the Spirit was poured out from on high, and such a number of souls [were] gathered into the fold of the Great Shepherd."[129]

Despite its growth, at that time, American Methodism remained dependent on the Anglican Church for certain sacraments and continued

120. Richey, *Methodism in the American Forest*, 113.

121. MEC, *Minutes of the Annual Conferences*, 1:6.

122. Fisk, "Dr. Fisk's Travels," 459; MEC, *Minutes of the Annual Conferences*, 1:6.

123. Duewel, *Revival Fire*, 50.

124. Myles, *Chronological History*, 128.

125. Frank, *American Revolution*, 159.

126. Powell, "Methodist Circuit Riders in America," 7.

127. Butler at al., *Religion in American Life*, 139.

128. Simpson, *Cyclopaedia of Methodism*, 283.

129. Jarratt and Coleman, *Life of the Reverend Devereux Jarratt*, 95.

to be under the authority of Wesley.[130] Thus, it can be argued that from this Annual Conference (1773) the American circuit rider ministry was born—still in its initial stages of development but on its way to reaching its full future potential.

The Christmas Conference and Official Beginning of the American Circuit Rider Ministry

Indeed, while it can be argued that the early American circuit rider ministry began during the Annual Conference of 1773, it is largely recognized that the official American circuit rider ministry was established during the Christmas Conference of 1784. After the American Revolutionary War ended (1783), there was a desire to break association with British governing systems.[131] This spirit of independence also inspired American Methodism to separate from English Methodism; it was mainly looking to sever its dependence on the Anglican Church and, to a degree, the direct control of Wesley.[132] Due to political confusion and issues after the war, even more of the English circuit riders and Anglican clergy returned to England.[133] On the other hand, there were some English circuit riders, such as Asbury, who felt that they still had work ahead of them in America.[134]

In the mid-eighteenth century, prior to the official circuit rider ministry formation, American church attendance was considered to be around 75 to 80 percent; however, during the American Revolutionary War, church attendance dropped to a concerning 17 percent.[135] This decline was mostly considered to be a byproduct of the divided loyalties in the American church (and other spheres of society).[136] However, after the war ended, a unified vision emerged to make "God and liberty" a vital

---

130. Bernard and Guyot, *Johnson's (Revised) Universal Cyclopaedia*, 388.

131. Outler, *John Wesley*, 84. See also Karsten, *Encyclopedia of War*, 492.

132. Wentz, *American Religious Traditions*, 183.

133. Powell, "Methodist Circuit Riders in America," 9; Redmile, *Apostolic Succession*, 185.

134. See also Reid et al., *Concise Dictionary of Christianity in America*, 26; Wheatherfield, "Rise and Progress," 4.

135. Finke and Stark, *Churching of America*, 15–16.

136. Bonomi, *Under the Cope of Heaven*, 177, 213–16.

component of America's identity and future.[137] Thus, as in decades past, there was once again an increase in interest and energy to pursue God and to do so in a way that was distinctly American. As discussed in the upcoming chapters, the circuit riders and their innovative evangelistic strategies (including the supernatural component) were at the forefront of this new movement, which led to Methodism's extraordinary expansion during that period (up 639.4 percent from the previous decade).[138]

Also, prior to the Christmas Conference, there were occasions when various American circuit riders petitioned to be allowed to administer the sacraments and become ordained Methodist ministers in America.[139] Asbury, out of a sense of respect, insisted on waiting for answers from Wesley regarding these matters.[140] In the meantime, back in England, as a result of the American Revolutionary War and the reported new needs of American Methodism, Wesley "ordained [as] Presbyters" Whatcoat and Vasey to support American Methodism in its independence. He also appointed Coke as "Superintendent"[141] in order to implement new changes within American Methodism (mainly regarding ordination and sacraments).[142] At the same time, as previously noted, Wesley commissioned Coke to go to America and ordain Asbury so that both of them could co-superintend American Methodism and the circuit rider ministry.[143]

Asbury, however, wanted to first have his proposed ordination by Wesley approved by the other American circuit riders, with whom he was laboring. Hence, Asbury (and Coke) called all "scattered circuit-riding preachers"[144] to gather on December 24, 1784, in Lovely Lane Chapel in Baltimore, Maryland.[145] This meeting was, thus, named the *Christmas Conference* because it was held on Christmas Eve. Technically,

---

137. Hinton, *History of the United States of America*, 1:499.

138. For more information regarding the growth of Methodism during this period, see appendix B.

139. See also Stevens, *History of the Religious Ministry*, 556.

140. Pyke, *Dawn of American Methodism*, 101.

141. Coke and Moore, *Life of the Rev. John Wesley*, 459.

142. Stevens, *History of the Methodist Episcopal Church*, 2:166; Coke and Moore, *Life of the Rev. John Wesley*, 458–59; Coke, "Journal of Thomas Coke," 240; Atkinson, *Centennial History of American Methodism*, 93.

143. Hurst, *John Wesley the Methodist*, 234–36; Noll, *Rise of Evangelicalism*, 203.

144. UMC, *Minutes of the West Michigan Annual Conference*, 180.

145. Balmer and Silk, *Religion and Public Life*, 63.

it was the first Methodist General Conference.[146] By this point, there were eighty-one official American circuit riders, and approximately sixty of them were present at the conference.[147] During this conference, in which a divine presence was reportedly felt, Asbury was ordained as an elder and deacon, and Asbury and Coke were unanimously approved as co-superintendents of American Methodism.[148] It was also during this conference that "the American circuit riders"[149] (including Asbury and Coke) founded the MEC.[150] However, without Wesley's approval, Asbury was appointed as a "bishop" of the MEC;[151] Coke happily announced to all gathered there that "[he had] ordained brother Asbury a bishop," though Wesley was displeased with the term.[152] Thereafter, American circuit riders served as part of the MEC, though their goal remained the same: to labor for and witness the "spread [of] the gospel . . . and revival of religion" across America.[153] This event marked the official birth and formation of the American circuit rider ministry.[154]

As this new American Methodist denomination was founded, it was done so as an intentional split from British Methodism and its ties to "the Anglican ecclesiastical structure,"[155] although the MEC still implemented and followed Wesleyan principles and teachings (which featured the supernatural component discussed in chapter 2).[156] While, in a way, Wesley appointed Coke (followed shortly by Asbury) as a step toward disconnecting American Methodism, Coke reported that, later in his life, Wesley felt "sorry for the separation."[157]

146. See also May, *Evangelism and Resistance*, 107.

147. Bangs and Garrettson, *Life of the Rev. Freeborn Garrettson*, 136; Murphy and Truesdell, *Separate Denominations*, 926.

148. Coke, "Journal of Thomas Coke," 290–91; Frank, *American Revolution*, 164.

149. Noll et al., *Fides Et Historia*, 20–21:46.

150. Tigert, *Constitutional History of American Episcopal Methodism*, 516.

151. M'Caine, *History and Mystery of Methodist Episcopacy*, 21–23; Wesley, *John Wesley and Modern Wesleyanism*, 5–6; Waller, *John Wesley*, 122–23.

152. Coke, "Journal of Thomas Coke," 291; Atkinson, *Centennial History of American Methodism*, 94.

153. Lee, *Short History of the Methodists*, 290. See also Morrow, *History of Warren County*, 318; Asbury, *Journal of the Rev. Francis Asbury*, 1:162.

154. MECS, *Journal of the General Conference*, 1:586.

155. Feinman, "Itinerant Circuit-Riding Minister," 44.

156. Even Asbury read Wesley's work. For instance, see Asbury, *Journal of the Rev. Francis Asbury*, 1:208. See also MECS, *History of the Organization*, 209.

157. Wesley and Coke, *Letters*, 15. See also Vickers, *Thomas Coke*, 178; Peurifoy,

Additionally, during this conference, the *Discipline* of the MEC was created, which contained Wesleyan governing and doctrinal principles (Thirty-Nine Articles, combined with the liturgy of the Anglican Church).[158] Asbury insisted that, in addition to living according to the Bible, Methodists needed to be further governed by the "doctrine and discipline" outlined in the *Discipline*; they were required to be familiar with Wesley's works, as well.[159] Lastly, the conference also officially ordained twelve other circuit riders and established the right to administer the sacraments and ordain future circuit riders through Methodist conferences.[160]

It is important to restate that even though Asbury and Coke were co-superintendents, Asbury was generally regarded as the primary leader of the American circuit rider ministry (and the MEC). Even Coke himself viewed Asbury as the primary leader, declaring: "In the presence of brother Asbury I feel myself a child. He is, in my estimation, the most apostolic man I ever saw, except Mr. Wesley."[161] After Coke departed for England in 1785, Asbury remained the sole leader and bishop of the MEC (including the circuit rider ministry) for the following thirty-one years.[162] As previously noted, because Asbury was considered to be an extraordinary American circuit rider and leader, he would later be named "the father of American Methodism"[163] and "one of the most famous"[164] figures in the entire history of the MEC.

The Circuit Riders Featured in This Work

While, by 1815, there were "more than seven hundred"[165] American circuit riders, the list of circuit riders selected for this study echoes the

Tekel of Methodism, 10; Coke and Moore, *Life of the Rev. John Wesley*, 458–59; Gray, *History of the Rise and Progress*, 11.

158. Jones, *United Methodist Doctrine*, 48.

159. Asbury, *Journal of the Rev. Francis Asbury*, 1:55, 205, 328. See also Powell, "Methodist Circuit Riders in America," 54–55.

160. Coke, *Extracts of the Journals* [1793], 72.

161. Ware, *Sketches*, 109.

162. Powell, "Methodist Circuit Riders in America," 4.

163. Johnson, *Frontier Camp Meeting*, 6.

164. Gaines and Merrill, *When God Comes to Church*, 79.

165. Mudge, "Short History," 43. See also Thacker, "Methodism and the Second Great Awakening," 52.

lists compiled by contemporary Methodist historians, scholars, and theologians who considered these circuit riders to be the "notable,"[166] "prominent"[167] "leaders"[168] and the "revivalists that contributed to the [Methodist] movement's populist appeal"[169] from the 1770s through the 1830s. These circuit riders were featured in the scholarly writings of Wigger,[170] Hatch,[171] Richey,[172] Taves,[173] Evans,[174] J. Williams,[175] O'Byrne,[176] Turner,[177] Lyerly,[178] and Ruth.[179]

It can be argued that there are at least two reasons why these particular circuit riders were studied by contemporary scholars. The first reason, considering this matter from a historical perspective, is that these circuit riders were considered by other circuit riders of the day to be "the great evangelists"[180] and spiritual models; it seems that they were viewed as "model" circuit riders due to their ministerial "zeal and devotion" combined with the amount of conversions that their ministries produced, which "increased [Methodism] from a little company of ten or twelve to upward of a million."[181] This identification is evident in the writings of other circuit riders and historians of the day, such as Finley,[182]

---

166. Richey et al., *American Methodism*, 5.

167. Turner, "Redeeming the Time," 1.

168. Hatch, *Democratization of American Christianity*, 244–303.

169. Evans, "Most Distinctive Contribution of Methodists," 1500.

170. Wigger, *Taking Heaven by Storm*, 19–22, 38–39, 43–44, 54, 106–7, 163, 181, 219, 246–49, 266.

171. Hatch, *Democratization of American Christianity*, 20, 89, 102, 121, 139, 174–75, 193–94.

172. Richey et al., *American Methodism*, 5, 18, 24–29, 32–34, 37.

173. Taves, *Fits, Trances, and Visions*, 17–18, 84, 94–96, 148, 155, 386.

174. Evans, "Most Distinctive Contribution of Methodists," 1499–501.

175. Williams, *Religion and Violence in Early American Methodism*, 220–28.

176. O'Byrne, "How Methodists Were Made," 186–87, 244, 261–62.

177. Turner, "Redeeming the Time," 31–34, 96–97, 112–13, 121–24, 140, 245–48, 282–89.

178. Lyerly, *Methodism and the Southern Mind*, 23, 45, 58, 61, 81–82, 110, 130, 152, 193, 198, 207.

179. Ruth, *Little Heaven Below*, 10–12, 24–29, 30–33, 76, 83–84, 88, 100–101, 129, 149–59, 214–18, 249–62. See also Vickers, *Thomas Coke*, 385–94.

180. Stevens, *Planting and Training of American Methodism*, 508.

181. Finley, *Sketches of Western Methodism*, 21.

182. Finley, *Sketches of Western Methodism*, 18–21.

Stevens,[183] and Wakeley.[184] The second reason why these circuit riders were selected as "a case study" by modern scholars is because these circuit riders generally left behind the most writings, especially in the form of "journals and autobiographies."[185]

Bearing this in mind, following is the list of the circuit riders featured in this study (brief biographical introductions are footnoted).[186] The list is presented in order by date of birth and includes: Benjamin Abbott (1732–1796),[187] James O'Kelly (1735–1826),[188] Richard Whatcoat (1736–1806),[189] George Shadford (1739–1816),[190] William Watters (1751–1833),[191] Philip Gatch (1751–1834),[192] Freeborn Garrettson

183. Stevens, *Planting and Training of American Methodism*, 507–9.

184. Wakeley, *Heroes of Methodism*, 3–10. See also Mode, *Frontier Spirit in American Christianity*, 179–81.

185. Robinson, *Divine Healing*, 124.

186. This book also includes material from a few circuit riders, such as Snethen, Daughaday and W. P. Finley, that was referenced in some of the journals or autobiographies of other circuit riders; because of the minor part their material plays in this research, these circuit riders are not featured in the above list.

187. Abbott was born in Pennsylvania and was converted to Christianity through Methodist sermons in 1772. Soon after his conversion, he became a circuit rider and was ordained in 1790. He served in various circuits, such as the Long Island circuit in Salem, New Jersey, and the Cecil circuit in Maryland. For more information, see Abbott and Ffirth, *Experience and Gospel Labours*, 177, 201–2, 206; Wakeley and Boehm, *Patriarch of One Hundred Years*, 21.

188. O'Kelly was born in North Carolina and was converted in 1774. He mostly ministered in Virginia and Maryland. O'Kelly appealed to reform the MEC's episcopal system; however, his appeal was denied, and in response, he established the Republican Methodist Church in 1792. For more information, see MacClenny, *Life of Rev. James O'Kelly*, 11; Kelly, *Author's Apology*, 6–7, 79–87.

189. Whatcoat was born in Gloucestershire, England. In 1758, he was converted through a supernatural encounter with the Spirit of God, and he became a Methodist in 1769; soon after, Wesley ordained him and sent him, together with Coke, to America. In 1800, he was also elected as a bishop of the MEC. For more information, see Phoebus, *Memoirs*, 9–29.

190. Shadford was born in Lincolnshire, England. After his conversion, he served as a circuit rider in England; later, in 1773, Wesley appointed him as a circuit rider in America; were he mostly served in Virginia. For more information, see Jackson, *Lives of Early Methodist Preachers*, 6:137–81.

191. Watters was born in Maryland and, in 1771, received his conversion. In 1772, he became a circuit rider and was also known to be the first American-born circuit rider; he ministered in Virginia, Pennsylvania, and Maryland. For more information, see Watters, *Short Account*, 17, 48; *First American Itinerant of Methodism*, 13, 32.

192. Gatch was born in Maryland. In 1773, he became a circuit rider, and his

(1752–1827),[193] William M'Kendree (1757–1835),[194] Jesse Lee (1758–1816),[195] Henry Smith (d. 1840),[196] Thomas Ware (1758–1842),[197] Ezekiel Cooper (1763–1847),[198] Benjamin Lakin (1767–1849),[199] John Collins (1769–1845),[200] William Burke (1770–1855),[201] Billy Hibbard

main ministerial circuits were in New Jersey, Pennsylvania, and Maryland. For more information, see Gatch, *Sketch of Rev. Philip Gatch*, 6–17, 72, 123, 170.

193. Garrettson was born in Maryland; in 1776, he became a Methodist circuit rider. His main traveling circuits were in New York, Delaware, Maryland, and Virginia. In spreading American Methodism, he became one of the most renowned circuit riders. For more information, see Garrettson, *Experience and Travels*, 26–28; Bangs and Garrettson, *Life of the Rev. Freeborn Garrettson*, 35–37, 66, 70–75; Tipple, *Freeborn Garrettson*, 62, 11.

194. M'Kendree was born in Virginia and became a Christian convert in 1787; he was led to become a Methodist circuit rider the following year. His main traveling circuits were in South Carolina, Maryland, Tennessee, Kentucky, and Illinois. In 1808, M'Kendree was also elected as a bishop of the MEC. For more information, see Paine, *Life and Times*, 1:17, 51, 57, 150; Richey, "Early American Methodism," 58–59.

195. Lee was born in Virginia. He was converted and became a Methodist through the preaching and mentoring of Williams. Shortly after reaching the age of nineteen, he felt that he was called to be a circuit rider. His first appointment was in North Carolina in 1783. However, Lee was remembered for establishing Methodism in the New England region and was known as the "Methodist Apostle of New England." For more information, see Lee, *Memoir*, 10, 124, 130, 290, 295; Crook, *Ireland and the Centenary of American Methodism*, 139; Hall, *American Religious Leaders*, 214.

196. H. Smith was born in Maryland and became a circuit rider in 1793. His main traveling circuits were in Virginia, Maryland, Pennsylvania, Ohio, and Kentucky. For more information, see Smith, *Recollections and Reflections*, 7–39.

197. Ware was born in New Jersey to his Presbyterian mother. Soon after his conversion, he was appointed by Asbury in 1783. His main places of ministry were in Virginia, New York, Delaware, Maryland, and Pennsylvania. For more information, see Ware, *Sketches*, 13, 73, 172; Sprague, *Annals of the American Pulpit*, 7:119–22.

198. Cooper was born in Maryland and was converted through Garrettson's preaching. His main appointed circuits were in Maryland, North Carolina, South Carolina, and New England. For more information, see Cooper, *Beams of Light*, 3–18, 149.

199. Lakin was born in Maryland and was converted in 1791. In 1794, he became a circuit rider and served in Tennessee, Alabama, and Ohio. For more information, see Finley, *Sketches of Western Methodism*, 164–78; Sweet, *Methodists*, 230; Sprague, *Annals of the American Pulpit*, 7:267–73.

200. Collins was born in New Jersey and became a circuit rider after his conversion in 1794. He mostly served in New Jersey and Ohio. For more information, see Finley, *Sketches of Western Methodism*, 298–317.

201. Burke was born in Virginia. Soon after his conversion experience in 1791, he became a circuit rider. He mostly served in Ohio. For more information, see Finley, *Sketches of Western Methodism*, 22–27.

(1771–1844),[202] William Beauchamp (1772–1824),[203] E. F. Newell (1775–1864),[204] Henry Boehm (1775–1875),[205] Thomas Smith (1776–1844),[206] Jacob Young (1776–1856),[207] Lorenzo Dow (1777–1834),[208] Jacob Gruber (1778–1850),[209] Seth Crowell (1781–1826),[210] James Bradley Finley

202. Hibbard was born in Connecticut, and he became a circuit rider in 1794. His circuits were primarily in New York, Massachusetts, and Connecticut. For more information, see Hibbard, *Memoirs*, 129–30; Sprague, *Annals of the American Pulpit*, 7:298–306.

203. Beauchamp was born in Delaware; soon after his conversion in 1810, he became a circuit rider. His circuits were mostly in Baltimore, New York, Boston, and Philadelphia. For more information, see Finley, *Sketches of Western Methodism*, 248–50; Sprague, *Annals of the American Pulpit*, 7:235–39.

204. Newell was born in Massachusetts and was converted in 1800. He became a circuit rider in 1806 and served mostly in New England. For more information, see Newell, *Life and Observations*, 5–41, 99.

205. Boehm was the son of the famous preacher Martin Boehm who co-founded the Church of the United Brethren in Christ denomination. Boehm was born in Pennsylvania and, in 1793, he received his conversion. In 1798, he became a circuit rider, and his traveling circuits were in Virginia, Maryland, and Pennsylvania. For more information, see Wakeley and Boehm, *Patriarch of One Hundred Years*, 6–17.

206. Smith was born in Maryland and, in 1798, became a circuit rider. He served in Philadelphia, Maryland, and Virginia. For more information, see Smith and Dailey, *Experience and Ministerial Labors*, 9–30.

207. Young was born in Pennsylvania and, in 1802, became a circuit rider; his primary ministries were in Kentucky, Ohio, and the West Liberty (Pittsburg) circuit. For more information, see Young, *Autobiography of a Pioneer*, 11–23, 143; DePuy, *Methodist Year-Book*, 33.

208. Dow, known as "Crazy Dow," was born in Connecticut. In 1796, he was appointed as a circuit rider and served in New England, Mississippi, Alabama, North Carolina, and New York; he also ministered in Canada, Ireland, England, and the West Indies. After his death, Dow's autobiography became the second bestselling book in America (after the Bible) during the mid-nineteenth century. For more information, see Dow, *History of Cosmopolite*, 11–29.

209. Gruber was born in Pennsylvania and became a circuit rider in 1800; he ministered mostly in New York, Maryland, Virginia, Ohio, and Pennsylvania. For more information, see Strickland, *Life of Jacob Gruber*, 5–34; Eaton, "Jacob Gruber's 1818 Camp Meeting Sermon," 242–48.

210. Crowell was born in Connecticut and, in 1801, became a circuit rider. He ministered in New York, Vermont, Connecticut, and Canada. For more information, see Crowell, *Journal of Seth Crowell*, 5–24.

(1781–1856),[211] Dan Young (1783–1831),[212] Charles Giles (1783–1867),[213] Thomas S. Hinde (1785–1846),[214] Peter Cartwright (1785–1872),[215] Joseph Travis (1786–1858),[216] John Emory (1789–1835),[217] Willbur Fisk (1792–1839),[218] and Henry Bidleman Bascom (1796–1850).[219] In addition, appendix A contains a list of names, years of birth and death,

211. Finley was born in North Carolina. He received his conversion in 1801 in Kentucky; in 1809, he was licensed as a circuit rider. His main place of ministry was in Ohio. For more information, see Finley, *Life among the Indians*, 3–5, 282; Knepper, *Ohio and Its People*, 165.

212. D. Young was born in New Hampshire and soon after his conversion (mostly through the ministry of Lee) become a circuit rider in 1804. He was mostly known for his ministry in New England. For more information, see Young, *Autobiography of Dan Young*, 13–29.

213. Giles was born in Connecticut and became a circuit rider in 1804; his main traveling circuits were in New England, Ohio, and New York. For more information, see Giles, *Pioneer*, 11–107.

214. Hinde, known as "Theophilus Arminius," was born in Virginia and become a circuit rider soon after his and his family's conversion in 1798. He ministered in Kentucky, Illinois, Indiana, and Missouri. For more information regarding Hinde, see Capers, "Recollections of Doctor Thomas Hinde," 120–28; Hinde, "Recollections of Mrs. Todd Hinde," 121–32.

215. Cartwright, known as the "Backwoods Preacher" and the "Lord's Plowman," was born in Virginia. In 1802, he became a circuit rider. He ministered in Kentucky, Tennessee, and Illinois. In Illinois alone, it was estimated that he preached fifteen thousand sermons and baptized twelve thousand people. For more information, see Cartwright, *Backwoods Preacher*, 1–30, 74, 77, 104, 118, 277.

216. Travis was born in Maryland. In 1803, he was converted, and he became a circuit rider in 1806. His main circuits were in Virginia, North Carolina and South Carolina, Georgia, Alabama, and Mississippi. For more information, see Travis, *Autobiography*, 9, 27–28; MECS, *Minutes of the Annual Conferences*, 24, 80.

217. Emory was born in Maryland; he was converted in 1806 and became a circuit rider in 1810. He ministered in Pennsylvania, Maryland, and Virginia. Emory was known for his academic contributions to American Methodism. For more information, see Emory, *Life of the Rev. John Emory*, 11–66.

218. Fisk was born in Vermont; in 1818, he became a Methodist circuit rider. His main preaching circuits were in New England. He was mostly known for his academic contributions to American Methodism. For more information, see Prentice and Fisk, *Wilbur Fisk*, 2; Holdich, *Life of Wilbur Fisk*, 44.

219. Bascom was born in New York and, in 1808, he was converted. In 1813, he became a circuit rider and ministered in Ohio, Tennessee, and Kentucky. For more information, see Henkle, *Life of Henry Bidleman Bascom*, 11–44; Sprague, *Annals of the American Pulpit*, 7:534–40.

and years of appointment for every circuit rider (between the 1770s and 1830s) referenced in this study.[220]

Brief Summary

In order to present a clear picture of the American circuit rider ministry, this chapter began with the historical and structural formation of the ministry followed by biographical introductions (in-text or footnoted) to the circuit riders featured in this study (including Asbury).[221] As discussed, Wesley's legacy in appointing the circuit riders was continued and further developed (especially by Asbury) to match the ministerial needs of America.[222]

More specifically, in order to further understand the backbone of the American circuit rider ministry, the beginning works of early American Methodism were introduced. As such, the lives and ministries of a few early Methodist figures were briefly discussed. Introductions began with the first officially appointed Methodists of the American circuit rider ministry (Boardman, Pilmore, and Williams), followed by introductions to the Methodists who were not officially appointed by Wesley (Strawbridge, Embury, and Webb). This was followed by the biographical introductions of Rankin, Coke, and Asbury (especially).

In order to further outline the historical formation of the American circuit rider ministry, the first Methodist Annual Conference (which birthed the early American circuit rider ministry) and the Christmas Conference (which birthed the official American circuit rider ministry and the MEC) were both discussed. Following these two events, a list was presented indicating the circuit riders selected for this study; the scholarly rationale behind the selections was also provided.

Although this chapter was chiefly designed to be a historical presentation, it can be observed that even in this early stage of American Methodism and its official creation of the circuit rider ministry (and the MEC), the supernatural played a pivotal role. Circuit riders believed that God was working ahead of them and supernaturally setting up the main

---

220. For a great resource regarding the early lives and ministries of circuit riders, see MEC, *Minutes of the Methodist Conferences*.

221. For a comprehensive list of the circuit riders referenced in this study, please see appendix A.

222. See also Kuiper, *Church in History*, 356.

figures and events, as in a game of chess, so that the creation of American Methodism would be possible. For instance, this is evident in Asbury; while he is known for his instrumental role in the official formation of the American circuit rider ministry (and the MEC), before he was even offered a position to serve in America by Wesley, it was the supernatural presence that kindled a new desire in him to go and minister in America.[223] Moreover, during the Christmas Conference, the circuit riders noted a tangible supernatural presence within the meeting as "the Lord . . . was peculiar[ly] present."[224]

Because "Methodism was launched as a Holy Spirit-infused" movement, the creation of the circuit rider ministry was not achieved merely through human efforts or strategies; rather, God was leading, supporting, and guiding the circuit riders throughout its formation.[225] Indeed, the circuit riders believed that the circuit rider ministry was divinely orchestrated and set apart in its work; they declared that the early Methodists were God's own "people" whose mission was divine and "right" before God.[226]

223. Asbury, *Journal of the Rev. Francis Asbury*, 1:1.

224. Coke, "Journal of Thomas Coke," 291.

225. Wesley Covenant Association, *Firm Foundation*, 57.

226. Abbott and Ffirth, *Experience and Gospel Labours*, 17.

Part II

The Role of the Supernatural and the Rise of Early American Methodism

Chapter 4

Private Supernaturalism

THIS CHAPTER IS DIVIDED into three parts. Firstly, it researches the role of the supernatural within the private lives of the circuit riders (specifically, within their conversions, callings, and sanctification). Secondly, it analyzes the circuit riders' evangelistic strategies, which were inspired by the personal supernatural experiences in their conversions, callings, and sanctification. Lastly, it examines the phenomena of spiritual warfare, which the circuit riders believed affected their private lives (in conversions, callings, and sanctification) and their evangelistic labors.

The Supernatural in the Circuit Riders' Private Lives

The below section outlines private supernaturalism in the circuit rider ministry. It endeavors to demonstrate how supernatural phenomena served as the catalyst in the personal lives of the circuit riders.

The Supernatural and Circuit Rider Conversions

As specified in previous chapters, Wesley's[1] and Asbury's[2] first personal (supernatural) experiences with the Spirit of God were essential to receiving their spiritual conversions.[3] Similarly, the supernatural was

1. For more information regarding Wesley's spiritual conversion, see chapter 2.
2. For more information regarding Asbury's spiritual conversion, see chapter 3.
3. For more information regarding the Wesleyan and early Methodist theology

a major factor in the personal conversions of most other circuit riders; in fact, the circuit riders presented the impression of the supernatural serving as the primary kindling force in their conversions or spiritual rebirths in which "the Holy Spirit had convicted"[4] and converted people.[5] Cartwright declared that the power and presence of "the Holy Spirit awaken[ed] [people's] sensibility"[6] because, as Asbury confirmed, a "conversion . . . was produced in the heart . . . by the Holy Ghost."[7] Garrettson concluded that, for the circuit riders, it was a "privilege to have [supernatural] evidence from God . . . [or] assurance that [they were] his adopted children."[8] These spiritual experiences led circuit riders to embrace their new identities as children of God. Typically, prior to the dawn of their ministries, the circuit riders were introduced to the experiential power of religion through convicting acts performed by the Spirit of God.[9] Therefore, their experiences with the supernatural began their transformational journeys and ultimately led them to their circuit rider roles.[10]

In general, these personal spiritual experiences were very intense or dramatic. For example, Abbott's conversion began with various divine dreams.[11] In one of these dreams, he arrived in hell with demons and was about to be tortured with fire. In another dream, he saw God and his mother in heaven; however, a voice told him in the dream that heaven was "not for [him] yet." After a while, Abbott experienced another divine dream; this time, he saw Jesus Christ who declared the forgiveness of his sins. Soon afterward, the Spirit of God suddenly descended on him "in such a manner that [he] fell flat to the floor." This encounter caused him to "lay" in a condition, as Abbott described, "as one strangling in

---

(including that of the American circuit riders) of spiritual conversion and the full assurance of faith, see chapter 3.

4. Cartwright, *Backwoods Preacher*, 136.

5. For instance, see Asbury, *Journal of the Rev. Francis Asbury*, 1:160–61.

6. Asbury, *Journal of the Rev. Francis Asbury*, 1:116.

7. Holmes, *Methodist Preacher*, 318.

8. Garrettson, *Letter to the Rev. Lyman Beecher*, 24.

9. Cartwright, *Backwoods Preacher*, 307; Abbott and Ffirth, *Experience and Gospel Labours*, 18–26; Garrettson, *Experience and Travels*, 32–34; Lee, *Memoir*, 10; Watters, *Short Account of the Christian Experience*, 30.

10. Wesley, *Sermons on Several Occasions* [Emory], 21; Watters, *Short Account of the Christian Experience*, 30; Asbury, *Journal of the Rev. Francis Asbury*, 1:38.

11. See also Knight, *Anticipating Heaven Below*, 135.

blood." Abbott testified that he then felt the supernatural power and presence of God "running through every part of [his] soul and body, like fire consuming the inward corruptions of [his] fallen depraved nature."[12] According to Abbott, it was through these supernatural experiences that he received his conversion.[13]

Modern historian Rawlyk noted that, like Abbott, Garrettson "had a traumatic conversion experience";[14] he was converted as a result of divine dreams and visions along with the audible hearing of God's voice.[15] For instance, at one point, Garrettson claimed that he heard the "awful [awe-inspiring] voice" of God in "a human voice as loud as thunder." The voice commanded: "Awake, sinner, for you are not prepared to die." During this time, Garretson was undergoing his spiritual conversion, and he felt "the good Spirit [setting] forth to [his] inmost mind the beauties of religion." At another point, the Lord spoke to Garrettson in the form of a vision, stating: "I have come once more to offer you life and salvation, and it is the last time: [choose], or refuse." After these words were spoken to him, Garrettson felt that he "was instantly surrounded with a divine power: heaven and hell were disclosed to view, and life and death were set before [him]." In light of all of these experiences, Garrettson realized that "man hath power to choose or refuse in religious matters," at which point he wholeheartedly chose to receive God's salvation and follow God by putting his "hands together, [and crying] out, Lord, I submit."[16]

Dow's conversion also began through various divine dreams. When he was thirteen years old, he had "a dream of the night" in which Wesley came to converse with him, urging him to pray and seek conversion. After this "dream . . . from God," Dow began to slowly seek and pray halfheartedly and "in secret." After some time passed, circuit rider Hull was scheduled to preach near Dow's home, and "people flocked out from every quarter to hear" him preach. During the sermon, Hull supernaturally "told [Dow] all [the things] that [he] ever did." Following this, Dow became interested in obtaining religion; thus, he prayed and fell into a "slumber" in which he saw another dream where "two devils" grabbed him and were taking him into "hell"; immediately after the

12. Abbott and Ffirth, *Experience and Gospel Labours*, 8, 15–16, 20, 33.

13. See also Finley, *Autobiography*, 167–69.

14. Rawlyk, "Freeborn Garrettson and Nova Scotia," xx, 145.

15. Garrettson, *Experience and Travels*, 11–13. See also Knight, *Anticipating Heaven Below*, 135.

16. Garrettson, *Experience and Travels*, 28, 35–37.

dream, Dow "heard the voice of God" declare that he has was not ready to die. In response, Dow earnestly prayed "for several hours," and during this prayer, Dow visibly "saw the Mediator [Jesus Christ] step in" to his room. Jesus called Dow his "son" and assured him that all of his sins were "forgiven . . . faith ha[d] saved [him]." Through this experience, Dow received his conversion.[17]

In a large religious meeting in 1801,[18] Finley experienced the Spirit of God being poured out, causing "a peculiarly-strange sensation" such as he "had never felt before." He immediately fell to the ground as "a strange supernatural power" seemed to permeate his mind. It appears Finley resisted this supernatural force; however, in doing so, he became "so weak and powerless that [he] found it necessary to sit down." At first, Finley disregarded these experiences and tried to excuse himself from surrendering his will to God, claiming that these experiences were "inspired by songs and eloquent harangues." However, in the midst of this reasoning, he witnessed "at least five hundred swept down in a mo-ment [by the power of God], as if a battery of a thousand guns had been opened upon them, and then immediately followed shrieks and shouts that rent the very heavens." As a result, Finley was terrified and "fled for the woods" and wished he had never attended the meeting. Soon after this experience, another experience occurred "by the Spirit of God." This encounter caused him to finally remove "the scales from [his] sin-blinded eyes," and he divinely comprehended "the awful truth, that if [he] died in [his] sins [he] was a lost man forever." This revelation prompted Finley to seek God in prayer, and as his knees reached the ground, he "cried aloud for mercy and salvation, and fell prostrate." This was his exposure to the supernatural that resulted in his conversion experience, through which, Finley stated, "the goodness and power of God [were] manifested."[19]

In a similar fashion, Lee experienced God supernaturally. He recalled that a "manifestation of the presence and power of God" was poured out on him, causing him to "completely . . . remove all his doubts, and enable[d] him to say, 'now I know in whom I believe.'" This experi-ence led to his spiritual conversion and full "assurance" of faith; thereaf-ter, he was ready to share the gospel with the world.[20]

17. Dow, *History of Cosmopolite*, 12–19.

18. Finley experienced his conversion during a camp meeting. For more information regarding camp meetings, see chapter 7.

19. Finley, *Autobiography*, 167–69, 191.

20. Lee, *Memoir*, 10.

Watters received his conversion after hearing a Methodist sermon about new birth. This conversion "was a notable miracle" because, after praying to God, the Spirit's "supernatural power penetrated every faculty of [his] soul and body," and he proclaimed that the prophetic words of Malachi 3:3 "were literally fulfilled in [his] conversion to God." Moreover, the apparent transformational effect in Watters's life was "so undeniable to all present that they appeared greatly affected and confident that the Lord had descended in the power of his Spirit and wrought a glorious work" in Watters, which encouraged and verified to the people that God was visibly working in their midst.[21]

During a circuit rider meeting, the Holy Spirit was reportedly poured out. After much distress and prayer, Burke was touched in a profound way, and the Spirit caused him to fall down "senseless to the floor." Following this spiritual encounter, he began to "recollect" that he had been on his "feet giving glory to God in loudest strains, to the astonishment of many." Soon after these experiences, "God gave [him] the witness of the Spirit," meaning that he received his spiritual conversion.[22]

Hibbard described his supernatural encounter during his conversion. After much distress resulting from the "wicked" life that he lived, Hibbard experienced fear that he would be condemned to hell, so he sought God and prayed for forgiveness. After one of his prayers in which he "kneeled down and closed his eyes, with [his] hands uplifted toward the heavens," he encountered a vision wherein he "saw Jesus Christ at the right hand of God looking down upon [him], and God the Father looking upon him." On perceiving his gaze, Hibbard felt that Jesus had "removed the burden of [his] sins." Jesus then spoke to him, saying: "Be faithful unto death and this shall be thy place of rest [referring to heaven]." For Hibbard, this was considered to be a miraculous revelation, and he testified that he "never had seen Jesus Christ before, nor heard his voice, nor ever had a sense of [Jesus's] intercession at the right hand of God for [himself] till now." However, later on, Hibbard struggled with the idea of predestination (that he was not elected to be saved) coupled with, it seems, demonic impressions that led him to doubt his spiritual rebirth or conversion until, at another point, the Lord spoke to him "with an audible voice" that was "as plain as it could have been spoken to [his] outward ears." Jesus assured Hibbard that "any poor sinner" who believes

---

21. Watters, *First American Itinerant of Methodism*, 30–32.
22. Finley, *Sketches of Western Methodism*, 25–26.

"may be saved" as salvation is a universal gift "which God gives to every [individual]" who is willing to repent and live in accordance with the gospel. This encounter finalized Hibbard's conversion and served as confirmation that the election "doctrine was false; for it contradicted the Scriptures."[23]

Cartwright encountered his conversion during a large religious meeting.[24] One Methodist circuit rider "preached with great power," followed by an outpouring of "the power of God . . . wonderfully displayed." This caused Cartwright to experience conviction and a desire for conversion. He "went, with weeping multitudes, and bowed before the stand, and earnestly prayed for mercy." During this time, Cartwright recorded a supernatural impression "as though a voice" said to him that his "sins [were] all forgiven." After this encounter, Cartwright had another supernatural encounter in which a "divine light flashed all round [him, bringing him] unspeakable joy in [his] soul." The experience continued as he rose to his feet, feeling as if he were "in heaven," and he and his family praised God for this conversion.[25]

During Young's conversion, he was touched by "a glorious display of Divine power" wherein he "could compare it to nothing but a storm of wind." Upon encountering this phenomenon, Young's tears began to flow, and he felt that he "had lost the power of speech." The experience continued, however, as his "knees became feeble, and [he] trembled like Belshazzar." This divine influence increased until he began to lose his "strength" and, ultimately, as he "fell upon the floor—the great deep of [his] heart appeared to be broken up." Following this encounter, he returned home weeping where he "fell upon the floor, and there [he] lay many hours, having no recollection of anything that passed." During this supernatural experience, he saw a vision of a divine light from heaven that miraculously brought him "from the power of darkness into the kingdom of God's dear Son." Through these supernatural encounters, Young indicated that he received his conversion.[26]

As illustrated in the above examples, it is evident that the supernatural was vital to the spiritual conversions of the circuit riders. Furthermore, it should be noted that these supernatural conversion experiences are

23. Hibbard, *Memoirs*, 9, 19–24, 28–39, 41–42.

24. As with Finley, Cartwright was converted during a camp meeting. For more information regarding camp meetings, see chapter 7.

25. Cartwright, *Backwoods Preacher*, 13.

26. Young, *Autobiography of a Pioneer*, 41–43.

also described in the Bible as a necessary step in becoming a Christian. The circuit riders understood, drawing from biblical principles, that after individuals received spiritual conversion, though they were still natural humans, they became children of the "heavenly Father"[27] who, through Jesus Christ, gave them "the Holy Spirit" who spiritually lived within them and "led" them.[28] This is evident in John 3:5–6, in which Jesus stated: "Truly, truly, I say to you, unless one is born of water and the Spirit, he cannot enter the kingdom of God." Hence, the circuit riders' conversion experiences enabled them to be "born of the Spirit."[29]

To summarize this section, circuit riders experienced their conversions supernaturally through the intervention of "the power of the Holy Ghost."[30] As Burke personally discovered, for an individual to be converted, they needed to somehow experience the spiritual "ecstasy" or immeasurable joy that confirmed that they were, indeed, "born again" of the Spirit.[31] Often, conversions were quite dramatic in nature and many times featured supernatural powers that overshadowed their souls and bodies.[32] Also, it was demonstrated that early Methodists[33] considered conversion to be an "unmerited and merciful favor of God" derived from "the powerful operation of the Holy Spirit."[34]

Additionally, Giles testified that it was "the supernatural work of regeneration" that enabled the circuit riders to become children of God.[35] This new identity as children of God was not something that was received through mere human knowledge; rather, it was received through the Holy Spirit in their conversions.[36] Consequently, personally experiencing God's conversion became the foundation on which circuit riders further

27. Cartwright, *Backwoods Preacher*, 261.

28. Finley, *Sketches of Western Methodism*, 164.

29. Holmes, *Methodist Preacher*, 57.

30. Cooper, *Beams of Light*, 18.

31. Finley, *Sketches of Western Methodism*, 26.

32. For instance, see Watters, *First American Itinerant of Methodism*, 30–32.

33. Hereinafter, when referring to "early Methodism" or "Methodists," unless otherwise specified, these terms describe early American Methodism and American Methodists from the 1770s through the 1830s.

34. Holmes, *Methodist Preacher*, 312. See also Cooper, *Beams of Light*, 18.

35. Giles, *Pioneer*, 80. See also Sprague, *Annals of the American Pulpit*, 7:119.

36. Holmes, *Methodist Preacher*, 318; Finley, *Autobiography*, 167–69; Garrettson, *Experience and Travels*, 27–29; Hibbard, *Memoirs*, 19–23; Watters, *First American Itinerant of Methodism*, 30.

built their Christian faith; it became the beginning of their spiritual journey.[37]

Moreover, like Wesley, the early Methodists believed that if those who professed to be followers of Christ had "not the Spirit of Christ [living in them] . . . [then] none [of them were] his."[38] If individuals identified as Christian but never witnessed the "renewing grace"[39] performed by "the power of the Holy Ghost,"[40] then it could be argued that those individuals were not his children as they had not personally experienced God. Moreover, according to circuit rider theology, if people did not belong to Christ, then they must "belong to the devil, for they two [Christ and the devil] share the world between them."[41] Thus, for circuit riders, the need for people to experience personal conversions became paramount because, through these experiences, people were transferred from the devil's kingdom of darkness "into the kingdom of God."[42]

Indeed, through their conversion experiences, the circuit riders (similar to Wesley) understood that they had escaped the fires of hell and found the narrow road, in Jesus Christ, that led to heaven.[43] They admittedly considered salvation to be their greatest treasure, even greater than their own earthly lives.[44] As such, the supernatural became the

---

37. Young, *Autobiography of a Pioneer*, 41–43; Cartwright, *Backwoods Preacher*, 13–15; Giles, *Pioneer*, 81–83; Finley, *Autobiography*, 180; Cooper, *Beams of Light*, 20; Gatch, *Sketch of Rev. Philip Gatch*, 18–19; Smith and Dailey, *Experience and Ministerial Labors*, 17–18.

38. Jackson, *Lives of Early Methodist Preachers*, 6:49.

39. Sprague, *Annals of the American Pulpit*, 7:119.

40. Cooper, *Beams of Light*, 18.

41. Jackson, *Lives of Early Methodist Preachers*, 1:114.

42. Finley, *Autobiography*, 292.

43. Abbott and Ffirth, *Experience and Gospel Labours*, 7–12; Garrettson, *Experience and Travels*, 42–44; Young, *Autobiography of a Pioneer*, 42; Finley, *Sketches of Western Methodism*, 26. Spiritual freedom, in the life of the circuit rider, is scripturally supported, especially in Jesus's statement in John 8:34–36: "Truly, truly, I tell you, everyone who sins is a slave to sin. A slave is not a permanent member of the family, but a son belongs to it forever. So, if the Son sets you free, you will be free indeed."

44. Watters, *Short Account of the Christian Experience*, 100–101. Also, this notion is scripturally supported; in fact, Jesus emphasized being a Christian's first love. He stated the following in Matthew 10:37–39: "Anyone who loves his father or mother more than Me is not worthy of Me; anyone who loves his son or daughter more than Me is not worthy of Me; and anyone who does not take up his cross and follow Me is not worthy of Me. Whoever finds his life will lose it, and whoever loses his life for My sake will find it." At the same time, see Revelation 2:4–6.

inspiration for the circuit riders to willingly "choose" God, followed by the laying down of their past lifestyles and perspectives while replacing them with a willingness to pursue their newfound religion wholeheartedly.[45]

However, some members of other mainline denominations (such as Presbyterians and Congregationalists) did not approve of Methodist experiential conversion; thus, they "denounce[d] it as [the theology of] an impostor, and a 'damnable heresy.'" These critics argued that this theology was merely a form of "self-conversion"[46] and that those who accepted it were operating under a "delusive spirit." Nevertheless, the circuit riders maintained that the conversion experience served as authentic "evidence of pardon and [brought] peace to the mind."[47]

The Supernatural and Circuit Rider Ministerial Callings

Just as the supernatural became the catalyst in circuit rider conversions, it also became the catalyst in circuit rider callings. As indicated in their personal journals, it was divine supernatural occurrences that exposed the circuit riders' callings to become ministers of the gospel. Their callings (and giftings) were indicated by the "motion of the Holy Spirit,"[48] which was often followed by strong spiritual "convictions"[49] in their hearts.[50] Some circuit riders were reportedly instructed by God's audible voice to go into the world and, despite the anticipated hardships, share the gospel message.[51] Regardless, Scudder explained that "every itinerant" (or circuit rider) in the early Methodist undertaking "felt that he was called and directed in his work by God." As demonstrated below, the circuit riders' "impulsion to preach was a real inspiration from above."[52]

45. Cross, *Burned-Over District*, 27. See also Merritt, "Letters on Methodism," 447; Wesley, *Sermons on Several Occasions* [Emory], 175–84.

46. Smith, *Recollections and Reflections*, 225–26. Also, see Abbott and Ffirth, *Experience and Gospel Labours*, 132–33; Finley, *Autobiography*, 287–89.

47. Dow, *History of Cosmopolite*, 14, 324.

48. Garrettson, *Letter to the Rev. Lyman Beecher*, 24.

49. Watters, *Short Account of the Christian Experience*, 22.

50. Lee, *Memoir*, 267.

51. For instance, see Finley, *Autobiography*, 180; Cooper, *Beams of Light*, 20; Garrettson, *Experience and Travels*, 42–44; Abbott and Ffirth, *Experience and Gospel Labours*, 11, 20.

52. Scudder and Cummings, *American Methodism*, 339.

While, in their callings, most circuit riders experienced an array of strong spiritual impressions and ministerial convictions, which were largely considered to be the result of "divine supervision"[53] or were "understood to be a divine" product of "the Holy Spirit,"[54] some experiences can be considered more "dramatic" in nature than others.[55] For the purpose of this study, the following section predominantly includes testimonies arguably more dramatic in substance.

Travis classified his calling to be a circuit rider as "divine." Even when he was a young boy and never anticipated becoming a circuit rider, he "dreamed that there were twelve preachers," including Asbury, in his father's home. One of the preachers scooped Travis onto his lap, explaining that he "must go with them" and become a circuit rider. According to Travis, the dream indicated that he was gifted and called to be a preacher and that he must not bury the preaching "talent that the Lord ha[d] given [him]." Later in his life, Travis prayed that if it truly was God's will for him to become a circuit rider, then God "would give [him] a token by L. Dow," who was scheduled to soon preach in his neighborhood. Travis attended Dow's preaching, and during his sermon, suddenly, Dow "with his finger pointed at [Travis], sa[id], 'There stands a young man that the Lord intends to make a preacher.'" This answered Travis's prayer and confirmed that the Lord was divinely calling him to join the circuit rider ministry and share the gospel; at the same time, his childhood dream was confirmed.[56]

After Abbott received his conversion, he understood that his calling as a circuit rider was directed by God. He claimed that God instructed him by saying: "You must join the Methodists, for they are my people, and they are right." After this and a few other occasions, he was "fully convinced, that a dispensation of the Gospel was committed to [him]." As a final confirmation, Abbott saw a divine dream in which God stated: "You must go and preach, for you must speak for me." Upon hearing this, he experienced a mysterious sensation as though his "outward and inward man were both animated," causing him to feel "as if [he] could

---

53. Giles, *Pioneer*, 81.

54. Young, *Autobiography of a Pioneer*, 51–52, 55.

55. See also Fry, *Life of Rev. William M'Kendre*, 21.

56. Travis, *Autobiography*, 30–31.

have sprung from the bed to the fire, which was about fifteen feet." Thus, Abbott began to preach the gospel.[57]

Giles expressed that, while standing near his father's house, he felt that "the forest was hewn down around it," and immediately, "the Spirit of God came down upon [him]." This spiritual visitation brought about a "mysterious manner" in which Giles felt that God had "called [him] to preach the everlasting gospel." This ministerial calling was confirmed through God's "perceptible, inward voice," to which Giles replied with "a willingness of mind to do whatsoever [his] Lord and Master required at [his] hands." It was at this time that Giles became "an ambassador for Christ" and felt that he was entrusted "with the great message of salvation to a fallen world."[58]

Following Hibbard's conversion, he confessed that whenever he had the opportunity to publicly engage "in prayer and exhortation," he felt that his "soul was truly happy in God." Hence, Hibbard knew that God had called and gifted him to preach. However, in response, Hibbard "would s[it] down and weep, and pray [to] the Lord to take those [spiritual] impressions" of preaching away from him. Even those who knew him recognized that God was calling Hibbard to preach, but Hibbard insisted that he could not "travel and preach." This struggle continued until he divinely "dreamed that [he] came . . . into an open field" and saw people waiting for him "to come and administer the sacrament" to them. In this dream, while all were engaged in prayer, the heavens "open[ed]" and Hibbard saw "Jesus at the right hand of God, and the Heavenly hosts surrounding the throne, adoring the Father and Son in the most sublime strains." He then felt that his soul "caught the heavenly fire," and in his sleep, he "began to clap [his] hands, and cried out, glory." After he awoke, he further received a spiritual "impression" regarding the meaning of the dream that confirmed that God would meet all of his ministerial needs because "whom God calls, he qualifies."

However, Hibbard later began to doubt his dream; thus, he "fasted and prayed" so that the Lord might "deliver" him from "those impressions to preach." Since the impressions would not leave him, Hibbard then prayed to the Lord that if his "impressions to preach were from [God], [he] might open the Bible on some text, clearly expressing the duty of one called of God to preach." However, if God was not calling him

57. Abbott and Ffirth, *Experience and Gospel Labours*, 17, 24.
58. Giles, *Pioneer*, 82.

to preach, then Hibbard asked that he would open the Bible on some text that would express the need of "running before [he] was sent." He closed his eyes, opened his Bible, and found his finger on the biblical passage of "Ezekiel 3:17, 18," which reads: "I [God] have made thee a watchman . . . therefore, hear the word at my mouth . . . to warn the wicked from his wicked way, to save his life." Soon after this confirmation, Hibbard revealed these spiritual experiences to his wife, repented of his "Jonah-like" attitude, and decided to become a circuit rider.[59]

During Finley's conversion process, he heard the audible voice of God "as though someone had spoken to [him, saying:] 'Go preach my Gospel.'" Finley, in awe, instantly responded to God's calling by replying: "Yes, Lord, if thou wilt go with me." Immediately after these experiences, Finley "did not stop to confer with flesh and blood" but rushed out "as fast as [he] could" to fulfill his new calling. Beginning with his "nearest neighbor . . . [he] called all the family together" and described to them the spiritual work that the Lord "had done for [his] soul." This incident was instrumental in Finley's calling to preach the gospel.[60]

Cooper was called by God through hearing a "forcibly impressed" voice which said: "Am not I He that sendeth by whom I will send? Dost thou doubt my promise?" God explained to Copper that he only needed to "open [his] mouth," and God would divinely "fill it" with the necessary words and signs so that people could be convinced and spiritually converted. God then presented Cooper with a ministerial commission to "go forth and . . . declare salvation in [Jesus's] name." After this experience, Cooper "wore away to a mere skeleton; many thought [he] would die. [He] continued in this low condition for several months, being incapable of any business" until he chose to accept his divine call to be a circuit rider. However, Cooper first petitioned to "the Lord [that if he] would restore [him] to [his] former [healthy] state of body and mind, [then Cooper] would preach, provided [that he] felt the same impressions to it." Hence, Cooper was restored, and it was "more than ever confirmed in the impression that it was the will of God that [he] should preach." Consequently, Cooper became a circuit rider.[61]

Garrettson's divine calling began when he heard the Lord speak to him with "that same blessed voice which had spoken to [him in the past]."

59. Hibbard, *Memoirs*, 123–35.
60. Finley, *Autobiography*, 180.
61. Cooper, *Beams of Light*, 20.

This voice spoke to him of the issue of slavery, insisting that it was not right for people to keep their "fellow-creatures in bondage . . . [they] must let the oppressed go free." Prior to this revelation, although Garrettson was not a slave owner, he had "never suspected that the practice of slave-keeping was wrong." Following this spiritual encounter, however, a desire grew in Garrettson "to spread [his] Redeemer's glory to the ends of the world." As Garrettson was "brought into gospel liberty," he believed that it was his divine "duty to open religious meetings in several places" and share the liberating gospel. Garrettson then began to practically preach the gospel to his "friends . . . neighbors . . . [and] families." However, he had not been preaching long before he felt "weary of life," so he prayed intensely for God's further guidance and slept and dreamed. In his dream, he struggled with the devil (there was also a "good angel" later present in the dream). The struggle continued until he wholeheartedly declared: "I am willing to go and preach [the] gospel." When he awoke from the dream, all of his weariness and "every cloud was dispersed, and [his] soul was enraptured with the love of [his] Savior."[62] From this final divine encounter, Garrettson was fully convinced of his calling to be a circuit rider. Indeed, after becoming a circuit rider, Bangs recorded Garretson's vocational conviction that the Holy Spirit had "set [him] apart . . . for the work of the ministry."[63]

Gatch, who "felt that [he] was called to exercise the gift of exhortation," made some wrong decisions after his conversion that he attributed to bringing him to "a bed of affliction" that was so severe that many thought he would soon die. However, while in this state, Gatch prayed and, in his "extremity, like Jonah, [he] promised the Lord that if he would spare [him, he] would speak his word" by becoming a circuit rider. Following this, the Lord gave him a dream wherein he "used a certain remedy and recovered." After Gatch "awoke, [he] told [his] dream, the remedy was provided, and [he] at once began to [miraculously] recover." For Gatch, the divine dream and healing were the final confirmation that he should become a circuit rider.[64]

Following Dow's conversion, during a time of prayer, he felt that God spoke "words [that] were suddenly impressed on [his] mind," saying: "Go ye into all the world and preach the gospel to every creature."

---

62. Garrettson, *Experience and Travels*, 31–38, 46–48, 146–47.

63. Bangs and Garrettson, *Life of the Rev. Freeborn Garrettson*, 45. See also Simpson, *American Methodist Pioneer*, 53.

64. Gatch, *Sketch of Rev. Philip Gatch*, 19, 20, 22.

Dow first resisted these impressions to preach, rationalizing that he was only "a child" and "an ignorant, illiterate youth." Time went on and the impressions and resistance continued until, at one point, Dow "was seized with an unusual weakness" and could not see; his physicians and friends believed he would "die." However, Dow prayed and, "beyond the expectation of all," God "rebuked the disorder" and his health began to be "restore[d]" until he was completely healed. Dow then again had "strong impressions" from God to preach and, this time, he responded by fasting; "on the 23rd day" of his fast, God confirmed Dow's calling though "an uncommon [spiritual] manner [in which the] light of God's countenance shined forth into [his] soul." This experience "fully convinced" Dow that he was called to preach, and "all [his] doubts and fears . . . [were replaced] with [God's] love." After overcoming some resistance from "the enemy," Dow became a circuit rider.[65]

Smith's calling began with a divine dream in which he was going upward into heaven while the conductor (a spiritual being) was going back down to earth. The conductor told him: "You cannot go to heaven now the Lord has a work for you to do." However, Smith considered this dream to be insufficient proof of his divine circuit rider calling; as a result, he later "fasted and prayed" and became "moved by the Holy Ghost to minister in holy things, and to preach the unsearchable riches of Christ." Smith then became a circuit rider.[66]

The (unofficial) traveling Methodist preacher Jea recorded an unusual story of his calling through a divine vision. Initially, Jea desired to minister to the world, but he felt that he was not equipped to do so because he did not speak or read the languages of the people to whom he wanted to minister (English and Dutch). However, this changed after Jea experienced a vision in which the Lord sent an angel to teach him to read, saying: "[You] desired to read and understand this book [the Bible], and to speak the language of it both in English and Dutch; I will therefore teach [you], and now read." Furthermore, Jea testified that the angel instructed him on how to read, beginning with the first chapter of the biblical book of John. After successfully reading the whole chapter, both the angel and the Bible were "gone in the twinkling of an eye." This experience "astonished [Jea] very much," especially since it became "dark immediately" after they departed. Jea considered this encounter to be a

65. Dow, *History of Cosmopolite*, 21–28.

66. Smith and Dailey, *Experience and Ministerial Labors*, 17–18.

sign that he should become a preacher, and thereafter, he was able to read, speak, and minister in both English and Dutch.[67]

Thus, whether through an audible hearing of the voice of God or through various supernatural impressions or dreams, the circuit riders were spiritually steered toward becoming ministers. They felt that they were supernaturally set apart or "called [by] God to preach" and share their personally experienced gospel with the lost world around them.[68] Hence, the supernatural was instrumental in inspiring, preparing, and sending the circuit riders to their ministerial destinations.[69]

However, at that time, an individual typically became a minister of a mainline denomination by undergoing various denominational and, especially, educational requirements.[70] In this, the circuit riders were distinct because exclusively educational ministerial qualifications were seen by the early Methodists as "a hindrance." Instead, they promoted spiritual "experience"[71] as the "satisfactory evidence"[72] of an individual's calling, and it was the "sole . . . criterion for admittance into the ministry."[73] As Cartwright expressed, it was understood by the circuit riders that "God . . . [would] qualify [a minister] for the work [even] if he never saw a college."[74] Asbury confirmed this by stating that circuit riders were not in much need of "the learned" as these ministers tended to depend on human strength as King Saul depended on his "armor"; instead, Asbury declared that the circuit riders should depend on God's strength, and in doing so, they would receive their spiritual "sling and the stone" that would cause "the gigantic Goliath [to] fall."[75]

While the circuit riders largely did not resemble mainline Protestant ministries, in ways they did resemble the ministry of the Apostolic Church. For instance, they believed that, in their callings,

67. Jea, *Life, History, and Unparalleled Sufferings*, 35–36.

68. Giles, *Pioneer*, 61.

69. Asbury, *Journal of the Rev. Francis Asbury*, 1:31, 261.

70. Cartwright, *Backwoods Preacher*, 39.

71. Plunkett, "Conversion," 854.

72. McElroy, "Deceased Preachers," 276.

73. Carey, "Education, Theology," 209. See also Bangs and Garrettson, *Life of the Rev. Freeborn Garrettson*, 290. However, especially after the 1830s, Methodists began to resemble other mainline denominations in their ministerial qualifications; my future research discusses this matter in detail.

74. Cartwright, *Backwoods Preacher*, 237.

75. Asbury, *Letters*, 475–78.

circuit riders underwent experiences similar to the apostle Paul or "Saul of Tarsus." Saul was called supernaturally when God took hold of him and shook "him a while over hell, then knock[ed] the scales from his eyes" and commissioned him "to preach Jesus and the resurrection." Just as Saul's calling was purely spiritual, "without any previous [Christian] theological training," so it was with the circuit riders; God called them supernaturally, reminding them that their strength was not in education, but rather, as in the Apostolic Age, it was in his power and presence.[76] Thus, the personal supernatural experiences in circuit rider callings (including their spiritual conversions) became paramount as, even in the face of future ministerial difficulties, these experiences of God's power and presence served as an encouragement to further fulfill their callings as they "settled into an acquiescence to the Divine will" for their lives.[77]

At the same time, it should be noted that while the supernatural played a crucial role in prompting the circuit riders' ministerial callings, according to circuit rider testimonies and their Arminian theology, they were willing to choose and respond to their divine callings themselves.[78] Indeed, they believed that God, although he called them, offered them a choice (and did not force them) in regard to whether they would accept his calling.[79] However, since the supernatural experiences of the circuit riders were so influential, although they had a responsive choice, it became difficult for them to resist their callings and "not preach the Gospel."[80]

Also, their spiritual experiences made them feel accountable and aware of the need to fulfill their callings.[81] It was their belief that God was truly almighty, and as he was revealing to them his wish and purpose for their future, some circuit riders, such as Finley, felt that if they rejected this call, God might be dissatisfied with them.[82] This assumption added to their list of reasons for responding to God's calling and preventing any future regret in rejecting the call they felt so evidently laid upon them.

76. Cartwright, *Backwoods Preacher*, 237.

77. Finley, *Autobiography*, 189.

78. Giles, *Pioneer*, 130. See also Holmes, *Methodist Preacher*, 135.

79. See Cartwright, *Backwoods Preacher*, 38–41.

80. Finley, *Autobiography*, 189.

81. This concept is also evident in the biblical text. For instance, Luke 12:48 states: "Everyone to whom much was given, of him much will be required, and from him to whom they entrusted much, they will demand the more."

82. Finley, *Autobiography*, 188–89.

The Supernatural in Sanctification
and a Biblically-Oriented Lifestyle

After experiencing the supernatural in both their conversions and callings, the circuit riders also recorded feeling a distinct supernatural longing for personal holiness. Inspired and motivated by their extraordinary transformational experiences, the circuit riders willingly chose to be continuously sanctified in relationship with the Spirit of God; in accordance with the scriptural writings, they desired to maintain a holy, biblically-oriented lifestyle.[83] As noted in chapter 2, the early Methodists (in England and America) understood sanctification to be "that work of the Holy Spirit by which the child of God is cleansed" or becomes holy "from all inbred sin" through constant "faith in Jesus Christ."[84] As the Methodist eyewitness and nineteenth-century historian Goss declared, circuit riders clearly emphasized "sanctification of the Spirit, consecration to God, resignation to the Divine will, and love and charity to [their] neighbor." Furthermore, for the circuit riders, sanctification was not merely "a doctrine" to be "believed and preached," but it was "inwardly experienced"[85] through the post-conversion indwelling of the "renewing Spirit of holiness."[86] Thus, in their spiritual transformation, relationship with the Spirit of God (along with biblical guidelines) became the circuit riders' main component in cultivating their Christian identity.[87]

For the circuit riders, the process of sanctification or holiness played such a vital role that even if individuals had experienced all of the supernatural phenomena of "religion . . . [or] spiritual life," if they did not also demonstrate "a strong disposition for holiness," then their Christianity was considered "delusive." Circuit riders believed that "real" Christian religion consisted of "real holiness" that was derived from the process of sanctification.[88] One of the ways that the circuit riders

---

83. Asbury, *Journal of the Rev. Francis Asbury*, 1:274; Watters, *Short Account of the Christian Experience*, 137. For more information regarding the biblical role of the Spirit and its connection with early Methodist theology, see Garretson, "Union of Fear," 252–57.

84. Wesleyan Methodist Connection, *Discipline of the Wesleyan Methodist Connection*, 13.

85. Goss, *Statistical History*, 186.

86. Holmes, *Methodist Preacher*, 107.

87. Asbury, *Journal of the Rev. Francis Asbury*, 1:274.

88. Asbury, *Journal of the Rev. Francis Asbury*, 1:90.

sought to maintain a gradual spiritual transformation was through their personal devotions. For instance, like other prominent Methodists of the time, Asbury practiced a strict and methodical devotional life.[89] In fact, Wigger claimed that one of Asbury's "central" goals was to maintain his solid devotional lifestyle.[90] At times, the majority of Asbury's "day was spent in private devotion" with the "expectation that [his] whole body [might] be full of light" or holiness from God.[91]

It appears that circuit riders' devotional lives mainly consisted of reading[92] and praying.[93] Regarding Asbury's devotions, aside from reading the available theological books of the day, his main reading focus was the Bible. Even throughout his busy schedule, Asbury strove to allot daily time for reading the Bible; at times, he would read "six chapters every day."[94] Circuit riders practiced reading so that they could increase their theological knowledge and further know God's character, thus leading them to a closer relationship with God while enabling them to maintain a biblically-oriented lifestyle.[95]

Regarding personal prayers, circuit riders were very active in maintaining their prayer lives.[96] For instance, at times, Asbury would "spend whole nights in prayer." Other times, he prayed up to "twelve times," and other times, he proclaimed "a fast, with prayer, for the Methodists, the health of the city, the general church, and the continent." Through their prayer lifestyle, circuit riders sought to experience more of the power and presence of God and be "filled with comfort under

89. Smith, "Religious Experience of Francis Asbury," 563.

90. Wigger, *American Saint*, 117.

91. Asbury, *Journal of the Rev. Francis Asbury*, 1:107.

92. For instance, see Asbury, *Journal of the Rev. Francis Asbury*, 1:103, 144, 145, 199; Gatch, *Sketch of Rev. Philip Gatch*, 9, 16, 184; Giles, *Pioneer*, 28.

93. For instance, see Asbury, *Journal of the Rev. Francis Asbury*, 1:7, 39, 154, 164, 165, 193; Finley, *Autobiography*, 162, 176–77, 183, 196; Abbott and Ffirth, *Experience and Gospel Labours*, 34, 41, 52, 93; Boehm, *Reminiscences*, 15, 17; Cartwright, *Backwoods Preacher*, 29, 73; Smith and Dailey, *Experience and Ministerial Labors*, 39, 50, 141.

94. Asbury, *Journal of the Rev. Francis Asbury*, 1:63, 103, 145, 154–55, 197, 199, 205, 211, 226, 229, 235.

95. For instance, see Young, *Autobiography of a Pioneer*, 39, 407; Abbott and Ffirth, *Experience and Gospel Labours*, 10, 21, 210; Finley, *Autobiography*, 162, 176, 232; Cartwright, *Backwoods Preacher*, 50; Hibbard, *Memoirs*, 89, 100, 276.

96. Frick, "Spirit of Methodism," 352.

all [of their] trials";[97] hence, they "mourned and wept, fasted, prayed, and truly longed to be sanctified throughout, soul, body, and spirit."[98] In their prayers, the circuit riders diligently sought to be "filled with his Holy Spirit" and "feel" God's power and presence "like a holy flame" so that they could live to be "more spiritual" and more "holy in heart and life." Asbury considered prayer to be "the sword of the preacher, the life of the Christian, the terror of hell, and the devil's plague."[99] Asbury also believed that without "fervent prayer . . . a man [could] not continue [to be] qualified to preach the Gospel";[100] for this reason, he found himself in "need to pray without ceasing."[101]

In essence, while circuit riders humanly sought sanctification, it was the power of the Spirit that actually enabled them to be sanctified.[102] Asbury expressed that "grace, almighty [spiritual] grace, must keep [him], otherwise all [efforts toward holiness, such as] reading, praying, and labours of every kind, would be ineffectual."[103] Hence, it is evident that the "instantaneous power"[104] of the Spirit impelled the circuit riders to desire sanctification, approach sanctification, and maintain a rich, biblically-oriented lifestyle.[105] This was achieved mainly through "steadfastly behold[ing] the divine glory" and supernaturally experiencing "a renewal of nature, a sanctification [given] through the Spirit."[106] Therefore, the circuit riders zealously sought to grow in "inward spiritual power,"[107] according to biblical principles, with the "hope to see much of the power of God."[108]

97. Asbury, *Journal of the Rev. Francis Asbury*, 1:138, 262, 289, 333.

98. Watters, *Short Account of the Christian Experience*, 137.

99. Asbury, *Journal of the Rev. Francis Asbury*, 1:5, 120, 222, 251, 274.

100. Asbury, "Letter CCCCX," 682.

101. Asbury, *Journal of the Rev. Francis Asbury*, 1:235.

102. See also Wigger, *American Saint*, 5.

103. Asbury, *Journal of the Rev. Francis Asbury*, 1:234.

104. Wesley, *Miscellaneous*, 717.

105. Due to early Methodism's strong emphasis on the process of sanctification, it sparked the nineteenth-century Holiness movement. See also Adewuya, *Holiness and Community*, 5; Hooton and Wright, *Extended Family*, 115.

106. Holmes, *Methodist Preacher*, 100, 107, 189, 280.

107. Goss, *Statistical History*, 185–86.

108. Asbury, *Journal of the Rev. Francis Asbury*, 2:41. See also Lee, *Life and Times*; *Memoir*, 86.

Thus, the power of the gospel (experienced through the Spirit of God) gave them new "meaning"; for some, after their conversions, they experienced shame in even reflecting on the ungodly actions that they had practiced in the past, but they were constantly pressed to change and become holier in their choices and lifestyles while being sustained by the supernatural.[109] However, the circuit riders believed that without "the power of religion," it was not possible for them to be sanctified or maintain a deep biblically-oriented lifestyle; their spiritual food was the direct strengthening power of the Spirit.[110] Asbury felt that "the operations of grace" enabled "believers to make advances in the Divine life" or sanctification.[111] This was also confirmed by Cooper who recalled that, at one point in his life and ministry, he "felt the power of God sensibly" enabling him to sustain a biblically-oriented lifestyle.[112]

The circuit riders, such as Gatch, also recommended that, in pursing sanctification, believers "ought always to keep in memory that" their spiritual "sufficiency is of God" as God's kingdom is not only one of "word, but [of] power" in the presence of the "Holy Ghost." Moreover, Gatch implied that Christians need the Pentecost powers in order to strengthen their souls and reach sanctification because "God knew that it was necessary for" those in the book of Acts "in Jerusalem [to be] endued with power from on high," and so it was also necessary for the Christians of his day to be partakers of the same spiritual power so that they could maintain a holy and a biblical lifestyle.[113] Largely through this mentality, American Methodism came to be considered "the means under God . . . of lifting this wicked, disquieted world into a purer, serener, and diviner region."[114]

Circuit Rider Evangelistic Strategies

As demonstrated, the supernatural played a vital role within the circuit riders' private lives (specifically, in their conversions, callings, and sanctification). This section of the chapter endeavors to illustrate how the

109. Young, *Autobiography of a Pioneer*, 35–44.

110. Cartwright, *Backwoods Preacher*, 307.

111. Asbury, *Journal of the Rev. Francis Asbury*, 3:31, 192.

112. Cooper, *Beams of Light*, 63.

113. Gatch, *Sketch of Rev. Philip Gatch*, 17, 123.

114. Goss, *Statistical History*, 186.

supernatural was also crucial in forming the circuit riders' evangelistic strategies. Indeed, it was through the circuit riders' personal supernatural experiences (in their conversions, callings, and sanctification) that such strategies were formed and implemented.

Evangelism was the focus of the circuit rider ministry; it included all of the organizational strategies and designated structures for accomplishing their mission of witnessing and reaching out to the world around them.[115] Evangelism included the labors of creating, riding, and managing specific circuits (presented in chapter 3), organizing various evangelistic indoor and outdoor meetings (presented in chapter 7), and sharing sermons (presented below).[116]

Circuit rider evangelism was inspired by Wesley but was further led and developed by the American circuit riders (mainly Asbury) who held that it was their Christian duty to share this experiential gospel with a world in need of God.[117] It was their belief that they were spiritually free to live on earth (with the assurance of eternal salvation) so that others could receive this spiritual freedom. As demonstrated by their lives, the circuit riders' implemented Wesley's moto: "You have nothing to do but to save souls. Therefore, spend and be spent in this work."[118] Moreover, even during the first American Methodist General Conference of 1784, circuit riders declared themselves to be an active ministry seeking to save the lost.[119] This conviction was reflected in their official statement: "Our Call is to save that which is lost. Now we cannot expect them to seek us. Therefore, we should go and seek them."[120]

The circuit riders believed that their greatest privilege was to lay down (self-sacrifice) their own lives for the good of others (especially in conversion and the salvation of souls).[121] For this reason, it was said that there was "no class" that "more identified with Christ in effort for the salvation of the lost than the ministry [of the circuit riders]."[122] Watters declared that, since the time that he "first knew the Lord," he never saw

115. Coke and Asbury, *Minutes*, 4.

116. See also Teasdale, *Methodist Evangelism*, 16–27.

117. Asbury, *Journal of the Rev. Francis Asbury*, 1:49, 146.

118. Emory, *History of the Discipline*, 41.

119. Whitehead, *Life of the Rev. John Wesley* [1793], 468.

120. Coke and Asbury, *Minutes*, 4. See also Tigert, *Constitutional History of American Episcopal Methodism*, 536.

121. Merritt, "Letters on Methodism," 447.

122. Goss, *Statistical History*, 168.

"anything in this world worth living an hour for," except ministering the gospel, thereby preparing for the "glorious kingdom, which shall be revealed at the appearing of our Lord and [Savior] Jesus Christ."[123] Through this principle, the circuit riders were imitating their God, Jesus Christ, who laid down his own life for the sake of others.[124] In "spread[ing] . . . the Gospel,"[125] the circuit riders hoped that, as it changed them and gave them salvation, it would do the same for the world.[126]

Evangelistic Conditions in the Early American Republic

Politically, the period of the Early American Republic was known for its establishment of a constitutional and "checks and balances" governmental system (containing the legislative, executive, and judicial branches).[127] Economically, this period was known for its capitalist development and budding industrial achievements that caused economic growth (e.g., America was able to purchase the Louisiana Territory from France); slavery played a part in this development, as well.[128] Socially and psychologically, the country encouraged "nationalism"[129] and a mindset of equality and independence through challenging hierarchical authorities.[130] Pioneer families were in the process of settling into unexplored frontier territory with the hope of beginning a new and better life.[131] During this time, the general public (especially on the frontier) was known to have received little formal education (with the exception of the clergy).[132]

123. Watters, *Short Account of the Christian Experience*, 100–101.

124. For instance, this is evident in 1 John 3:16: "This is how we know what love is: Jesus Christ laid down his life for us. And we ought to lay down our lives for our brothers and sisters."

125. Bangs and Garrettson, *Life of the Rev. Freeborn Garrettson*, 189.

126. Asbury, *Journal of the Rev. Francis Asbury*, 1:162.

127. Möllers, *Three Branches*, 17. See also Sharp, *American Politics in the Early Republic*, 1–13.

128. Berkin et al., *Making America*, 399; Northrup, "Land Policies," 429; O'Brien, *Atlas of World History*, 126–27.

129. O'Byrne, "How Methodists Were Made," 247.

130. Tocqueville, *Democracy in America*, 1:50–51.

131. Slaughter, *Whiskey Rebellion*, 65, 69; Volo and Volo, *Family Life in Nineteenth-Century America*, 380–81.

132. Stevens, *One Nation Under God*, 175. See also O'Byrne, "How Methodists Were Made," 249.

The circuit rider ministry seems to have adapted well to these conditions of the Early Republic. For instance, the circuit riders sought to share the gospel in every populated place, especially on the frontier but also in both rural and urban settings; as Feinman declared, the circuit riders endeavored to cover "a vast territory rather than being rooted in a single locality."[133] Furthermore, as America was establishing capitalism or a "free market" economy, a sort of religious market was also being formed. For instance, besides Presbyterian, Congregationalist, and Episcopal religious groups, there arose other religious groups, such as Methodist, Baptist, Mormon, Moravian, and Mennonite (Anabaptist).[134] Individuals had the opportunity to choose the religious group that they deemed most fitting for them.[135]

The circuit riders distinguished themselves from other groups in their active evangelistic pursuits through the use of circuits (a system that was admired for its practicality and accessibility);[136] the circuits and other Methodist evangelistic strategies were also attractive due to the characteristic supernatural displays that often accompanied the circuit rider ministry.[137] Additionally, the circuit riders distinguished themselves from traditional ministers or "university trained clergymen" by wearing the clothing of the "common people" (especially the lower classes) and by sleeping outdoors and staying as guests in the homes of the people to whom they ministered. The circuit riders' lack of formal education was also specifically appealing to the American pioneers because they were considered to be uneducated ministers ministering to uneducated people. In this way, they were able to understand and relate to the lifestyles, dreams, and struggles of the typical early American. In other words, they spoke the language of the common people. This proved to be effective for their ministerial success.[138]

To summarize this section, the circuit riders' evangelistic strategies (circuits, sermons, and meetings) matched the Early Republic's structures and circumstances; this was another confirmation for them

133. Feinman, "Itinerant Circuit-Riding Minister," 46. See also Tefft, *Methodism Successful*, 403–4.

134. Puy, *People's Cyclopedia of Universal Knowledge*, 2071–72.

135. See also Gaustad and Schmidt, *Religious History of America*, 163–65.

136. Noll, *Old Religion in a New World*, 60.

137. Wigger, "Holy, 'Knock-'Em-Down' Preachers," para. 12–16.

138. Hatch, *Democratization of American Christianity*, 34, 58, 104–6, 150–54, 162, 190.

that they were, indeed, set apart to minister in America for "such a time [as this]."[139] Finley confirmed that the circuit rider ministry was a God-driven movement formed specifically for spreading the gospel during the "circumstances of the [Early Republic]."[140]

Evangelism and the Supernatural

Regarding evangelism and the supernatural, for the circuit riders, re-counting to audiences their own supernatural experiences became an essential asset in their evangelistic (and preaching) strategies.[141] Echoing Wesley, and as they gleaned from their own spiritual experiences, the circuit riders held that without the intervention of the Holy Spirit, humanity could not be saved as human intellect was darkened and could not comprehend the gospel by mere reason or logic.[142] In other words: "The darkness of the human intellect with regard to religion, the depravity and deceitfulness of the heart, as also man's total incapability to do anything conducive to his salvation without supernatural direction and aid, are truths obviously exemplified in the conduct of fallen man."[143] Therefore, throughout their lives and missions, it was paramount for the circuit riders to heavily rely on the "demonstration"[144] of divine manifestations.[145] As Asbury suggested to a fellow circuit rider in an evangelistic meeting, "Feel for the power, feel for the power, brother."[146]

According to the circuit riders, being born and raised under Christian religious norms was not enough; it was imperative to experience spiritual conversion or the power of religion (as experienced by Wesley

139. M'Ferrin, *History of Methodism in Tennessee*, 1:323.

140. Finley, *Autobiography*, 368–69.

141. Cartwright, *Backwoods Preacher*, 30; Ruth, *Early Methodist Life and Spirituality*, 317–24.

142. Later, the new generation of circuit riders (beginning in the 1830s) gradually changed this belief by concluding that humans are intellectual beings and, therefore, they can receive even salvation through reason. For more information regarding this matter, see Bowen, "Missionary Discourse," 104–8; Wesley, *Sermons on Several Occasions* [Emory], 15–16, 388–89.

143. Buroes, "Sermon on Romans 8:16, 17," 402.

144. Finley, *Autobiography*, 232, 275.

145. Young, *Autobiography of a Pioneer*, 19; Cartwright, *Backwoods Preacher*, 277.

146. Boehm, *Reminiscences*, 441. See also Atkinson, *Centennial History of American Methodism*, 293.

and the circuit riders, themselves).[147] For instance, even though Abbott's wife was recognized as a "religious . . . [and even a] praying woman," according to him, this was insufficient because, in essence, "she knew nothing of experimental religion . . . [as] she never had experienced a change of heart." Later, as Abbott witnessed to her the love of Christ, his wife experienced her spiritual conversion, and Abbott testified that when God poured out his Spirit, his "wife was so wrought upon, that she cried aloud for mercy." Afterward, God created in her a "great . . . conviction" so powerful that, for the following three days, "she [neither ate nor] drank, [and] slept but little." Abbott recalled that it was during this time that his wife perceived her "lost condition" and identified herself, prior to this experience, as merely a Pharisee because her past form of religion was external rather than experiential.[148]

Scudder expressed that the circuit riders understood that even many "Christians were generally infidel[s] in respect to . . . [spiritual] experience." The circuit riders considered it their divine duty to share the experiential gospel with all, Christians and non-Christians alike; they preached spiritual "experience . . . [and] the doctrine that the Spirit of God dwelt in the hearts of believers, and gave them assurance of sins forgiven."[149] In other words, the circuit riders evangelized to the world with the hope that people would experience spiritual rebirth via the Spirit of God.[150]

It is evident in circuit rider writings that, while circuit riders performed their duties in sharing the gospel, they expected God to meet them by supernaturally pouring out his Spirit so that individuals might experience "the mighty power of God,"[151] be "baptized with the Holy

147. This belief is supported biblically, especially in John 3:5–6 wherein Jesus required everyone to be born of the Spirit: "Truly, truly, I tell you, no one can enter the kingdom of God unless he is born of water and the Spirit. Flesh is born of flesh, but spirit is born of the Spirit." For more information regarding Wesley, his conversion, and the supernatural, see chapter 3.

148. Abbott and Ffirth, *Experience and Gospel Labours*, 18, 25–26.

149. Scudder and Cummings, *American Methodism*, 152.

150. Lee, *Memoir*, 5. For more information regarding the Methodist understanding of spiritual rebirth, see chapter 2.

151. Cartwright, *Backwoods Preacher*, 223.

Ghost,"[152] and receive conversion.[153] Thus, it appears that the circuit riders relied on the supernatural as a primary component of their evangelistic "success."[154] While this notion is further investigated in upcoming chapters, a few examples of this circuit rider perspective are listed below.

Smith declared that the circuit rider ministry relied upon "the demonstration of the Spirit . . . in power." Often, circuit riders, such as Newell, prayed that God would "give [or allow them] to see [his] power and goodness displayed in the awakening and conversion of sinners."[155] Hibbard, in his life and ministry, witnessed "extraordinary cases of the power of God"; from these supernatural cases, numerous audience members in circuit rider "meetings fell as if slain in battle," which led to many receiving "conversions [that] were . . . [performed] with visible demonstrations of the power of God."[156] Atkinson recorded an incident during one circuit rider meeting when the Spirit of God descended and "a sudden sound was heard as of a rushing wind," audible from a distance. A sense of curiosity grew as people gathered to discern from where the rushing noise was coming. However, they beheld nothing with their natural eyes as not a "leaf quivered." Still, the noise continued, and the source was soon identified as, suddenly, audience members "by hundreds, fell upon the ground. Great cries arose from the startled and convicted multitude." Also, from this outpouring, Methodist membership expanded as "conversions quickly followed, and the work resulted, ultimately, in hundreds of additions to the Church."[157]

Hence, the role of the supernatural in evangelism was to proclaim the gospel via demonstrations of the Spirit of God as it was the Spirit of God who was "moving the heart of its subjects to feel [the gospel]."[158]

152. Finley, *Sketches of Western Methodism*, 97. See also Abbott and Ffirth, *Experience and Gospel Labours*, 95–97; Atkinson, *Centennial History of American Methodism*, 293; Holdich, *Life of Wilbur Fisk*, 67.

153. Asbury, *Journal of the Rev. Francis Asbury*, 1:70, 265.

154. Lee, *Memoir*, 40–41. This idea is biblically supported; for instance, Zechariah 4:6 states that greatness comes "not by [human] might nor by [human] power, but by [the] Spirit of [God]." At the same time, in his ministry, Jesus demonstrated that supernatural manifestations were essential for Christian ministry. In John 10:37–38, Jesus stated: "If I am not doing the works of My Father, then do not believe Me. But if I am doing them, even though you do not believe Me, believe the works themselves, so that you may know and understand that the Father is in Me, and I in the Father."

155. Newell, *Life and Observations*, 261.

156. Hibbard, *Memoirs*, 161, 208.

157. Atkinson, *Centennial History of American Methodism*, 225.

158. Scudder and Cummings, *American Methodism*, 339. See also Finley,

For the circuit riders, this was the gospel of the "living God"[159] who they believed could transform the entire human race, if they were but willing.[160] Whatcoat witnessed that God, through the circuit rider ministry, was bringing about rebirth, even in those as cold as "stones." He expressed that the preaching of "the Gospel, which is the power of God," stirred up members of the public and caused a spiritual light to touch them, "and of these stones [those present] did the supreme Ruler of the universe raise children to Christ." In addition, members of the public, who became "deeply experienced in grace," were also presented with "the gifts of the Holy Spirit" so that they could participate in gospel labors, as well.[161] Scudder observed that the circuit riders believed that spiritual conversion "depend[ed] on the enlightening, renewing, and sanctifying inworkings of the Holy Spirit"; a person was truly "saved" or converted "only, as he [became] the subject of this work of the Spirit."[162] Therefore, circuit riders demonstrated a ministry wherein supernatural powers caused Methodism to be "so successful in soul-saving."[163] As such, American Methodism, through its evangelistic strategies and the power of the Spirit, became "one of the chief exponents of the Great Revival which swept eastern and western America."[164]

Primary Preaching Strategies

In order to better understand the circuit rider ministry, one of the main components of circuit rider evangelism should be explored in greater depth: the preaching styles and strategies of the circuit riders (and their relationship to the supernatural). The circuit riders felt that they were "inward[ly] mov[ed] [by] the Holy Ghost to preach" the gospel as a "divine afflatus" was "impelling them with a spiritual power to declare it."[165]

Autobiography, 275; MEC, Minutes of the Forty-Third Session, 45–46.

159. Young, Autobiography of a Pioneer, 165.

160. Asbury, Journal of the Rev. Francis Asbury, 1:31.

161. Phoebus, Memoirs, 93.

162. Scudder and Cummings, American Methodism, 51.

163. MEC, Minutes of the Forty-Third Session, 45.

164. Williams, Garden of American Methodism, 29. See also Buckley, History of Methodism in the United States, 1:153; Asbury, Journal of the Rev. Francis Asbury, 1:75, 101.

165. Scudder and Cummings, American Methodism, 339. See also Giles, Pioneer, 237.

Dow confirmed this matter by stating that the circuit riders (including himself) felt "assisted by the supernatural grace of God" in preaching the gospel.[166] Therefore, circuit rider sermons deserve further attention and analysis, which this section supplies.

As Asbury was the primary leader of the entire circuit rider ministry, he was responsible for directing the American circuit riders in their preaching strategies (a tool of circuit rider evangelism). Asbury's main strategic aim, passed onto the circuit riders, was simply to preach the gospel everywhere and to everyone with the hope of seeing the divine power and presence make "way for the word of truth, and the Holy Spirit" to attend it so that it might be "spread in power and cover these [American] lands."[167] He especially implemented his lessons during and after the Revolutionary War when many of the prominent circuit riders left America (including Rankin).[168] During that time, Asbury began to lead and principally employ young American-born Methodists.[169] This leadership tactic proved to be very effective in spreading Methodist revivals as the American-born Methodists were strongly tied to their American roots and desired to see experiential religion proclaimed in their homeland.[170] Indeed, while modern scholar McClymond advised to not "overlook the [Methodist] ties between Britain and America,"[171] this study suggests that, despite keeping some post-war ties with British Methodism, American Methodism developed preaching strategies tailored to the environment of the Early Republic rather than Britain.[172] In fact, as the theologian Ward observed, American "Methodists made it possible to pull down an Anglican establishment" and erect something new.[173] This is evident in circuit rider preaching strategies.

In preaching, unlike the "college-educated" ministers of other denominations, such as the "Congregationalists, Presbyterians and Episcopalians,"[174] the circuit riders were encouraged to "give a good ac-

166. Dow, *History of Cosmopolite*, 111. See also Hempton, *Methodism*, 7–8.

167. Asbury, *Journal of the Rev. Francis Asbury*, 1:110.

168. Moore, "Methodism in War Times," 688–93.

169. Lawrence, *One Family Under God*, 200.

170. "Was John Wesley the Founder of American Methodism?," 623; Powell, "Methodist Circuit Riders in America," 10.

171. McClymond and McDermott, *Theology of Jonathan Edwards*, 444–45.

172. Hatch, *Democratization of American Christianity*, 3–4.

173. Ward, *Protestant Evangelical Awakening*, 295.

174. Wigger, "Fighting Bees," 88.

count of their [spiritual] experience[s]."[175] With this form of preaching, education held "a secondary place to experimental and practical religion" while the primary goal was to be "inwardly moved by the Holy Ghost . . . [which gave] evidence of their divine mission."[176] Asbury declared that Methodist circuit rider meetings "should be purely spiritual" and that the preacher should speak regarding his own spiritual experience because "in the preaching of the Gospel: First [comes] Christian experience."[177] Moreover, Wigger indicated that Asbury prompted Methodists to daily live their "sermons and [preach] from their daily [spiritual] experience[s]."[178]

The circuit riders implemented a preaching strategy in which they shared their sermons in direct and bold ways fueled by "zeal . . . [and] courage" and a sense of urgency;[179] their sermons were "anchored toward salvation,"[180] and "with earnestness [they] urged and beseeched men to flee the wrath to come."[181] For instance, it was common for circuit riders to question people "[if they were] born again [by the Holy Spirit]." They typically followed this question by asking: "Your sins are [they] forgiven?" If the answer was "no," then their responses were similar to the following: "You are in the broad road to hell, and if you die in this state you will be damned."[182] The circuit riders "could map out the path of life, and picture the glories of heaven and the glooms of hell with a vividness and a power that made all hearts feel their reality."[183]

In fact, due to the popular appeal of these zealous messages, some scholars identified the circuit riders' intensity as an intentional preaching strategy and largely attributed their success to this strategy. For instance, modern scholar Anderson argued that a circuit rider endeavored "to keep his audience awake and interested with voice tone modulations, shouts and displays of vigorous impassioned pleas."[184] However, as the circuit

---

175. Asbury, *Journal of the Rev. Francis Asbury*, 1:39.

176. Lee, *Memoir*, 5.

177. Asbury, *Journal of the Rev. Francis Asbury*, 3:119, 156.

178. Wigger, *American Saint*, 284.

179. Young, *Autobiography of a Pioneer*, 167.

180. Powell, "Methodist Circuit Riders in America," 101.

181. Goss, *Statistical History*, 166. See also Cheek Jr., "Original Diversity," 189.

182. Garrettson, *Experience and Travels*, 24–25.

183. Finley, *Sketches of Western Methodism*, 150.

184. Anderson, "Shaping of American Community," 6.

riders attested, their passion was authentic (as opposed to contrived) and was largely a response to the passion they encountered through their own spiritual experiences, which they greatly desired to share with their audiences. As the circuit riders began "to tell the people"[185] their personal testimonies (past and current) of God's power and "what God had done for"[186] their souls, this offered their audiences an opportunity to experience practical religion, as well.[187]

Circuit rider sermons were not mixed with "fine-spun metaphysical or philosophical theories,"[188] but they were heartfelt and gave the impression of sincerity. Their sermons were "delivered in plain, simple language—the language of the people,"[189] which frequently resulted in "[spiritual] spears running through"[190] audience members.[191] Through these bold and simple messages, the circuit riders anticipated that, as their sermons were considered to be filled with "experimental and practical divinity,"[192] their audiences would supernaturally receive experimental and practical religion, especially in regard to conversion.[193]

This view was expressed by Boehm who stated that circuit rider "preaching was more direct; they aimed at the heart, and looked for more immediate [spiritual] results [and responses]."[194] Goss confirmed this matter by stating that, "as a rule," a circuit rider "addresse[d] himself directly to the heart" of his audiences, "while many others [from other denominations] appeal[ed] to the intellect."[195] When the circuit riders shared their sermons, they expected that, through God's grace, their audience would, indeed, respond to the offered message of salvation.[196]

185. Dow, History of Cosmopolite, 19–20.

186. Abbott and Ffirth, Experience and Gospel Labours, 18.

187. Paine, Life and Times, 1:51; Chase, Recollections of the Past, 100; Knickerbocker, Bard of the Bethel, 2–4; Asbury, Journal of the Rev. Francis Asbury, 2:397–98; Finley, Autobiography, 165–66; Maynard, Experience of Sampson Maynard, 9–10.

188. Chase, Recollections of the Past, 101. See also Finley, Sketches of Western Methodism, 150.

189. Goss, Statistical History, 167.

190. Garrettson, Experience and Travels, 35, 25.

191. Smith, Recollections and Reflections, 35.

192. Chase, Recollections of the Past, 100.

193. Lee, Memoir, 5; Wakeley and Boehm, Patriarch of One Hundred Years, 492.

194. Boehm, Reminiscences, 492.

195. Goss, Statistical History, 166.

196. Powell, "Methodist Circuit Riders in America," 101.

This Methodist style of experiential preaching was something new for the American audience, and they were attracted to it;[197] consequently, it was highly effective on America soil as, in general, it has been argued that Americans were religious pragmatists, including Asbury and most Methodists.[198] Due to this American mindset, experiences seemed appealing because of the opportunity for immediate application.[199] Even the *Natchez Newspaper and Public Advertiser* published an article declaring how the "preaching" strategies "of Methodists [were] peculiarly profitable and welcome" in America as they did not "depend" on "human learning" or "polished Academia" but on practical "force of the truth" in order to "carry conviction to the hearts of [their] hearers."[200] Thus, the circuit riders continued in this ministerial strategy by sharing their simple messages of religious experiences throughout their circuits and then offering similar pragmatic experiences of "the power of religion"[201] to their audiences.[202]

Furthermore, based on circuit rider writings, it can be argued that whenever the circuit riders categorized a sermon (including a meeting) as successful, it was because, as Dow argued, the supernatural "presence of the Lord"[203] was apparent there in some shape or form.[204] Similarly, Sweet stated that early Methodism's ministerial "success" was connected to the outpourings of "great grace and peace."[205] Indeed, "the secret of [their preaching] success [was] realized . . . [to be] the Holy Ghost [who] was with the preachers and the word . . . [and through whom] signs and wonders followed."[206] Asbury confirmed this matter by declaring that the success of his circuit preaching was in "the power of God [that was]

197. Abbott and Ffirth, *Experience and Gospel Labours*, 36; Chase, *Recollections of the Past*, 14; Wigger, *Taking Heaven by Storm*, 78.

198. Powell, "Methodist Circuit Riders in America," 50; Wigger, *American Saint*, 106; Abraham and Kirby, *Oxford Handbook of Methodist Studies*, 328.

199. See also Bowden and Smith, *American Chemical Enterprise*, 40.

200. "Religious: The Methodist," 1.

201. Asbury, *Journal of the Rev. Francis Asbury*, 2:63.

202. See also Boehm, *Reminiscences*, 492; Asbury, *Journal of the Rev. Francis Asbury*, 1:261.

203. Dow, *History of Cosmopolite*, 81.

204. See also Scudder and Cummings, *American Methodism*, 339.

205. Sweet, *Circuit Rider Days*, 40.

206. Saxton, "Holy Spirit," 633. See also MEC, *Minutes of the Forty-Third Session*, 45.

present while [he] preached."[207] Therefore, according to Cartwright, the circuit riders relied on the supernatural power and presence in their evangelistic sermons so that they could preach more effectively because divine manifestations were considered to be "the success" of their missions.[208]

However, in the 1830s, as Methodist membership had already become substantial in many parts of America, Methodists entered the early stages of distancing themselves from this form of preaching and, instead, "plunge[d] right into" the preaching styles of other mainline denominations.[209] This began during the General Conference of 1816 (the year of Asbury's death). Bangs, who was highly educated and possibly motivated by other mainline denominations, recommended that the MEC require brief "informal" training for young Methodist preachers. This recommendation encountered "great opposition" from the circuit riders;[210] nevertheless, after several days of debate, it was recommended that "a course of reading and study proper be pursued by candidates for the ministry."[211] Although this training was approved, modern Methodist scholar Rowe observed that, because the training was merely recommended, it remained "irregular and spasmodic."[212] Indeed, attendance was low because the circuit riders, admittedly, were not supportive of the training occurring in other denominations largely because, without any formal educational training, the circuit rider ministerial strategies had proven to be successful in maintaining consistent growth.[213] However, pressure from the new generation of Methodist leaders and clergy continued. It was their desire to make Methodism "the next great educational ministry," especially during the 1830s when many theological books were being published.[214] As this pressure increased over the years, in 1848, the MEC finally approved to

207. Asbury, *Journal of the Rev. Francis Asbury*, 1:55.

208. Cartwright, *Backwoods Preacher*, 118.

209. Cartwright, *Backwoods Preacher*, 39.

210. Stevens and Bangs, *Life and Times of Nathan Bangs*, 171.

211. MEC, *Journals of the General Conference*, 151. See also Sweet, *Methodists*, 303.

212. Rowe and Maser, "Discovery," 60.

213. For more information on Methodist growth, see appendix B.

214. DePuy, *Methodist Year-Book*, 177.

"impose"[215] professional educational requirements on their clergy.[216] As Methodists began opening their own theological schools, they intended to train the next generation of "young preachers" in ministerial and preaching styles that were, according to Giles, "mere mechanical" in that they required "reading their sermons." It was lamented within the older generation of circuit riders that, with this change, Methodism began losing its "zeal and pathos to make the house of worship an interesting place."[217]

To summarize this section, Asbury led the American circuit rider ministry in discovering and employing the tools of evangelism through preaching.[218] Asbury presented a preaching vision that was empowered by the Wesleyan component of sharing personal (supernatural) experiences with the hope that, through the power of the Spirit, circuit rider audiences would respond to their sermons.[219] At the same time, Asbury directed the rest of the American circuit riders to understand the importance of being "moved by the Holy Ghost to speak for God."[220] Circuit riders came to the realization that the very best "aid" in preaching the gospel was, for them, speaking by and through the Holy Spirit;[221] hence, there were many times in which the circuit riders, such as Asbury, prayed for the "Holy Spirit [to be present] in [their] preaching" and implored, "Lord, preach thy word, by thy Holy Spirit."[222]

Furthermore, the circuit riders presented a ministry with "its supernatural reality" that "was indeed new, for the people [who] had not been so taught"; more specifically, they aimed to demonstrate "a religion to be 'felt and seen.'"[223] As Giles observed, the circuit riders preached with

---

215. Holifield, "Clergy," 176–79.

216. MEC, *Journal of the General Conference* [1848], 137–40, 158–59, 165–70, 186, 190–91, 209, 272, 307; Finke and Stark, *Churching of America,* 164.

217. Giles, *Pioneer,* 302, 325. See also Chase, *Recollections of the Past,* 99–101. This matter will be further discussed in my future research.

218. See also Wigger, *American Saint,* 417.

219. Boehm, *Reminiscences,* 492.

220. Asbury, *Journal of the Rev. Francis Asbury,* 1:70.

221. For instance, see Abbott and Ffirth, *Experience and Gospel Labours,* 118, 146, 162, 183; Finley, *Autobiography,* 180, 270, 297; Boehm, *Reminiscences,* 161; Young, *Autobiography of a Pioneer,* 119, 422–24; Giles, *Pioneer,* 82; Lee, *Memoir,* 61; Smith and Dailey, *Experience and Ministerial Labors,* 77; Paine, *Life and Times,* 1:51, 56, 58.

222. Asbury, *Journal of the Rev. Francis Asbury,* 1:75, 345.

223. Scudder and Cummings, *American Methodism,* 49.

the "divine Providence" that followed them as they were "endowed with [spiritual] power from above."[224] Hence, as the circuit riders preached, they did not do so in light of educational or professional training (as was the norm in other mainline Protestant denominations of those days); rather, they preached in sharing their personal supernatural testimonies and "in demonstration of the Spirit, [causing] many souls [to be] saved under [their] ministry."[225]

Endured Hardship in Evangelism

Because of both their confidence in their personal spiritual experiences and their zeal to evangelize, the circuit riders were willing to go to even the most remote and dangerous places;[226] as such, they became American frontier missionaries.[227] The circuit riders aimed "to experience [God], to do [ministry], and to suffer" for the gospel so that "men, women, children, and infants"[228] could be baptized and receive conversion. As noted briefly in previous chapters, while ministering in these hazardous places, circuit riders encountered various threatening situations (at times, even life-threatening ones), such as: sickness,[229] persecution,[230] prison,[231] severe weather,[232] potential attacks from mobs and American Indians, etc.[233]

For example, circuit rider Daughaday was known to have greatly "suffered . . . from a cough and pain in his breast; and frequently spit blood." Even in this condition, Daughaday did not cease his ministerial labors but, instead, exhausted the "feeble remains of dying nature,

224. Giles, *Pioneer*, 237.

225. Young, *Autobiography of a Pioneer*, 19. See also Chase, *Recollections of the Past*, 100–101; Boehm, *Reminiscences*, 492.

226. See also Kinghorn, *Heritage of American Methodism*, 57.

227. Foley, *Genesis of Missouri*, 272.

228. Asbury, *Journal of the Rev. Francis Asbury*, 3:85.

229. Young, *Autobiography of a Pioneer*, 143.

230. Cartwright, *Backwoods Preacher*, 79.

231. Bangs and Garrettson, *Life of the Rev. Freeborn Garrettson*, 103.

232. Cartwright, *Backwoods Preacher*, 231.

233. For instance, Young described his travel difficulties and his fear of being attacked by American Indians. For more information, see Young, *Autobiography of a Pioneer*, 7–13; Cartwright, *Backwoods Preacher*, 1.

in proclaiming salvation through Jesus Christ, to a lost and ruined world."[234] Also, once after Cartwright concluded a religious meeting, he traveled during a "day [that] was intensely warm" while being sick with a "fever." His condition worsened to the point that he "lay down" and was ready "to die" there. However, someone spotted him and carried him to a safe place. After Cartwright felt better, he immediately continued with his traveling.[235] Thus, it can be understood that the circuit riders were "daunted by no hardship" and were passionate about witnessing conversions. They "traveled their assigned districts year in and year out, devoting themselves wholly to propagating the gospel."[236]

At the same time, while circuit riders were going through these hardships, they also prayed in expectation of receiving a touch from the Holy Spirit that would spiritually empower them to minister effectively with "peace [and] love."[237] For instance, in his personal life, Coke cherished the times when he "felt much of the power of God"; he also acknowledged that, at times, when there was "little good . . . in [his natural] power . . . the grace of God" was poured out in his life, making it possible for him to preach "almost every evening, and sometimes in the morning, and three times on the Lord's day."[238]

Similarly, Collins witnessed that "with the sword of the Spirit, [and by] relying upon the strength" of God, he "went forth in [Jesus's] name," overcoming various ministerial hardships.[239] Whatcoat testified that what kept him strong in his life and ministry was "the power of God [that] came upon" him and caused his heart to become "remarkably melted with love to God and man."[240] When Boehm was exhausted from his ministerial labors and "had no time for 'rest week,'" nor any "time to rust out," he considered it a "happy toil [because] God was with [him], strengthening [him] with his Spirit, and cheering [him] with his presence."[241]

---

234. MEC, *Minutes of the Annual Conferences*, 1:507. Daughaday (1777–1810) was a circuit rider who, due to these kinds of hardships, died at the age of thirty-three. See MEC, *Minutes of the Methodist Conferences*, 507.

235. Cartwright, *Backwoods Preacher*, 149–50.

236. Cleveland, *Great Revival in the West*, 26.

237. Asbury, *Journal of the Rev. Francis Asbury*, 3:322.

238. Coke, *Extracts of the Journals* [1793], 72, 157.

239. Finley, *Sketches of Western Methodism*, 319.

240. Phoebus, *Memoirs*, 17.

241. Wakeley and Boehm, *Patriarch of One Hundred Years*, 80.

As illustrated, it appears that no ministerial hardships, not even threats of death, stopped the circuit riders from proclaiming the gospel.[242] According to the circuit riders, what carried them through these hardships was the divine inner power and the love that was reflected in their desire to reach others for the sake of the gospel.[243] Indeed, the divine "love of Christ and of souls ha[d] carried them forward against the world, the flesh, the devil, and . . . floods of calumny."[244]

The circuit riders braved these perils because of their spiritual experiences in conjunction with their "divine commission" to evangelize and witness to the lost.[245] These two factors (experience and commission) became their strength and were crucial to the ongoing success of their evangelistic ministry.[246] As noted previously, it was because these circuit riders gave their lives for the sake of both God and others in the midst of various hardships that, unfortunately, the majority of them passed away at a young age, many of them only in (or even before) their early thirties.[247]

242. Asbury, *Journal of the Rev. Francis Asbury*, 1:2, 8, 65, 348; Cartwright, *Backwoods Preacher*, 263; FUMC, *History of the First United Methodist Church*, 27.

243. Gatch, *Sketch of Rev. Philip Gatch*, 170.

244. Merritt, "Letters on Methodism," 471.

245. Powell, "Methodist Circuit Riders in America," 103. At the same time, in addition to experiencing many spiritual blessings, the biblical text warns believers to expect persecution and hardship. For example, John 15:19–21 states: "If you were of the world, the world would love you as its own; but because you are not of the world, but I chose you out of the world, therefore the world hates you. Remember the word that I said to you: 'A servant is not greater than his master.' If they persecuted me, they will also persecute you. If they kept my word, they will also keep yours. But all these things they will do to you on account of my name, because they do not know him who sent me." Also, 2 Corinthians 4:8–11 states: "We are afflicted in every way, but not crushed; perplexed, but not driven to despair; persecuted, but not forsaken; struck down, but not destroyed; always carrying in the body the death of Jesus, so that the life of Jesus may also be manifested in our bodies. For we who live are always being given over to death for Jesus' sake, so that the life of Jesus also may be manifested in our mortal flesh." Lastly, 2 Timothy 3:12 states: "Indeed, all who desire to live a godly life in Christ Jesus will be persecuted."

246. Asbury, *Journal of the Rev. Francis Asbury*, 1:24, 31, 211–12. See also Wakeley and Boehm, *Patriarch of One Hundred Years*, 21; Smith and Dailey, *Experience and Ministerial Labors*, 36.

247. Duewel, *Heroes of the Holy Life*, 166; Rhodes, *First United Methodist Church*, 4–5.

Spiritual Warfare in the Circuit Riders'
Private Lives and Evangelism

To begin, aside from some discussion in a book by J. Williams[248] and a couple of studies pertaining to Wesley, such as one article written by Rack[249] and one by Webster,[250] spiritual warfare in the circuit rider ministry has not been heavily researched by scholars. Thus, this work intentionally addresses this need in detail.

While circuit riders labored to evangelize America, they recorded that they continuously engaged in spiritual warfare with demonic beings because, as modern historian Gross observed, the circuit riders believed that one of their missions was "to wrest the new nation from the control of the devil."[251] Hence, the phenomenon of spiritual warfare played a large role in the circuit riders' private lives and ministries (which included their evangelistic labors); for this reason, spiritual warfare, and its effect on the circuit riders, is investigated at length in the following section.

In brief, the circuit riders perceived human existence to be regularly interrupted by satanic or demonic powers.[252] The demonic beings' "cunning"[253] thoughts were often "whispered"[254] in a deceptive way, making it largely difficult to discern whether these thoughts belonged to the believers themselves (including the circuit riders) or the devil. Therefore, the circuit riders believed that the devil's evil works could only be detected through their spiritual senses, which were empowered by the Spirit of God. Indeed, they perceived the devil to be "a liar"[255] and the "most subtile adversary."[256]

248. Williams, *Religion and Violence.*

249. Rack, "Doctors, Demons, and Early Methodist Healing," 137–52.

250. Webster, "Those Distracting Terrors of the Enemy," 373–85.

251. Gross, "Romance of American Methodism," 14.

252. Cooper, *Beams of Light*, 18; Abbott and Ffirth, *Experience and Gospel Labours*, 21, 23; Asbury, *Journal of the Rev. Francis Asbury*, 1:109; Garrettson, *Experience and Travels*, 16–18. This concept is also presented in the biblical text, especially Ephesians 6:11–12, which states: "Put on the whole armor of God, that you may be able to stand against the schemes of the devil. For we do not wrestle against flesh and blood, but against the rulers, against the authorities, against the cosmic powers over this present darkness, against the spiritual forces of evil in the heavenly places."

253. Asbury, *Journal of the Rev. Francis Asbury*, 1:90.

254. Travis, *Autobiography*, 27.

255. Horton, *Narrative of the Early Life*, 81.

256. Cooper, *Beams of Light*, 118.

In circuit rider writings, the words *devil*,[257] *devils* (plural),[258] and *Satan* were understood to indicate the "enemy of mankind."[259] As noted in chapter 1, these devils were identified as angelic beings who rebelled against God in the heavenly realms and, thus, became demonic beings.[260] According to the theology of the circuit riders, since all of these demonic beings were ruled by the devil, it was fitting to the circuit riders that they name their spiritual enemies *devils*;[261] this implied that all demonic beings fall under the same category of rebellious and destructive evil beings.[262] This logic is also present in the biblical text, especially in Mark 3:23–26, which displays how Jesus used the singular word *Satan* to describe the entire "kingdom" of demonic beings.

According to Unger, one of the most prominent modern scholars on exorcism, churches today (specifically, Pentecostal and Charismatic churches) view demonic beings largely the same as they did during the time of the circuit riders. Often, they are viewed as "sinister beings" that aim to influence and "enslave" people (even Christians) by promoting separation from God. Unger expressed that, as understood in the circuit rider ministry, the only way for people to be delivered from these evil beings is through prayer and exorcism.[263]

Circuit riders believed that in order to both be liberated from the oppression of these spiritual beings and become spiritually equipped to set others free (through their evangelistic missions), personally engaging in spiritual warfare or exorcism was paramount.[264] Therefore, for the circuit riders, spiritual warfare was a spiritual battle that was performed in faith through various prayers and supplications and ended in the expulsion of evil spirits through the power of God.[265]

257. Holdich, *Life of Wilbur Fisk*, 269.

258. Cartwright, *Backwoods Preacher*, 184.

259. Asbury, *Journal of the Rev. Francis Asbury*, 1:33, 53.

260. Staton and Thompson, *Angels*, 43–44.

261. Cartwright, *Backwoods Preacher*, 184.

262. The idea of Christian spiritual warfare with the devil and demonic beings was introduced in chapter 1.

263. Unger, *What Demons Can Do to Saints*, 13–14, 50–77.

264. See also Williams, *Religion and Violence*, 6.

265. For more information regarding the expulsion of demonic beings, see, Bryan, *Serpent and the Savior*.

Encountering Spiritual Attacks

One of the most common demonic attacks in the lives of the circuit riders came through various temptations to hinder them from living a biblical lifestyle and proclaiming the gospel. Many of the "powerful" temptations that crept into the lives of the circuit riders were attributed to having originated from the hand of "Satan."[266] For instance, Garrettson recalled times in which devils attempted to torture or distract him through various temptations so that he might be prevented from preaching. Garrettson once declared that "the devil strives very hard to hinder the spreading of the Gospel."[267] At another point, Garrettson spiritually discerned that the devil tried "very hard to keep [him] from going [and ministering] among [a certain group of] people." At various times, he recorded that he was deeply "tempted of the devil all the morning before preaching"; apparently, in this temptation, the devil attempted to "destroy or weaken [Garrettson's] faith."[268] Likewise, Fisk described a "temptation of the devil" in which Satan attempted to interrupt the proclamation of the gospel. Fisk further recorded that "the devil like[d] . . . destroying [the circuit riders'] zeal altogether."[269]

Many times, the temptations of the devil were associated with attacks of doubt.[270] According to the circuit riders, devils supernaturally transmitted influential thoughts into their minds or emotions in order to prompt them to question what they knew about God; this was done with the intent of causing the doubting and rejecting of God and returning the circuit riders to old lifestyle choices. Asbury described these demonic attacks as a form of thought "firebrands," and he was often very much "grieved by some involuntary [implying demonic] thoughts which crowded in upon [him]."[271] Finley exemplified this notion when he declared that the devil injected the temptation of doubt into his mind, causing him to consider that "Christ never died for" him and that he "had better kill [himself] with [his] gun," for the longer he lived, "the

266. Asbury, *Journal of the Rev. Francis Asbury*, 1:75.

267. Bangs and Garrettson, *Life of the Rev. Freeborn Garrettson*, 189.

268. Garrettson, *Experience and Travels*, 17, 30, 86.

269. Holdich, *Life of Wilbur Fisk*, 264, 269.

270. Garrettson, *Experience and Travels*, 24–28.

271. Asbury, *Journal of the Rev. Francis Asbury*, 1:100, 278.

more sin [he would] commit, and, hence, the greater [would] be [his] damnation."[272]

Similar to Finley, Garrettson recounted stories of the devil report-edly afflicting him so that he might reject God, abandon his evangelis-tic labors, and return to his old ways. For instance, the devil tortured Garrettson with a "powerful temptation" resembling "a powerful dart" intended to cause doubt in him. The devil spoke to him with these words: "The God . . . you are attempting to serve, is a hard Master; and I [the dev-il] would have you to desist from your [endeavor]." Garrettson described this experience as very intense and expressed that "carnal people know very little of this kind of [spiritual] exercise but [it] was as perceptible to . . . [him as if he were] conversing with [the devil as] two persons face to face." Later, the devil again injected thoughts of "atheism and deism against [him]" by insisting that Garrettson leave behind those "Meth-odists [who] are a set of enthusiasts," or mentally unstable individuals. In addition, the devil promised Garrettson that he would give him "all these things" and the "splendor [of] the world exhibited to [Garretson's] imagination" with the condition that Garrettson reject the God that he was "attempting to serve, and pray to him no more."[273] Similarly, Horton recalled a time of "temptation . . . [and] impression" from the devil who urged Horton to cease his ministerial work by offering him an "illusion" of "the glories, of the world, with its cities and kingdoms, [which] seemed spread out before [him] in all their beauty."[274]

In the same manner, Travis recalled how the devil afflicted him "by whisper[ing] in [his] ear" thoughts of rejecting God and turning to alcohol, instead, because he would "never get religion" or go to heaven. Travis, however, resisted these spiritual attacks. At another point, Travis recorded that the devil worked "hard to make [him] call in question the goodness and wisdom of a superintending Providence." During this spiritual attack, Travis described "a severe struggle for two or three days," but he emerged victorious and "felt a resignation to the will of [his] heavenly Father, who doeth all things well."[275]

Likewise, Abbott recalled times in which Satan brought to mind the Presbyterian doctrines with which he was raised, assuring him that he

272. Finley, *Autobiography*, 175.

273. Garrettson, *Experience and Travels*, 27, 31–34.

274. Horton, *Narrative of the Early Life*, 22–23.

275. Travis, *Autobiography*, 27, 157.

was destined for hell. At one point, the demonic torture was so severe that Abbott thought the devils had come to take his "soul and body."[276]

At times, the circuit riders described an atmosphere of spiritual battle wherein the attacks of the devil were so strong that they attempted to cause doubts regarding the circuit riders' personally experienced, supernatural conversions. For instance, Cooper declared that "the devil came and powerfully tempted [him] to doubt [his] conversion and regeneration."[277] Likewise, after Dow's conversion experience, his mother argued that he had not been converted and that his "peace [was] a false one." These words alarmed Dow and "the tempter" took advantage of his predicament by causing doubt. Dow admitted that "instead of going to God in prayer" he began to "reason with the tempter." This produced "unbelief" and a "restless mind." As a result, Dow decided "to [run through] the fields and woods, sometimes kneeling and walking"; there he prayed for further confirmation of his conversion, and "[his] Beloved" answered by causing him to experience the "Redeemer's love." To Dow, this served as evidence that he was, indeed, reborn of God.[278]

At times, these demonic thoughts were direct threats to the circuit riders, even prompting them to end their lives. For instance, prior to becoming a circuit rider, Smith was once praying and seeking God for conversion; however, he was in a dispute with his sibling during this time. As a result, "Satan took occasion, from this circumstance to tempt [him] to pray no more" for his conversion or any other thing. The devil persisted in oppressing and torturing Smith for a time, making him feel as if he were "of all beings most miserable" and insisting that it would be "better for [him] to die than to live." Smith explained that this spiritual "temptation was urged with such vehemence, that [he] set about devising a way [in his mind] to get out of the world." He continued to make these diabolic thoughts a reality as, at one point, he said goodbyes to his family and "went to the barn, the place of execution." There he had "hung a rope, suitable for a halter there stood a ladder leaning against a girder of the barn; and all things seemed prepared for the fatal deed." However, before he put the rope around his neck, God spoke to him and the following "thought rushed into mind: 'It is an awful thing to die—you had better pray first.'" This thought from God was so crucial to him that

276. Abbott and Ffirth, *Experience and Gospel Labours*, 10–11.

277. Cooper, *Beams of Light*, 18.

278. Dow, *History of Cosmopolite*, 20.

he abandoned his suicide and repented for his actions. In doing so, the devil retreated, and Smith received conversion, dedicated his life to God, and later became a circuit rider.[279]

Newell recalled that he experienced threatening thoughts that magnified the devil saying: "[Can] the roof prevent our thoughts from rising . . . Can the dim light of that small taper [candle] aid in opposing an evil angel, who, if permitted, could destroy any part of creation as the first-born in Egypt and Judea were destroyed." However, once Newell declared that he was "a child of God—an heir of Heaven," he testified that God, through his grace and power, enabled him to overcome these intense spiritual battles.[280]

In a similar fashion, Horton recalled times when the devil would "tell [him]" lies in order to prevent him from preaching the gospel; the devil declared that "the people would not believe [the gospel message] although it was the truth." The devil would then threaten Horton that, if he continued to preach, "the sin of their unbelief [would] be chargeable to [him]" because he was only "a poor deluded" and "illiterate creature."[281]

The circuit riders also witnessed times when a demonic being directly assaulted them. For instance, Asbury recalled that "sometimes [he was] greatly assaulted by Satan." Even during his many sermons in various circuits, he would, at times, feel that "Satan was close at [his] heels" ready to attack. Indeed, "Satan, that malicious enemy of mankind, [was] frequently striving to break [circuit rider] peace" by his various assaults.[282]

According to the circuit riders, the devil occasionally influenced individuals by stirring up in them thoughts and feelings of intent to physically attack the circuit riders. It appears that individuals who were being used by the devil were unaware that they were being used for this purpose. For instance, Garrettson claimed that during a funeral sermon "the devil sent out a woman with a pistol or two to shoot [him]." Even in the midst of this intense danger of being shot and killed, Garrettson recorded that, after the crowd pulled the woman out, God's power was "sensibly felt among the people," and with tears in their eyes, the people begged Garrettson to "pray for them" and to return and "visit them,

279. Smith and Dailey, *Experience and Ministerial Labors*, 11–21.

280. Newell, *Life and Observations*, 26, 38.

281. Horton, *Narrative of the Early Life*, 24–25, 28–29, 37–38.

282. Asbury, *Journal of the Rev. Francis Asbury*, 1:42, 48, 53.

and not to let the disturbance prevent [him from] coming among them again."[283]

Relating to this matter, Abbott recorded various incidents in which he noticed that, because of his preaching, "the devil was very angry" and, it appears, threw thoughts at people who, in turn, "threatened . . . to tar and feather" Abbott. At another time, Abbott testified that there arose persecution when a Presbyterian professor "became an instrument in the hand of the devil to oppose and lay waste the truth." Apparently, "under the cloak of religion," this professor's demonically-influenced persecution caused "much hurt to the cause of God." Abbott recorded another occasion in which, because of the success in circuits, "the devil got angry, and made one of his servants throw some stones."[284] Cartwright also recorded numerous incidents in which "the devil stirred up opposition" against him and caused him to be "tormented by the devils."[285]

Moreover, the circuit riders believed that the devil, at times, caused "wicked" people to undertake certain actions or commit certain sins so that the circuit riders might be deterred from spreading the gospel. As Asbury stated, "the power of Satan . . . do[es] all he can in stimulating his trusty servants [wicked people] to defend his cause" of disturbing the spreading of the gospel.[286]

When there were no signs of conversions during circuit sermons, the circuit riders perceived this as the result of being in the midst of a demonic "power" or stronghold that ruled that certain area.[287] Finley described a spiritual world in which the territories occupied by demonic "darkness [would] always excite a sturdy conflict [and] resistance to truth and righteousness [of the gospel]."[288] The devil used these unsuccessful meetings as an opportunity to discourage the circuit riders, as well. Asbury described this phenomenon in stating that, at times, "the power of Satan" was so substantial in certain places that it "depress[ed] the life and liberty of the speaker."[289]

283. Garrettson, *Experience and Travels*, 102–4.

284. Abbott and Ffirth, *Experience and Gospel Labours*, 49–50, 71, 197.

285. Cartwright, *Backwoods Preacher*, 97, 184.

286. Asbury, *Journal of the Rev. Francis Asbury*, 1:109.

287. Asbury, *Journal of the Rev. Francis Asbury*, 1:396. See also Paine, *Life and Times*, 2:196.

288. Finley, *Autobiography*, 203.

289. Asbury, *Journal of the Rev. Francis Asbury*, 1:396.

According to the circuit riders, demonic beings were also perceived as one of the main reasons why people persisted in their sins.[290] For instance, Watters presented a spiritual world wherein, before he received his conversion, he "was held in the chains of [his] sins, [and] too often a willing captive of the devil." However, after his conversion, he declared that his liberty was "so sensible" that it changed him "from darkness to light—from death to light—from the Devil and sin to Christ and grace, [and he] felt the importance of [his] Savior."[291] Likewise, Newell prayed to God that he might save people from "the cruelties of sin and Satan and make them happy in their God and King."[292]

Overcoming Spiritual Attacks

As it pertains to overcoming these spiritual attacks, the circuit riders portrayed a lifestyle in which, despite various demonic assaults on their lives and evangelistic labors, they were victorious in these spiritual battles and "came to [their] deliverance" through prayers and the power and presence of God.[293] While through these battles they suffered and were tremendously challenged, ultimately, these challenges contributed to their becoming "better acquainted with Satan's devices . . . [as they grew] in confidence in [their] blessed Savior."[294]

For instance, while the devil made "use of all his cunning and tricks" to damage Asbury's (and, through him, the circuit rider ministry's) work of spreading the gospel, Asbury was generally very successful in battling these demonic forces. Asbury's primary spiritual weapon was prayer; he followed this by "rebuk[ing]" the devil. Asbury testified that God gave him the ability and the "power to resist every temptation of Satan." Hence, Asbury recalled that he had no "injury [because of] . . . the power of God." At other points, Asbury identified himself as a conqueror in spiritual battles whenever he "call[ed] on the name of the Lord." According to

290. Regarding this matter, the apostle Paul wrote to the church in Corinth, describing how the devil keeps people in bondage so that they might not see the salvation of the gospel. In 2 Corinthians 4:4, he stated: "In their case the god of this world has blinded the minds of the unbelievers, to keep them from seeing the light of the gospel of the glory of Christ, who is the image of God."

291. Watters, *Short Account of the Christian Experience*, 3, 16.

292. Newell, *Life and Observations*, 261.

293. Horton, *Narrative of the Early Life*, 29–30.

294. Garrettson, *Experience and Travels*, 55–56.

Asbury, while the demonic beings, with their various attacks, attempted
to prevent him from spreading the gospel, after these spiritual battles,
Asbury would "enjoy a sweet and peaceful nearness to God." Also, because he was spiritually experienced, when Satan attacked, "the Lord gave
[Asbury] power to resist him." Throughout these spiritual battles, Asbury
concluded that "the Spirit of all grace comfort[ed] [his] heart" because
God's "grace [was] sufficient" for him.[295]

M'Kendree believed that "the devil [kept] possession of the people"
until the divine "power [of God was] displayed." He emphasized that the
only way for people to be liberated from the tortures of the devil was for
the supreme power of God to be manifested in them. Hence, according
to M'Kendree, the divine power of God liberated "the sinners" from
the snares of the devil.[296] Like M'Kendree, Garrettson felt himself to be
liberated and protected by God; Garrettson supernaturally overcame
the devil and was "blessed" because the Lord, through him, "greatly
weakened Satan's kingdom."[297] Similarly, through God's power and
presence, Watters was able to overcome demonic attacks; he "rejoiced"
because God "had broken the snare of the Devil."[298]

Not only were circuit riders often victorious in incidents of
personal spiritual warfare, but they also demonstrated that, through their
evangelistic labors, the kingdom of the devil was greatly damaged. As
Cooper testified: "The devil's kingdom suffered great loss; his power was
[badly] shaken. Religion now became the common topic of conversation
through . . . almost every company."[299]

Thus, for the circuit riders, spiritual warfare was considered to be
a lifelong battle that, as Asbury expressed, involved the "need of always
standing [with a spiritual] sword in hand, against [the] adversary the
devil."[300] In short, the circuit riders believed in a world wherein dark powers
attempted to interrupt their personal walk with God (through various
attacks, especially in doubt and unbelief),[301] thwart their expanding work

295. Asbury, *Journal of the Rev. Francis Asbury*, 1:42, 53–55, 75, 90, 134, 157, 223,
278. See also Williams, *Religion and Violence*, 3; Horton, *Narrative of the Early Life*,
22–23.

296. Paine, *Life and Times*, 1:103.

297. Garrettson, *Experience and Travels*, 132.

298. Watters, *Short Account of the Christian Experience*, 92.

299. Cooper, *Beams of Light*, 98.

300. Asbury, *Journal of the Rev. Francis Asbury*, 1:139.

301. Garrettson, *Experience and Travels*, 26–29.

in conversions and revivals,[302] and increase hardship in ministry (even stirring other people to attack the circuit riders physically).[303] Concerning this, Travis concluded that "the devil continues, as of old, 'going about seeking whom he may devour;' and those whom he well knows he cannot devour he is determined to worry, and to render their road to heaven as rough as he possibly can."[304] Regardless, the circuit riders actively worked to combat the devil's schemes through the might of the Holy Spirit.

Concluding Comments

This chapter endeavored to investigate the private supernaturalism of the circuit riders, mainly by focusing on the significance of the supernatural in their conversions, callings, and sanctification. This was followed by an examination of the role of the supernatural in developing and implementing their evangelistic strategies (which were inspired by their personal supernaturalism). Finally, the chapter ended with an analysis of spiritual warfare and its effect on the circuit riders' personal lives and evangelistic labors. In all of these matters, it was demonstrated that the supernatural played a vital part.

Beginning with their convictions and conversions, the circuit riders demonstrated that, although the gospel was presented to them by humans, it was the supernatural phenomena that made it possible for them to be convinced of the existence of God (and the spiritual meaning of the gospel); their spiritual conversions then followed. Indeed, the circuit riders did not receive their conversions through mere rational or philosophical arguments but, rather, through direct intervention of the Spirit of God. This led to the circuit rider belief that, without personally experiencing supernatural phenomena, true spiritual conversion was impossible.

Thus, following their personal spiritual conversions, circuit riders zealously shared the knowledge that everyone needed to privately obtain a spiritual conversion; in this way, like the circuit riders, everyone could

302. Cartwright, *Backwoods Preacher*, 19. See also Cartwright and Hooper, *Fifty Years as a Presiding Elder*, 151.

303. Garrettson, *Experience and Travels*, 103–4. See also Abbott and Ffirth, *Experience and Gospel Labours*, 38.

304. Travis, *Autobiography*, 326.

personally witness a "change in their hearts"[305] that served as evidence that they were "born of God."[306] It did not matter if, prior to their spiritual conversions, individuals were familiar with the concept of Christian conversion, considered themselves religious, or practiced "deism . . . Universalism . . . [or] skepticism,"[307] what mattered for them was that everyone simply experienced conversion, which "enlightened" Christians regarding "divine things."[308] Furthermore, the circuit riders evangelized with the assumption that, because prior to their spiritual conversions they thought that they knew of the experiential or "practical . . . gospel" and were in error, other members of the American public might also be in such a condition.[309] Hence, from these personal spiritual experiences (and inspired by Wesleyan theology), the circuit riders formed the understanding that, after Scripture, spiritual experience was one of the main cornerstones of Christianity and, as a result, needed to be proclaimed.[310]

Not only did "supernatural influence" serve as the primary catalyst in circuit rider conversions, but it was also the catalyst in their ministerial callings.[311] As circuit riders were introduced to experiential Christianity (during their conversions) through various supernatural acts, they were also personally called by God to share this experiential Christianity through preaching. Thus, these acts served as personal "evidence"[312] of their "divine call."[313]

Because circuit riders were divinely called to share the gospel on American soil, it should be noted that, in those days, the vast majority of the public already considered itself to be Christian. In fact, in the mid-eighteenth century, prior to the official circuit rider ministry formation, American church attendance was considered to be around "75 to 80 percent."[314] Consequently, in their calling to evangelize America,

305. Abbott and Ffirth, *Experience and Gospel Labours*, 53.

306. Garrettson, *Experience and Travels*, 243–44.

307. Cartwright, *Backwoods Preacher*, 229.

308. Garrettson, *Letter to the Rev. Lyman Beecher*, 27.

309. Giles, *Pioneer*, 176.

310. See also Boehm, *Reminiscences*, 441; Asbury, *Journal of the Rev. Francis Asbury*, 1:5, 120, 222.

311. Lee, *Memoir*, 295.

312. Finley, *Sketches of Western Methodism*, 407.

313. Bangs and Garrettson, *Life of the Rev. Freeborn Garrettson*, 290.

314. Hutson et al., "Religion in Eighteenth-Century America." See also Hurst, *America on the Cusp of God's Grace*, 23–24.

a dilemma arose in considering what and how to preach because most Americans already identified as Christians (indicating that they had been, to some degree, instructed in Christianity and the theology of conversion by parents, ministers of other denominations, etc.).

An additional aspect of this evangelistic dilemma was that the circuit riders were considered to be "illiterate"[315] with "bad grammar, low idioms, and the euphony of a nasal twang."[316] Because, at that time, Americans were generally used to hearing well-educated sermons, these uneducated and "rant[ing]" circuit riders were unlikely to make converts based on training or rhetoric.[317] However, the circuit riders were determined that their strength would not be in education but, rather, in the supernatural power and presence of God.[318] Thus, through their simple language, circuit riders became intermediaries between God and the public; while they preached, they believed that God's Spirit would be with them in "confirming the word with [supernatural] signs."[319]

The circuit riders also had to bear the added pressure that, unlike ministers of other denominations who had the chance to speak at least once a week to their congregations, when circuit riders shared the gospel, especially in new locations or circuits, they initially had only one opportunity to preach with the "intention"[320] of forming any "new . . . [Methodist] society."[321] Therefore, if people attended their evangelistic meetings, then in order to spark their interest (with the ultimate goal being spiritual conversions), circuit rider sermons needed to be something extraordinary (despite the fact that they were preaching the same gospel message as ministers of other denominations). Based on these disadvantages, the natural chance of the circuit rider ministry finding success in America was slim. However, as indicated, the circuit riders developed an evangelistic strategy that derived from their own personal supernatural experiences or testimonies, which proved to be highly successful.

315. Cartwright, Backwoods Preacher, 287.

316. Goodrich, Recollections of a Lifetime, 311.

317. Burritt, Methodism in Ithaca, 70.

318. Wakeley and Boehm, Patriarch of One Hundred Years, 492; Lee, Memoir, 5; Asbury, Journal of the Rev. Francis Asbury, 1:39.

319. Finley, Autobiography, 120. See also Giles, Pioneer, 170.

320. Asbury, Journal of the Rev. Francis Asbury, 1:53.

321. Giles, Pioneer, 140.

Compared to ministers of other denominations, circuit riders were considered to be performing extraordinary evangelism because they "were favored with the most powerful display of the divine power that had" ever been known to the Early Republic.[322] Using the concepts of God's love and forgiveness as examples in their sermons, not only did circuit riders share theological knowledge concerning God's love and forgiveness toward people, but, more importantly, they included opportunities within their messages for audience members to experience God's love and forgiveness for them through his power and presence. In other words, after the Methodist preacher shared his "preliminary exercises," he gave a direct "opportunity . . . [for his audience to witness a] relation of Christian experience." In this way, people in these meetings had the chance to theoretically know about God's love and forgiveness and then supernaturally experience these things as their "direct evidence." Indeed, as further presented in upcoming chapters, whatever circuit riders preached, they endeavored to demonstrate through the power of God. For example, if a person was reported to be tormented by demons or hunted by various "demon shapes," circuit riders would pray in anticipation of an immediate deliverance, which was usually followed by that individual "experienc[ing] religion . . . [and the circuit riders] receiving them into the Church."[323] Thus, as demonstrated, circuit rider ministerial strategies resembled more the Apostolic Age (especially as seen in the book of Acts) and the early Christian church and less the ministries of other mainline denominations in their time.[324]

Moreover, as the circuit riders progressed with their evangelistic strategies, they "challenge[d]"[325] both the established American religious system and social order of those days. Often leaders of "other denominations . . . [such as the] Presbyterians and Congregationalist[s]," who were expected to rely on their "educated ministry and theological training," considered circuit rider evangelism to be both unscriptural and ignorant; at times, circuit riders were referred to as "the

322. Cooper, *Beams of Light*, 149.

323. Finley, *Autobiography*, 197, 391. See also Asbury, *Journal of the Rev. Francis Asbury*, 1:258; Cartwright, *Backwoods Preacher*, 17; Garrettson, *Experience and Travels*, 139–40.

324. Giles, *Pioneer*, 237; Richards, "Review," 552; Asbury, *Journal of the Rev. Francis Asbury*, 2:59.

325. Young, *Autobiography of a Pioneer*, 42, 232.

monkey-catchers," implying that their ministry attracted the uneducated (i.e., the "monkeys").[326]

Furthermore, because of their emphasis on the experiential gospel (coupled with their stark break from the traditions of other denominations), circuit riders were occasionally perceived, as modern scholar Noll stated, to be "ecclesiastical upstarts [and] destroyers of families." Because the circuit riders challenged the established social rules of the day, especially in regard to the issue of slavery, they were also seen by some as "agents of social upheaval and worse."[327] Indeed, Asbury, Coke, and other circuit riders believed and promoted the belief "that slavery is contrary to the laws of God, man, and nature, and hurtful to society, contrary to the dictates of conscience and pure religion." The circuit riders pledged that they would "not cease to seek its destruction by all wise and prudent means."[328] Modern scholar Murray explains that, according to the circuit riders, people kept slaves because they "did not experience sufficient [spiritual or] religious enthusiasm to free their slaves."[329]

Ultimately, the circuit riders proved that they were not greatly bothered by these negative opinions surrounding their countercultural messages since they continued preaching about a spiritually-experienced gospel. Regardless of ministerial conflicts, various hardships, or spiritual warfare, the circuit riders strove to constantly support themselves in God, especially through the process of sanctification.[330] Their pursuit of holiness served as a source of divine empowerment, strengthening them in their ministerial labors.[331] Hence, when facing ministerial challenges, in combination with the strength drawn from their human contributions of personal commitment and discipline, God's supernatural fillings and

---

326. Cartwright, *Backwoods Preacher*, 39, 72.

327. Noll, *Rise of Evangelicalism*, 216.

328. MEC, *Minutes of the Methodist Conferences*, 25–26, 55. See also Douglass, *Anti-Slavery Movement*, 12; Russell, *American Methodism*, 21–22; Essah, *House Divided*, 57.

329. Murray, *Methodists and the Crucible of Race*, 13. See also Goodrich, *Recollections of a Lifetime*, 311; Southwell, *Apology for Atheism*, 9. In 1844, the MEC decided to split due to disagreements concerning the issue of slavery. For more information, see Farish, *Circuit Rider Dismounts*.

330. This practice is biblical. In Ephesians 3:16, the apostle Paul prayed for the church in Ephesus: "According to the riches of his glory [God] may grant you to be strengthened with power through his Spirit in your inner being."

331. Asbury, *Journal of the Rev. Francis Asbury*, 1:31, 90, 107, 274.

empowerments were proven to be instrumental in maintaining their ministerial strength.[332]

The circuit riders also testified that in order to maintain a biblical lifestyle and see progress in the spreading of the gospel, it was imperative for them to spiritually discern or recognize the attacks of the enemy and defeat them by engaging in spiritual warfare (dispelling demonic activity through the power of God).[333] Even in this, the circuit riders painted a picture wherein God was, in all things, superior;[334] hence, through God's Spirit, the circuit riders foiled the devil's plans.[335]

To conclude, throughout their ministry, circuit riders depended on the supernatural because they knew that if their ministry was going to be "successful,"[336] it would have to be solely due to the outpouring of the power of God.[337] In utilizing this evangelistic tool (i.e., the power of God), the circuit riders, despite their religious and social critics, would be remembered by many as "preachers [who] would have the most telling impact."[338]

332. See also Wigger, *American Saint*, 189.

333. Garrettson, *Experience and Travels*, 16–18. This concept of the devil and his demonic hosts being the main enemy of mankind is also present in the biblical text. For instance, 1 Peter 5:8 states: "Be alert and of sober mind. Your enemy the devil prowls around like a roaring lion looking for someone to devour."

334. The biblical text expresses this concept. For example, Romans 8:37 states that, through God, Christians "in all these things . . . are more than conquerors through him who loved us."

335. Asbury, *Journal of the Rev. Francis Asbury*, 1:55, 278; Watters, *Short Account of the Christian Experience*, 92; Finley, *Autobiography*, 270.

336. MEC, *Minutes of the Forty-Third Session*, 45.

337. Asbury, *Journal of the Rev. Francis Asbury*, 1:55; Phoebus, *Memoirs*, 17; Paine, *Life and Times*, 1:103; Finley, *Autobiography*, 197; Giles, *Pioneer*, 62; Newell, *Life and Observations*, 273.

338. Wigger, *American Saint*, 9.

Chapter 5

Public Supernaturalism

JUST AS THE CIRCUIT riders relied on the supernatural in their personal lives (the category of private supernaturalism discussed in the previous chapter), they also relied on the supernatural throughout their evangelistic meetings and believed that the supernatural, derived from the "power and presence"[1] of the Holy Spirit, impacted and advanced their ministerial works (the category of public supernaturalism).[2] As such, this investigation features a section on various visible appearances of the power and presence of God followed by a detailed examination of the circuit riders' understanding and significance of other common supernatural phenomena that originated from the outpourings of God, such as: being slain in the Spirit, enthusiastic emotional expressions, dreams, visions, trances, exorcisms, healings, the raising of the dead, and divine weather shifts.

Appearances of the Power and Presence of God

As discussed in chapter 1, *the power and presence* served as the physical evidence of God's active supernatural involvement in the circuit rider ministry; thus, the circuit riders witnessed various visible demonstrations of the power and presence in their meetings.[3] For them, these incidents

1. Finley, *Sketches of Western Methodism*, 75.

2. Asbury, *Journal of the Rev. Francis Asbury*, 2:58–59; Giles, *Pioneer*, 237; Richey et al., *American Methodism*, 12.

3. Atkinson, *Centennial History of American Methodism*, 225.

were generally "a mysterious [divine] presence [or appearance]."[4] Asbury concluded that the "instantaneous manifest[ions]" of the power and presence of God were, to him, a mystery as he could not fully comprehend "these things [of the Spirit]," but since he witnessed them so many times (in his life, through his audiences, and with various circuit riders), he knew "that [these phenomena] do exist,"[5] and he "was pleased"[6] when they appeared.

The main reason why the appearances of the Spirit were mysterious to the circuit riders was because they could not predict the outpourings. While, at times, they could see them with their physical eyes, at other times, they could not; however, they could "sense"[7] them spiritually in their lives and meetings.[8] Although the appearances of the Spirit were a mystery to the circuit riders, they often attempted to better understand and explain these appearances by likening them to natural or physical phenomena, such as: fire, wind, cloud, energy/force, electric shock, radiant light, and rain. Hence, to better understand the supernatural in the circuit rider ministry, the following sections are dedicated to the investigation of the nature and role of these visible appearances of the Spirit of God.

The Spirit's Appearance as Fire

Circuit riders witnessed the appearance of the power and presence of the Spirit as fire.[9] This image of the Spirit appearing as fire is also found in Acts 2:3, in which the first apostles described the appearance of the Spirit being poured out on the Day of Pentecost: "Fire appeared to them and rested on each one of them." The circuit riders, at times, witnessed similar appearances of the Spirit. For instance, once when Asbury was preaching a sermon, suddenly, "the sacred fire was felt." For Asbury and the circuit riders, when the term *fire* was used, it was occasionally in reference to a natural burning fire;[10] however, they also used this term, as in the book

---

4. Bergland, *Journeys of Robert Williams*, 67.

5. Asbury, *Journal of the Rev. Francis Asbury*, 3:114.

6. Asbury, *Journal of the Rev. Francis Asbury*, 2:244.

7. Abbott and Ffirth, *Experience and Gospel Labours*, 212.

8. See also Cartwright, *Backwoods Preacher*, 13.

9. Hebrews 12:29 states: "For our God is a consuming fire."

10. For instance, see Asbury, *Journal of the Rev. Francis Asbury*, 1:54, 70; Finley,

of Acts, in reference to a spiritual fire.[11] Thus, when the circuit riders referenced a "sacred fire," they were referring to the Spirit and the "word of the Lord as a [tangible spiritual] fire."[12]

Often, when the Spirit appeared as a divine fire, it caused in people a spiritual sensation of burning fire.[13] As Lee expressed, "the power of the Lord came down on the assembly, and it seemed as if the whole house was filled with the presence of God. A [spiritual] flame kindled and ran from heart to heart."[14] Cooper declared that the preaching circuits were spiritually "flaming: the Preachers [were] much alive: the [spiritual] fire [ran] as in stubble."[15] The role of this appearance was that it caused people to be "deeply convicted of sin; many mourners were filled with consolation, and many believers were so overwhelmed with love, that they could not doubt but God had enabled them to love him with all their heart."[16]

At one point, while Dow was preaching, people "observed that they saw something fall from the sky like a [spiritual] ball of fire . . . [that was] the bigness of a man's hat-crown." The moment that this ball of fire reached the crowd, many "fell like men shot in the field of action . . . [and some] cried for mercy."[17] Similarly, M'Kendree testified how, in another instance, "the power of the Lord came down—the word was like fire among the people: some that never heard a Methodist before . . . sunk to the floor and cried for mercy [because of this spiritual fire] . . . [as] yielding sinners."[18] Burke recalled times when "the heavenly flame spread . . . [and the place was] caught [by] the holy fire [similar to the book of Acts], and in a short time hundreds attended [circuit rider] night meetings . . . the mourners were down in the house and all over the yard,

---

Autobiography, 23, 38; Cartwright, *Backwoods Preacher*, 3.

11. For instance, see Gatch, *Sketch of Rev. Philip Gatch*, 87; Abbott and Ffirth, *Experience and Gospel Labours*, 135, 201; Garrettson, *Experience and Travels*, 223; Asbury, *Journal of the Rev. Francis Asbury*, 1:124; Finley, *Autobiography*, 239; *Sketches of Western Methodism*, 26; Boehm, *Reminiscences*, 12, 44; Giles, *Pioneer*, 302; Cartwright, *Backwoods Preacher*, 118; Travis, *Autobiography*, 111; Scudder and Cummings, *American Methodism*, 242; Smith and Dailey, *Experience and Ministerial Labors*, 53.

12. Asbury, *Journal of the Rev. Francis Asbury*, 2:31, 241, 355.

13. Smith, *Recollections and Reflections*, 233–43.

14. Lee, *Short History of the Methodists*, 55.

15. Cooper, "Account of the Work of God," 409.

16. Lee, *Short History of the Methodists*, 55.

17. Dow, *History of Cosmopolite*, 135.

18. Paine, *Life and Times*, 1:92.

crying mightily to God for mercy."[19] Boehm also witnessed a time when "a wall of [spiritual] fire" was around their meetings.[20] Shadford recounted that when he would "speak for [God], [God's] word was like the flaming sword, which turned every way, to every heart; for sinners trembled and fell before it, and were both convinced and converted to God."[21]

The Spirit's Appearance as Wind

The power and presence of the Lord occasionally manifested as a strong or "mighty wind."[22] This adopted form is also evident in the Bible, especially on the Day of Pentecost.[23] As found in Acts 2:2: "And suddenly there came from heaven a sound like a mighty rushing wind, and it filled the entire house where they were sitting." The circuit riders described many similar appearances of the Spirit materializing as a mighty rushing wind. For instance, Rankin witnessed that, due to the Spirit's outpouring in a meeting, many audience members were so stunned that they were "ready to faint and die under His Almighty hand." For approximately "three hours the gale of the Spirit" proceeded to spiritually "breathe" upon the public's "dry bones." As for himself, Rankin "scarcely knew" whether he was in his "body or not," and they did not know how or when to conclude the meeting as the environment's spiritual intensity continued.[24] Smith recalled a time when the Spirit of the Lord was poured out like "a rushing, mighty wind"; encountering this visible appearance, the public "fell before it, and lay in heaps all over the floor." As a result of this outpouring, members of the public continued flowing in, and the gospel labor persisted for "thirteen days and nights without interruption."[25] Cartwright also recorded an event when the power and presence of God descended as "the sound of a mighty rushing wind." Consequently, masses of "mourners" gathered and kneeled for repentance while the effects of the occasion continued

19. Finley, *Sketches of Western Methodism*, 75.

20. Wakeley and Boehm, *Patriarch of One Hundred Years*, 70.

21. Shadford, "Short Account of Mr. George Shadford," 184.

22. Smith and Dailey, *Experience and Ministerial Labors*, 77.

23. Strong similarities are also found in the story of Elijah and God (1 Kgs 19:11–13).

24. Jackson, *Lives of Early Methodist Preachers*, 5:203.

25. Smith and Dailey, *Experience and Ministerial Labors*, 77.

to "spread all over." Moreover, as a result of this spiritual wind, around 250 "professed religion," and around 210 joined the Methodist societies.[26]

The Spirit's Appearance as a Cloud

At times, the mysterious power and presence of God was present in the form of a visible cloud or mist; as seen above, similar manifestations occurred in the biblical text, most notably in the book of Exodus.[27] For instance, in a meeting with Asbury, Rankin recorded that "in a moment the cloud [of God] broke, and the power of God rested" on their meeting.[28] The circuit riders further described incidents in which "the cloudy" Spirit erupted and the actual "heavens appeared to open with blessings," causing God's nearness to be "felt by many present."[29]

The Spirit's Appearance as a Divine Energy/Force

At other times, the power and presence of God appeared as a divine spiritual "energy" or force.[30] For instance, once while Asbury preached on Romans 2:8–10, he recognized that "much of the power of God [that had descended] was felt; a [tangible] divine energy went forth amongst the people that night in town."[31] During another meeting, Abbott testified that the Spirit was manifested as a "divine energy" that caused "the devil [to flee] . . . and the people fell down before the Lord, as men slain, in the battle . . . [emitting] cries and screeches . . . clapping their hands, [and] shouting praises to God, and the Lamb, for the manifestation of his love."[32]

26. Cartwright, *Backwoods Preacher*, 104.

27. For more information, see Exodus 13:21–22; 14:19–20; 40:34–38.

28. Jackson, *Lives of Early Methodist Preachers*, 5:191.

29. Watters, *Short Account of the Christian Experience*, 125.

30. Dow, *History of Cosmopolite*, 355.

31. Asbury, *Journal of the Rev. Francis Asbury*, 1:109.

32. Abbott and Ffirth, *Experience and Gospel Labours*, 209, 227.

The Spirit's Appearance as an Electric Shock

At times, when the power and presence of God was poured out intensely, it manifested as an electric shock that went forth into the audience. Burke observed this phenomenon, stating that the Spirit of God "appeared like an electric shock" in an assembly. From this outpouring, people fell to the ground "like men slain in the field of battle." The meeting proceeded until late and further developed with "astonishing power [and] hundreds were converted to God."[33]

The Spirit's Appearance as a Radiant Light

The power and presence of the Lord appeared, at times, as a radiant light; this was sometimes identified as "the light of God's countenance."[34] For instance, during a circuit rider meeting, Cartwright pointed out that the Spirit descended on their assembly resulting "in the whole encampment [becoming] lighted with the glory of God." The people who were gathered were "greatly blessed," and many "hardened sinners were brought to bow before the Lord, and some of them were soundly converted."[35] Boehm also witnessed occasions when the Spirit was poured out as he witnessed the meeting room being "filled with [radiant] glory."[36] At the same time, like Moses after his meetings with God in which his face shone by reflecting the light of God, the circuit riders also witnessed this phenomenon;[37] there were cases when the radiant light was reflected on certain individuals, and their faces, such as the face of M'Kendree, "beamed with [radiant] glory."[38]

The Spirit's Appearance as Rain

At other times, circuit riders witnessed the power and presence of God appear as rain. The description of God as water or living water is found

---

33. Finley, *Sketches of Western Methodism*, 84.

34. Dow, *History of Cosmopolite*, 21, 252.

35. Cartwright, *Backwoods Preacher*, 223.

36. Wakeley and Boehm, *Patriarch of One Hundred Years*, 33.

37. For more information regarding the story of Moses and his shining face, see Exodus 34:29–35.

38. Finley, *Sketches of Western Methodism*, 83–84.

within the biblical text, as well.[39] For instance, circuit rider Bascom recorded an event wherein the Spirit "seemed to fall like rain on the assembly, and the outbursts of deep feeling could no longer be held in restraint."[40] There were also recordings, by the circuit riders, in which this form of the Spirit's appearance was "poured down for more than forty days."[41]

The Significance of the Visible Manifestations of the Power and Presence of God

Many of the Spirit's appearances within the circuit rider ministry were not seen with physical eyes, but they were felt through their spiritual senses, and they were apparent in circuit rider lives and meetings.[42] However, from this analysis, it can be concluded that there were also numerous times in which, within the circuit rider ministry, the power and presence of God appeared in visible and tangible supernatural forms. Generally, the circuit riders associated these supernatural appearances with natural phenomena, such as: fire, wind, cloud, energy/force, electric shock, radiant light, and rain.

Moreover, it seems that on the occasions when the Spirit resembled a natural phenomenon, the effects of that particular natural phenomenon were produced. For instance, when the Spirit appeared as fire, certain effects were produced that were related to natural fire; hence, the appearance of spiritual fire led to a form of burning sensation in people.[43] Likewise, when the Spirit appeared as an electric shock, it caused individuals to experience effects of a physical electric shock; it could even knock people out instantly, similar to the way people would respond upon encountering

39. For more information regarding God being identified as living water, see John 4:14; 7:37–39. Also, 1 Corinthians 12:13 states: "For in one Spirit we were all baptized into one body—Jews or Greeks, slaves or free—and all were made to drink of one Spirit."

40. Henkle, *Life of Henry Bidleman Bascom*, 148.

41. Asbury, *Journal of the Rev. Francis Asbury*, 1:161.

42. Asbury, *Journal of the Rev. Francis Asbury*, 3:114; Sprague, *Annals of the American Pulpit*, 7:383; Marsden, "Of the Methodist Doctrines," 211.

43. Garrettson, *Experience and Travels*, 223; Asbury, *Journal of the Rev. Francis Asbury*, 1:124; Finley, *Autobiography*, 239; Abbott and Ffirth, *Experience and Gospel Labours*, 135, 201; Finley, *Sketches of Western Methodism*, 26; Gatch, *Sketch of Rev. Philip Gatch*, 87.

a physical electric shock.[44] At other times, the Spirit appeared as a cloud or as a radiant light in order for people to witness God's existence and also in order to alert the circuit riders and their audiences to the fact that God was ready to go into action, to approve their evangelistic labors and perform supernatural acts.[45]

As noted, these various supernatural appearances of God's Spirit were common within the biblical text, especially in the book of Acts (and, particularly, on the Day of Pentecost). Therefore, it can be concluded that the visible appearances of the power and presence of God manifested in the Apostolic Age were also similarly operative in the lives and ministries of the circuit riders.[46]

Introduction to the Common Encounters Found in Public Supernaturalism

The outpouring of the power and presence of God in the circuit rider ministry (whether appearing as fire, wind, rain, electric shock, or bearing no connection to any natural phenomena) gave birth to other forms of supernatural phenomena, such as: being slain in the Spirit, enthusiastic emotional expressions, dreams, visions, trances, exorcisms, healings, the raising of the dead, and divine weather shifts. It should be noted that, within circuit rider writings, there are so many instances of these manifestations that one can write volumes on the subject; however, while this book presents some instances of these phenomena below, it does so in order to demonstrate the theology and, ultimately, the significance of these supernatural events within the circuit rider ministry.

The Phenomena of Being Slain in the Spirit

While O'Byrne argued that "divine communications [including dreams]" were the "most . . . [common] supernatural elements" in early Methodism, this book's research suggests that the experience of "falling down" or

---

44. Finley, *Sketches of Western Methodism*, 76, 84.

45. Cartwright, *Backwoods Preacher*, 223; Watters, *Short Account of the Christian Experience*, 125.

46. See also Gatch, *Sketch of Rev. Philip Gatch*, 17.

being "slain in the Spirit" along with religious enthusiastic expressions became the most common supernatural occurrences in Methodism.[47]

During the time of the circuit rider ministry, the effect of being slain in the Spirit was also known as the "Knock-'Em-Down."[48] Presbyterian minister Stone,[49] who Cartwright described as having ministered with Methodist circuit riders (such as Page and Burke) in the famous multi-denominational camp meeting of Cane Ridge, Kentucky (1801),[50] thoroughly described this manifestation (along with a few others) and documented its occurrences during the meeting.[51] In short, however, Stone described the supernatural event of being slain in the Spirit as follows: "With a piercing scream, [they fell] like a log on the floor or earth, and appear[ed] as dead."[52]

Moreover, circuit riders recorded that when individuals were slain in the Spirit by "an overwhelming power of the Divine Being,"[53] they later emphasized that they could not help but act the way that they did; indeed, they were admittedly "slain to the floor"[54] with a force and frenzy that rendered them "unable to stand."[55] To be more specific, when people were slain in the Spirit, their bodies encountered a direct "loss . . . [of] the power of voluntary motion, which was common among the Methodists of those days."[56] Finley examined a case of an individual who was slain in the Spirit, stating: "He exhibited no signs whatever of life; his

47. O'Byrne, "How Methodists Were Made," 76–90.

48. Wigger, "Holy, 'Knock-'Em-Down' Preachers," para. 1.

49. Because of his in-depth accounts, it was common for Methodist historians (especially during the nineteenth century) to use his testimonies in their works; thus, this study does the same. For instance, see McTyeire, *History of Methodism*, 492–93; Price, *Holston Methodism*, 1:379–82; M'Ferrin, *History of Methodism in Tennessee*, 1:347–52; Arminius, "Introductory Remarks," 223.

50. Due to the importance of Methodist camp meetings, they are also discussed at length in chapter 7.

51. Cartwright, *Backwoods Preacher*, 9–13, 124; Finley, *Autobiography*, 165. Cartwright also accused Stone of spreading heresy regarding the divine nature of Jesus Christ. For more information, see Cartwright, *Backwoods Preacher*, 10, 124.

52. Stone, *Biography*, 39.

53. Paine, *Life and Times*, 1:51.

54. Crowell, *Journal of Seth Crowell*, 79.

55. Paine, *Life and Times*, 1:51. See also Abbott and Ffirth, *Experience and Gospel Labours*, 55.

56. Sprague, *Annals of the American Pulpit*, 7:372.

limbs were rigid, his wrists pulseless, and his breath gone."[57] Hence, it seems that when people were slain in the Spirit, they were involuntarily "speechless,"[58] and then they "fainted" in the presence of the Lord.[59] Pilmore described that "people were so affected that they fainted away and all were as solemn as death . . . [because] the Spirit of the Lord was poured out from high."[60]

To an outside observer, when individuals were slain in the Spirit, they typically appeared to be dead. Lee noted that, at times, they would be "lying and struggling as if they were in the agonies of death."[61] Other times, as Smith explained, they were seemingly "shot down in battle"[62] or, as Cartwright described, "as men slain in battle"[63] or, according to Abbott's observation, "like dead men."[64] Circuit rider Granade described the manifestation in greater detail, recalling that "the people fell as if they had been slain by a mighty weapon, and lay in such piles and heaps . . . that it was feared they would suffocate."[65]

Audience size appears to have been irrelevant in regard to being slain in the Spirit as when people were exposed to this spiritual phenomenon, they "instantly . . . fell right and left, and cried aloud for mercy."[66] In fact, the average number of people slain in the Spirit fluctuated; sometimes there was only one person,[67] at times a dozen,[68] at times "twenty and thirty,"[69] at times "three hundred,"[70] and at other times "hundreds [fell] prostrate under the mighty power of God."[71] For instance, Burke

57. Finley, *Autobiography*, 364.

58. Wakeley and Boehm, *Patriarch of One Hundred Years*, 104.

59. Lee, *Memoir*, 277; Abbott and Ffirth, *Experience and Gospel Labours*, 190.

60. Pilmore, *Journal of Joseph Pilmore*, 169.

61. Lee, *Short History of the Methodists*, 131.

62. Hibbard, *Memoirs*, 147.

63. Cartwright, *Backwoods Preacher*, 9.

64. Abbott and Ffirth, *Experience and Gospel Labours*, 67.

65. M'Ferrin, *History of Methodism in Tennessee*, 1:405. See also Dow, *History of Cosmopolite*, 153.

66. Cartwright, *Backwoods Preacher*, 42.

67. Cartwright, *Backwoods Preacher*, 30, 98, 223. See also Asbury, *Journal of the Rev. Francis Asbury*, 1:144.

68. Abbott and Ffirth, *Experience and Gospel Labours*, 87.

69. Asbury, *Journal of the Rev. Francis Asbury*, 1:165.

70. Hyde, *Story of Methodism*, 160.

71. Cartwright, *Backwoods Preacher*, 9. See also Asbury, *Journal of the Rev. Francis Asbury*, 1:173.

recorded an incident when "not less than five hundred were at one time lying on the ground."[72] Indeed, there were times in which the preacher was surrounded by an unconscious audience; he would be left upon the stage, waiting to resume the message until his audience members returned to their senses. Moreover, as it pertains to area, sometimes God's presence was manifested and caused people to be slain in the Spirit only within the confines of a certain meeting place;[73] however, sometimes individuals "more than a quarter of a mile off"[74] from the main meeting place were affected by the manifestation.[75]

It appears that from the time that the Spirit touched people to the time that it took them to fall down was mere seconds or the blink of an eye.[76] Also, the length of time in which individuals remained in this state varied; however, the typical length in which people "lay helpless"[77] or remained motionless and "without strength [was] from half an hour, to two hours"[78] or "all the time of the sermon"[79] or "for hours."[80] Occasionally, especially when God's outpouring "continued . . . [for] days and nights,"[81] reports indicated that people laid "powerless and motionless for days, sometimes for a week at a time, without food or drink."[82]

Most often, it appears that when people were exposed to or touched by the "visible"[83] power and presence of God, they were filled with the Spirit, which brought about a form of spiritual "ecstasy,"[84] causing people to be instantly slain in the Spirit. When people experienced this spiritual ecstasy, apparently, "they would arise happy in God."[85] In other words, though people fell, they encountered tremendous joy and happiness,

---

72. Finley, *Sketches of Western Methodism*, 78.

73. Abbott and Ffirth, *Experience and Gospel Labours*, 97.

74. Garrettson, *Experience and Travels*, 95.

75. Young, *Autobiography of a Pioneer*, 41.

76. Cartwright, *Backwoods Preacher*, 42.

77. Lee, *Memoir*, 314.

78. Hibbard, *Memoirs*, 147.

79. Asbury, *Journal of the Rev. Francis Asbury*, 1:59.

80. Bangs and Garrettson, *Life of the Rev. Freeborn Garrettson*, 224.

81. Smith and Dailey, *Experience and Ministerial Labors*, 77.

82. Cartwright, *Backwoods Preacher*, 21.

83. Asbury, *Journal of the Rev. Francis Asbury*, 1:163.

84. Finley, *Sketches of Western Methodism*, 25.

85. Hibbard, *Memoirs*, 147.

especially those who experienced conversions.[86] For example, Abbott recalled a story in which the Spirit descended and stirred a nonbeliever who "soon fell on the floor, as one dead . . . [and] his blood appeared stagnated." The man remained in this state for some time, and when he returned to his senses, he happily "praised God" and was converted.[87] Similarly, Asbury recorded the story of a woman who was known to be "a mocker." However, God loved her, and on that day, he poured out his presence on her, causing her to fall "down" by the Spirit. After this occurrence, she was convicted of her sin and cried out "for mercy." She confessed "her sins before all the people" and happily found faith in Christ.[88]

The act of being slain in the Spirit transcended genders and socioeconomic classes as well as Christians and non-Christians;[89] in other words, the experience "was very common among all classes, the saints and sinners of every age and grade."[90] As such, the circuit riders recorded a ministry in which even "some of the wicked and the wise fell to the floor."[91] Finley captured this matter in recording the story of a reportedly "wicked" man (the leader of a large "wicked" company) who deliberately interrupted a circuit rider meeting. Immediately, he was slain in the Spirit, and "as if smitten by lightning, he fell from his horse." Witnessing this, Finley feared that God, in his judgment, had "killed [this] bold and daring blasphemer." Also fearing his death, the man's company rushed to his side, and as they approached him, "the power of God came upon them, and they [also] fell like men slain in battle." Their leader remained in this condition "for thirty hours" and, to all who were gathered there, he appeared to be "dead." Suddenly, the leader returned to his senses, praising God. Finley exclaimed that, because of God's love, even the most wicked were converted. Hence, the instant that supernatural powers descended, even "sinners fell as men slain in mighty battle."[92]

Travis recorded that often "profane sinners, downright skeptics, and God-defying wretches" approached their meetings and, by the power of the Spirit, in less than "ten minutes the very vilest of all such

---

86. See also Garrettson, *Experience and Travels*, 36–37; Lee, *Short History of the Methodists*, 131.

87. Abbott and Ffirth, *Experience and Gospel Labours*, 172.

88. Asbury, *Journal of the Rev. Francis Asbury*, 3:113.

89. Finley, *Autobiography*, 240.

90. Stone, *Biography*, 39.

91. Lee, *Short History of the Methodists*, 275.

92. Finley, *Autobiography*, 364–65, 367.

would be stricken to the floor." They remained "speechless, breathless, and pulseless," appearing to those around them as "perfectly dead," as if directly hit "by a deadly arrow." Travis reported that, during his ministry, people who were slain in the Spirit generally remained in this state for an hour; upon recovering, their faces reflected a "heavenly smile" followed by shouts of "Glory, glory to God!"; ultimately, their spiritual conversions ensued. Hence, according to Travis, becoming slain in the Spirit was a very effective means of conversion.[93]

Cartwright also described this manifestation when the "tremendous" power of the Spirit descended on an assembly and touched a "gang of rowdies" who were immediately slain in the Spirit and "fell by dozens on the right and left." In this meeting, there was also a man who strongly opposed the circuit rider ministry; Cartwright identified him as his "special persecutor." This persecutor was suddenly slain in the Spirit, as well, and he "fell suddenly, as if a rifle-ball had been shot through his heart." The persecutor remained in this immobilized state until the following morning when he awoke and experienced his spiritual conversion with "shouts of glory and victory."[94]

At another time, Cartwright observed that when the power and presence of God descended on his audience, numerous people who were gathered inside a building were slain in the Spirit. The intensity of the outpouring was reported to be so great that even those outside of the building began to be slain and fall "like men shot in battle." Many cried out for mercy from God, including "five bullies."[95] Hence, Cartwright also witnessed that even the reportedly wicked were spiritually converted when they were touched by the outpouring of the Spirit.[96]

At other times, those who mocked Methodist spiritual experiences were touched by God's Spirit and instantly fell down.[97] For example, Asbury recorded an account of a circuit rider who shared a story of a young woman who was scorning the ministry's actions of "falling down" on the ground or being "slain" by God's touch. On one occasion, she insisted, out of judgement and malintent, on helping those who were falling down. However, during that meeting, "the power of God soon seized her,"

93. Travis, *Autobiography*, 24.

94. Cartwright, *Backwoods Preacher*, 79.

95. Cartwright and Hooper, *Fifty Years as a Presiding Elder*, 85.

96. Cartwright, *Backwoods Preacher*, 78–79.

97. For more information on the spiritual experiences of Methodist critics, see chapter 6.

causing her to fall down on the ground. In an act of irony, the woman "wanted help [for] herself" in getting up. In return, it was "the Spirit of grace [who] helped her, by giving her faith in Christ [or conversion]."[98]

At other times, when the power of God was present, some people became frightened and ran away from the circuit rider meetings; however, while they ran away, the Spirit occasionally caught them like fish in a net.[99] For instance, Abbott described an event in which "a number fell to the floor." One gentleman tried to "run off"; however, he was slain in the Spirit as "God laid him down at the door" of their meeting-house. A woman also attempted to run from the meeting, but as she did, God "arrested her," and slain in the Spirit like the gentleman, she "fell back into the house just as she was going out of the door." At another time, there was one "very wicked woman" who was affected by the power and presence of God; however, sensing that she would be slain in the Spirit and fall, the woman resisted God's touch and grabbed a cheese press to steady herself. She then began to run from the meeting but did not go far as, upon "passing through a skirt of wood," God grasped her and "convinced her of [his] omnipotent power; and trembling, she went home and threw herself on the bed" and later experienced conversion.[100]

Further regarding those who ran away from acute spiritual environments and occurrences of the Knock-'Em-Down, Smith recorded an interesting event in which the Spirit's power descended upon a meeting, causing many to cry out to God. Some, however, ran away from this meeting. One of the participants, overwhelmed by the intensity of the supernatural occurrences, began to run, exhibiting shocking emotions and continuously exclaiming, "God will sink the place."[101]

Despite the fact that, at times, the public reacted negatively to audience members being slain in the Spirit, the circuit riders learned how to deal with these negative reactions while still continuing with their evangelistic goals. For instance, during one of Garretson's meetings, the husband of a wife who was slain in the Spirit "was much offended, [and] threatened [Garrettson], as he said, for killing his wife." However, it seems that this manifestation and threat was rather common for Garrettson

98. Asbury, *Journal of the Rev. Francis Asbury*, 1:166–67.

99. Smith and Dailey, *Experience and Ministerial Labors*, 53.

100. Abbott and Ffirth, *Experience and Gospel Labours*, 73–74. This woman's story was unusual because she later rejected her faith. For more information, see Abbott and Ffirth, *Experience and Gospel Labours*, 75–77.

101. Smith and Dailey, *Experience and Ministerial Labors*, 53.

because he calmly continued to "spen[d] some time in praying" and carried on with the meeting.[102]

Thus, it can be concluded that it was "common . . . [in Methodist meetings] for men and women to fall down as dead."[103] During the circuit rider meetings, people experienced God's outpouring via the involuntary effect of being slain in the Spirit or falling down on the ground.[104] These experiences were unpredictable, yet they were anticipated and prayerfully requested by the circuit riders.[105] When they occurred, people fainted (from one individual to hundreds of them at a time) under "the presence and power of God";[106] according to the observations of outsiders, they appeared to be without living consciousness, resembling dead bodies.[107] The event of being slain in the Spirit lasted for minutes or for hours or, at times, for a week.[108] It can be argued that the spiritual goal of individuals falling down (believers and nonbelievers alike) was that, at the time they returned to their senses, they typically were spiritually refreshed and exhibited joy in the Lord (because they met God in this extraordinary fashion);[109] moreover, nonbelievers were often converted.[110]

The Phenomena of Emotional Enthusiastic Expressions

In the circuit rider ministry, in addition to being slain in the Spirit, it was also very common for people who were reportedly touched by the power and presence of God to be inspired to emotionally express this touch in various enthusiastic ways; hence, as introduced in chapter 2 and discussed at length in chapter 6, these intense emotional expressions were often labeled as "religious enthusiasm."[111] The most common ways in

102. Garrettson, *Experience and Travels*, 86–87.

103. Asbury, *Journal of the Rev. Francis Asbury*, 1:165.

104. Finley, *Autobiography*, 364; Cartwright, *Backwoods Preacher*, 79.

105. Asbury, *Journal of the Rev. Francis Asbury*, 1:165.

106. Crowell, *Journal of Seth Crowell*, 17–20, 49, 79.

107. Abbott and Ffirth, *Experience and Gospel Labours*, 52; Finley, *Autobiography*, 364; Hyde, *Story of Methodism*, 160; Wallace, *Parson of the Islands*, 30.

108. Bangs and Garrettson, *Life of the Rev. Freeborn Garrettson*, 224.

109. Finley, *Autobiography*, 240.

110. Hibbard, *Memoirs*, 147.

111. Cartwright, *Backwoods Preacher*, 21–22. While religious enthusiasm was discussed in chapter 2, because this matter plays a great role in the circuit rider ministry, it is extensively investigated in chapter 6, as well.

which individuals emotionally expressed these spiritual experiences were through spontaneous joy, weeping, shouting, singing, dancing, physical jerking, making animal noises (barking and roaring), holy laughing, sobbing and groaning, and emotional melting. Furthermore, these phenomena were reported to have occurred in almost every meeting; in other words, whenever there was an outpouring of God's Spirit, some sort of emotional outburst typically followed. This section describes the role of supernatural emotional responses within the circuit rider ministry.

One of the most commonly recorded emotional outbursts was crying. Cooper stated that this occurred because "the word was like a sword in the hearts of some who cried out . . . to God" and, as a result of this, "tears flowed on every hand; the countenances of the people bespoke the effect of the truth in their souls."[112] At times, the cries were so intense that people's "streaming eyes, and faces [were] bathed in tears."[113] Sometimes believers cried, other times nonbelievers cried, and the majority of the time, both groups present unpredictably cried as they were moved by "the power of God."[114] It was common after such an incident occurred for people to receive conversions, so this phenomenon was significant because people received spiritual refreshment and, moreover, because the labor of the gospel was "spread in a manner which human language cannot describe."[115]

The circuit riders recorded that people also unpredictably wept (a more intense form of crying) and exhibited "weeping eyes, and indeed there was a shower of tears amongst [them]."[116] At times, weeping was followed by mourning as Garretson observed that there was "a great weeping and mourning among poor sinners."[117] Sometimes, the Spirit was poured out, and the entire meeting's "floor was pretty well covered with weeping mourners."[118] Indeed, in the circuit rider meetings, there were often "weeping multitudes."[119] Methodist altars became full with

112. Cooper, *Beams of Light*, 135.
113. Lee, *Short History of the Methodists*, 57.
114. Hibbard, *Memoirs*, 151.
115. Finley, *Autobiography*, 367.
116. Jackson, *Lives of Early Methodist Preachers*, 6:169. See also Cartwright, *Backwoods Preacher*, 263.
117. Garrettson, *Experience and Travels*, 91.
118. Young, *Autobiography of a Pioneer*, 54.
119. Cartwright, *Backwoods Preacher*, 13.

"old and young, parents and children, weeping together and praying."[120] There were other occasions in which the Methodist "preachers and people wept" together; the circuit riders themselves, at times, "mourned and wept" that they might see God's power demonstrated in their lives and meetings.[121] In other words, it can be concluded that the cause of individual and collective outbursts of cries, tears, weeping, and mourning was a touch by "the divine power [that] was glorious among the people"[122] and that these forms of expression served as spiritual nourishment that also gave birth to conversions.[123]

In the circuit rider ministry, it was also common for the circuit riders, and particularly for their audiences, to express their spiritual experiences with spontaneous joy.[124] The manifestation of joy, according to Galatians 5:22–23, was considered to be one of the primary fruits of the Spirit of God, given to all believers as a "God-imparted emotion."[125] It seems that joy, at times, was a byproduct of individuals being "filled with [spiritual] amazement";[126] feelings of joy were directly bestowed by God and, as a result, individuals often spontaneously shouted "aloud for joy."[127] Largely as a result of the Spirit's touch, especially in experiences of salvation, people "rejoice[ed] with a joy unspeakable [that was] full of glory," and they often became "refreshed in [their] spirit." In other words, in the circuit rider ministry, the language of joy was very closely connected to happiness, especially for new converts; because of this fact, at times, tremendous "joy [came] from happy converts." According to the circuit riders, the new converts were transformed from "a dark and heavy cloud" to a "glorious [spiritual] light . . . [where the] distress left . . . and the anguish of . . . [the] heart was turned into joy."[128] Moreover, in circuit rider meetings, people occasionally witnessed the appearance of God as a "divine light" that "flashed all round" and brought to people's hearts a vivid and "unspeakable joy." In addition to joy being a pivotal part of conversion, believers experienced this joy, as well, sometimes directly

120. Newell, *Life and Observation*, 235.

121. Watters, *Short Account of the Christian Experience*, 137.

122. Smith and Dailey, *Experience and Ministerial Labors*, 29–30.

123. Finley, *Autobiography*, 367; Young, *Autobiography of a Pioneer*, 195.

124. Lee, *Memoir*, 94.

125. Washington, *Letters from the Wilderness*, 81.

126. Ware, *Sketches*, 62.

127. Young, *Autobiography of a Pioneer*, 195.

128. Finley, *Autobiography*, 224, 239, 203.

imparted by God and sometimes in witnessing the conversions of others and beholding their "great . . . joy."[129]

Audiences commonly expressed their spiritual experiences through shouts;[130] when the supernatural power of God descended on people there was "such a shout [that they] never heard." The observers of these events thought that sometimes "there were upward of two hundred people who shouted at one time."[131] During various meetings, there were occasions when "every few minutes [people would rise] in shouts of triumph."[132] At times, nonbelievers were touched by the Spirit of God so intensely that they "screamed";[133] at other times, their shouts were "shouts of victory over the powers of darkness."[134] Regardless, people typically "shouted aloud"[135] as a result of their supernatural experiences, especially conversion experiences, which often produced shouts that were mixed with joy and actively "prais[ed] the Most High for his abounding grace."[136] In short, people shouted "aloud the praise of God"[137] with "shrieks and shouts . . . [that] rent the very heavens"[138] and originated "from hundreds."[139]

During circuit rider meetings, people frequently sang songs.[140] Similar to the act of shouting, people sang out of a (somewhat involuntary) need to burst into song upon encountering a spiritual manifestation;[141] they also incorporated prayers and praise into song form.[142] At times, it appears that this form of singing was supernatural as people sang harmoniously "not from the mouth or nose, but entirely in the breast, the sounds issuing thence." The noise was apparently captivating and "most

129. Cartwright, *Backwoods Preacher*, 13, 232.
130. Young, *Autobiography of a Pioneer*, 195.
131. Wakeley and Boehm, *Patriarch of One Hundred Years*, 47.
132. Finley, *Sketches of Western Methodism*, 78.
133. Lee, *Religious Experience*, 48.
134. Shipp, *History of Methodism in South Carolina*, 331.
135. Henkle, *Life of Henry Bidleman Bascom*, 55.
136. Smith and Dailey, *Experience and Ministerial Labors*, 29–30.
137. Cartwright, *Backwoods Preacher*, 263.
138. Finley, *Autobiography*, 167.
139. Cartwright, *Backwoods Preacher*, 207.
140. Paine, *Life and Times*, 1:42.
141. Young, *Autobiography of a Pioneer*, 54.
142. Garrettson, *Experience and Travels*, 53–55.

heavenly; none could ever be tired of hearing it."[143] There were also many encounters in which "the songs of joy [flowed] from happy converts."[144]

When individuals witnessed and experienced God's Spirit, this often led to individual and corporate "dancing"[145] while "professing religion."[146] Dow observed that this form of "dancing" was "a strange exercise" because, while it was considered to be "involuntary," it also "require[d] the consent of the will." If people resisted the overpowering urge to dance, it brought "deadness and barrenness over the mind." However, if people "yield[ed]" to this urge, they felt "happy" and exhibited "a great cross [between] a heavenly smile and solemnity on the countenance." This form of dancing also reportedly caused "conviction" and produced a child-like mentality in that those who danced and "fixed [their eyes] upwards" on God disregarded behavioral propriety "below."[147] Furthermore, to spectators, religious dancing was viewed as "heavenly . . . The smile of Heaven shone on the countenance of the subject, and assimilated to angels appeared the whole person"[148] as they danced and shouted "aloud for joy."[149]

There were times when people in circuit rider meetings engaged in the controversial "exercises known as jerks" or "jerking."[150] While, as noted above, dancing was considered to be a cooperation between an involuntary urge and the human will, in general, jerking was described as an intense and fully "involuntary"[151] physical jerk (comparable to a seizure) and, as a result, it was little connected to emotions; however, the reason why it is incorporated in this emotional expressions section is because, in the circuit rider ministry, physical jerking was traditionally considered to be a part of "emotions"[152] or religious enthusiasm (which was often seen as "emotional wildness").[153]

For Cartwright, jerking was occasionally considered to be a "judgment" from God, "first, to bring sinners to repentance," and second, to

143. Stone, *Biography*, 41–42.

144. Finley, *Autobiography*, 239.

145. Paine, *Life and Times*, 1:153.

146. Stone, *Biography*, 40.

147. Dow, *History of Cosmopolite*, 213.

148. Stone, *Biography*, 40.

149. Smith and Dailey, *Experience and Ministerial Labors*, 29–30.

150. Paine, *Life and Times*, 1:153.

151. Cartwright, *Backwoods Preacher*, 21.

152. Dow, *History of Cosmopolite*, 182, 213.

153. Gregoire, "History of Religious Sects," 7.

demonstrate to people that the Lord could "work with or without means, and that He could work over and above means." Cartwright believed that, despite the controversy surrounding them, if it "seemeth [to] Him good," God would use the jerks to further his purpose of "the salvation of the world" and the demonstration of "the glory of His grace."[154] Similar to Cartwright, Dow perceived "the jerks [to be] a sign of the times"; he believed that God sent the jerks for two main reasons—as a "judgment for the people's unbelief" and "as a mercy to convict people of divine realities."[155]

While some during that time attempted to explain the jerks through natural means, circuit riders expressed that one could "not account for it on natural principles" as the source of this phenomenon was divine.[156] Finley described this supernatural manifestation, explaining that sometimes hundreds at a time jerked back and forth with "great rapidity and violence." This jerking was so intense that people's "bodies would bend so as to bring their heads near to the floor." Often, when women experienced this phenomenon, their hair would "crack like the lash of a driver's whip." There were also those who jerked "from side to side, so quickly that the features of the face could not be distinguished"[157] or would make "a kind of grunt or groan."[158] Occasionally, audience members would stop, "rise up, and dance" in order "to obtain relief" from the involuntary exercise.[159] While, to an observer, jerking could have appeared to be a painful experience, those who encountered it reported to have had "no bodily pain."

It was described that, at times, "about one hundred and fifty appeared to have the jerking exercise."[160] At other times, circuit riders witnessed occasions wherein they had "seen more than five hundred persons jerking at one time." It seems that the phenomenon of jerking was more prevalent in larger meetings and less so in smaller meetings; nonetheless, in circuit rider meetings, the "jerks were very prevalent."[161]

154. Cartwright, *Backwoods Preacher*, 21.

155. Dow, *History of Cosmopolite*, 182–84.

156. Dow, *History of Cosmopolite*, 185.

157. Stone, *Biography*, 40.

158. Dow, *History of Cosmopolite*, 183.

159. Cartwright, *Backwoods Preacher*, 20.

160. Dow, *History of Cosmopolite*, 183.

161. Cartwright, *Backwoods Preacher*, 20–21.

Also, as further investigated in chapter 6, this form of expression played a large part in the public's increasing criticism of Methodism.[162] It became common for "some wicked persons [to mock] the jerks." However, those who mocked these expressions were many times touched by the Spirit so that they themselves "were thrown to the earth with violence."[163] Finley noted that the jerks were not restricted to any specific class or type within the audience, but rather, "saint, seeker, and sinner were alike subject to these wonderful phenomena."[164] Dow confirmed this by declaring that, in his ministry, "black and white, the aged and the youth, rich and poor, without exception" were subject to the jerks.[165]

In addition, audience members occasionally exhibited animal roaring and barking. This was also a controversial manifestation in those days; however, circuit riders generally considered this exercise to be divinely inspired and believed that it functioned as a means of enabling conversions or increasing knowledge of God. In this exercise, individuals engaged in "roaring out in the disquietude of their spirits," which caused a noise that sounded as "though heaven had come into their souls."[166] In a similar fashion, there was the animal "barking exercise" in which people would "make a grunt or a bark" as a result of a spiritual encounter.[167]

When the Spirit of the Lord was poured out, it was common for people to experience holy laugher, a kind of "loud, hearty laughter . . . [that] was truly indescribable." However, while this phenomenon was identified as laughter, at times "it excited laughter in none that heard it." Rather, it "excited solemnity" in those present, both "saints and sinners."[168] There were times in which holy laughter lasted for long periods of time. New converts would often spontaneously begin to "laugh, and would continue doing so for [hours]." There was a recorded case in Kentucky in which a woman "laughed all day and all night."[169] Also, it seems that

162. The upcoming chapter is dedicated to public criticism surrounding religious enthusiasm, including jerking.

163. Stone, *Biography*, 40.

164. Finley, *Autobiography*, 165.

165. Dow, *History of Cosmopolite*, 184.

166. Sandford, *Memoirs*, 371.

167. Stone, *Biography*, 40–41. See also Cartwright, *Backwoods Preacher*, 21; Lee, *Memoir*, 206; Ware, *Sketches*, 253–54.

168. Stone, *Biography*, 41.

169. Sweet, *Circuit-Rider Days in Indiana*, 48–49. See also Brown, *Global Pentecostal and Charismatic Healing*, 220.

this phenomenon was more commonly experienced in larger meetings and was predominately considered to be divine—a sign of overpowering and uncontrollable joy. However, it should be noted that some scholars (including modern scholars) have disputed the fact that holy laughter was divinely inspired.[170]

In addition to the above emotional expressions, individuals occasionally expressed their spiritual encounters through emotional melting: "The melting power of God was felt and [through it, many] were blessed.[171] In some meetings, there was such a great display of the power of God that it reportedly caused a "great melting" within the audience.[172] While this term was not explicitly defined by the circuit riders, it was largely understood to represent a heart being softened as a result of spiritual influence. This can be contrasted with the instance within the biblical text in which God caused Pharaoh's heart to be hardened.[173] Thus, within these circuit rider meetings, it appears that God emotionally melted the hearts of those present.

Within circuit rider meetings, there were other forms of emotional expression that occurred less frequently. For example, when "the power of the Highest was manifestly upon the audience," it occasionally caused people to be "attested by sobs and groans from every part."[174] In meetings, there were "cries for mercy [that] seemed as though they would rend the heavens"; at times, the cries were considered to be very loud—so loud that in meetings "little could be heard, except . . . strong cries to God for mercy."[175] Sometimes, people expressed the touch of God by "wringing their hands, smiting their breasts, and begging all to pray for them."[176] There were also cases in which the power of the Spirit descended, causing many to feel as if they had been "impaled."[177]

From this section, it can be concluded that audience members in the circuit rider ministry expressed their supernatural encounters through various emotions (also known as "religious enthusiasm"). Spiritual

170. For more information, see Rhodes, *What Does the Bible Say About*, 310.

171. Newell, *Life and Observations*, 235.

172. Asbury, *Journal of the Rev. Francis Asbury*, 2:50.

173. For more information, see Exodus 9:12.

174. Buckley, *History of Methodism in the United States*, 164.

175. Lee, *Short History of the Methodists*, 55–57.

176. Asbury, *Journal of the Rev. Francis Asbury*, 1:165.

177. Paine, *Life and Times*, 1:41.

166 THE SUPERNATURAL AND THE CIRCUIT RIDERS

experiences were expressed sometimes with crying, weeping, shouting, singing, dancing, jerking, roaring, laughing, sobbing, and groaning. As Ware observed, because the "great power [of God] attended the word; many wept aloud, some for joy, and some for grief; many, [were] filled with amazement."[178] One of the main functions of these supernatural phenomena was to serve as a source of spiritual refreshment. Most importantly, however, the phenomena served as a means of producing new converts (which, in turn, caused growth in American Methodism). As Cartwright summarized, in the circuit rider ministry, "sinners wept, quaked, and trembled, and saints shouted aloud for joy" resulting in many individuals being "born into the kingdom of God."[179]

The Phenomena of Divine Dreams, Visions, and Trances

Although dreams, visions, and trances were mentioned in previous chapters, this section details the meaning of dreams, visions, and trances from a spiritual perspective; it is followed by an examination of their significance within circuit rider audiences.

 Dreams (found in the New Testament text as ὄναρ or ἐνύπνιον)[180] are understood to be a common byproduct of sleep and can "be reflections of reality, sources of divination, curative experiences, or evidence of unconscious activity."[181] *Visions* (found in the New Testament text as ὅραμα)[182] are largely understood to hold more clarity than dreams and are largely known to originate as a result of a spiritual or "religious experience"; they can be seen as a form of "a dream,"[183] a "trance, or as a supernatural apparition."[184] Lastly, *trances* (found in the New Testament text as ἔκστασις,)[185] often involve a form of "spiritual ecstasy";[186] trances can

178. Ware, *Sketches*, 62.

179. Cartwright, *Backwoods Preacher*, 232.

180. For instance, see Matt 1:20; 2:12, 19, 22; 27:19; Acts 2:17.

181. "Dream" (*EBO*).

182. For instance, see Matt 17:9; Acts 7:31; 9:10, 12; 10:17, 19; 11:5; 12:9; 16:10; and 18:9.

183. "Vision" (*CED*). See also Schreuder, *Vision and Visual Perception*, 671.

184. "Vision" (*OED*).

185. For instance, see Acts 3:10; 10:10; 11:5; 22:17; 2 Cor 12:2; Mark 5:42; 16:8; Luke 5:25.

186. For instance, this word was used in the biblical Greek to describe Peter's trance in Acts 10:10: "ἐγένετο δὲ πρόσπεινος καὶ ἤθελεν γεύσασθαι. παρασκευαζόντων δὲ αὐτῶν ἐγένετο ἐπ᾽ αὐτὸν ἔκστασις."

also be understood as "a mental state between sleeping and waking" in which an individual "does not move but can hear and understand what is being said."[187] Occasionally, those who experience a trance feel as if they are "out of"[188] their physical bodies; the condition is also "characterized by an absence of response to external stimuli."[189] Furthermore, a trance can be understood as "a preternatural, absorbed state of mind preparing for the reception of the [spiritual] vision."[190]

The circuit riders believed that many of their dreams, visions, and trances were divinely orchestrated and "were sent by God, in his mercy, for [the] good [of believers]."[191] According to the circuit riders, divine dreams, visions, and trances were another way in which God communicated with the circuit riders and their audiences; these divine dreams, visions, and trances also typically served as a form of spiritual encouragement.[192] For example, in his journal, Gatch copied down the following text from Joel 2:28 because he felt that it applied to his ministry, as well: "I will pour out my Spirit upon all flesh, and your sons and your daughters shall prophesy . . . your old men shall dream dreams, your young men shall see visions."[193] These divine phenomena were encountered in various places, such as evangelistic meetings, ministerial circuits, and people's private homes.

Just as the circuit riders encountered divine dreams, visions, and trances in their private lives, their audiences also encountered such phenomena. It appears that some divine dreams, visions, and trances in circuit rider audiences were experienced for the purpose of conversion. For instance, Garretson recorded a story that happened during a Methodist meeting in which a man who was known for "wickedness came cursing and swearing" and was then supernaturally touched by God and became a believer. This man relayed that, during his short period of conversion, he experienced a vision or trance of hell wherein he "thought every

187. "Trance" (*CED*).

188. Easton, "Trance."

189. "Trance" (*OED*).

190. *Bible Dictionary*, 2:530.

191. Gatch, *Sketch of Rev. Philip Gatch*, 9.

192. For more information, see also Asbury's sermon on Joel 2:28–29 in Asbury, *Journal of the Rev. Francis Asbury*, 3:169; Horton, *Narrative of the Early Life*, 134–36; Young, *Autobiography of Dan Young*, 28–31.

193. Gatch, *Sketch of Rev. Philip Gatch*, 61.

minute [he would] fall," apparently, into hell. In that moment, he decided to trust in Christ, for he "saw a beauty in him."[194]

Cartwright recalled a story of a woman who was touched by the power of God but was not willing to acknowledge Jesus Christ's divine nature. The reason for this was because an Arian demon or devil[195] "still claimed a residence in this woman's heart." So, Cartwright, the lady, and a few others prayed, and it appeared that "the bending heavens came near." This caused the lady to lose "her assumed good feelings, and [she] sunk down into sullen, dumb silence." The woman continued in this condition for weeks until, one night, she experienced a divine "dream or vision" in which Jesus appeared to her "in all His supreme glory." In her dream or vision, Jesus "told her she was wrong . . . [and] forgave her" of her errors and unbelief. After this experience, she became a firm believer in Christ's divinity and joined the MEC.[196]

Sometimes it seems that divine dreams, visions, and trances appeared in order to elicit an immediate response from the dreamer. For example, Asbury, who was a believer in divine dreams and visions, recorded an incident of a woman who "dreamed three times that the Indians had surprised and killed them all." After she had these divine dreams, "she urged her husband to entreat the people to set a guard." When the people heard the news from her husband's description of the dreams and his request for a guard, not only did they not believe him, but they also "abused him, and cursed him." Seeing that the people would not respond to the warnings that came from the divine dream, the woman and her "husband sprung away, one east, the other west, and escaped"; the dream came true, and American Indians attacked the residence.[197] Likewise, Young once recorded a prophetic "dream or vision" of an American Indian woman who, upon having a dream, urged the chief of her tribe not to harm a certain preacher who was attempting to minister to the American Indians.[198]

Travis recalled a female who dreamed of attending a ball. In this dream, she died and was taken into heaven but did not enjoy the "the company of saints and angels"; thus, she "was hurled down to flames

194. Garrettson, *Experience and Travels*, 91–92.

195. Arianism is a belief considered to be a form of Christian heresy; it dates back to the fourth century. For more information, see Green, *Unholy Hands on the Bible*, 410.

196. Cartwright, *Backwoods Preacher*, 125.

197. Asbury, *Journal of the Rev. Francis Asbury*, 2:74; 3:169.

198. Young, *Autobiography of a Pioneer*, 368.

and burnings." When a minister heard this dream, he discerned it was a divine dream and warned the female "not to go" to the ball. However, the woman disregarded the warning and attended; then "all the particulars of her dream relating to this world came to pass."[199]

Some of the divine dreams, visions, and trances were prophetic foretellings. For instance, Bangs recorded Garrettson's story of Mrs. Basset who "had been praying for her husband's conversion." She then saw a prophetic dream in which "God had converted [her husband's] soul." Later, when her husband returned to his home, he told all his family what the Lord had done for him as, apparently, he experienced a conversion. Mrs. Basset, who divinely foreknew this event, confessed to her husband: "I know it . . . [because] the blessed God told me so."[200]

Coke recorded an account of a certain dream by a "poor [Caribbean] man." In this man's dream, "two Ministers came to [his home on the] Island." The dream made such an impression on the man that he remembered it vividly, and "as soon as he saw Mr. Baxter and [Coke] enter the Church," he knew them "immediately to be the very same persons who had been represented to him in his dream."[201] Also, during Shadford's ministerial work, one of his audience members, who had never met him before that day, told him: "I saw you in a dream last night."[202]

To summarize this section, it can be concluded that divine dreams, visions, and trances were common supernatural manifestations in the circuit rider ministry.[203] It appears that the main role of these phenomena was to serve as a form of divine communication between an individual and God. For instance, Boehm argued that, through supernatural dreams, the spiritual realm communicated with humanity; moreover, for Boehm, these phenomena (such as divine dreams) derived either from "an evil source [the demonic spirits] . . . or from a good source [God]." According to Boehm, one could discern the source of a spiritual dream by its fruit; one usually knew when dreams issued from God as they exhibited "some good purpose."[204]

199. Travis, *Autobiography*, 232–33.
200. Bangs and Garrettson, *Life of the Rev. Freeborn Garrettson*, 100.
201. Coke, *Extracts of the Journals* [1816], 145.
202. Jackson, *Lives of Early Methodist Preachers*, 6:165.
203. See also O'Byrne, "How Methodists Were Made," 76–90.
204. Wakeley and Boehm, *Patriarch of One Hundred Years*, 62.

It appears that divine dreams, visions, and trances were a crucial part of the circuit rider ministry because, through them, conversions took place,[205] people obtained spiritual empowerment,[206] and divine messages were received.[207] Some of these messages required immediate responses from the seers and others were prophetic messages that disclosed specific future events.[208] Horton and D. Young recorded incidents in which God used these phenomena to enable readers of the Bible to "understand passage[s]" that had previously puzzled them.[209] Also, Asbury recorded occasions wherein these phenomena served as a catalyst in people becoming more "sanctified."[210]

Moreover, not only did the circuit riders believe that dreams, visions, and trances were largely divine, but they demonstrated "great reliance"[211] on them as valuable sources of divine communication that "greatly strengthened [their] blessed work,"[212] just as in the Apostolic Age.[213] Indeed, these phenomena were perceived as a means of divine revelatory guidance, and they "intend to see the result" of them.[214] For instance, Garrettson was aware that "some suppose[d] that [they] ought not to put any dependence in dreams and visions"; however, he introduced the theology and understanding that people should depend on them because even the "wise and good men ha[d] done [so] in all ages . . . [such as the apostles] Peter, Paul."[215] Horton echoed this viewpoint by

205. Abbott and Ffirth, *Experience and Gospel Labours*, 14–20.

206. Garrettson, *Experience and Travels*, 9–11, 146–47; Jea, *Life, History, and Unparalleled Sufferings*, 35–36; Lee, *Memoir*, 271; Travis, *Autobiography*, 54; Young, *Autobiography of a Pioneer*, 47; Wakeley and Boehm, *Patriarch of One Hundred Years*, 62.

207. Coke, *Extracts of the Journals* [1816], 145; Jackson, *Lives of Early Methodist Preachers*, 6:163.

208. Asbury, *Journal of the Rev. Francis Asbury*, 2:74–75; Horton, *Narrative of the Early Life*, 93; Jackson, *Lives of Early Methodist Preachers*, 6:165.

209. Horton, *Narrative of the Early Life*, 58. See also Young, *Autobiography of Dan Young*, 29–30.

210. Asbury, *Journal of the Rev. Francis Asbury*, 1:278.

211. Strickland, *Life of Jacob Gruber*, 120.

212. Horton, *Narrative of the Early Life*, 60.

213. The first apostles witnessed and relied on divine dreams, visions, and trances as a crucial form of spiritual guidance. For more information, see Acts 7:56; 9:4–5; 10:9–16; 16:6–10.

214. Dow, *History of Cosmopolite*, 204.

215. Garrettson, *Experience and Travels*, 172–73.

arguing that "some say there is nothing [divine] in" these phenomena, but he thought "otherwise" because, through them, individuals "received many signal manifestations of the divine goodness in the course of [their] pilgrimage."[216]

It also should be noted that early Methodists were aware that some dreams, visions, and trances were the product of mere "self-induced manifestations"[217] that, at times, "misled [people], by pride and a warm imagination."[218] They also believed that dreams and trances could originate from angels and from various "demonic activity."[219] It seems that circuit riders could spiritually discern (and actively endeavored to discern) the origins of these phenomena, and they identified many of them as direct God-messages.[220] Thus, in the circuit rider ministry, people "dreamed dreams, saw visions" and experienced trances that they perceived to be biblical; furthermore, the circuit riders recommended that individuals rely on these divine phenomena as the early apostles did.[221]

The Phenomena of Spiritual Warfare and Exorcism

As discussed in chapter 4, while personal, experiential lessons in spiritual warfare taught the circuit riders how to recognize and thwart the works of the devil in their own lives, they also reportedly instructed the circuit riders on setting others free (via exorcism) from various demonic oppressions and even, at times, possessions of the entire human will.[222] As

216. Horton, *Narrative of the Early Life*, 134–35. See also Young, *Autobiography of Dan Young*, 28.

217. Elliott, "How Miracles Helped," para. 11.

218. Wesley, *Sermons on Several Occasions* [Drew], 413. See also Wesley, *Sermons on Several Occasions* [Jackson], 714.

219. Elliott, "How Miracles Helped Spread," para. 11. See also Wesley, *Sermons on Several Occasions* [Drew], 413; Taves, *Fits, Trances, and Visions*, 53.

220. For instance, see Gatch, *Sketch of Rev. Philip Gatch*, 61; Abbott and Ffirth, *Experience and Gospel Labours*, 8–20; Young, *Autobiography of a Pioneer*, 47; Wakeley and Boehm, *Patriarch of One Hundred Years*, 62; Asbury, *Journal of the Rev. Francis Asbury*, 2:74; Travis, *Autobiography*, 232–33; Jackson, *Lives of Early Methodist Preachers*, 6:165. Furthermore, 1 Corinthians 12:10 states that discerning the origin of a spiritual revelation is one of the gifts of the Holy Spirit bestowed by God on Christians.

221. Peck, *Early Methodism*, 187.

222. A demonically possessed individual is considered to be strongly oppressed by the powers of the devil. For example, see also Pilmore, *Journal of Joseph Pilmore*, 73.

Scudder observed, in general, the circuit riders' "work often appear[ed] semi-miraculous, and [it was] as if Christ were [physically] again present, casting out demons, and clothing the delivered ones with a right mind."[223]

Asbury recorded a story of a woman named Achsah Borden who, upon facing severe temptation, chose to participate in sinful activities. These sinful acts brought her to a place of "deep distress." Borden's family members, in an effort to protect her, locked her in a room and removed all knives from her house because they were afraid that she would harm herself. Soon after, Borden lost her ability to speak. Asbury described her by saying that in "silence, she would not work at all, nor do the smallest thing." However, she heard about the Methodists who purportedly engaged in productive spiritual prayers. As a result, Borden wanted the Methodists to pray for her with the hope of being healed. She was later directed to a place "where a number [of Methodists] met for prayer." Asbury explained that when the "brethren saw into her case," they immediately supernaturally discerned that "a dumb spirit" was living in her. Whether from her sinful acts, distress, or the trauma of being locked away, the dumb evil spirit took advantage of her weaknesses and afflicted her with a speechless life. Asbury also stated that the Methodists were sure that "God would cast [the evil spirit] out." So, they joined together in prayer and prayed for "part of three days" consecutively; on "the third day at evening she cried for mercy, soon spoke and praised God, from a sense of comforting, pardoning love." The dumb evil spirit was cast out of Borden, and because of this exorcism, she was set free from the burden of her speechless life. Her relationship with God was also restored, and she sensed his pardoning love.[224]

Garrettson recorded a similar story of a girl who was a believer; however, at one point in her life, she wandered away from the Lord, and the devil tortured her severely by making her appear as a societal outcast. During this time, as a result of all of these difficulties, she reportedly became "dumb for two years." After she heard about the Methodists and their spiritual reputation, she desired to attend their meetings, and upon doing so, she heard the sermon and a call for experiential prayer. She passionately began to pray and then "went into a private room, [and] kneeled down to prayer" where she remained in a state of persistent prayer "till the Lord blessed her soul." In that moment, the girl was delivered and

223. Scudder and Cummings, American Methodism, 89.
224. Asbury, Journal of the Rev. Francis Asbury, 1:258.

"her tongue was loosened, and she could speak forth the praises of Israel's God." After this experience, Garrettson took her back to her home. When her family saw her restored and with a healthy appearance, they marveled and "some thought [that] the Methodists could work miracles." For the rest of her life, the girl was "able to speak and work as well as usual."[225]

Garrettson recorded the exorcism of a man "who was troubled with an evil spirit." This man recalled that "for a long time the devil had followed him, and that he had frequently seen him with his bodily eyes." This man was seemingly "under [Christian] conviction" but did not have knowledge regarding how to deal with evil spirits. As a result, Garrettson, being experienced in spiritual warfare, "gave him good directions" to overcome this spiritual battle. Following their conversation, they prayed together, and the man "was troubled no more . . . and he became one of [Garrettson's] quiet hearers."[226]

Garrettson also described an incident in which he became lost on his way to a circuit. He then stopped at the nearest house and there encountered a woman who had previously worshiped the devil. She confessed to Garrettson that she had "sold [her] three little children to the devil" and was convinced that the devil would soon come to claim their souls. As a result, "she had carried a razor in her bosom for three weeks with an intention, first, to take the lives of her children before the day came that she thought the devil was to come for them, and then to take her own life." Garrettson, however, insisted that her children "belong[ed] to God" and not the devil. He preached to her, prayed for her, and read the Bible. At first, due to the strong demonic influence on the family, it seemed that whatever Garrettson said was "all in vain." However, Garrettson persisted in his efforts as he believed "it pleased the Lord to visit her soul in mercy." Finally, the mother was filled with "rapture of joy" and began to bless and praise God as she experienced her personal conversion.[227]

Finley recalled an exorcism of a young man who appeared to "have been possessed of the devil." Due to demonic influence, the man was considered to be full of "ravings and blasphemy," which "shocked all who heard him." He "boastingly" criticized divine manifestations and even "defied the power of God." Regarding those who were slain in the

225. Garrettson, *Experience and Travels*, 137–39.

226. Garrettson, *Experience and Travels*, 183.

227. Garrettson, *Experience and Travels*, 180–82. Horton recorded a similar story of Satanists (from Africa) sacrificing animals and newborn children to the devil; for more information, see Horton, *Narrative of the Early Life*, 183–88.

Spirit, the young man argued that they were simply "overcome by the influence of fear, or nervous weakness." However, to his amazement, the young man was "suddenly" slain in the Spirit himself, and down he "fell on the floor lifeless to all appearance." He remained in this state for eight hours and, during this time, was intermittently "seized with convulsions of such an intense and powerful character, that [it seemed] he must die from the agony." After the experience, he rose to his normal state and began "praising God for his salvation." Not only was this man spiritually converted, but he also began to urge "all his friends to seek an interest in the Savior. His conversion [and spiritual deliverance] was a matter of astonishment to all." Finley considered this account to be a "demonstration of the power of God, [as well as an] irresistible conviction."[228]

Finley described another story of a Catholic woman who appeared to have been kept under condemnation of the devil and harbored many fears. She also believed that a child she had lost was a punishment from God for her wickedness. Finally, she prayed wholeheartedly, and "a dark and heavy cloud, which had rested upon her, pass[ed] away, and she was surrounded with a glorious light." From this supernatural encounter, she felt that "all her distress left her, and the anguish of her heart was turned into joy." Unfortunately, this peace did not last long because the devil "tempted her and darkness again surrounded her." However, as the woman had become familiar with the concept of spiritual warfare and was confident in her past spiritual breakthroughs, even "in this state of mind," she pursued the Lord in prayer. Again, the Lord visited the woman, and she "was happily delivered from the snare of the devil." After her demonic deliverance, she became a dedicated Methodist.[229]

Pilmore was known to have experienced spiritual battles with demonic beings; through them, he became familiar with seeking the Lord and rebuking the devil. Pilmore recorded a severe case of exorcism performed on a lady who was known to be "possessed by the devil"; after much prayer, she was fully delivered.[230]

Among these spiritual struggles, the circuit riders recorded unusual cases in which people allegedly experienced such profound spiritual enslavement by the devil that they became mentally unstable and, consequently, refused deliverance; thus, they remained in these conditions,

---

228. Finley, *Autobiography*, 232.
229. Finley, *Autobiography*, 255.
230. Pilmore, *Journal of Joseph Pilmore*, 16, 73.

and often their cases eventually ended in death. For instance, Cartwright recalled a story revolving around the devil's work in tormenting a new, impressionable Christian to death. A woman was slain in the Spirit by the power of God and was thriving spiritually; however, she had not yet reached a state of Christian maturity. Satan took advantage of this state and "tempted her to believe that she was a reprobate, and that there was no mercy for her." Arising from these temptations, the woman came to the belief that "she was Jesus Christ," and as such, she "took it upon her . . . to bless and curse [all who] came to see her." Things worsened as she "refused to eat, or drink, or sleep." The woman remained in this poor condition of demonic delusion and captivity for thirteen days and, ultimately, died because she refused to get well or receive deliverance.[231]

Abbott recorded another unusual case during one of his meetings in which one "very wicked" woman was touched "by the mighty power of God" and, after returning home, "shook to that degree, that the bed on which she lay trembled under her." When people heard of her condition, they went to visit her, along with Abbott; whenever the woman became capable of speech, she warned the people to not sin as she had because they would end up worse than her. Abbott assured everyone that these shakings were from God, and after a few days, the woman became happily converted and lived a devout life of faith. However, six months after her conversion, her husband had a dispute with a Methodist society member, and being much affected by it, the woman renounced her faith and returned to her old practices, wherein she became a "worse child of hell than at the beginning." Eighteen months later, it became apparent that the woman was dying, so Abbott and his daughter Rebecca went to visit her, imploring her to repent again, but she would not. Finally, in a moment of terror, she cried: "Do not you see the devils there ready to seize my soul and drag it to hell . . . I feel as much of the torturing torments of the damned as a mortal can feel in the body." Those present assured the woman that she was "out of her senses," but after these words, in front of all present, "her flesh rotted on her bones, and fell from one of her sides, so that her entrails might be seen. In this awful, terrible situation, she left this stage of action [died]." Abbott then warned that this is what would happen to those who backslid in their faith and denounced God in their words and actions.[232]

231. Cartwright, *Backwoods Preacher*, 43.

232. Abbott and Ffirth, *Experience and Gospel Labours*, 74–75. An individual who was formerly a biblical Christian but no longer claimed to be a Christian or did not

At times, Methodists recorded stories wherein the devil was the main influence in prompting people to murder. For instance, Jea, who encountered various experiences of spiritual warfare, recorded the tragic story of his wife who, largely because of "the temptations of Satan," mistreated and then killed their own baby. She also threatened to kill her husband Jea because she was convinced in her heart by demonic beings that she was destined "to go to eternal misery; and therefore, she was determined to do all the mischief she could." His wife was then sent to a court and was punished and "suffered according to the law." Despite this tragedy, Jea found power and healing in God who "gave [him] grace to withstand the temptations of the Devil."[233]

As demonstrated, the circuit riders recorded various incidents of spiritual warfare or individual exorcisms performed directly by them or other Methodists of the day. Cartwright summarized these experiences, saying: "Satan was in many who cried so lamentably for him to be cast out. And out of many he was cast, by the power of the Holy Ghost, through faith in Jesus Christ. They were first torn by Satan, then healed by Christ."[234]

Thus, as noted in chapter 4, it is evident that the supernatural activities of spiritual warfare and exorcism were frequently experienced within the circuit rider ministry. This battle was fought in faith, with prayer, and through God's Spirit by expelling demons from people's lives. Indeed, circuit riders displayed a ministry in which they frequently engaged in and performed spiritual deliverances (i.e., exorcisms) over their audiences.[235] In doing so, Newell testified that the power and presence of God descended, and "lovely children and youth were brought from the power of Satan unto God."[236] However, regarding unbelievers, the circuit riders expressed that all unbelievers were unprotected subjects of "stimulat[ion]"[237] and captivity "from the powers of Satan"[238] and were in need of spiritual conversion by being rescued "from the bondage of

---

live a life compatible with biblical principles was identified by the circuit riders as a *backslider*. For more information regarding the term, see Baxter, *Christian Directory*, 351–55.

233. Jea, *Life, History, and Unparalleled Sufferings*, 46–47.

234. Cooper, *Beams of Light*, 89.

235. Cooper, *Beams of Light*, 89.

236. Newell, *Life and Observations*, 131.

237. Asbury, *Journal of the Rev. Francis Asbury*, 1:109.

238. Lee, *Short History of the Methodists*, 271.

Satan to the liberty of the children of God."[239] Moreover, the circuit riders believed (echoing 2 Cor 4:4) that the devil or "the god of this world blind[ed] the minds of mankind"[240] so that they would not receive the salvation that is presented in the gospel.[241]

Lastly, O'Byrne noted that, in other denominations, "supernaturalism was not nearly as common as it would be in early Methodist narratives."[242] Expanding on this observation, the circuit riders themselves believed that one of the main reasons why so many ministers of other denominations did not experience the supernatural of "the day of Pentecost" was because the Holy Spirit was "so destructive to Satan's kingdom that [Satan would] stir up all his powers against it, and those ministers" who endeavored to walk in the same power as seen on the day of Pentecost; as a result, such ministers were hunted by the enemy "as lambs among wolves." Thus, works of the devil were considered by circuit riders to be largely responsible for the lack of supernatural activity in the church (specifically, some non-Methodist denominations) of their day.[243]

The Phenomena of Divine Healings

Modern scholar Hiatt explained that, within the circuit rider ministry, a "divine healing [was considered to be a] healing by the direct intervention of God."[244] Before examining the supernatural instances of divine healings witnessed within the circuit riders' audiences, it should be noted that the circuit riders also recorded numerous occasions in which they themselves were physically sick or in pain. For instance, Asbury recorded times when he had "a violent pain in [his] head. After service, [he] went to bed, and was very ill." In another instance, he also recorded that when

239. Finley, *Autobiography*, 270.

240. Asbury, *Journal of the Rev. Francis Asbury*, 1:87.

241. This concept is present in the biblical text as, at one point, Jesus pointed out that because of sin, people willingly or unwillingly join the devil and demonic powers. This is also seen in John 8:44: "You are of your father the devil, and your will is to do your father's desires. He was a murderer from the beginning, and does not stand the truth, because there is no truth in him. When he lies, he speaks out of his own character, for he is a liar and the father of lies."

242. O'Byrne, "How Methodists Were Made," 75.

243. Abbott, *Life and Labours*, 180.

244. Hiatt, "John Wesley & Healing," 90.

he "laid down on the floor upon [his] nightgown; [he] slept in pain."[245]
These physical sicknesses and pains came about as a result of the circuit
riders' lack of rest and tremendous physical strain, sparked by their
continuous horseback riding through various harsh weather conditions.
It is natural, when exposed to such damaging circumstances, for one's
physical immune system to be rendered defenseless against many germs
or viruses.[246]

Nevertheless, due to the power and presence of God, the circuit riders witnessed various displays of divine (and often immediate) physical
(and even emotional) healings; it appears that, in God's compassion and
mercy, circuit riders occasionally observed that "the power of the Lord
was present . . . to heal."[247] For instance, Asbury once "went to bed with
a fever on [him]; and the morning felt so much pain that [he] thought
of not going to the Court–house [to preach]." However, he reported that
the Lord healed him and "rewarded [his] weak [endeavors] with liberty,
power, and consolation." Because of this supernatural healing, Asbury
could preach "the next day." Similarly, during one of Asbury's circuit travels, he was under severe "affliction of body." However, God intervened
supernaturally, and through his "perfect love, [there was] peace within
[him]," and Asbury witnessed a "harmony" in which "every [part of his]
malady" was healed. The next day, Asbury was able to continue with his
regular circuit schedule.[248]

Furthermore, it should be noted that divine healings were occasionally associated with the level of faith of the circuit riders or the audience
members.[249] The circuit riders observed that God's power and presence
was always there to heal people (physically or emotionally), but faith was
required to actually receive spiritual or physical healing. Consequently,
faith was the bridge that brought supernatural healings from the Spirit
of God into people. Regarding this matter, Gatch recalled an important
spiritual revelation wherein he "felt the power of God . . . affect [his]
body and soul." During this time, according to Gatch, God spoke to him
saying that his "power [was] present to heal . . . if [Gatch would] believe."
Afterword, he "instantly submitted to the operation of the Spirit of God,

245. Asbury, *Journal of the Rev. Francis Asbury*, 1:8, 295. See also Morrell, *Journals*, 25–27.

246. For more information on this matter, see "Out in the Cold," para. 2.

247. Ware, *Sketches*, 115. See also Asbury, *Journal of the Rev. Francis Asbury*, 1:312.

248. Asbury, *Journal of the Rev. Francis Asbury*, 3:125, 179.

249. See also Stevenson and Cook, *Biographical Sketch*, 31–32.

and [his] poor soul was set at liberty. [He] felt as if [he] had got into a new world."[250]

Similarly, when Horton had "severe pain in [his] right side" to the degree that he was unable to do anything, the Lord "spoke unto [him]," saying that if he would "believe, [his] side [would] be healed." Horton accepted this and in faith responded that God was "able to heal." After this faith declaration, Horton testified that "in that very moment" he felt "the power" of God entering him "as sensible as [he] ever felt the hand of a person upon any part of [his] body," and his "cure was instantaneous and perfect."[251]

Regarding another instance of faith-associated healing, Lakin once described a woman "who was afflicted with a disease pronounced by her physicians incurable." After Lakin prayed for her, he recommended that she have faith in receiving supernatural healing because "the Lord, in His own good time, [would] rebuke [this incurable] disease and restore her to health." It appears that the woman put this faith recommendation into practice because she recovered. Lakin later witnessed that she was "still living, at an advanced age, able to perform a considerable amount of labor."[252]

Regarding additional supernatural healings, Lakin recorded a divine healing of a young woman whose "speech was taken from her." Her symptoms were so severe that, although she had the ability to sit up, she was "entirely inclined to lay." This woman remained in this condition for nine days; she then began to zealously pray, and after much prayer, "her speech was restored and she arose with her usual strength, and her body in no ways emaciated, but in full flesh and [vigor]." Rejoicing in this miracle, Lakin declared that "the Lord's doings . . . [were] marvelous in [their] eyes."[253]

Newell recorded the divine healing of "a sick man who appeared near the gates of death." Apparently, this man had "returned from [a] sea [journey]" wherein he had encountered "a tremendous gale"; he and others on the ship believed that they would die and, thus, "wicked as [they] were, unitedly called on God for help." God "delivered" them safely, but the man later "forgot the vows" he made to God during his

250. Gatch, *Sketch of Rev. Philip Gatch*, 12–13.

251. Horton, *Narrative of the Early Life*, 134–35.

252. Sprague, *Annals of the American Pulpit*, 7:272. See also Horton, *Narrative of the Early Life*, 13–15.

253. Finley, *Sketches of Western Methodism*, 183.

distress and had entirely "broken the solemn promises of [his] heart." The man, admittedly, had continued to live a life of "sins." As a result, he thought that the root of this sickness, which brought him "into the very jaws of death," was his decision to turn his back on God and live a sinful lifestyle (despite the fact that God had miraculously rescued him from the storm). Considering his physical condition, the man believed that he would die but was "unprepared to die." The man "requested [Newell] to pray for him." Consequently, they "joined in prayer" and felt that the spiritual "water of life flowed [and that] his disease was rebuked" in an act of divine healing. Newell also testified that soon after this experience, the man "raised up" and declared to people "what great [a] thing the Lord had done for his soul."[254]

Garrettson described an incident with "two of [his] friends" who, through his ministry, had reportedly experienced spiritual conviction but were struggling in their process of conversion, causing them to be "under deep distress" regarding their spiritual state. The men became "tempted of the devil" to believe that in order for them to become converted, they had to burn all of their valued possessions, including their money. When Garrettson heard this news, he was concerned and made his way to see his friends. Upon arriving, he discovered that one of them had incurred burns; he found him in bed with a doctor tending to him and applying "several blister-plasters" to his burns. First, Garrettson explained (through biblical passages) that conversion was a gift from God and only required the application of faith. Following this teaching and a prayer, Garrettson "sensibly felt that the Lord was present" and about "to heal." As such, Garrettson, believing that God had healed his friend, instructed him to "take his blister-plasters off." In accordance with Garrettson's faith, God had "restored [his friend] . . . in a natural" sense, and his skin was instantly healed. Additionally, Garrettson expressed that God poured out his Spirit and restored his friends in a "spiritual" sense, as well, as they experienced spiritual conversion. When people heard of this encounter, they began to gather there until they reached "about three hundred souls." Garrettson took advantage of this opportunity to preach, and "the Lord touched the hearts of many," causing a new Methodist "society" to be formed in the area.[255]

254. Newell, *Life and Observations*, 124–25.

255. Garrettson, *Experience and Travels*, 177–79.

Abbott recalled the divine healing of his wife. She "had been in a poor state of health for about seven years." Finally, she wholeheartedly "besought God to deliver her from her affliction of body, which she had so long [suffered] under." Abbott recorded that, as soon as this petition was made, "in a moment she was restored to as perfect health as she had ever enjoyed, and continued so until the day of her death."[256]

When Asbury was preaching "at Mr. R.'s, and at Mr. L.'s" congregation, he was "informed that Mrs. P. was dangerously ill." Upon hearing this news, Asbury immediately "rode about twenty miles to see her." While this is not recorded, knowing that Asbury practiced a lifestyle of methodical prayer, it can be assumed that he was likely praying for a divine intervention for Mrs. P. while he made his way to her home. When he "arrived at the house about nine o'clock," Asbury witnessed a supernatural healing and "a miracle of saving grace" as the power of the Lord had made Mrs. P well and "happy in the love of God." After witnessing this supernatural act, Asbury declared that "the power and the glory of this and of every other good work, belong[ed] unto the Lord."[257]

Also, while Asbury was once "returning after preaching," he found Brother Bailey "with all the symptoms of a severe bilious attack, and like a dead man in appearance." Apparently, Brother Bailey passed the first "night in great distress." However, after much "prayer . . . [was] made for him," Asbury acknowledged that, "through [God's] mercy," much of his "fit went off."[258]

Young, who recorded many personal struggles with sicknesses and pains, also often prayed for others to receive miraculous healings. For instance, Young recalled the story of a man who was "dangerously ill." After much prayer, "in the morning the sick man was better."[259]

Some of the circuit riders became famous for their supernatural phenomena. As such, even though members of the public or "neighbors" often mocked Methodists because of their experiential religion, when they were "sick," these neighbors "began to send for" the Methodist preachers, such as Abbott, "to pray with and for them [for divine healing]." After

---

256. Abbott, *Life and Labours*, 91.

257. Asbury, *Journal of the Rev. Francis Asbury*, 1:218.

258. Asbury, *Journal of the Rev. Francis Asbury*, 1:218, 312.

259. Young, *Autobiography of a Pioneer*, 101–2, 279.

many of them recovered, they often felt "ashamed" for previously having "laughed" at Methodist spirituality.[260]

To summarize this section, it can be concluded that the circuit riders believed in, practiced, and witnessed supernatural healings both in body and soul. It appears that divine healings occurred because of God's compassion combined with the faith of those who were praying to encounter or receive divine healing. Divine healings were vital to the lives and ministries of the circuit riders, especially as they caused people to draw closer to God by experiencing and witnessing God's power, love, and care for those who were hurting.[261]

The Phenomena of Raising the Dead

The circuit riders also recorded stories featuring the supernatural act of raising people from the dead. These were intense incidents that required extraordinary faith, with constant crying "···~· the Lord with all [one's] heart"[262] and petitioning "as if speaking to God face to face."[263] Despite the fact that raising the dead was seen as an impossible act by the public, the circuit riders declared that there was nothing impossible or irreversible for God—not even natural death itself.

No circuit rider presented this matter in as much detail as Hibbard; he demonstrated that the seemingly impossible act of raising an individual from the dead could, indeed, be successful through persistent prayer and unwavering trust in God's power. In one of his testimonies, Hibbard recorded two supernatural events that occurred at the same time: one of a person who was raised from the dead (Rachel) and another of a person who was divinely healed (Brother W.). Hibbard went to visit and attend a prayer meeting at the house of Sister W. whose husband, Brother W., "lay sick with the lake-fever." Her sister, Rachel, was present, as well. While Hibbard was praying for unbelievers, a heavy storm came about, at which point he prayed three times the same prayer: "O Lord, thunder conviction to the sinner's heart." After each of these prayers, he witnessed that

260. Abbott and Ffirth, *Experience and Gospel Labours*, 25.

261. Gatch, *Sketch of Rev. Philip Gatch*, 13; Asbury, *Journal of the Rev. Francis Asbury*, 3:192.

262. Hibbard, *Memoirs*, 163. See also Garrettson, *Experience and Travels*, 19–21; Asbury, *Journal of the Rev. Francis Asbury*, 2:112.

263. Young, *Autobiography of a Pioneer*, 317–18.

in an "instant the lightning, like a sheet of fire, flashed, and an awful clap of thunder shook the house." Immediately afterward, Hibbard found that "the two sisters [Sister W. and Rachel] lay as dead upon the floor." On the other hand, Brother W. "was getting out of bed." Suddenly, Brother W. exclaimed: "Don't be frightened, this is the power of God; glory to God, I am healed." Hence, Brother W. was miraculously healed. However, while Sister W. immediately rose from the floor, Rachel did not get up. They checked her pulse "but found she had none." Hibbard "perceived" that Rachel had "no symptoms of life, her eyes and jaws were set, and her head, neck, and arms, were cold." She lay down for hours. Sister W. "said mournfully, 'She is dead.'" Hibbard would not accept this; instead, despite her complete lack of pulse, he declared in faith that Rachel was not dead. Hibbard vehemently prayed to "the Lord" to raise her up. However, it seems that these attempts "failed. Sister W. [again] said, 'It is in vain, she is dead.'" Again, Hibbard chose not to believe these facts and did not let them discourage him. He said to Sister W., "Don't say so, but rub away, and pray to the Lord." They continued rubbing, inflated the lungs, and prayed for another two hours until, finally, Rachel "gave the first symptom of returning life." It appears that Rachel was not happy that she was brought back to life because she complained: "O why have I come back again?" Soon after this, Hibbard "ordered her [to] drink" and rejoiced that "Rachel was alive" and even saw that she "was happy." Hence, Hibbard's persistent faith was rewarded by God with both a divine healing and a resurrection from the dead.[264]

Garrettson recalled a testimony of his brother (by birth) John who was raised from the dead, as well. John was "dangerously ill," and many of

---

264. Hibbard, *Memoirs*, 161–64. This testimony resembles one of Jesus's testimonies as described in Luke 8:41–42, 49–56, which states: "And there came a man named Jairus, who was a ruler of the synagogue. And falling at Jesus' feet, he implored him to come to his house, for he had an only daughter, about twelve years of age, and she was dying. As Jesus went, the people pressed around him. . . . While he was still speaking, someone from the ruler's house came and said, 'Your daughter is dead; do not trouble the Teacher anymore.' But Jesus on hearing this answered him, 'Do not fear; only believe, and she will be well.' And when he came to the house, he allowed no one to enter with him, except Peter and John and James, and the father and mother of the child. And all were weeping and mourning for her, but he said, 'Do not weep, for she is not dead but sleeping.' And they laughed at him, knowing that she was dead. [However, Jesus was determined to not accept the reality that the girl was dead, thus] taking her by the hand he called, saying, 'Child, arise.' And her spirit returned, and she got up at once. And he directed that something should be given her to eat. And her parents were amazed, but he charged them to tell no one what had happened."

his "relations and friends came to see him expecting every minute that he would breathe his last." At one point, Garrettson feared for his brother's "soul, which seemed to be just launching into eternity," suspecting that it was unprepared. It seems that his brother's soul left his body and "was summoned to appear in the world of spirits, and that hell was his doom." Troubled by all of this, Garrettson clung to his faith, believing that God would raise his brother from the dead; hence, he began to pray intensely for his brother's soul. After he was "done praying," the Lord gave John the power to move "his lips." The words that came out of his mouth were a plea for God to "have mercy on [him] and raise [him] up, and give [him] a longer space, and [he would] serve [God]." After further prayers, "the Lord answered [them], and granted him a longer space." Garrettson "immediately rose from [his] knees, and told the waiting company they need not be uneasy, for the Lord would raise him again." Later, Garrettson testified that his brother "was able to walk about his room . . . and [received] . . . his recovery." A few years after these experiences, Garrettson recognized that his brother "was really changed in heart, he lived two years and eight months happy in the service of God, and died a witness of perfect love."[265]

Asbury personally interviewed Dorcas Brown and recorded the testimony of her son. The boy "had been captured by the Indians, and was returned killed." However, "in contradiction to this account, and the general belief" of the population, Asbury recorded that Dorcas was determined in her heart to pronounce in faith "that she should again see him [alive and] in the flesh . . . contrary to the expectation of all but herself." She remained in the spirit of prayer and of this expectation for "three years and eight months." After the eighth month passed, Asbury recorded that her prayers and perseverance payed off: her son was raised from the dead and "return[ed]" to her in the flesh. Asbury recalled this miracle as one of the most marvelous "experience[s] . . . [of the] manifestations of the power of God, and of the interposition of his providence in answer to prayer."[266]

265. Garrettson, *Experience and Travels*, 19–22.

266. Asbury, *Journal of the Rev. Francis Asbury*, 2:112.

The Phenomena of Divine
and Extraordinary Weather Shifts

The circuit riders recalled stories wherein, during some of their evangelistic meetings, the weather conditions became harsh; in faith, they prayed to God that the weather conditions would shift. Indeed, according to their faith, they witnessed divine weather changes. This was yet another supernatural phenomenon that, it seems, required a great amount of faith in the impossible. Thus, similar to exorcisms, healings, and the raising of the dead, in order for weather changes to occur, the circuit riders petitioned God (via prayer) to divinely alter the situation.

The circuit riders believed that God valued the conversion of souls above all else and, therefore, was willing to divinely stop the "water[ing of] the earth"[267] or a hurricane in order to bring about conversions.[268] Hence, if weather conditions were threatening an event that was designed to convert souls, then the circuit riders, in an attempt to align with God's will, had a great amount of boldness and faith in petitioning God (through prayer) to divinely intervene and alter the weather conditions so that God's will could be done.[269]

This is best illustrated in the ministry of circuit rider Easter (which was recorded by M'Kendree, an eye-witness, and described in Atkinson's writings, as well).[270] Easter was a man known to possess "a powerful, conquering faith"[271] that was considered "far more surprising than any recorded of those days of the Son of Man."[272] His ministry was known for its frequent supernatural encounters since he and his audiences often experienced visitations "of the displays of divine power."[273] At one of Easter's

267. Paine, *Life and Times,* 1:54–57. See also Wakeley and Boehm, *Patriarch of One Hundred Years,* 159.

268. Lockwood, *Western Pioneers,* 170. These types of supernatural events are recorded in the Bible, as well. For instance, in his ministry, Jesus once commanded the strong winds to cease. Mark 4:39 states: "He [Jesus] got up, rebuked the wind and said to the waves, 'Quiet! Be still!' Then the wind died down and it was completely calm." For more information on divine weather shifts, see 1 Kgs 18:41–19:8; Ps 107:28–31.

269. Wakeley and Boehm, *Patriarch of One Hundred Years,* 159.

270. For more information regarding Easter and divine weather shifts, see Paine, *Life and Times,* 1:55–56; Atkinson, *Centennial History of American Methodism,* 224–225.

271. Atkinson, *Centennial History of American Methodism,* 224.

272. Lee, *Life and Times,* 205.

273. Paine, *Life and Times,* 1:57.

large open-air meetings, during "a time of considerable drought, it began to thunder, and drops of rain fell." Seeing this, Easter prayed to the Lord to stop the rain and assured people that they "might keep [their] seats . . . [stating in faith] that it would not rain to wet [them]."[274] Easter was fully confident that the Lord would "withhold the rain until evening— [and instead] pour out his Spirit [and] convert the people." Despite these confident assurances and prayers, "the appearance of rain increased—the people began to get uneasy—some moved to take off their saddles." Easter further prayed to the Lord, believing that there were "sinners there that must be converted or be damned," so he petitioned with urgency that God might "stop the bottles of heaven until the evening."[275] After this demonstration of intense faith through prayer, the clouds began to part, and there was "a fine rain on both sides of [the people but] there was none where [they] were until night." In this evangelistic meeting, instead of witnessing the rain being poured out, as everyone expected, the unimaginable happened, which is what Easter expected and prayed for: a divine shift in weather conditions so that the meeting could continue. Moreover, in this meeting, "the Lord's Spirit was poured out in an uncommon degree, [wherein] many were convicted . . . [on] that day."[276]

In the same manner, Boehm recorded a testimony of a supernatural weather change performed through faith and prayer by circuit rider Dr. Chandler.[277] This event occurred in a meeting as "a dark, thick cloud gathered," followed by a strong "prospect of a tremendous shower." When people witnessed these weather conditions, they "showed symptoms of alarm, and began to disperse." However, confident that God would divinely alter the weather conditions and make it possible for the meeting to proceed so that people could receive conversion, Chandler "requested [people] to be seated." Then, he "prayed that God would fold up the clouds, and that the rain might not descend upon the encampment." Immediately after this prayer, "the clouds parted when right over the camp, and it rained on either side, but no sprinkling on the camp ground." Boehm "was an eye-witness" of this event and testified that "this

---

274. Atkinson, *Centennial History of American Methodism*, 224.

275. Paine, *Life and Times*, 1:55.

276. Atkinson, *Centennial History of American Methodism*, 225.

277. See also Mariner, "William Penn Chandler," 135–40.

rough expression [demonstrated God's] power," especially since it came in combination with determined faith.[278]

Circuit riders also encountered life-threatening weather conditions that, after faith prayers, ended in God supernaturally saving lives without the incurring of any injuries. For instance, at one point during a great hurricane in North Carolina, Pilmore testified that the Lord supernaturally spared his life and that "not a hair of [his] head ha[d] been injured."[279]

Concluding Comments

This chapter was dedicated to the detailed analysis of public supernaturalism in the circuit rider ministry. Specifically, this chapter focused on investigating the source(s) of supernatural phenomena and researched the nature and role of some of the most common phenomena experienced within the ministry. It was demonstrated that, in the circuit rider ministry, the outpouring of the Spirit birthed various supernatural acts. Furthermore, as demonstrated in this chapter and confirmed by Asbury, because there were such frequent and "very uncommon circumstances [or occurrences] of a supernatural kind," it is evident that the supernatural was a regular part of the circuit rider ministry.[280] Even some newspapers of the day, such as *The National Gazette*, publicly acknowledged this by reporting that Methodist ministers operated in a "supernatural" realm, which sparked conversion experiences in many individuals, such as Maffitt who witnessed a descending "light from heaven" through which he "distinguished his Savior" and later became a circuit rider.[281]

There were times in the circuit rider ministry when the Spirit of God visibly appeared in supernatural forms. These appearances, although spiritual in nature, were often identified as resembling natural or physical phenomena, such as: fire, wind, cloud, energy/force, electric shock, radiant light, and rain. Whether the Spirit's appearances were visible or not, when the Spirit was poured out, various other phenomena were also produced. Some of the most common phenomena experienced in the

278. Wakeley and Boehm, *Patriarch of One Hundred Years*, 158–59.

279. Pilmore, *Journal of Joseph Pilmore*, 190. See also Lockwood, *Western Pioneers*, 170.

280. Asbury, *Journal of the Rev. Francis Asbury*, 2:58.

281. Maffit, "Life of John N. Maffit," 1.

circuit rider ministry (derived from God's Spirit) were reportedly the acts of being slain in the Spirit, various enthusiastic emotional expressions, divine dreams and visions and trances, spiritual warfare, healings, the raising of the dead, and divine weather shifts.

It was also demonstrated that many phenomena, such as the visible appearances of the Spirit, being slain in the Spirit, various emotional expressions (such as the jerks), and dreams, visions, and trances, generally were received involuntarily and were caused by a direct touch of the Spirit's power and presence. Other phenomena (i.e., spiritual warfare, miraculous healings, the raising of the dead, and divine weather shifts) were also performed by the power and presence of God but were in co-operation with personal faith and petition via prayer.

Each investigated supernatural manifestation was orchestrated for a divine purpose: principally, to cause empirical demonstration of the existence of God and, ultimately, to make it possible for people to experience conversion through the work of the circuit riders. For instance, when the power of God was poured out, causing people to be involuntarily slain in the Spirit, they rose from this state and experienced conversion. Thus, in general, the significance of all of the above phenomena, such as the raising of the dead or the changing of weather conditions, was that it gave an opportunity for all gathered to not only be convinced and believe but also to personally experience God and receive conversion, therein becoming children of God. Additionally, these phenomena many times served as a means of spiritually refreshing, empowering, and encouraging those who were already converted (such as those who belonged to Methodist societies).

Moreover, people began to view the circuit riders with awe because what they preached, they also frequently demonstrated via visible acts; through them, people were slain in the Spirit, healed emotionally and physically, delivered from demonic oppression, and raised from the dead, among other extraordinary things. Therefore, they exhibited preaching with direct "demonstration of the power of God."[282]

282. Finley, *Autobiography*, 232. See also Peck, *Early Methodism*, 465; Maffitt, *Memorial of Philip Embury*, 35; Asbury, *Journal of the Rev. Francis Asbury*, 1:161; Asbury, *Journal of the Rev. Francis Asbury*, 3:114; Lee, *Memoir*, 86; Finley, *Autobiography*, 239; *Sketches of Western Methodism*, 26; Giles, *Pioneer*, 302; Paine, *Life and Times*, 1:92; Smith and Dailey, *Experience and Ministerial Labors*, 77; Cartwright, *Backwoods Preacher*, 9, 104; Watters, *Short Account of the Christian Experience*, 126; O'Byrne, "How Methodists Were Made," 239; Abbott and Ffirth, *Experience and Gospel Labours*, 67.

Consequently, the supernatural, aside from filling the circuit riders "afresh with the Holy Ghost and fire," became an effective instrument in engaging the public.[283] As noted in chapter 4, because Americans were partial to pragmatism, supernatural experience became a religious form through which members of the public thrived. Manifestations made Methodism very attractive among Americans; especially because of these manifestations, people experienced conversions as the gospel was spiritually transmitted into "hearts . . . with power."[284] Also, while the circuit riders were responsible for preaching (and preparing) their sermons, they acknowledged that the supernatural was the component that made their sermons influential to the public. In other words, the supernatural in the circuit rider ministry was a "resistless influence"[285] that enabled the public to be immediately "filled with faith and the Holy Ghost."[286]

Additionally, as further delineated in chapter 7 of this study, it appears that the more bizarre the supernatural displays, the easier the conversions. Also, the more massive the outpourings of the Spirit, the more numerous the conversions. Hence, the supernatural made the work of the circuit riders easier and more extensive in that, when it appeared, the circuit riders generally did not need to convince people of the truth of the gospel as the displays greatly contributed to their work of convicting and converting.[287]

The circuit rider ministry was "successful" because it introduced the Early Republic to an intimate Christianity, one in which the "agency of the Divine Spirit of God" was personal and relational.[288] This God was not passive and did not perform signs and wonders only in the past; instead, he was active and continued in his signs and wonders. In addition, the God of the circuit riders was willing to live, through his Spirit, inside of believers and daily interact in all areas of their lives.

In other words, the early Methodists, through "supernatural powers," introduced a Christianity that resembled an intimate relationship

283. Marsden, "Of the Methodist Doctrines," 211.

284. Stevens, *History of the Methodist Episcopal Church*, 1:389.

285. Prentice and Fisk, *Wilbur Fisk*, 123.

286. Abbott and Ffirth, *Experience and Gospel Labours*, 209.

287. For more information regarding the correlation between the supernatural and Methodist revivals, please see chapter 7.

288. Cartwright, *Backwoods Preacher*, 118.

between a father and a child.[289] More specifically, it resembled the biblical relationship between God (the Father) and Jesus (the Son). Jesus performed a ministry that featured continuous loving fellowship with God; Jesus spoke to God, and God spoke back to Jesus. Circuit riders imitated this kind of relationship in their ministry wherein they spoke to God, and God supernaturally spoke back to them. Furthermore, the circuit riders demonstrated that this same relationship with God was available to their audiences. In doing so, Methodists revolutionized the idea of a personal God who could be tangibly experienced through supernatural acts as in the early church.[290] This form of intimate Christianity, experienced through "the unction or baptismal fire of the Holy Ghost," became so striking and desirable to people that it caused Methodism to further grow.[291] In fact, as further discussed in chapter 7, the promotion of relational and experiential Christianity was an instrumental tool in America encountering the Second Great Awakening.

Moreover, while perhaps, up until this point, supernatural acts were something new to eighteenth and nineteenth-century America, they were long-established within the history of Christianity. These acts flowed from the same God, and so the circuit riders, who were performing these phenomena in "power," encountered incidents that paralleled biblical accounts (especially those present in the books of Exodus and Acts) and the early Christian church.[292] Because their ministry resembled biblical accounts, especially accounts of the first apostles, manifestations in the circuit rider ministry were largely considered to be scripturally supported. Thus, the circuit riders made it possible for America to experience the same God, with the same supernatural acts, of biblical times; consequently, biblical supernaturalism was reactivated.

The ministry of the circuit riders can also be compared, in addition to the ministries of Jesus and the early apostles, to the ministry of Moses. In the Old Testament, Moses served as an intermediary between God and Israel; during this time, Israel witnessed numerous supernatural manifestations.[293] In the same way, the circuit riders, who (like Moses)

289. Garrettson, "Account of the Revival," 307.

290. For more information regarding supernatural activity in the early church, see Middleton, *New Edition of a Free Inquiry*, 6–178.

291. Cartwright, *Backwoods Preacher*, 118.

292. Stevens, *History of the Methodist Episcopal Church*, 1:389.

293. For more information regarding supernatural phenomena and the ministry of Moses, see the book of Exodus, especially chapters 3–11; 16–17; 19–20; 33–34.

were "full of love and [beamed] radiant with glory" from God's Spirit, became intermediaries of the power of the gospel and of many diverse supernatural manifestations.[294] Also, as Israel looked to Moses for guidance and deliverance, so the circuit riders became the public's Moses from whom they expected and received their guidance and deliverance.

294. Finley, *Sketches of Western Methodism*, 150.

Chapter 6

Religious Enthusiasm: Criticism and Controversy

WHILE THE TERM *RELIGIOUS* enthusiasm (and the controversy surrounding it) in Wesley's ministry was examined in chapter 2, and the
description of common religious enthusiastic displays in the circuit rider
ministry was discussed in chapter 5, criticism by the American public
and the circuit riders' views (and defenses) regarding religious enthusiasm's controversial nature have not yet been examined. Thus, in order to
better understand the function of the supernatural within the American
circuit rider ministry, these varied perspectives are examined in detail
within this chapter.[1]

Similar to the situation with Wesley in England, due to the many
"strange" and uncommon supernatural manifestations that occurred in
America, early Methodism was, at times, severely criticized by the public
and, in a derogatory way, labeled religiously "enthusiastic."[2] The majority
of criticism was in response to the various wild emotional expressions
(such as physical jerking, barking, roaring, shrieking, and dancing) and,

1. For more information regarding the meaning of *religious enthusiasm* in the
eighteenth and nineteenth centuries, see chapter 2.

2. Watters, *Short Account of the Christian Experience*, 16. Similarly, the Bible
indicates that the public, especially the religious leaders of the day, accused Jesus by
attributing the source of his supernatural acts to the devil. For instance, in Matthew
12:24, the religious leaders said of Jesus that "it is only by Beelzebub, the prince of
demons, that this man casts out demons." At one point, even Jesus's mother and
siblings accused him of being insane, as described in Mark 3:21: "When his family
heard about this, they went to take charge of him, for they said, 'He is out of his mind.'"

to a lesser degree, dreams, visions, and trances along with prophecies and being slain in the Spirit.[3] Furthermore, while the majority of the circuit riders were actively supportive of religious enthusiasm, a small number of circuit riders were uncomfortable with the "wild" enthusiastic displays present within specific meetings.[4] In brief, this chapter is separated into three major sections: the criticism from the American public toward Methodist religious enthusiasm, the general circuit rider support and defense of religious enthusiastic experiences, and the uneasiness and disapproval of a small number of circuit riders who considered aspects of religious enthusiasm to be too controversial.

Brief Description of Enthusiastic Experiences and Spiritual Ecstasy

To begin, in considering those who exhibited religious enthusiasm or emotional expressions (as also described in chapter 5), when these individuals experienced supernatural encounters or spiritual ecstasies, it seems that they, in varying degrees, lost control of their bodies, which led to socially indecent "enthusiastic" displays.[5] Others experienced the intensity of the gospel through various feelings, such as joy, which made them cry, clap their hands, shout, and even dance.[6] Hence, one can argue that these spiritual experiences were so profound in people that they surpassed the need for maintaining a sense of propriety.[7] It appears that those who experienced them suddenly became like little children, dismissing ordinary social norms and enjoying their spiritual experiences (especially in conversions) that produced freedom in a form of spiritual ecstasy.[8]

This Christian spiritual ecstasy was traditionally compared to wine.[9] The apostle Paul noted this relationship in Ephesians 5:18–19: "And do

3. For more information regarding the criticism of religious enthusiasm, see Trapp, "Nature, Folly, Sin, and Danger," 39–40; Cartwright, *Backwoods Preacher*, 21–22.

4. Wigger, *American Saint*, 83.

5. Cartwright and Hooper, *Fifty Years as a Presiding Elder*, 85; Finley, *Sketches of Western Methodism*, 26.

6. Lee, *Memoir*, 94; Abbott and Ffirth, *Experience and Gospel Labours*, 195, 209.

7. Cartwright, *Backwoods Preacher*, 231.

8. See also Finley, *Sketches of Western Methodism*, 26.

9. MacDonald, *Colossians and Ephesians*, 318.

not get drunk with wine, for that is debauchery, but be filled with the Spirit, addressing one another in psalms and hymns and spiritual songs, singing and making melody to the Lord with your heart."[10] In the book of Acts, when the first apostles were enthusiastically filled with the power of the Spirit on the Day of Pentecost, the public around them observed their enthusiastic expressions and declared that the apostles were drunk with wine when, in fact, they were in their "spiritual ecstasy"; following this, those who did not experience or understand the supernatural source of these enthusiastic expressions mocked and criticized the religious enthusiasm of the first apostles.[11] It seems that, in a similar fashion, people mocked and accused the circuit rider ministry.[12] However, according to the first apostles and the circuit riders (along with most of their audience members), both groups were simply filled with the supernatural phenomenon of spiritual ecstasy. Indeed, Finley replied to those who accused him of being drunk with wine (and crazy) by saying that, like the first apostles, he was simply "filled with the Spirit."[13]

Public Criticism of Religious Enthusiasm in the Circuit Rider Ministry

Clearly, the circuit riders faced tension from the public as a result of the enthusiastic expressions displayed in their meetings. This is unsurprising. To put this in perspective, many members of the public decided to attend these meetings (for a number of personal reasons); in doing so, they typically beheld, before their eyes, a visible and mysterious spiritual power and presence manifested as burning fire[14] or mist[15] covering the entire meeting, followed by hundreds of people falling down (as if shot in battle)[16] along with some crying loudly and others shouting praises[17]

10. See also Rech, *Wine and Bread*, 58–59.

11. Ramsay, *Westminster Guide to the Books of the Bible*, 375. For more information regarding the Day of Pentecost, see Robertson, *Conversations with Scripture*, 18–23.

12. See also Atkinson, *Centennial History of American Methodism*, 237.

13. Finley, *Autobiography*, 180.

14. Asbury, *Journal of the Rev. Francis Asbury*, 2:356.

15. Jackson, *Lives of Early Methodist Preachers*, 5:191.

16. Hibbard, *Memoirs*, 161; Finley, *Autobiography*, 167; Cartwright, *Backwoods Preacher*, 9; Hyde, *Story of Methodism*, 160; Atkinson, *Centennial History of American Methodism*, 219–20.

17. Wakeley and Boehm, *Patriarch of One Hundred Years*, 46–47. See also Cooper,

and proclaiming healings[18] and prophetic dreams and visions[19] at the top of their lungs while others danced,[20] jerked (as if touched by an electric shock),[21] barked like dogs or "hallooed [howled]" like wolves,[22] "roar[ed]" like lions, and "scream[ed]" loudly.[23] Thus, overall, the natural reaction of the Early American Republic was to experience thoughts and feelings of wonder and/or shock. According to the circuit riders, a typical visitor responded to these displays by bowing down and declaring that these supernatural acts were, indeed, of God; this was followed by repentance and conversion.[24]

However, the circuit riders also recorded responses of those who witnessed these phenomena and reacted with insults and accusations, though this appears to be less typical.[25] For instance, Cartwright observed this reaction during one of his circuit rider meetings wherein "the power of God [was poured out and] arrested many careless sinners, and waked up many old formal professors of religion." Many in this meeting were converted by the display of the power of God. Conversely, in this same meeting, there was a company "who came to look on and mock; and so ignorant were they."[26] In other words, there were those who were converted, and in the same meeting, there were also those who witnessed the power of God but criticized circuit riders because of their "insane"[27] enthusiasm or their "'Methodist fits,' as they called the [enthusiastic] exercises that were going on."[28]

Beams of Light, 87; Travis, *Autobiography*, 24.

18. Gatch, *Sketch of Rev. Philip Gatch*, 13. See also Asbury, *Journal of the Rev. Francis Asbury*, 3:179.

19. Jackson, *Lives of Early Methodist Preachers*, 6:166. Within the biblical text, dreams and visions were common occurrences. For more information, see Gen 15:1; 1 Sam 28:6; Judg 7:12–15; 1 Kgs 3:5; Dan 2–3; Matt 1:20; Acts 9:10; 10:9–15; 18:9–11.

20. Paine, *Life and Times*, 1:153.

21. Stone, *Biography*, 40.

22. Horton, *Narrative of the Early Life*, 25–26; Sandford, *Memoirs*, 371.

23. Lee and Lee, *Short Account*, 22.

24. Abbott and Ffirth, *Experience and Gospel Labours*, 96. See also Cooper, *Beams of Light*, 87.

25. Atkinson, *Centennial History of American Methodism*, 237.

26. Cartwright, *Backwoods Preacher*, 231.

27. Lyles, *Methodism Mocked*, 35–37.

28. Cartwright, *Backwoods Preacher*, 231.

Atkinson described the critics of enthusiasm as individuals who were "violently offended" and stated that some "were wicked enough" to call these acts "the work of the devil—madness, disorder, and delusion."[29] Others labeled Methodist religious enthusiasm as enchanted, witchcraft, or having derived from the demonic realm.[30] This criticism of the ministry's spirituality caused some to step back and disassociate themselves from it.

Cooper expressed that "a general query passed to and from among the citizens" regarding religious enthusiasm in early Methodism. It seems that the public was mostly concerned about the emotional outbursts in Methodist meetings because they "were very noisy, with penitential cries and shouts of praise." Also, since the critics, admittedly, had not personally experienced supernatural religious expressions, they could not comprehend them, and consequently, "many could not bear this, but reprobated it as insufferable madness in places of worship."[31] Moreover, the circuit riders, such as Abbott, believed that just as "the miracle of speaking with tongues, at the day of Pentecost" was "explained away by infidels," so these supernatural phenomena experienced in the circuit rider ministry were being explained away through the criticism of those who had not experienced them.[32]

For example, even during the earliest days of Methodist presence in America, there were newspapers, such as the *Virginia Gazette*, that criticized Methodists harshly for their religious enthusiasm and dismissed their spirituality.[33] The Vermont newspaper *Universalist Watchman* labeled the Methodists as "religious fanatics" who were operating under their "enthusiastic imagination."[34] The *N. Carolina Chronicle* published an article that painted Methodist enthusiasm in a negative light, particularly in regard to Dow whom the paper referred to as an "imposter."[35]

29. Atkinson, *Centennial History of American Methodism*, 237.

30. Abbott and Ffirth, *Experience and Gospel Labours*, 109–10, 122.

31. Cooper, *Beams of Light*, 87.

32. Abbott, *Life and Labours*, 180.

33. "Williamsburg," 2. See also Wigger, *American Saint*, 154; Cooper, *Beams of Light*, 87; Richey et al., *American Methodism*, 42; Turner, "Revivalism and Preaching," 128–30; Urban, *Gentleman's Magazine and Historical Chronicle*, 335.

34. Tinker, "Drama of Life," 4.

35. "Friday, June 1," 3. However, in other places in North Carolina and Mississippi, Dow was welcomed, and his visits were announced in newspapers. For more information, see "Dow's Preaching Appointments," 3; "Lorenzo Dow Will Deliver a Sermon," 3.

As discussed in chapter 2, criticism of religious enthusiasm was influenced and reinforced by Enlightenment thinking.[36] Such thinking considered enthusiastic phenomena to be a product of irrational behavior and emotional instability or disorder.[37] According to the psychological perspectives of those days, religious enthusiastic experiences (which were especially prevalent in revivals) were viewed, "in the name of science," as "hysterical" disorders, "convulsive seizures," or "abnormal manifestations of emotional" communication that stemmed from some form of "mental malady" and, as such, were considered to be in no way divine.[38]

However, while the enlightened approach and psychological perspectives validated and empowered public criticism, what seems to have puzzled the public was the fact that those who attended circuit rider meetings and, consequently, experienced and participated in religious enthusiastic expressions were reportedly sound of mind prior to attending the meetings. Therefore, it appeared to the public that something extraordinary had seized the participants, causing them to exhibit a variety of enthusiastic expressions.[39]

Furthermore, these kinds of emotional enthusiastic expressions were rarely experienced within other mainline denominations, likely because, as Noll noted, "religious thinkers gradually accommodated theology to the demands of science, reason, and law."[40] Unfortunately, this further puzzled the public. As aforementioned, the majority of the American public at that time was familiar or affiliated with such denominations; they were aware that typical church services in those days practiced preaching and worship in a structured, premediated fashion that was compatible with social norms and behaviors. Yelling, shouting, crying, jerking, and barking were not present in their services.[41] Hence, not only were these critics unaccustomed to experiencing religion through any of these expressions, they also had never been encouraged to experience such things in their religious settings and, in many cases, they had never

36. Giles, *Pioneer*, 19–23. See also Hempton, *Methodism*, 32–54.

37. Winslow, *Journal of Psychological Medicine*, 12:xlvii–xlix; Lyerly, *Methodism and the Southern Mind*, 147.

38. Winslow, *Journal of Psychological Medicine*, 12:xlvii–xlix.

39. For instance, see Finley, *Autobiography*, 167.

40. Noll, "Irony of the Enlightenment," 150.

41. See Peck, *Early Methodism*, 200; Chase, *Recollections of the Past*, 100–101; Goodrich, *Recollections of a Lifetime*, 311; Bangs and Garrettson, *Life of the Rev. Freeborn Garrettson*, 228–29; Garrettson, *Letter to the Rev. L. Beecher*, 8.

even previously heard of these expressions.[42] With this in mind, public criticism of religious enthusiasm (in addition to stemming from spiritual inexperience) can also be seen as a product of theological confusion.

Circuit Rider Responses to Public Criticism

The responses of the circuit riders to criticism varied; generally, they either responded by logically defending Methodist religious enthusiasm, or they responded by praying that their critics would personally experience these phenomena themselves and become witnesses to the fact that religious enthusiasm was inspired by God.

Logically Defending Methodist Religious Enthusiasm

Cartwright defended Methodist enthusiasm by saying that if sinners, who were being saved, reflected their conversion experiences through forms of religious enthusiasm, then this was acceptable as "the Almighty chooses" these various acts, including enthusiastic displays, for "the further manifestation of His work." In other words, the reason that God employs these means is because he wants "His power to be known," and so he "awakens the attention of a drowsy world."[43]

Dow viewed the critics of religious enthusiasm as "awful [and] delusive" because they hindered people from personally experiencing the power of religion. He insisted that, in rejecting the gospel's enthusiastic component, these critics (who were often leaders of other denominations) had "taken the shell for the kernel" and led the church toward becoming a social "union [that is only a] form of ceremony [and] is not religion." According to Dow, Christianity consisted of experiencing a "union of heart in the Spirit of the gospel of Christ," which, at times, resulted in enthusiastic displays.[44]

Bangs acknowledged that there were meetings in which "some disorder" occurred as, within these meetings, there were instances of "words and gesticulations not in accordance with strict religious decorum." However, Bangs defended these enthusiastic instances, claiming that they were in accordance with "the book of God" and that they were

---

42. Cartwright, *Backwoods Preacher*, 38, 121–22.

43. Cartwright, *ackwoods Preacher*, 315.

44. Dow, *History of Cosmopolite*, 323–25.

also common in the "church at different periods." He further stated that when the human "mind and body" was supernaturally touched by sensations "unknown to sensual minds," it was normal for these sensations to elicit "sudden flashes" of enthusiastic expression. At the same time, Bangs assured critics that the individuals experiencing these phenomena were reportedly living "peaceable lives, in all godliness and honesty."[45]

Cooper argued that the main reason why early Methodists allowed (and encouraged) these religious expressions was because these phenomena were produced as a result of God working in an "extraordinary manner" since spiritual "power [was] attending" the circuit rider ministry. Cooper further argued that it was not the noise from enthusiastic expressions that produced the supernatural effects; conversely, it was the supernatural "effects of the power which produced" the enthusiastic noise. These various religious expressions were "principally the effect of God's power among the people." While, to the critics, they likely appeared as madness, to those who were experiencing these phenomena, they were considered "a great blessing." Cooper delighted in the exhibits of religious enthusiasm because they were not "for evil doing" but, rather, "for righteousness' sake." Cooper felt that if the circuit riders suffered because of them, they should "be glad with exceeding joy" as they originated from God. Moreover, Cooper was "awfully" afraid that many would "lose their souls" by rejecting religious enthusiasm out of fear of "reproach" or for a "good name among men."[46]

As noted above, the circuit riders also understood that the reason why people labeled these supernatural phenomena using the derogatory term *religious enthusiasm* was because their critics "ha[d] not experienced anything of the sort."[47] Cooper referred to those who criticized the circuit rider ministry's religious enthusiasm as "poor creatures" because "they knew not what they said," as they knew anything about the real "power of God." Consequently, if these people were not operating through the Spirit of God, then Cooper questioned "what manner of spirit [they] were of."[48]

Finley asserted that those who criticized Methodist "enthusiasm ought to tell what they understand by the spirit of Christianity." He declared it was evident that the enthusiastic move of the Spirit in

45. Bangs, *History of the Methodist Episcopal Church*, 4:113–17.
46. Cooper, *Beams of Light*, 91.
47. Watters, *Short Account of the Christian Experience*, 16–17.
48. Cooper, *Beams of Light*, 87.

Methodist gatherings "was the most extraordinary that ever visited the Church of Christ." Furthermore, he argued that these enthusiastic gatherings were even "peculiarly adapted" to the needs of the country.[49] Watters justified Methodist enthusiasm with the argument that, during people's conversions, "the heavens" were opened over them, resulting in mass conversions, and those present were "happy, day and night, in God [their] Savior."[50] Thus, circuit riders believed that their critics were filled with "prejudice or obstinacy" that prevented them from acknowledging that these manifestations were "a display of God's glory and power among men" and that, as a result of them, many experienced spiritual conversion.[51]

In a particular incident, when Brother C. witnessed the nature of wild religious enthusiasm, he asked Abbott why he did not command those affected "to be silent." Abbott answered that this work was "the power of God." As such, he maintained that "if every cry was as loud as ever [he] had heard a clap of thunder, [he] would not forbid them."[52]

Moreover, it should be noted that the circuit riders became familiar with these enthusiastic phenomena because they often experienced them within their private lives; this resulted in the circuit riders remaining largely unaffected and unshaken by the criticism of religious enthusiasm.[53] Atkinson declared that these public opinions, in the end, did not deter the Methodists "from pursuing the best of causes—to wit, that of sinners' conversion to God."[54]

Finally, the circuit riders' advice regarding those who took offense to religious enthusiasm was that if individuals "could not be reconciled to these shoutings and powerful conversions, to let them alone, lest they should be found fighting against God." They held that if these enthusiastic expressions were "of man," then it would come to nothing, "but if of God, [one] could not overthrow it."[55] Therefore, they continued to logically

49. Finley, *Autobiography*, 368.

50. Watters, *Short Account of the Christian Experience*, 17.

51. Cooper, *Beams of Light*, 92.

52. Abbott and Ffirth, *Experience and Gospel Labours*, 82, 177, 201–2, 206.

53. Jackson, *Lives of Early Methodist Preachers*, 6:154; Watters, *Short Account of the Christian Experience*, 17; Abbott and Ffirth, *Experience and Gospel Labours*, 16–18, 87–90; Garrettson, *Experience and Travels*, 24–26; Lee, *Memoir*, 10; Finley, *Autobiography*, 232; Young, *Autobiography of a Pioneer*, 137.

54. Atkinson, *Centennial History of American Methodism*, 237.

55. Cooper, *Beams of Light*, 92.

and biblically defend, encourage, and welcome enthusiastic expressions because they were believed to be from God. For the circuit riders, the frequent conversions that followed these expressions served as proof of their divine origin.

Praying for Critics to Personally Experience These Phenomena

As noted above, in the circuit rider ministry, when words did not affect their critics, then the other main response from the circuit riders was to pray for the power and presence of God to touch the critics so that they might be personally exposed to supernatural phenomena and, thus, become convinced that religious enthusiasm was God's doing, as opposed to a human's or the devil's. There are numerous records of this form of response. For example, Methodist preacher Bennett observed that in "many instances the manifestations of Divine power struck terror into the hearts of [scoffers] who sought fun and frolic at the meetings";[56] hence, the following section is dedicated to presenting some of these accounts.

Abbott was known to rely on God's displays of power as a sort of verification that his message, along with its supernatural component, originated from God. At one point, Abbott was frequently followed by a Presbyterian opponent who accused his ministry of being from the devil. During one of his circuit rider meetings, the Presbyterian opponent was in attendance; when Abbott saw him, he prayed to God that if anyone were to be slain in the Spirit, it would be that man. Then, as Abbott was preaching, he "heard several cry-out, 'water water—the man is fainting!'" Abbott looked around and saw his "old opponent trembling like Belshaz-zar." As a result, the audience became anxious, but Abbott recommended that they leave the opponent "alone, and to look to themselves, for that it was the power of God that had arrested him." With this, the people let Abbott proceed, and "down [the man] fell on the floor, struggled a while, and then lay as one dead." When the meeting concluded, Abbott instructed some of his friends to move the man aside "as he was in [their] way," and they needed to attend a Methodist class meeting. After the class, Abbott went back to see his old opponent and asked him: "Is this the work of the devil, or not?" However, the man said "nothing to him."

56. Bennett, *Memorials of Methodism in Virginia*, 88.

Abbott was rhetorically implying that it was God who had done the work and not the devil.[57]

Abbott recorded additional stories in which the Lord displayed his power in such a manner that "many fell to the floor; their cries were very great." In witnessing these incidents, some "sprang to the doors and windows, and fell one over another in getting out." One woman in the meeting accused Abbott by saying, "You are a devil!" Others gathered around her and rebuked her by saying that this was the true work of God. Later, another woman accused Abbott, also claiming that his work was not from God; however, she was touched by the power of God and "fell to the floor, and cried out, 'Lord, have I called [your] servant an enchanter?'" After she personally experienced the supernatural, she proclaimed that these works were "of the Lord," and she continued to praise God as she lay on the floor. Again, it was God who was verifying that Abbott's sermons and the signs that followed him were, indeed, divine.[58]

Travis recalled an unusual story of a young man, reputed to be of talent, birth, and education, who was "a professed infidel." This young man attended a circuit rider meeting, deliberately "defying any power, human or divine." However, it was recorded that ten minutes later, to the man's surprise, the power of God touched him, causing him to fall "prostrated on the floor at his full length . . . [where] breathless and pulseless he lay for an hour or more." He then awoke and, reportedly, "of all the loud shouting and incessant shouting" that Travis had ever heard, this young man "took the lead." Not only was he converted, but also, the man later became a minister.[59]

Dow recorded an instance of "a young man from N. Carolina" who mocked and "mimicked" those who experienced the jerks; while doing this, he "was seized with them himself" to such a degree that he was visibly "ashamed" while he was "attempting to mount his horse." Seeing this, others assisted him, and when he was finally able to mount his horse, he could "not sit alone" because of the jerks. Dow approached the young man, and he repented of his attitude and asked Dow to pray for him because he believed that "God sent [the jerks] on [him] for [his] wickedness, and [for] making so light of [the jerks] in others."[60]

---

57. Abbott and Ffirth, *Experience and Gospel Labours*, 87–89.

58. Abbott and Ffirth, *Experience and Gospel Labours*, 57, 94, 104.

59. Travis, *Autobiography*, 25.

60. Dow, *History of Cosmopolite*, 184–85.

Cartwright recorded a story of another young man who was known to mock the enthusiastic work of God within Methodism. However, during a circuit rider meeting, Cartwright witnessed that "the glory of the stupendous grace of God" was poured out, and the young man was "overtaken" by this power and "awfully shaken as it were over hell." After this supernatural experience, the man fell down prostrate before all those he had "so much disturbed and persecuted" and begged God "for mercy as from the verge of damnation" until he felt that God had fully "reclaimed him."[61]

Another incident occurred with two brothers and two sisters, "finely dressed," who attended one of Cartwright's meetings. At one point, the brothers left while the young sisters "took the jerks, and they were greatly mortified about it." When their brothers heard of this, they swore they would "horsewhip" Cartwright for giving their sisters "the jerks." However, as they approached Cartwright with the intent to harm him, Cartwright exclaimed: "Yes; if I gave your sisters the jerks, I'll give them to you." This statement alarmed the brothers, and they ran away, causing Cartwright to laugh. Later, it was confirmed that Cartwright had the pleasure of seeing "all four soundly converted to God, and [he] took them into the Church."[62]

In one of Finley's meetings, in which the Spirit's power was displayed and many were converted (including one young man who was reputed to be wicked and demonized), another man, identified as the "gainsayer," publicly opposed the manifestations and labeled Methodist enthusiasm as "the work of the devil." In response, like many circuit riders of his day, Finley argued that God, in demonstrating his power, was justifying the divine works of the circuit riders. Finley challenged the people by stating that if Methodist religious enthusiasm was truly the work of the devil, then when the "wicked" young man recovered from being slain in the Spirit, he would "curse and swear as formerly; but if it be a work of God, his oaths and curses [would] be turned into prayers and praises." Since, upon waking, the young man praised God, the gainsayer was without further comment (Finley did not record whether the gainsayer was later converted himself).[63]

---

61. Cartwright, *Backwoods Preacher*, 223.
62. Cartwright, *Backwoods Preacher*, 20.
63. Finley, *Autobiography*, 232.

Cartwright described an unusual incident within a circuit rider meeting in which two young men, "ringleaders in wickedness," mocked the audience's enthusiastic exercises. After the men departed without receiving forgiveness, one of them was dashed against a tree by his horse, which rendered him instantly breathless and permanently unable to speak.[64]

Like the above incident that ended tragically, Cartwright described another unusual story that occurred during a large religious meeting in which enthusiastic expressions (specifically, the jerks) were prevalent. There was a "company of drunken rowdies" with bottles of whisky who came to disturb the meeting. A man from this company "cursed the jerks" (which had been occurring) and even "all religion." Nevertheless, shortly afterward, God poured out his Spirit on this man, and when he took the jerks himself, he began to run but "jerked so powerfully he could not get away." Regardless, the man would not repent and instead "swore he would drink the damned jerks to death"; however, while he tried, he could "not get the bottle to his mouth" because he was jerking to such a great degree. This continued until, finally, with a sudden jerk, the bottle was thrust from his arm and shattered on a tree. The man was livid, swearing profusely, though the jerks continued to increase. Cartwright recorded that, ultimately, he experienced a "very violent jerk" that broke his neck, and the man died "with his mouth full of cursing and bitterness." Thus, it appears that the jerks provided the man with an opportunity to experience God and repent as others did in the meeting; however, as he remained unrepentant, in this case, Cartwright recorded that the jerking became, for him, "a judgment sent from God."[65]

As noted in chapter 5, and as seen in some instances above, those who were in "much opposition to what was sometimes called 'the Methodist power'" became frightened at times and began to run away from circuit rider meetings upon witnessing the magnitude of the power of God.[66] In larger meetings, people sometimes experienced the so-called running exercise.[67] As Stone described, this was "nothing more than that persons feeling something of these bodily agitations, through fear, [and] attempt[ing] to run away and thus escape from them." These people often

64. Cartwright, *Backwoods Preacher*, 263.

65. Cartwright, *Backwoods Preacher*, 21.

66. Sprague, *Annals of the American Pulpit*, 7:372. See also Abbott and Ffirth, *Experience and Gospel Labours*, 129–30.

67. Cartwright, *Backwoods Preacher*, 21.

did not run far "before they fell, where they became so agitated they could not proceed any farther." For instance, there was a young physician from a renowned family who came some distance to a religious meeting and then felt the need to run for his life. He "did not proceed far until he fell down, and there lay until he submitted to the Lord." After this divine experience, he "became a zealous" Christian.[68]

To summarize this section, the circuit riders responded to their critics mainly through logical defenses and through relying on the practical and evident power of God to demonstrate that their ministry was from the Lord and not from humans or the devil. The circuit riders' other main response to their critics was to pray to God that their critics would enthusiastically experience his Spirit. When this happened, critics personally witnessed and understood that Methodist experience, as Cooper insisted, was not an "enthusiastical madness"[69] and did not originate from the devil; rather, it was a form of spiritual ecstasy that flowed directly from the Spirit of God.[70]

Methodist Contention Surrounding Religious Enthusiasm

While the majority of the circuit riders strongly supported religious enthusiasm in their meetings and encouraged people to be open-minded regarding the idea of enthusiasm, there was a small group of circuit riders who generally supported and practiced the milder forms of religious enthusiasm in their meetings but rejected the wilder forms and even condemned those who practiced them (due, it seems, to the cultural controversy they sparked and the negative light they shed on the Methodist movement).[71]

One Methodist work, *Methodist Error, or, Friendly, Christian Advice*, published anonymously (in 1819) but inscribed by John Watson, was written exclusively about the controversial nature of religious enthusiasm;[72] more specifically, it was a theological book purportedly

---

68. Stone, *Biography*, 40.

69. Cooper, *Beams of Light*, 87.

70. Abbott and Ffirth, *Experience and Gospel Labours*, 93; Cartwright, *Backwoods Preacher*, 79.

71. Finkelman, *Encyclopedia of African American History*, 142; Abbott and Ffirth, *Experience and Gospel Labours*, 68–69.

72. See *Methodist Error*; Taves, *Fits, Trances, and Visions*, 76.

written for the Methodists' "benefit" in order to both expose the "enthusiasm and error that crept" into Methodism and argue that Methodism was generally like any other nineteenth-century mainline denomination. Contrary to testimonies documented by the circuit riders themselves, Watson declared that "the major part" of Methodism ran a "decen[t]" church whereas, he asserted, "the minor part [was] very zealous for the literal practice of shouting, leaping and jumping and other outward signs of the most heedless emotion." He urged individuals to distrust other religious books that promoted these phenomena, labeling them as propaganda. Watson claimed that, in his conversion, he experienced the divine power of "the Holy Ghost," but because he had not "lost the sense of decency" and had never personally experienced the need for enthusiastic expressions, he concluded that these expressions were neither divine nor scriptural and that they painted Methodism in a negative light; furthermore, he asserted that these expressions might be "the devices of Satan." Watson endeavored to support these convictions through the writings of John and Charles Wesley as well as the Methodist *Discipline*. Moreover, most of Watson's book contained unusual interpretations of particular biblical passages and maintained that God's aim for the church was to have it act in "order." Watson argued that "the unstable and irregular" acts of religious enthusiasm opposed the biblical text and needed to be abandoned entirely within Methodism. Watson also labeled some acts of enthusiasm as "evils," especially those that came from the ministry of the enthusiastic circuit rider Dow, whom he considered to be the "prey of imagination, dreams and impressions."[73]

Aside from Watson, who was a Methodist lay leader, there were a small number of circuit riders who were displeased with wild enthusiastic expressions, especially as they became a point of contention with the public.[74] For instance, Rankin criticized the ministry's practices when he witnessed the wild emotional expressions of Methodist revivals, especially in the southern states.[75] Although various forms of supernatural phenomena were often witnessed in Rankin's ministry (including milder religious enthusiasm),[76] in order to protect Methodist reputation from

73. *Methodist Error*, 5, 9–10, 16, 21–23, 31–33, 37, 39–40, 42–45, 48–50, 78–84, 86, 100–117, 119, 157–59.

74. Williams, *Religion and Violence in Early American Methodism*, 73.

75. Jackson, *Lives of Early Methodist Preachers*, 5:203; Wigger, *American Saint*, 83.

76. For instance, see Jackson, *Lives of Early Methodist Preachers*, 5:147–49, 156, 163–64, 167, 203–4.

further public embarrassment, he insisted that a "stop must absolutely be put to the prevailing [religious enthusiastic] wild-fire." In fact, Ware perceived that Rankin "was ashamed to say that some of his brethren, the preachers, were infected with" this controversial wildness.[77]

However, when Asbury heard of Rankin's criticism of the enthusiastic circuit rider revivals, he "became alarmed at these imprudent remarks." Ware witnessed that Asbury then "interposed to put a stop" to the remarks in a way that was satisfying to the circuit rider "preachers generally, and mortifying to" Rankin. Ware also explained that Asbury proudly allowed and advocated these controversial expressions of religious enthusiasm to be practiced by the circuit riders and their audiences. Indeed, according to Asbury, any contention such enthusiasm generated needed to be put aside as he felt it was perfectly acceptable for the circuit riders to experience religious enthusiasm and for the preachers and the "saints [to emotionally] . . . cry out and shout."[78] As Asbury exclaimed regarding a Methodist meeting: "If [people] will shout, why let [them] shout."[79] Asbury added that it was fitting for the "guilty mortals [to emotionally] tremble at God's word, for to such the Lord will look."[80]

Regarding the arguments that Rankin and Asbury had over religious enthusiasm, Ware expressed that they were so severe that if the American Revolutionary War had not occurred, there might have been a split in American Methodism.[81] On one side of this hypothetical split would have been the non-enthusiasts (the minority), and on the other side would have been the pro-enthusiasts (the majority).

In further considering Asbury's support of enthusiastic expressions, it has been argued that he "believed that everything should be done decently and in order and communicated this constantly to his preachers."[82] While it is true that Asbury believed the Methodist apparatus (i.e., the circuits) should be run in a methodical and orderly fashion, he did not believe that the meetings themselves or the religious expressions found within them should be run in such a fashion. Rather, Asbury believed (and frequently communicated to the circuit riders) that it was more important to be

77. Ware, *Sketches*, 253.

78. Ware, *Sketches*, 253–54.

79. Asbury, *Journal of the Rev. Francis Asbury*, 2:87.

80. Ware, *Sketches*, 253–55. See also Murray, *Methodists and the Crucible of Race*, 13.

81. See also Wigger, *Taking Heaven by Storm*, 114–15.

82. Thacker, "Methodism and the Second Great Awakening," 51.

"moved by . . . [the Spirit of] God" so that the circuit riders and their audiences could experience the fullness of the gospel, which included wild enthusiastic displays.[83] Furthermore, Asbury occasionally shouted disorderly, spontaneous praises during his meetings, proclaiming things such as: "Oh, my God! Display thy power."[84]

Aside from the argument with Rankin, Asbury recorded a letter written by a circuit rider (D. J.) who referred to religious enthusiasm in a derogatory way. In his letter, D. J. acknowledged that the meetings "where the greatest number of souls . . . [were] converted to God" were the meetings in which there occurred "the most outcries, tremblings, convulsions, and all sorts of external signs." However, D. J. feared that these external signs, while beneficial to the individual, would damage the reputation of the ministry. As a result, he attempted to keep emotional expressions "within bounds" so that Methodist "good might not be evil spoken of." D. J. feared that intense forms of religious expression could further embarrass Methodism and even create "a great tendency to hinder the work of God." For this reason, he recommended that "hot-brained enthusiasts" exercise restraint.[85]

It seems that Lee was on the fence regarding religious enthusiasm (especially in its wild form). Although Lee regularly experienced enthusiastic expressions within his ministry, because the expressions were outside of the ecclesiastical standards of other denominations (especially in New England, where he mostly ministered) and because he perceived that parts of his audiences were offended by them, he was skeptical about recommending the expressions and viewing them as divinely inspired. For instance, Lee recorded an incident in which "wild enthusias[tic]" expressions were present in a particular Methodist meeting. This was a story of a "certain female" who, during the meeting, "exhibited at sometimes the jerking exercise," at other times "the dancing exercise, and not unfrequently the basking exercise." Lee described these expressions as a "ridiculous . . . set of exercises" that the woman used to draw the attention "of the multitude" to her and away from the sermon; thus, he opposed them.[86]

---

83. Asbury, *Journal of the Rev. Francis Asbury*, 1:70.

84. Asbury, *Journal of the Rev. Francis Asbury*, 3:84, 243; 2:86–87.

85. Asbury, *Journal of the Rev. Francis Asbury*, 1:168.

86. Lee, *Memoir*, 294–95.

During other revival meetings, there were "some things which might be called imprudent" that Lee considered to be on the questionably wild side of enthusiasm, and he feared that these activities might tarnish the Methodist reputation. However, Lee also acknowledged that since "there were so many souls brought to God," attempting to appease the offended public by stopping these imprudent activities "was thought to be dangerous" because, in doing so, it could hinder the "gracious work which the Lord was so strangely carrying on." Regarding all other "milder" forms of enthusiastic expressions that were not considered too controversial, such as crying, shouting, and even falling as if dead, Lee welcomed and practiced these in his life and ministry. In other words, it seems that Lee (like Wesley and Rankin) was concerned about Methodism's image within society, and so he took precautions to preserve it while still trying to ensure that the Holy Spirit's work was unhindered. In certain contexts (such as the above incident with the woman), it appears that what largely bothered Lee was the attention that wild religious enthusiasm claimed from other audience members. Lee desired the people to give their undivided attention to the Lord and opposed other distractions and interruptions.[87]

As aforementioned, Cartwright was actively supportive of religious enthusiasm;[88] however, in Cartwright's journals, he recorded a particular meeting in which he was agitated by "strange and wild exercises," such as running, jumping, and barking. However, it seems that what disturbed Cartwright was the fact that, from these exercises, a "great evil arose from the heated and wild imaginations." Some members of the audience declared that they had "seen heaven and hell" and even communicated with "spirits of the dead in heaven and hell"; they also prophesied under the pretense of divine inspiration, predicting "the time of the end of the world, and the ushering in of the great millennium." This caused great concern in Cartwright because he did not believe that the visions and prophecies that followed the exercises were scriptural. Cartwright explained that this presented "the most troublesome delusion" that was an "appeal to the ignorance, superstition, and credulity" of the public. These "visionar[ies]," however, insisted that if people opposed them, God would send "fire down from heaven and consume" them. Apparently, Cartwright "never saw [such a case] before," and he even declared that

---

87. Lee, *Memoir*, 53–55, 205–6, 270, 313. See also Lee, *Short History of the Methodists*, 313.

88. For instance, see Cartwright, *Backwoods Preacher*, 223–63.

"the Methodist preachers generally preached against [such] extravagant wildness."[89]

It appears that these acts were a sizable distraction within the revival. Consequently, Cartwright decided to oppose their faulty theology publicly and "proclaimed open war against these delusions." He made arrangements and "drew multitudes together" in order to biblically demonstrate that their delusions were false. As a result, some of the "visionary men and women" predicted that God would kill Cartwright. Although these phenomena seemed supernatural, since they resulted in division and did not conform to the biblical text, Cartwright declared that they were the product of "self-deluded [and] false prophets."[90]

It should, again, be noted that Cartwright experienced diverse supernatural encounters in his own life. In fact, Cartwright defended Methodist enthusiasm, identifying it as "wonderful [emotional] excitement following or preceding conversions."[91] However, Cartwright was known to be a devout student of the Bible, and if he discerned that a supernatural thought or expression opposed the biblical text, it perturbed him; consequently, he attempted to stop that unbiblical message.[92] This approach is evident in one of his books (featuring an aggressive title), *A Letter Purporting to Be from His Satanic Majesty, the Devil*, which was written against the doctrine of predestination (and, specifically, against Presbyterians).[93] The book ardently defended the concept of free will, which Methodism supported and believed to be biblically-based.[94]

Aside from the above enthusiastic incident that he considered to be unscriptural, Cartwright, like Lee, criticized "enthusiastic persons" who seemed to be "supremely wrapped up in self . . . [and simply wanted] to be seen of men." In fact, at one point, Cartwright went so far as to state that those who participated in enthusiasm for the benefit of self were destined for "hell" and causing "the ignorant and gaping crowds" to go to hell with them, as well. Hence, while religious enthusiastic expressions were, ordinarily, a celebrated part of Cartwright's life and ministry, there were two occasions in which Cartwright identified religious enthusiastic

89. Cartwright, *Backwoods Preacher*, 21–22.

90. Cartwright, *Backwoods Preacher*, 22.

91. Cartwright, *Backwoods Preacher*, 79, 315.

92. Watters, *Peter Cartwright*, 26–27; Cartwright, *Backwoods Preacher*, 22.

93. The reference for this work is Cartwright, *Letter Purporting to Be from His Satanic Majesty.*

94. See Cartwright, *Autobiography*, 219.

exercises as both destructive and a serious impediment to successful ministry.[95]

There was an incident connected to religious enthusiasm in which the circuit rider Snethen (who was serving as a settled pastor at that time) wrote a letter to the British Methodists in order to prevent Dow from effectively ministering during one of his trips to England. Apparently, Snethen did not approve of Dow's excessive interest in and practice of enthusiastic expressions and even wrote that Dow "succeeded so well in deceiving or duping" circuit riders and audience members alike with this "rhapsody." However, in carefully considering this letter, it seems that Snethen's greatest issue was not with Dow's religious enthusiasm but, rather, with his "filthy" outward appearance and his uneducated preaching that was "clownish in the extreme . . . [and] an insult to the gospel." Interestingly, it was later reported that Snethen "had mostly lost his congregation" as a "consequence" of this letter and the Methodists' disapproval of his actions against Dow.[96]

There was another incident involving Dow and a certain Methodist local pastor Hardy. This case was reported in *The Carolina Federal Republican* and explained that, as a result of Dow's enthusiasm and "clownish manners," Hardy (who was based in Richmond) refused to allow Dow to preach in a chapel.[97] It appears that Hardy made this decision in order to appease some of Dow's critics in the area. However, four days later, the same newspaper reported that Hardy publicly apologized to Dow for having "mistaken [his] character."[98]

During this time period, there were no other negative opinions or criticisms made by the circuit riders and/or Methodists, in general (although, it appears that Pilmore was not a great supporter of extreme religious enthusiasm, either).[99] As Lyerly explained, "most [of the circuit riders] defended religious enthusiasm . . . many [of them] felt that it was better to allow some excess [in enthusiastic expressions] than to dampen the spirit."[100]

95. Cartwright, *Backwoods Preacher*, 21, 159, 231, 315.

96. Dow and Dow, *Dealings of God*, 126, 163. See also Price, *Holston Methodism*, 2:72–73.

97. Hardy, "Lorenzo Dow," 2.

98. Hardy, "Henry Hardy," 3.

99. Wigger, *Taking Heaven by Storm*, 112.

100. Lyerly, *Methodism and the Southern Mind*, 38.

Concluding Comments

While religious enthusiasm was discussed in previous chapters (i.e., its definition, detailed description, and relationship to Wesley and his ministry), this chapter exclusively investigated the controversy surrounding religious enthusiasm in the circuit rider ministry. Specifically, it investigated three things: the offended public's opinion concerning religious enthusiasm, the general defenses of the circuit riders in response to their critics, and the objection of a small number of circuit riders toward wild enthusiastic activity. It was demonstrated that the clear majority of circuit riders were supportive and appreciative of the religious enthusiasm present in Methodism; as observed by Finley, this enthusiasm was "believed . . . [to be a direct] work of God's Spirit on the hearts of the people, and . . . [as a result of it] thousands were genuinely converted to God."[101] Indeed, while the circuit riders were, at times, surprised by an enthusiastic "outpouring of the Spirit," they were not so much shocked by it as they were, seemingly, thankful for it.[102]

Asbury was such a serious advocate of religious enthusiasm that he considered it to be the heart of the ministry's growth.[103] He stated that the circuit rider ministry should experience the entire gospel, including the "wild-fire" of religious enthusiasm.[104] In addition, Asbury warned that "to be hasty in plucking up the tares, [was] to endanger the wheat."[105] In other words, if God poured out his Spirit in an enthusiastic manner, humans should not attempt to cease or manipulate his outpouring because, in doing so, conversions could be hindered. Asbury held that by choosing to cooperate with only selected parts of God's outpouring, people might also interrupt and endanger the revivals.[106] Thus, for Asbury and the majority of the circuit riders, religious enthusiasm was a part of biblical Christianity with its supernatural acts originating from God.[107]

101. Finley, *Autobiography*, 363.

102. Asbury, *Journal of the Rev. Francis Asbury*, 1:161.

103. Wigger, *Taking Heaven by Storm*, 112.

104. As noted earlier in the chapter, this word was used by Rankin in criticizing American Methodism's religious enthusiasm. For more information, see Ware, *Sketches*, 253.

105. Ware, *Sketches*, 254. See also Conlin, *American Past*, 1:294.

106. For more information, see Ware, *Sketches*, 254.

107. See also Westerkamp, *Women in Early American Religion*, 120.

However, it seems that in observing the ministry from the outside, the public was often genuinely shocked. When the public witnessed the atmosphere and acts produced in the American circuit rider meetings (such as shouting, physical jerking, barking, dancing, crying, prophesying, and being slain in the Spirit), it was beyond their understanding.[108] They could not comprehend that environment because, as demonstrated in this study, the source of these experiences was spiritual and, therefore, beyond ordinary natural experiences. Regarding the matter of the natural encountering the supernatural, even Wesley concluded that the natural mind has "no inlets for the knowledge of spiritual things."[109] Since the public was not capable of understanding these expressions naturally, it seems that, while most chose to respond with conversion, others responded with fear, which bred criticism and insult.

Cooper explained that many of those who criticized and insulted religious enthusiasm attended Methodist religious meetings in protest; however, as illustrated, the presence of the Holy Spirit often touched them, causing the former critics to join in the emotional religious outcries of those whom they had previously insulted. Furthermore, it appears that when individuals experienced the touch of the Holy Spirit, to them it was deemed more valuable and meaningful to continue in that experience and endure the insults of outsiders.[110]

The circuit riders understood that this kind of public criticism was also common in England during the days of Wesley as his *Journals* featured "instances of wonderful excitement . . . [and] opponents of religion, who, ridiculing these [enthusiastic] scenes, [were suddenly] brought to their knees, and compelled to cry to God for mercy." In the same way that negative public opinions did not hinder Wesley from progressing in his ministry, it was also demonstrated that public criticism did not hinder the American circuit riders from further progressing in their ministry.[111]

At the same time, it was demonstrated that a small number of circuit riders (such as the prominent circuit rider Lee) expressed some confusion and wariness concerning wild religious enthusiasm in their meetings. On one hand, they supported and practiced forms of enthusiastic expression in their ministry (even some wild forms, such as jerking

108. Arminian Methodists, "Review of Bogue & Bennett," 340.

109. Wesley, *Sermons on Several Occasions* [Emory], 78–79.

110. Cooper, *Beams of Light*, 87–91.

111. Cartwright, *Backwoods Preacher*, 315.

and being slain in the Spirit). On the other hand, however, they disputed the divine origins of particular enthusiastic incidents in order to placate the offended public and better align Methodism with the ecclesiastical standards of those days. Unlike Asbury and most other circuit riders who were entirely supportive of religious enthusiasm in all contexts, these circuit riders exercised caution so that, echoing circuit rider D. J., God's work might not be publicly criticized as a result of unnecessary emotional outcries (particularly those that they considered to be both wild and voluntary, such as shrieking and howling).[112] Thus, in their own way, these circuit riders endeavored to protect early Methodism and its supernatural component from purportedly needless controversial activities and the accusations they generated.

While it has been argued that the circuit riders merely practiced religious enthusiasm in "moderation" or milder forms, as opposed to wilder forms, this research has demonstrated that only a small number of circuit riders restricted themselves to milder forms of enthusiasm. Most circuit riders (including Asbury) promoted and included wilder forms of enthusiasm in their lives and ministries.[113]

In fact, despite the confusion and criticism surrounding American Methodism and its religious exercises, the historian Holmes observed in 1823 that "the Methodists in America [were] more [religiously] enthusiastic than those in England." Holmes concluded that they moved on by the Spirit of God as a countercultural ministry in which they seemed "determined to take heaven by storm." For example, each morning was often begun by "singing, praying, and telling 'their [spiritual] experience.'" Following this, there were numerous sermons, resulting in the whole day being gladly "taken up in religious exercises."[114] In other words, the supernatural components of Methodism, which were sometimes identified as "religious enthusiasm" or "Methodist fits," were welcome and frequently manifested in circuit rider meetings; in many cases, these "extraordinary" expressions were "almost-beyond belief."[115] As demonstrated, these controversial phenomena generally served, together with other forms of supernaturalism, as a means of bringing fame to the circuit rider ministry and expanding its labors through

112. Cartwright, *Backwoods Preacher*, 122.

113. Turner, "Redeeming the Time," 95.

114. Holmes, *Account of the United States of America*, 388.

115. Cartwright, *Backwoods Preacher*, 231, 315.

convictions, conversions, and nation-wide revivals (as examined in the following chapter).[116]

---

116. Hibbard, *Memoirs*, 209. See also Watters, *Short Account of the Christian Experience*, 17; Abbott and Ffirth, *Experience and Gospel Labours*, 81–82; Lee, *Memoir*, 270; Young, *Autobiography of a Pioneer*, 137; Finley, *Autobiography*, 232; Cooper, *Beams of Light*, 87.

Chapter 7

The Supernatural
and Methodist Expansion

THIS CHAPTER STUDIES THE circuit riders' application of supernatural phenomena (discussed at length in chapter 5) in their evangelistic revivals in an attempt to unearth the role of the supernatural in their ministry, at large, as well as its effect on the ministry's growth. A portion of this chapter investigates Methodist camp meetings as they were one of the circuit riders' primary evangelistic tools, often producing nationwide revivals. The general characteristics of revivals are also discussed as well as additional revival information by American state.[1] Following this is a section on the criticism of Methodist revivals by leaders and members of other denominations as well as portions of the American public. While it was demonstrated in previous chapters that private and public supernatural phenomena were a regular and vital part of the circuit rider ministry, this chapter heavily researches and ultimately demonstrates, via circuit rider writings, the correlation between the supernatural and the growth of American Methodism (from the 1770s through the 1830s).

---

1. Prior to 1840, the twenty-six American states were as follows: Delaware, Pennsylvania, New Jersey, Georgia, Connecticut, Massachusetts, Maryland, South Carolina, New Hampshire, Virginia, New York, North Carolina, Rhode Island, Vermont, Kentucky, Tennessee, Ohio, Louisiana, Indiana, Mississippi, Illinois, Alabama, Maine, Missouri, Arkansas, and Michigan. See Geiger, *Perspectives History Higher Education*, 25:43–44.

Introduction to Revivals in the Circuit Rider Ministry

Early Methodist revivals were understood to occur, as Cartwright stated, when "the mighty power [and presence] of God" descended on various circuit rider meetings and touched multitudes of people by the tens or "hundreds"; at times, even "between one and two thousand souls [were] . . . happily and powerfully converted to God."[2] While the majority of Methodist revivals occurred in prearranged camp meetings (discussed in the next section),[3] revivals also commonly occurred spontaneously in smaller Methodist religious meetings,[4] held in: barns,[5] houses,[6] churches,[7] schools,[8] neighborhoods,[9] town-centers,[10] quarterly meetings,[11] open-air meetings,[12] and other "impromptu settings."[13] The mid-nineteenth-century Methodist preacher H. Turner stated that revivals also occurred in "prayer-meetings, love-feasts, and the administration of the holy sacraments. Revivals . . . frequently [grew] out of them and always should."[14]

Goss asserted that "Methodism originated with revivals; its life-power [was] drawn from them, [and] it can only exist by their continued use."[15] Scudder confirmed that it was the revivals that drew the "attention

2. Cartwright, *Backwoods Preacher*, 9. Since Methodist revivals were produced through the power and presence of the Holy Spirit, then these revivals can also be called *spiritual revivals* as they aimed to introduce experiential Christianity and generate conversions.

3. Dow and Dow, *Dealings of God*, 267.

4. For instance, see Hibbard, *Memoirs*, 257; Finley, *Sketches of Western Methodism*, 37, 48, 84.

5. For instance, see Atkinson, *Centennial History of American Methodism*, 220.

6. For instance, see Boehm, *Reminiscences*, 32; Asbury, *Journal of the Rev. Francis Asbury*, 1:204.

7. For instance, see Young, *Autobiography of a Pioneer*, 49, 54.

8. For instance, see Finley, *Autobiography*, 318.

9. For instance, see Abbott and Ffirth, *Experience and Gospel Labours*, 35.

10. For instance, see Hibbard, *Memoirs*, 178.

11. For instance, see Boehm, *Reminiscences*, 34; Asbury, *Journal of the Rev. Francis Asbury*, 1:232.

12. For instance, see Asbury, *Journal of the Rev. Francis Asbury*, 1:361.

13. Ditchfield, *Evangelical Revival*, 104.

14. Turner, *Genius and Theory of Methodist Polity*, 57. See also "Revivalism" (*EBO*).

15. Goss, *Statistical History*, 173.

of the people to [Methodism], and proved its claim to the divine approval" as these revivals were produced by the Holy Spirit; thus, the spiritual "energy" present in Methodist revivals originated from "the unction of the Holy One," or God's Spirit, which was "quickening and impelling the body, and producing what [the Methodists] call revivals."[16] This was openly confirmed by *The Vermont Journal*, which declared that it was the "the Holy Spirit" who was at work in Methodist "revivals" to "convince [and convert]" people through the "displays of Divine Sovereignty."[17]

The circuit riders recorded so many local and nationwide revivals that one can write volumes on them; furthermore, the circuit riders recorded abundant conversions that occurred through these local and nationwide revivals.[18] It was through these frequent spiritual revivals or awakenings (the main ones stemming from camp meetings) that "Methodism grew"[19] throughout America to the point that, by the early 1830s, the MEC had become the largest denomination in America.[20] During this time, as discussed further in the chapter, revivals became so substantial that historians have identified this period as America's Second Great Awakening.[21]

Camp Meetings in the Circuit Rider Ministry

Since Methodist camp meetings were considered to be one of the primary components of Methodist revivals, this section is designated to describing camp meetings and determining the role of the supernatural

16. Scudder and Cummings, *American Methodism*, 252, 289. See also Boehm, *Reminiscences*, 32.

17. Godard, "Religious Intelligence," 1.

18. For instance, see also Cooper, *Beams of Light*, 247.

19. Handy, "American Methodism and Its Historical Frontier," 46.

20. Harrell et al., *Unto a Good Land*, 1:202; Garnett and Matthew, *Revival and Religion*, 127; Kirby at al., *Methodists*, 177; Reid, *Evangelism Handbook*, 103; Cartwright, *Backwoods Preacher*, 64. Some historians, such as Hudson, concluded that the MEC became the largest denomination during the 1820s. However, this argument is questionable because, during this time, the Baptists increased in number and they, at times, could be considered the largest denomination (especially during the early 1820s). Thus, most prominent historians have supported the argument that the MEC became the largest denomination during the early 1830s. See Hudson, *Religion in America*, 116–17.

21. Revivals were also common in other mainline American denominations, such as the Baptists and Presbyterians. For more information regarding the Second Great Awakening, see Hankins, *Second Great Awakening*, 1–5.

in this form of evangelistic enterprise. As the general population of the Early American Republic was in a state of continuous growth (in 1800, the recorded population was 5,305,937; by 1830, the recorded population was 12,866,020), there was a need to implement fresh ways to minister on American soil.[22] Especially at the beginning of the nineteenth century, due to population increase, Methodist open-air style preaching became more and more prominent, which ultimately led to the need for incorporating camp meetings.[23]

Defining Camp Meetings

In brief, Finley defined Methodist camp meetings as outdoor meetings that were held for the "practical exhibition of religion . . . [and] unfeigned and fervent spirituality."[24] They were considered to be special religious events that were generally advertised (sometimes through newspapers)[25] and prearranged in a certain location and place, much like a modern-day rock concert.[26] "Thousands"[27] came from great distances to attend camp meetings so that people could receive "salvation for their souls"[28] or experience spiritual refreshment.[29] These religious camp meetings became so renowned that individuals and families "often pitched tents to stay for the entire event"[30] so that they could practically experience religion, hear worship music, and take communion.[31]

In the circuit rider ministry, it was Asbury who directed and promoted this new strategy of ministering to the American population through massive camp meetings.[32] He tremendously enjoyed being part

22. Goss, *Statistical History*, 154.

23. Powell, "Methodist Circuit Riders in America," 97. See also Hankins, *Second Great Awakening*, 1–5.

24. Finley, *Autobiography*, 315. See also "Camp Meeting" (*EBO*).

25. For instance, see "Friday [in] Edenton," 3; "Religious News," 3; "Wednesday, May 3," 3.

26. Rieser, *Chautauqua Moment*, 20; Semple, *Lord's Dominion*, 129.

27. Cartwright, *Backwoods Preacher*, 9.

28. Jones, "Account of the State of Religion," 209.

29. Finley, *Sketches of Western Methodism*, 209.

30. Danielson, "Methodist Camp Meetings and Revival," 160. See also Cartwright, *Backwoods Preacher*, 45; Brigham, *Observations on the Influence of Religion*, 148–50.

31. Pease, "Revival of the Work of God," 71; Ruth, "Camp Meeting," 560.

32. Barlow, *Profiles in Evangelism*, 19; Johnson, *Frontier Camp Meeting*, 83; Richey et al., *American Methodism*, 41; Parker, "Camp Meeting on the Frontier," 188.

of these events, stating that the camp meetings had "been blest to [his] mind" because he enjoyed "preaching [during them] every day."[33] Asbury also urged the circuit riders to participate in the camp meetings, declaring that circuit riders "must attend to camp meetings, [because] they [made their] harvest times."[34]

Brief History of Camp Meetings

Although it is not exactly known when the first American camp meeting occurred, there are two common beliefs regarding the origin of the camp meeting. According to some scholars, the first camp meeting was held in the summer of 1799 in Kentucky through the leadership of the McGee brothers, William (a Presbyterian) and John (a Methodist).[35] According to other scholars, camp meetings began in July of 1800 in Kentucky through the primary leadership of McGready, a Presbyterian.[36] In any case, in Tennessee on October 21, 1800, Asbury participated in one of the first camp meetings in the country. Regarding this experience, he stated that "[t]he ministers of God, Methodists and Presbyterians, united their labours, and mingled with the childlike simplicity of primitive times [the Apostolic Age]" to proclaim the gospel.[37]

In 1801, the concept of the camp meeting received nationwide and international fame after the successful multi-denominational meeting held in Cane Ridge, Kentucky (which was briefly mentioned in chapter 5).[38] This camp meeting was considered to be organized and hosted by the Presbyterian minister Stone, although Methodists, such as circuit riders Page and Burke, participated and preached, as well.[39]

Following this, circuit rider interest in camp meetings rapidly spread. Especially after discovering that the MEC had only grown 12.6

33. Asbury, "Chapter 13."

34. Asbury, *Journal of the Rev. Francis Asbury*, 3:272.

35. Gorham, *Camp Meeting Manual*, 14.

36. Adams, *Johnson's Universal Cyclopedia*, 2:605.

37. Asbury, *Journal of the Rev. Francis Asbury*, 2:397. See also Clark, *1844*, 37.

38. Cartwright, *Backwoods Preacher*, 13; Danielson, "Methodist Camp Meetings and Revival," 160; Galli, "Revival at Cane Ridge." Especially in the southern states during 1801, religious meetings were known to feature Presbyterians and Methodists united in spreading the gospel in America. For more information, see Arminius, "Introductory Remarks," 223; M'Ferrin, *History of Methodism in Tennessee*, 1:351–53.

39. Finley, *Autobiography*, 166; McGuire, "Cane Ridge Meetinghouse," 164.

percent from 1790 to 1800 (whereas, in the previous decade [1780–1790] the growth was estimated to be 571.92 percent), concerns began to surface that the circuit approach was growing stale.[40] The influence of the Age of Enlightenment was also increasing at this time (especially in urban settings), which brought forth skepticism of supernatural phenomena; this was especially problematic because the circuit riders relied on such phenomena to maintain a vibrant and dynamic ministry. In search of an innovative approach that addressed the mindset of the newest American generation as well as the accelerated population growth, the circuit riders began to orchestrate camp meetings, which accommodated significantly larger crowds. In turn, these large-scale venues (which often became the talk of the town) drove up local interest in Methodism and, consequently, Methodist supernaturalism.

Upon further witnessing their future potential, Methodists began to incorporate camp meetings as one of their primary tools of mass evangelism and expansion.[41] Asbury was a passionate supporter of this; he identified the camp meeting as a "great instrument" and declared that the "Methodists [were] all for camp meetings." This fact is also clearly demonstrated in Asbury's journals; while prior to 1802, camp meetings were very infrequently mentioned, after 1802, Asbury described (at times, extensively) at least fifty-four camp meetings.[42] Johnson, an expert in the study of nineteenth-century camp meetings, observed that, in time, camp meetings of other denominations were considered "relatively insignificant when measured against Methodist utilization of the forest revival [or camp meeting]."[43] Thus, while Methodists were not the only ones who led and participated in camp meetings (there were also Baptists and Presbyterians), camp meetings eventually became mostly associated with Methodism.[44]

Moreover, when Methodism was still predominately led by Asbury (until 1816), it was recorded that more than four hundred camp meetings occurred annually.[45] Even following Asbury's death in 1816, by the year

40. For more information on Methodist growth statistics (1773–1840), see appendix B.

41. Ahlstrom, *Religious History of the American People*, 437; Richey et al., *American Methodism*, 42.

42. Asbury, *Journal of the Rev. Francis Asbury*, 3:121, 289, 340.

43. Johnson, *Frontier Camp Meeting*, 80.

44. Ingersoll, *Baptist and Methodist Faiths in America*, 25.

45. Asbury, *Journal of the Rev. Francis Asbury*, 3:321–22; Matthews, *Timetables of History*, 61; Cairns, *Endless Line of Splendor*, 101.

1820, it was estimated that there was an increase of Methodist camp meetings as around five hundred occurred annually.[46] It was customary for camp meetings to be held during the month of September, after the harvest season.[47] The typical duration of these camp meetings was between four to seven days and, at times, up to eight days and nights.[48]

However, after the 1830s, especially beginning in the 1840s and culminating in the 1860s, revivalist camp meetings started to drastically fade away in the Methodist church, and it was observed that the "effectiveness of Camp meetings [was] lessened"[49] in Methodism but continued elsewhere.[50] Indeed, the effectiveness of post-1860s camp meetings was diminished because the Methodists experienced a decline in the supernatural and evangelistic zeal (and an increase in "wealth and education") at that time in their ministry.[51] As a result, Johnson observed that the Methodists began to approach camp meetings as not "necessary" for their ministry, and they felt that their ministerial importance had "passed away."[52]

It should be noted that, still today, "hundreds of 'old time' [Methodist] camp meetings are held each year" that serve as a source of "spiritual renewal." However, while modern Methodist denominations (such as the UMC) hold camp meetings that outwardly resemble the "old time" meetings by including a stage, music, and preachers, the overall goals and practices of these meetings greatly differ from the circuit rider camp meetings. The goal of these modern camp meetings is a "renewal" of current Christians' spirituality as opposed to the circuit riders' primary goal of reaching the unchurched with the gospel. Furthermore, while supernatural displays were welcome, common, and even expected in circuit

46. Danielson, "Methodist Camp Meetings and Revival," 160. See also "Methodist Camp Meeting," 59; Brown, "Camp Meeting Movement," 62.

47. Powell, "Methodist Circuit Riders in America," 97.

48. Cartwright, *Backwoods Preacher*, 104; Ruth, "Camp Meeting," 560.

49. Barclay, *Methodist Episcopal Church*, 90–91.

50. Finke and Stark, *Churching of America*, 168.

51. Turner, "Redeeming the Time," 100.

52. Johnson, *Frontier Camp Meeting*, 250–51. On the other hand, however, they prospered in education and adopted ministerial strategies similar to those of other mainline denominations of the day. This information is further explored in my upcoming research.

rider camp meetings, these displays are not evident in modern Methodist camp meetings.[53]

Circuit Rider Camp Meetings and the Supernatural

From the time that camp meetings were first introduced, circuit riders perceived that they were largely appealing to the Early American Republic because of their supernatural displays;[54] Johnson noted that this was because "supernatural forces were personalized in persuasive fashion."[55] In fact, all of the supernatural phenomena discussed in chapters 5 and 6 were prevalent in camp meetings.[56] Circuit riders indicated through their journals that camp meetings were highly marked by the outpourings of the Spirit of God, which especially resulted in the act of being slain in the Spirit and in various forms of religious enthusiasm (e.g., shouting, weeping, running, jumping, and barking).[57] Gorham, who wrote a manual on how to conduct nineteenth-century camp meetings, witnessed that camp meetings were "not dry, dogmatic theorizing; not metaphysical hair splitting"; instead, they were "plain, clear, evangelical, Bible truth" that featured "the Holy Ghost sent down from heaven."[58] Due to their popularity and renown for experiential religious conversions, Cartwright observed that "people in those days thought no hardship of going many miles to a camp meeting"[59] for the purpose of a tangible divine experience.[60] Examples of such divine experiences and supernatural manifestations are described below.

Asbury declared that Methodist camp meetings often contained divine "fires blazing here and there" that illuminated the spiritual darkness; as a result, the cries of the "redeemed captives" and the exclamations of

53. Brown, "Camp Meeting Movement," 62.

54. Parker, "Camp Meeting on the Frontier," 188; Barlow, *Profiles in Evangelism*, 19.

55. Johnson, *Frontier Camp Meeting*, 171.

56. Lee, *Memoir*, 13; Ingersoll, *Baptist and Methodist Faiths in America*, 25.

57. Young, *Autobiography of a Pioneer*, 41; Finley, *Autobiography*, 167; Ingersoll, *Baptist and Methodist Faiths in America*, 25; Cartwright, *Backwoods Preacher*, 13, 136; Finley, *Autobiography*, 350. For more information regarding circuit rider religious enthusiasm, see chapter 6.

58. Gorham, *Camp Meeting Manual*, 163.

59. Cartwright, *Backwoods Preacher*, 104.

60. See also Taves, *Fits, Trances, and Visions*, 154.

souls "struggling into life" broke "the silence of midnight."[61] Asbury even prayed that there might be "twenty camp meetings in a week" and that the Lord's power and presence would be poured out "in every direction."[62]

Cartwright described a camp meeting and its supernatural activity, stating that the meeting continued "by night and day." Arriving on foot or horseback, in carriages or wagons, thousands had the opportunity to hear of "the mighty work." As the power of God was poured out, hundreds were slain in the Spirit "under the mighty power of God, as men slain in battle." From this encounter alone, "between one and two thousand souls" experienced conversion. Moreover, the "heavenly [spiritual] fire" blazed in almost every direction, and more than "one thousand persons broke out into loud shouting all at once," producing a sound that could be heard from miles away. Cartwright recounted another camp meeting that lasted eight days; while the circuit riders preached, "the power of God attended, sinners by the score fell; the altar, though very large, was filled to overflowing."[63]

Finley described a certain camp meeting in which the public "experienced religion," and the manifestations of the Holy Spirit were so extensive that "multitudes were converted" and hundreds left the meeting feeling "deeply and powerfully" touched by the power of God. At another camp meeting, Finley described how the presence of the "supernatural" was evident and brought forth conversions.[64]

Lee witnessed that during various camp meetings, he was "greatly honored" to watch the work of the power and presence convert "precious souls." He recalled that, frequently, he heard of "fifty or a hundred souls" receiving conversion, and he believed that a "revival of religion" was extending, as a result.[65] Likewise, Young witnessed that, often in circuit rider camp meetings, a "display of Divine power followed . . . [and caused people] to fall upon the floor like trees thrown down by a whirlwind."[66]

It should also be noted that, while all camp meetings were designed to produce revivals in the form of massive spiritual awakenings or conversions (which the majority of them succeeded in doing), not all

61. Asbury, *Journal of the Rev. Francis Asbury*, 2:397.

62. Asbury, *Journal of the Rev. Francis Asbury*, 3:274.

63. Cartwright, *Backwoods Preacher*, 9, 104.

64. Finley, *Autobiography*, 167, 202, 398–99.

65. Lee, *Short History of the Methodists*, 309.

66. Young, *Autobiography of a Pioneer*, 41.

camp meetings actually sparked spiritual revivals.[67] For instance, Young recalled a camp meeting (even while Dow was present) in which there were no signs of achieved revival as, of that meeting, it was said that "nothing special took place." Indeed, the circuit riders felt that a small number of camp meetings did "not succeed" in reaching their intended evangelistic goals; this was largely because, for some reason, there were not enough supernatural displays present.[68] However, as demonstrated below, the camp meetings that were associated with the outpouring of the "tremendous power [of the Spirit]" (which were the clear majority) brought forth Methodist revivals.[69]

Analyzing the Correlation between the Supernatural in Circuit Rider Revivals and Methodist Growth

As noted throughout this work, the circuit riders believed that "the Church was enlarged"[70] exclusively through the "Divine Presence."[71] In early Methodism, both small and great revivals (especially camp meetings) were derived from, as Peck witnessed, "wonderful outpourings of the Holy Spirit," which caused numerous small and large-scale conversions and, consequently, resulted in "the multiplication of circuits and stations" (i.e., Methodist expansion).[72] For instance, Atkinson recorded Boehm's opinions about Asbury's dependence on the Holy Spirit in revival meetings; Boehm believed that, like the first apostles, Asbury's sermons "depended much on the divine influence." Asbury was confident (echoing Zechariah 4:6) that "it was not by might, nor by power, but by the Spirit of the Lord" that revivals and, ultimately, Methodism would expand.[73]

---

67. For more information regarding the nature of early Methodist revivals, see also Sutcliffe, *Divine Mission of the People Called Methodists*, 28–42.

68. Young, *Autobiography of a Pioneer*, 191, 235. Circuit riders identified the devil's spiritual strongholds as more substantial in particular people groups and territories; as a result, circuit riders further believed that this could negatively affect the success in their revivals. For more information on this matter, see chapter 6.

69. Cartwright, *Backwoods Preacher*, 79.

70. Paine, *Life and Times*, 1:150.

71. Maffitt, *Memorial of Philip Embury*, 35. For more information regarding this matter, see chapters 4–5.

72. Peck, *Early Methodism*, 465.

73. Atkinson, *Centennial History of American Methodism*, 293. See also Scudder and Cummings, *American Methodism*, 209.

In the circuit rider ministry, when the power and presence of God was manifested, consequently sparking revivals, there was a direct response in numeric growth (beginning with conversions and measured, ultimately, by Methodist membership).[74] For example, in Asbury's journals, he recorded an incident in which God poured out "his Spirit on men, women, and children." From this outpouring of the Spirit, a revival broke out that was considered so powerful that people had "never" seen such things "with [their] eyes," which led to numerous conversions. At another time, it was recorded that the Spirit's power and presence was poured out for "more than forty days." As a result of these outpourings, the labor became "more deep than ever, extended wider, and was swifter in its operations"; throughout many circuits and counties, the supernatural power "came down," causing massive conversions.[75]

Finley witnessed that, because the Lord visited the circuit rider ministry "with a great and powerful revival," numerous souls embraced spiritual conversion and began "to rejoice with a joy unspeakable and full of glory." From this outpouring of the Spirit, masses were also "added to the Church, and the people of God were greatly refreshed in spirit." Finley noted that "the revival flame spread" throughout circuit appointments, and there were evident "displays of Divine power in awakening and conversion."[76]

Lee witnessed "a very great display of the power and love of God" that resulted in "many souls" becoming converted and, ultimately, "added to the [Methodist] Society." Displays of the divine in another revival caused "shaking among the dry bones" that was amplified "from week to week." This revival reportedly impacted all ages; the "old and grey headed," the middle-aged, the youth, and even the "little children were the subjects of this work."[77] Burke witnessed a time in which "a powerful and extensive revival" developed. From this revival, "hundreds" were added to the Methodist societies, and Burke categorized it as "among the greatest revivals that was ever known."[78]

Boehm testified that, after numerous prayers for growth, the Holy Spirit "filled" their house. From this point onward, the labor of "revival

---

74. See also Henkle, *Life of Henry Bidleman Bascom*, 56.

75. Asbury, *Journal of the Rev. Francis Asbury*, 1:161, 172, 218.

76. Finley, *Autobiography*, 224, 270.

77. Lee, *Short History of the Methodists*, 54, 279.

78. Finley, *Sketches of Western Methodism*, 66.

commenced" with many "cries of distress [and] the prayers for mercy heard." Boehm exclusively connected the circuit rider ministry's growth with the display of "the power of God" among the people through which "the work of revival continued; sinners were crying for mercy, and many obtained pardons."[79] Furthermore, Cartwright recalled how God's Spirit had blessed him, causing revivals to spread "almost through the entire country, and great additions" were made to the MEC. Thus, it was because of the outpouring of "the Holy Spirit" upon audiences, coupled with the determination of the circuit riders, that many "glorious" revivals were born. Clearly, the circuit riders acknowledged that their revivals "broke out" through God's hand as "young [and old] . . . were converted."[80]

An interesting pattern evident in the circuit rider ministry is that, even during the height of revivals, circuit riders continued to pray that the Holy Spirit would be poured out and supernaturally fall on Methodist meetings so that they might repeatedly, and in new ways, "feel it as well as see it."[81] For instance, as recorded in Asbury's journal, at one point in Virginia, despite the fact that the circuit riders had been experiencing revivals in their midst, the circuit riders "earnestly recommended" the Methodist societies to pray even more for "the prosperity" of the ministry and "a larger out-pouring of the Spirit of God. They did so; and not in vain." What followed was a "refreshing" revival that lasted for two years and was "as great [a revival] as perhaps ever was known." Moreover, after those two years, the Spirit of God was poured out again in a supernatural way that they "had not seen before." This then extended itself as in "almost every assembly . . . [there were] signal instances of divine power . . . Here many old stout-hearted sinners, felt the force of truth, and their eyes were open to discover their guilt and danger."[82]

The circuit riders expressed that the various displays of the supernatural prompted spiritual breakthroughs in specific people groups or areas that, in the past, exhibited no interest in religion and rejected the gospel. This notion was described by Finley who recorded a revival that "contributed greatly to increase the interest" in experiential Christianity including among masses who "previously paid no attention to the subject of religion." Finley (echoing 1 Kgs 19:11–12) noted that divine

79. Wakeley and Boehm, *Patriarch of One Hundred Years*, 32, 46.

80. Cartwright, *Backwoods Preacher*, 64, 102, 117, 226.

81. Lee, *Memoir*, 86. See also Maffitt, *Memorial of Philip Embury*, 33, 35; Cooper, *Beams of Light*, 112.

82. Asbury, *Journal of the Rev. Francis Asbury*, 1:159–60.

supernatural acts were behind this transformation because the power of God was demonstrated "not only in the earthquake and the fire, but in the still small yet powerful voice." Hence, from the Spirit's outpourings, the number of those spiritually converted "was great, and the work extended almost every-where."[83]

Cartwright further illustrated this notion by describing a circuit in which a significant number of citizens were "very wicked" and continuously "resisted and rejected" the gospel despite hearing numerous sermons. However, God then poured forth his Spirit and their "wicked" town was "awfully shaken" by the power and presence as many began to "quail" and tremble under God's Spirit. Moreover, Cartwright witnessed that the Spirit's influence was so poignant that whatever wickedness controlled the town was transformed into godliness as "deism gave way, Universalism caved in, skepticism, with its coat of many colors, stood aghast, hell trembled, devils fled, drunkards awoke to soberness." In other words, supernatural manifestations caused "all ranks and grades of sinners" to repent and receive conversion. From the outpouring, there later came a revival in that area in which more than one hundred individuals "were converted, and joined the Church."[84] Thus, many times in the circuit rider ministry, the supernatural served as an impetus in causing religious interest (and, ultimately, church growth) in people and areas that were previously not attracted or welcoming to the Christian gospel.

Consequently, as noted in chapter 5, circuit rider revivals also became agents in transforming social morals in the locations where revivals occurred. Even in places "notorious for wickedness, and, especially, for drunkenness," through various supernatural displays, many became "happy converts" and began lifestyles that pursued Christian holiness.[85] Hence, circuit riders believed that revivals not only produced membership growth through supernatural displays, they also believed that revivals became a catalyst in changing the social norms (from wickedness to godliness) in those affected areas.[86] In other words, circuit riders identified the "many signal manifestations of the power and grace

83. Finley, *Autobiography*, 239.

84. Cartwright, *Backwoods Preacher*, 229.

85. Finley, *Autobiography*, 239.

86. See also Asbury, *Journal of the Rev. Francis Asbury*, 3:349.

of God"[87] as the means by which people were first internally and then externally "affected in an extraordinary manner," and soon after, "great" revivals took "place in [their] settlement, and a considerable number [of people were] converted" on a daily basis.[88]

In addition to the conversions sparked by various supernatural phenomena, these revivals also became popular because of their poignant salvation messages. As discussed in chapter 4, it was common in Methodist circles for the core message presented in these revivals to be of God's love and salvation that was offered to everyone, regardless of race, gender, or socioeconomic class. This message, directed toward conversion, seems to have especially gained popularity, as Asbury noted, among "the poor and lower classes."[89] For this reason, the membership of early American Methodism largely consisted of what was considered to be the lower classes of the nation.[90]

Often, Methodist revivals, with their characteristic supernatural displays and their unprejudiced supplications for conversion and social change, also made a way for new Methodist societies and congregations to be formed. Asbury illustrated this when, during a circuit sermon at Brother Connelly's, he acknowledged that there was a "revival of religion." Due to this revival, there was a formation of "a large" Methodist society there. Also, during one of his visits to Mr. S's society, Asbury witnessed another "appearance of a revival" that he anticipated would cause that society to grow in numbers.[91] Hence, the circuit riders demonstrated that, through these spiritual revivals, "many professed to obtain regenerating grace, and [many] joined the [Methodist] Church."[92]

At the same time, as Cooper illustrated, revivals were also an opportunity for many "backsliders" to be reclaimed and "old believers" to develop more passion for "the glory of God and the salvation of souls" and join the Methodist movement.[93] In addition to church membership growth, circuit riders reported that revivals "also produced a great

87. Ware, Sketches, 172.
88. Gatch, Sketch of Rev. Philip Gatch, 103.
89. Danielson, "Methodist Camp Meetings and Revival," 160–61.
90. Buy, "Four Types of Protestants," 194.
91. Asbury, Journal of the Rev. Francis Asbury, 1:204, 395.
92. Paine, Life and Times, 1:146.
93. Cooper, Beams of Light, 253.

increase" in the number of circuit riders themselves.[94] For instance, during various revivals, some of the prominent circuit riders felt called to ministry, such as Cartwright[95] and Finley.[96]

Thus, in the circuit rider ministry, "the demonstration of the Spirit and power" was the key factor in the popularity and success of the circuit riders' evangelistic revivals.[97] It appears that significant growth occurred only during times when God poured out his Spirit through "Pentecost[al]" or supernatural effects, enabling audiences to experience God directly.[98] Indeed, in these revivals (including camp meetings), while people "heard . . . Methodist" sermons, growth in revivals was achieved through the Spirit's "power, [through which] hundreds were awakened and happily converted to God."[99] According to the circuit riders, in these "glorious"[100] Methodist revivals, while sermons played a great role, it is evident that a far greater role was played by the Spirit of God as, essentially, the circuit riders spread the experiential gospel in various circuits not only with "words"[101] but also with "demonstration[s]"[102] of "much power."[103] They continuously labored and prayed that revivals might "spread in power, and cover these" American lands.[104] Clearly, the circuit riders understood that, through the hand of the "Holy Ghost," Methodism would "grow and multiply with greater rapidity . . . [working] to break down every barrier, to overcome sin, [and] to defeat the common foe of God and man . . . [by extending] light and truth and religion through the world."[105]

94. Finley, *Sketches of Western Methodism*, 74.

95. Cartwright, *Backwoods Preacher*, 13.

96. Finley, *Autobiography*, 167–68.

97. Finley, *Sketches of Western Methodism*, 326. For more information regarding this matter, see also Abbott and Ffirth, *Experience and Gospel Labours*, 155–57, 175, 215–16.

98. Wakeley and Boehm, *Patriarch of One Hundred Years*, 21. See also Smith and Dailey, *Experience and Ministerial Labors*, 96.

99. Finley, *Sketches of Western Methodism*, 334.

100. Young, *Autobiography of a Pioneer*, 74.

101. Pilmore, *Journal of Joseph Pilmore*, 186.

102. Finley, *Sketches of Western Methodism*, 326.

103. Pilmore, *Journal of Joseph Pilmore*, 57.

104. Gatch, *Sketch of Rev. Philip Gatch*, 104; Stevens, *History of the Methodist Episcopal Church*, 1:234.

105. Saxton, "Holy Spirit," 633–44.

In general, this was the pattern of early Methodist growth in America (through the work of the circuit rider ministry): numerous souls became "awakened and converted,"[106] not naturally or through mere human intellectual persuasion but, rather, through the supernatural displays of the "power [and presence] of God."[107] Cartwright confirmed the distinct correlation between the supernatural and Methodist expansion and specified that the circuit riders could not, by their own abilities, cause Methodism to grow.[108] He stated the following:

> It is true we could not, many of us, conjugate a verb or parse a sentence, and murdered the king's English almost every lick. But there was a Divine unction attended the word preached, and thousands fell under the mighty power of God, and thus the Methodist Episcopal Church was planted firmly in this Western wilderness, and many glorious signs have followed, and will follow, to the end of time.[109]

Methodist Laity Participation in Evangelism

The zeal of the circuit riders to evangelize America was passed on to the members of the Methodist laity, as well, and they also began to share the gospel anywhere they could.[110] For instance, Finley recorded a testimony of a Methodist lawyer who used an opportunity in court to proclaim the gospel. Finley expressed that this lawyer was talking about his case and then preaching to those present "so much so that the judges and jury alike began to shed tears." The lawyer even rose from his seat and cried

106. Bangs and Garrettson, *Life of the Rev. Freeborn Garrettson*, 182. For instance, Garrettson recalled a meeting in which, initially, there were only four members, praying and singing to the Lord; suddenly, the power of God descended in an extraordinary manner, causing those four individuals to grow to twenty people who were then added to that Methodist society.

107. Finley, *Autobiography*, 275. Some of the circuit riders, however, such as Beauchamp, were known to be both intellectually persuasive and experienced in supernatural phenomena. For more information, see Finley, *Sketches of Western Methodism*, 252.

108. For more information regarding Methodist membership growth from 1773 to 1840, see appendix B.

109. Cartwright, *Backwoods Preacher*, x. See also Abbott and Ffirth, *Experience and Gospel Labours*, 220, 227, 237.

110. For more information about Methodism and the ministry of laity, see Warner, *Method of Our Mission*, 70–73.

out to God to visit the courtroom and "send more power to these sinners' hearts." It appears that this Methodist lawyer anticipated that God would use his preaching so that people in that court might be "awakened . . . and that they would soon all be at the mourner's bench crying for mercy."[111]

Thus, in general, "every member" of the MEC became a laboring member who contributed to "the growth of the denomination . . . [as] in a special sense, [Methodist growth could also] be attributed to its efficient system of lay operations."[112] Even many of the Methodist laymen felt spiritually drawn to imitate the circuit riders in sharing the experiential gospel with whomever they could. In this way, the early Methodists as a whole "spread" the spiritual "flame" of the gospel "through their respective neighborhoods."[113]

Characteristics of Circuit Rider Revivals

In order to provide a fuller understanding of Methodist revivals, the following section is dedicated to the analysis of the appearance and duration of revivals as well as the distance covered within them and their participant and conversion statistics. As noted previously, such revivals were often held "in the open air [i.e., camp meetings], [tents], in the chapel[s], and the barn[s]."[114]

The customary length of circuit rider revivals varied; according to Asbury, their duration was directly connected to the duration of the "outpouring of the Spirit of God."[115] If the Spirit was sensed in revivals, then those revivals were considered continuous or ongoing; however, if the Spirit was no longer sensed, then those revivals generally began to wane and soon came to a close.[116] However, when the Spirit's presence in some meetings was no longer sensed with the intensity it was before, then the circuit riders, in faith and prayer, typically petitioned to God for "the

111. Finley, *Sketches of Western Methodism*, 207.

112. Goss, *Statistical History*, 176.

113. Asbury, *Journal of the Rev. Francis Asbury*, 1:162.

114. Atkinson, *Centennial History of American Methodism*, 220.

115. Asbury, *Journal of the Rev. Francis Asbury*, 1:159, 172.

116. Cartwright, *Backwoods Preacher*, 229; Finley, *Sketches of Western Methodism*, 66.

Spirit of the Lord" to continue being present within those revivals. In this case, then, the duration of revivals often persisted for longer periods.[117]

That being said, some revivals in the circuit rider ministry lasted for days and some "for weeks."[118] Some revivals were experienced continuously for many nights, or they "continued all day and most of the night."[119] Other revivals lasted for several seasons; some occurred during the fall season and still others occurred during (or for the full duration of) "spring . . . [or] summer."[120] There were many "marvelous" and significant revivals that lasted for a year; as Smith witnessed, sometimes they continued for up to or even more than "two years with very little intermission."[121]

As far as it pertains to the distance from which the impact of revivals was felt, this varied, as well. Sometimes revivals were localized, occurring only in one particular place. Most often, however, revivals spread. For example, Asbury noted in his journal that one revival "extended itself in some places, for fifty or sixty miles [a]round [and] it increased still more in the following year."[122] Revivals sometimes began in a certain place and then spread over a county or two; such was the case, as Finley recorded, when a revival spread "at Elk Garden, head of Clinch river, at Bickley's Station, and at several other preaching-places."[123] Often, the effect of revivals "extended to other Churches" and circuits, as well.[124] Indeed, the outpouring of the Spirit in revivals occasionally "extended itself, more or less, through most of the circuits, which takes in a circumference of between four and five hundred miles."[125] At other times, revivals spilled over from one state to another state, such as in "Virginia and North Carolina" where the circuit rider ministry "had a great revival," or as in another significant revival that spread "through Delaware state, to Pennsylvania."[126]

---

117. See also Asbury, *Journal of the Rev. Francis Asbury*, 1:159–61.

118. Travis, *Autobiography*, 56.

119. Wakeley and Boehm, *Patriarch of One Hundred Years*, 32. See also Young, *Autobiography of a Pioneer*, 143.

120. Lee, *Memoir*, 198. See also Powell, "Methodist Circuit Riders in America," 97.

121. Smith and Dailey, *Experience and Ministerial Labors*, 96. See also Watters, *Short Account of the Christian Experience*, 134.

122. Asbury, *Journal of the Rev. Francis Asbury*, 1:159.

123. Finley, *Sketches of Western Methodism*, 34

124. Finley, *Autobiography*, 270.

125. Lee, *Short History of the Methodists*, 54–55.

126. Phoebus, *Memoirs*, 29, 34.

As it pertains to the typical number of audience members in these revivals, this also greatly varied. Numbers were tied to the population density of certain geographical areas in which revivals occurred.[127] That being said, the number of participants sometimes consisted of tens but typically "hundreds, and sometimes thousands." For example, during one revival, Atkinson recorded that the audience contained "no less than five thousand the first day; and the second day of twice that number."[128]

As it pertains to the usual number of participants who actually received conversion, this varied, as well, and was tied to the number of participants, duration, and geographical distance of the Spirit's influence within particular revivals. At times, as Lee expressed, "it was quite common to hear of fifty or a hundred souls being converted."[129] At other times, "above a hundred whites, besides as many negroes, found peace with God." Sometimes, there were around "four hundred,"[130] "sixteen hundred . . . eight hundred,"[131] "twelve hundred,"[132] or "not less than fourteen hundred . . . ha[d] been converted"[133] and then added to the MEC.

It should also be noted that there were times when the circuit riders recorded the exact number of conversions, such as "one thousand eight hundred and three" converts.[134] However, generally, convert numbers per revival were closely approximated when described by the circuit riders, and so it is common to read of how "hundreds were brought to God."[135]

Circuit Rider Ministry Revivals by American State

As demonstrated above, due to both the "wonderful display[s] of the power and presence of God in the conversion of souls" and the circuit riders' ministerial labors, Methodist revivals spread throughout all parts

127. For more information regarding the historical demographics of America, see Haines, *Population History of North America*.

128. Atkinson, *Centennial History of American Methodism*, 220, 224.

129. Lee, *Short History of the Methodists*, 309.

130. Atkinson, *Centennial History of American Methodism*, 219, 224.

131. Lee, *Short History of the Methodists*, 134.

132. Paine, *Life and Times*, 1:36.

133. Asbury, *Heart of Asbury's Journal*, 264.

134. Watters, *Short Account of the Christian Experience*, 137.

135. Lee, *Short History of the Methodists*, 134.

of America.[136] The following section outlines Methodist revivals by state; appendix B also features charts of Methodist statistical data from 1773 to 1840.

Circuit riders and historians of those days recorded revivals in Virginia that began from their "fourteen counties."[137] One of the most influential revivals began in 1776, and by 1823, Virginia had fifty-four circuits, attended by at least ninety-seven ministers.[138] During this time, Atkinson described "the wonderful scenes" of this divine "drama" as "in the powerful awakening . . . the revival swept like flames through a dry forest."[139] In general, as described by the eyewitness and nineteenth-century historian Bennet, revival work in Virginia was known to have included "the power of God . . . manifested in a most extraordinary manner."[140]

Methodist circuit riders, eye-witnesses, and historians recorded revivals that spread throughout the state of Maryland, especially in 1789.[141] Cooper referred to this as a "little Pentecost" because the sermons were "so accompanied by the energy of the Holy Ghost" that people felt the "mighty" presence as they "tremble[d] and we[pt]," resulting in numerous conversions."[142] Asbury also reported that God's work was "glorious through the continent" and that, specifically in Baltimore, the labor went on "rapidly." There, Asbury anticipated that "an earthquake" of divine power would reach from "north to south, and from east to west."[143]

There were also revivals in New Jersey, especially during and after 1782, in which Asbury witnessed the display of supernatural manifestations as "preachers and people wept." He further stated that

136. Lee, *Short History of the Methodists*, 356. See also Dieter, "Revivals and Revivalism," 255–57; Arminius, "Short Sketches of Revivals," 28–35.

137. Asbury, *Journal of the Rev. Francis Asbury*, 1:172. See also Paine, *Life and Times*, 1:71; Jackson, *Lives of Early Methodist Preachers*, 6:169–71; Powell, "Methodist Circuit Riders in America," 5; Lee, *Memoir*, 97.

138. Bennett, *Memorials of Methodism in Virginia*, 698.

139. Atkinson, *Centennial History of American Methodism*, 218.

140. Bennett, *Memorials of Methodism in Virginia*, 149. See also Lee, *Short History of the Methodists*, 44.

141. Lee, *Short History of the Methodists*, 74, 140, 279; Asbury, *Journal of the Rev. Francis Asbury*, 1:172; Armstrong, *History of the Old Baltimore Conference*, xi, 12, 24, 196; Wakeley and Boehm, *Patriarch of One Hundred Years*, 48, 69.

142. Cooper, "Account of the Work of God," 410. See also Porter, *Comprehensive History of Methodism*, 272; Atkinson, *Centennial History of American Methodism*, 236.

143. Asbury, "Chapter 3." See also Atkinson, *Centennial History of American Methodism*, 241; "Revival in Baltimore," 2.

New "Jersey flames with religion; some hundreds [were] converted" and circuit riders "labored for a manifestation of the Lord's power."[144] For example, the newspaper *The Post-Boy* reported in 1805 that a "revival of religion" occurred in Trenton, New Jersey, and at least "five hundred souls were brought to God during [a] meeting."[145]

There were revivals "through[out] Kentucky";[146] one of the most recognized was the great revival of 1799.[147] As described by the eighteenth-century historian Redford, in Kentucky, a "great . . . display of Divine power" descended with such intensity that there was "almost a visible manifestation of the Holy Spirit." As a result of this phenomenon, even "the most reckless sinners turned pale and trembled while they felt its awful presence."[148]

There are records of Methodist revivals in North Carolina, especially in 1802.[149] Nineteenth-century Methodist historian Moore expressed that, during these revivals, the Spirit was present, gathering numerous "poor sinners" who supernaturally "felt" his power causing them to "testify" that their sins were forgiven.[150] Some newspapers, such as the *Weekly Raleigh Register*, reported a few of these revivals and publicly acknowledged that the "display of [God's] power . . . [through] the outpouring of his Spirit was visible" to the public.[151] By 1802, the MEC in North Carolina reached 200 circuits, and 358 circuit riders were appointed to minister to 86,734 members.[152]

There were also revivals in South Carolina.[153] Nineteenth-century Methodist minister Shipp described how, during these revivals, the Spirit of God supernaturally descended and "one universal cry for mercy was

144. Asbury, *Journal of the Rev. Francis Asbury*, 2:47, 77. See also Atkinson, *Centennial History of American Methodism*, 243; *Memorials of Methodism in New Jersey*, 221, 420.

145. "From the Trenton Federalists," 1.

146. Young, *Autobiography of a Pioneer*, 108.

147. Smith, *History of Methodism in Georgia and Florida*, 497.

148. Redford, *History of Methodism in Kentucky*, 2:188–89. See also Paine, *Life and Times*, 1:153; Sweet, *Circuit-Rider Days in Indiana*, 49.

149. Stevens, *History of the Methodist Episcopal Church*, 1:186.

150. Moore, *Sketches of the Pioneers of Methodism*, 96, 257.

151. "For the Register," 3.

152. Lepley, "Circuit Riders," para. 5.

153. Gatch, *Sketch of Rev. Philip Gatch*, 88; Shipp, *History of Methodism*, 281, 355, 357.

heard all through the vast concourse of people." In this meeting, many were slain in the Spirit while "others, rising to fly from the scene, fell by the way." From these outpourings, "hundreds" rejoiced because they became spiritual converts, or "heaven-born souls," and their cries of "victory over the powers of darkness" were heard throughout the area.[154]

From the time that the circuit riders began to minister in Tennessee, especially during 1787, the state experienced Methodist revivals.[155] Nineteenth-century Methodist minister M'Ferrin reported that "many thousands" of individuals joined circuit rider meetings and that, during them, "the mighty power and mercy of God" was displayed. Audience members were slain in the Spirit "like corn before a storm of wind" and, upon returning to their senses, were filled "with divine glory" that caused their faces to shine. These displays were so startling that they reportedly caused even the "stubborn sinners" to "tremble." Also, there were times when, during these revivals in Tennessee, "thousands of souls" were converted, and numerous Methodist "societies were organized."[156]

Eighteenth (and even nineteenth) century New England[157] was known to predominately consist of Congregationalist churches that practiced a theology containing Calvinist doctrines (of predestination) derived from the early Puritans and Pilgrims.[158] However, as Methodist work began there (from 1789), there was an increase of various Methodist revivals, most notably in Vermont.[159] These revivals started especially after 1797 and often caused many to be slain in the Spirit or "struck helpless to the floor."[160]

In Indiana, as investigated by Methodist historian Sweet, by 1832, Methodist membership had expanded to approximately twenty thousand. Throughout the 1820s, there were several "remarkable revivals" in various locations throughout the state. Through them, "converts were

154. Shipp, *History of Methodism in South Carolina*, 331.

155. Paine, *Life and Times*, 1:153; M'Ferrin, *History of Methodism in Tennessee*, 1:43; MEC, *Minutes of the Annual Conferences*, 2:50.

156. M'Ferrin, *History of Methodism in Tennessee*, 1:141, 296.

157. The New England states are Connecticut, Maine, Massachusetts, New Hampshire, Rhode Island, and Vermont.

158. *Evangelical Repository*, 95; Murphy and Truesdell, *Separate Denominations*, 453.

159. Lee, *Short History of the Methodists*, 274; Allen and Pilsbury, *History of Methodism in Maine*, 26–27; Crawford, *Centennial of New England Methodism*, 489.

160. Meredith, *Jesse Lee*, 98.

won . . . [and] the greatest religious revivals were conducted out in the open air." In these Methodist revivals, it was reported that often "strange and seemingly supernatural things happened."[161]

There were also various recorded revivals in other states, such as New York, especially in 1790;[162] Atkinson witnessed that, at one point, approximately four hundred were converted in around eight weeks. Moreover, there were "two hundred accessions" throughout the revival, and afterward, numerous "others joined" the church.[163] By the year 1800, nineteenth-century historian Smith observed that "the great revival tide which swept over America came in blessing to Georgia," and so there were various Methodist revivals there.[164] Furthermore, in the late eighteenth and early nineteenth century, there were Methodist (and Baptist) "great religious revivals"[165] in the state of Mississippi, which originated from and "depended" on various spiritual gatherings, specifically camp meetings.[166] Additionally, in 1803, there were revivals in Ohio that circuit riders believed to have been some of "the most powerful revivals" of the labor of God, which caused the "awakening and the conversion of sinners";[167] indeed, the *Buffalo Emporium and General Advertiser* reported in 1824 that there was an "extensive revival of religion" in Ohio that successfully spread to other parts of the country, as well.[168] Beginning in 1804, there were various revivals in Illinois, especially one in 1820 in which, due to the power of God, it was recorded that many were slain in the Spirit, resembling dead people "in battle."[169] Additionally, by 1828, there were recorded revivals in the state of Florida.[170]

161. Sweet, *Circuit-Rider Days in Indiana*, 48.

162. Ware, *Sketches*, 230.

163. Atkinson, *Centennial History of American Methodism*, 241.

164. Smith, *History of Methodism in Georgia and Florida*, 89.

165. Sparks, "Religion In Mississippi," para. 5–6.

166. Jones, *Complete History of Methodism*, 1:138–39, 223–24.

167. Finley, *Sketches of Western Methodism*, 200. See also Paine, *Life and Times*, 1:153; Barker, *History of Ohio Methodism*, 118.

168. Griffin, "Moral and Religious," 1.

169. Leaton, *History of Methodism in Illinois*, 36, 55, 167.

170. Smith, *History of Methodism in Georgia and Florida*, 236, 238. See also Gatch, *Sketch of Rev. Philip Gatch*, 121.

Criticism Surrounding Methodist Revivals

It appears that the majority of Americans from other denominations approved of Methodist revivals and the strategies and practices surrounding them. Unity and peace were prevalent because many leaders "among the different denominations" of those days worked together and formed "great union[s]" for the purpose of seeking revivals, especially in interdenominational camp meetings.[171] For example, the well-known Presbyterian revivalist Finney praised the Methodists and their revival strategies, stating the following: "Look at the Methodists. Many of their ministers are unlearned, in the common sense of the term . . . and yet they have gathered congregations, and pushed their way, and won souls everywhere . . . Few Presbyterian ministers have gathered so large assemblies, or won so many souls."[172] Hence, their mutual desire for revival caused them to set aside their ecclesiastical and theological differences and focus on converting souls and empowering believers, thus furthering the Second Great Awakening.[173]

However, there were instances in which "religious leaders"[174] and loyal members of other denominations were unhappy with Methodist revivals and strove to stop them. According to Hatch, some of "the learned and orthodox distained early Methodism's new revival measures."[175] For example, *The Universalist Watchman* reported that a number of Presbyterian leaders in New England and Pennsylvania had "condemned" Methodist "revivals" for their "scenes of moral misuse and desolation."[176] It appears that these individuals were content with religious life within the Early Republic (largely because most of America at that time was

171. Giles, *Pioneer*, 307. See also Asbury, *Journal of the Rev. Francis Asbury*, 2:397; Clark, *1844*, 1:37; Cartwright, *Backwoods Preacher*, 9–10.

172. Finney, *Lectures on Revivals of Religion*, 259.

173. Some prominent non-Methodist ministers who were famous for their early nineteenth-century revivalist efforts were as follows: Charles Grandison Finney, Lyman Beecher, Barton Stone (who was introduced in chapter 5), Edward Everett, Benjamin Randall, and Thomas and Alexander Campbell. Interestingly, many of these revivalists continued to use Methodist ministerial strategies (especially in including camp meetings and supernaturalism) even after the 1830s, which was a period of time when Methodism itself began to move away from the circuit riders' practices in order to more closely resemble the ministerial strategies of other mainline denominations (resulting in a notable decline in evangelism and supernaturalism).

174. Howe, *What Hath God Wrought*, 186–87.

175. Hatch, *Democratization of American Christianity*, 14.

176. Williamson, "Occasional Sermon," 2.

considered to be church friendly); for that reason, they leaned toward the notion that laboring for revival was unnecessary and potentially harmful, especially coming from the uneducated and "overly emotional" Methodists and their "shallow and unorthodox" theology.[177]

Indeed, it seems that the Presbyterian church (as well as other denominations) during that time was divided between "the old and new school." The old school Presbyterians generally maintained a distaste for the Methodist experiential gospel and revivals; however, the new school Presbyterians, with which Finney identified, were in agreement (and even co-labored with) the circuit riders by pursing the experiential gospel and revivals. Consequently, there was notable contention within the denomination concerning Methodism and its work.[178]

One of the main reasons why other denominations were against Methodist revivals was because Methodism absorbed members of these denominations. Circuit rider revivals were attended by people "of all denominations, sects, and conditions . . . [who would] come out to [listen to their] preaching";[179] as a result of the divine encounters within the circuit rider revivals, a number of these people then "joined . . . [a Methodist] society" or church.[180] When other denominational leaders witnessed the decline of their church membership, some became "much alarmed at [Methodist] success." As a result of this, there were instances in which these leaders would "oppose [the circuit riders] openly"[181] and "persecution began to be waged against"[182] circuit rider labors.

Peck noted that, although it seemed "strange" for Christians to participate in these schemes, leaders of other denominations created "union meeting[s]" for the purpose of "straining every nerve to keep the Methodists down." These meetings occurred before Methodists met at their potential revival locations and, because of the fact that the other

177. Howe, *What Hath God Wrought*, 186. For more information regarding early nineteenth-century criticism of revivals, including Methodist revivals, see Reeves, "Countering Revivalism and Revitalizing Protestantism," 1–8, 263–65; Baldwin, "Devil Begins to Roar," 94–119; Bratt, *Antirevivalism in Antebellum America*, xv–xxii; Butler, "Enthusiasm Described and Decried," 305–25.

178. Finney, *Memoirs*, 7, 234, 237–40, 343.

179. Finley, *Autobiography*, 260. See also Abbott and Ffirth, *Experience and Gospel Labours*, 137–38.

180. Garrettson, *Experience and Travels*, 93, 224.

181. Asbury, *Journal of the Rev. Francis Asbury*, 1:351, 376.

182. Finley, *Autobiography*, 171. See also Lee, *Short History of the Methodists*, 74; Abbott and Ffirth, *Experience and Gospel Labours*, 71.

denominational leaders and members "had possession of [the desired] ground," they endeavored to prohibit any "Methodist revivals" from taking place on their land. These leaders also met with the local public in order to paint the circuit riders as "intruders" who would create contention within the community; thus, the goal of these leaders was to prevent ministerial success in the local circuit rider revivals.[183]

As Methodism expanded, its episcopal system expanded, as well. There were times when religious leaders of other denominations criticized the circuit rider ministry for operating under this system and, for this reason, attempted to prevent Methodist ways from further spreading throughout the country via their revivals. This criticism was mostly regarding the amount of power given to the Methodist bishops (in appointing the circuit riders to various circuits). For some Americans of those days, this episcopal system was not considered democratic. One of the most vocal critics of this system was the Baptist minister Graves; in one of his letters addressed to the MEC, he accused Methodism of being "a harlot and an abomination," imitating the tyrannical papal system and, therein, becoming a descendant of "the Church of Rome—the great whore and mother of harlots—also called Antichrist."[184] Another outspoken critic was the Congregationalist minister E. Smith who argued that the Methodist episcopal system was an "antichristian government . . . in opposition with the great Bishop Jesus Christ" and that Methodist bishops were a "cause of divisions and contentions" within the American Protestant churches.[185] There was also an incident inside the MEC in which circuit rider O'Kelly petitioned to reform the episcopal system. This was unsuccessful, however, which prompted O'Kelly to form his own denomination, the Republican Methodist Church, in 1792.[186]

Methodist growth also contributed to the spread of Arminian doctrine, which as historian Smith explained, featured "free-will and universal

183. Peck, *Early Methodism*, 197–98. See also Cooper, *Beams of Light*, 334; Asbury, *Journal of the Rev. Francis Asbury*, 1:147.

184. Graves, *Great Iron Wheel*, 33.

185. Smith, *Age of Enquiry*, 46–47. E. Smith was also known for publishing the first religious newspaper in America, the *Herald of Gospel Liberty* (1808). See also Smith, "Address to the Public," 1.

186. This denomination later became known as the "Christian Church" or "Connection." For more information, see Cartwright, *Backwoods Preacher*, 139; O'Kelly, *Author's Apology*, 6–7, 79–87; Buckley, *Constitutional and Parliamentary History*, 70–80.

salvation."[187] Previously, American religion was known for holding "most rigidly to the doctrines of unconditional election and reprobation" in which only a select number, or the "predestined," could receive salvation. In other words, predestination or Calvinist doctrines "filled the whole country." Because Methodists introduced and practiced a vastly different salvation theology, tension grew within the American church (and was most notably felt by the Presbyterians and Congregationalists). According to Finley, no other denomination (except Methodism) was "sufficiently fearless and independent to call [predestination] in question."[188] Thus, because the Methodists believed that their salvation theology was closer to the biblical teachings, they openly preached against doctrines of Calvinism (while other denominational leaders preached against Methodist Arminianism).[189] This further contributed to the criticism of Methodism and the deterrence of Methodist revivals.

The expansion of Methodism with its "experimental religion and practical piety"[190] also specifically discouraged "drinking" alcohol, which, consequently, incited social conflict.[191] Asbury desired the public to "lay aside the use of wine and strong drink in general. [In doing so, he believed that] God would suddenly and certainly work."[192] As a result of this Methodist stance, those who "refused to drink [liquor] were called, by way of reproach, Methodist fanatics." This stance not only upset much of the public, it also especially seemed to anger the liquor (mostly whiskey) manufacturers. This was another reason why the circuit riders became a target of "opposition," and their revival meetings were unwelcomed in certain places. Regardless, the circuit riders continued to speak "out publicly against this monster evil."[193]

187. Smith, *Revivalism and Social Reform*, 24–25. See also Olson, *Arminian Theology*, 108.

188. Finley, *Autobiography*, 369.

189. Finley, *Sketches of Western Methodism*, 216. See also Peck, *Early Methodism*, 200; Cartwright, *Backwoods Preacher*, 106–11; Abbott and Ffirth, *Experience and Gospel Labours*, 182–83; Cooper, *Beams of Light*, 66; Ware, *Sketches*, 119.

190. Finley, *Autobiography*, 369. See also Boase, *Methodist Circuit Rider*, 1:63–65; Hempton, *Methodism*, 77–79.

191. Boase, *Methodist Circuit Rider*, 1:63–65. See also Rorabaugh, *Alcoholic Republic*, 5–10.

192. Asbury, *Letters*, 256.

193. Finley, *Autobiography*, 247–49. See also Cartwright, *Backwoods Preacher*, 186–87; Asbury, *Journal of the Rev. Francis Asbury*, 1:347; Giles, *Pioneer*, 89–91; Young, *Autobiography of a Pioneer*, 108–10.

Largely due to the conflict surrounding Methodism, there were cases of new Methodist followers who became targets of "persecution and the vilest reproach everywhere followed them." For example, there were instances in which youths were converted during revival meetings and publicly announced that they desired to become Methodists; however, this apparently displeased their parents (who were members of other denominations), and in response, their "parents cruelly whipped their children till the blood ran down to the ground."[194] Similarly, it became evident that revival meetings were attractive to females; in fact, modern scholar Hempton argued that Methodism became "preponderantly a women's movement."[195] As such, there were instances in which women expressed a desire to become Methodists; however, their husbands, who supported other mainline denominations, persecuted them and "turned [them] out of doors in the darkness, [in] cold and storm."[196]

While contention existed between the Methodists and some "other Protestants," it should be noted that there is no recorded contention within early American Methodism itself regarding revivals, at least not in the existence of the revivals, the laboring toward them, or the importance of them.[197] The only conflict that arose among the Methodists during their revivals was in regard to religious enthusiastic exercises, although as noted in the previous chapter, even opposition to these exercises was minor.[198]

To conclude this section, circuit riders believed it was their divine duty to bring about revivals throughout America.[199] As a result, though some non-Methodists pressured them in their revival labors, the circuit riders remained steadfast in their mission.[200]

194. Young, *Autobiography of Dan Young*, 25–27.

195. Hempton, *Methodism*, 5.

196. Young, *Autobiography of Dan Young*, 26–28.

197. Reeves, "Countering Revivalism and Revitalizing Protestantism," 16.

198. For more information regarding religious enthusiasm in the circuit rider ministry, see chapters 5–6.

199. Coke and Asbury, *Minutes*, 4; Bangs and Garrettson, *Life of the Rev. Freeborn Garrettson*, 189; Tigert, *Constitutional History*, 536.

200. Peck, *Early Methodism*, 197–98, 323; Asbury, *Journal of the Rev. Francis Asbury*, 1:162; Atkinson, *Centennial History of American Methodism*, 225; Williams, *Garden of American Methodism*, 29.

Concluding Comments

The aim of this chapter was to explore the importance and effect of supernatural phenomena within circuit rider revivals along with the correlation between such phenomena and the expansion of early American Methodism. The chapter began by defining and describing Methodist revivals and camp meetings (including their general characteristics and influence by state); it used these revivals as a model for assessing the role of the supernatural in the circuit rider ministry (which often revolved around such large Methodist meetings). Ultimately, this work demonstrated that the supernatural generated numerical growth in American Methodism.

The circuit riders presented a ministry wherein the constant out-pourings of the "divine"[201] power and presence in their evangelistic meetings (particularly camp meetings) gave birth to "the phenomena of revivals"[202] that took place both locally and nationwide.[203] The circuit riders demonstrated that when "the power and grace of God"[204] was poured out, it often came in an extraordinary form, such "as the sound of a mighty rushing wind."[205] Furthermore, it occasionally felt that "the foundations of the place would seem to be shaken, and the people to be moved like the trees of the forest by a mighty tempest."[206] From such astounding incidents, revivals were sparked. In these revivals, the supernatural clearly played a singular role in that, through displays within evangelistic meetings (especially camp meetings), spiritual conversions were produced by the power and presence of God, which further generated public interest and amplified the movement's growth.

Early Methodist camp meetings were considered to be a rather new mission strategy (having been introduced between 1799 and 1801);[207] however, they rapidly became pivotal in bringing about massive religious

---

201. Lee, *Memoir*, 13.

202. Scudder and Cummings, *American Methodism*, 254. See also Asbury, *Journal of the Rev. Francis Asbury*, 1:160–61.

203. Phelan, *History of the Expansion of Methodism in Texas*, 118.

204. Bangs, *History of the Methodist Episcopal Church*, 2:101.

205. Cartwright, *Backwoods Preacher*, 104. See also Lee, *Short History of the Methodists*, 313.

206. Paine, *Life and Times*, 1:56.

207. Rieser, *Chautauqua Moment*, 20. See also Schmidt, *Kentucky Illustrated*, 99.

conversions and Methodist "expansion"[208] from the 1800s to the 1830s.[209] In fact, Richey labeled the camp meeting as "a hugely successful engine of [early] Methodist growth."[210] For the circuit riders, the camp meeting became one of their strongest organizational tools because it enabled them to exercise their preaching strategies (discussed in chapter 4) among large crowds while also offering an immediate opportunity for those crowds to experience the gospel supernaturally (discussed in chapters 5–6). A similar model of large-scale evangelism through camp meetings was used in future American ministries; for example, even in the twentieth century, camp meetings were instrumental to the ministry of the well-known evangelist Billy Graham.[211]

There are no accounts in circuit rider writings in which any form of revival occurred solely based on evangelistic or preaching efforts. Although circuit riders' ardent labors were key in producing their revivals, the circuit riders gave credit to God or "the Divine power" for the "awakening and conversion of sinners."[212] The circuit riders acknowledged that, "without God" and his evident works, the circuit riders could "do nothing" as divine acts endowed the circuit riders with "miraculous power."[213] To them, without these heavenly supernatural manifestations, "the greatest talents [were] rotten wood, and the most profound learning [was] a broken reed."[214]

Moreover, it was inconsequential whether revivals occurred through prearranged meetings (such as camp meetings) or in smaller spontaneous meetings; what is evident is that in order for any Methodist meeting to have been counted as a successful revival (one that contributed to membership expansion), it had to be visited by the supernatural. The circuit riders made it clear that, in their revivals, it was "the Spirit [who] would apply the truth with demonstrative power to the heart," making it the chief factor in circuit rider ministerial achievements.[215] Indeed,

208. Ahlstrom, *Religious History of the American People*, 437.

209. Some parts of America, such as the West, experienced revivals and camp meetings up until the 1840s and even, sporadically, up until the 1860s. For more information, see Barclay, *Methodist Episcopal Church*, 90–92.

210. Richey et al., *American Methodism*, 42.

211. See also Reid, *Evangelism Handbook*, 333–37.

212. Young, *Autobiography of a Pioneer*, 272.

213. Allen, "Walking by Faith," 205.

214. Newell, *Life and Observations*, 273.

215. Finley, *Sketches of Western Methodism*, 209. See also Goodsell, "Camp Meeting

their labors were "direct results of the power of the Holy Spirit, and manifest proofs of His presence and approval of the work."[216] Hence, the relationship between the supernatural and Methodist growth was vital because circuit riders depended on supernatural displays as "a perpetual guarantee of their success" in causing Methodist membership to expand nationwide.[217]

With the frequent unusual and intense displays in these revivals, people began to believe that the "days of [the apostolic] miracles [were] not past."[218] The magnitude of these supernatural manifestations was to such a degree that they produced sights that "eyes never saw before, nor read of, either in Mr. Wesley's *Journals*, or any other writings, except the account in Scripture of the day of Pentecost." Prior to attending these revivals, audience members generally had not witnessed such displays but knew them, theoretically, to have existed in the Apostolic Age and the early church.[219] It was the same Spirit who "affected the disciples on the day of Pentecost"[220] who also affected the circuit rider ministry and produced numeric growth.[221] Newell confirmed this matter when

on the Champlain District," 483–85; Cartwright, *Backwoods Preacher*, 12–17; Finley, *Autobiography*, 170–73; Young, *Autobiography of a Pioneer*, 197, 300.

216. Buckley, *History of Methodism*, 1:261. See also Whitby, "Extract with Dr. Whitby's Discourses," 57–61. Although James Buckley admitted the reality that divine influence caused early Methodism to expand, in his own life, ministry, and writings, he was admittedly against the supernatural phenomena that was believed and practiced in Methodism during and after the 1860s. For more information regarding this matter, see Buckley, "Faith-Healing and Kindred Phenomena," 222–36.

217. Scudder and Cummings, *American Methodism*, 339. For interpretations and conclusions regarding early Methodist growth, see Handy, "American Methodism," 46; Sargant, *Battle for the Mind*, xx, 106–7, 220–21, 225; Watson, *Class Meeting*, 19–31; Turner, "Redeeming the Time," 148, 224–25; Wigger, "Fighting Bees," 93–95, 105–7; *Taking Heaven by Storm*, 4–20; Hatch, *Democratization of American Christianity*, 40, 89, 140; O'Byrne, "How Methodists Were Made," 8–11, 213–50; Hempton, *Methodism*, 5, 30–33, 41–47, 140, 201; Billman, *Supernatural Thread in Methodism*, 43–44; Ruth, *Little Heaven Below*, 186–88, 209–22; Ruth, *Early Methodist Life and Spirituality*, 7, 161–89; Richey, *Methodism in the American Forest*, 6–7, 26–27, 63–64.

218. Porter, *Comprehensive History of Methodism*, 219. See also Snethen, *Snethen on Lay Representation*, 122.

219. Atkinson, *Centennial History of American Methodism*, 220.

220. Scudder and Cummings, *American Methodism*, 541.

221. Similar to the circuit riders, the apostle Paul summarized his ministry in Romans 15:18–19 by stating: "For I will not venture to speak of anything except what Christ has accomplished through me to bring the Gentiles to obedience—by word and deed, by the [supernatural] power of signs and wonders, [derived] by the power of

he concluded that the circuit rider ministry's "success, like that of the Apostles, depended entirely on the presence and power of God, and the riches of his grace."[222] Methodists openly declared that their expansion and revivalist "success resembled the revival of [the Day of] Pentecost" wherein "converts were multiplied by scores, sometimes by hundreds."[223] In other words, as also noted in previous chapters, the circuit riders directly compared their ministry, not to the denominations around them, but rather, to one of the most supernatural and pivotal incidents in the New Testament: the descent of the Holy Spirit as tongues of fire upon the believers. Because of the supernatural, public reputation of Methodist revivals, as revitalizers of the biblical signs and wonders, "spread all over" America;[224] as a result, masses poured into their meetings and "felt [the] power of God in [their] souls,"[225] causing the "conversion of thousands [at once]."[226]

In the majority of recorded revivals, supernatural manifestations affected, in varying degrees, all present: believers and nonbelievers, those who rejected the gospel, backsliders and "people [who] had been accustomed to a dry, cold, life-less ministry, and a 'form of godliness' without the power."[227] Their past understandings of religion were altered during these revivals as circuit rider "preaching"[228] had "power in it."[229] As noted in chapter 6, even many who attended these revivals in order to ridicule Methodist religious experience became spiritually converted;[230] they mocked "till the power of the Lord laid hold of them, and then they fell [down or were slain by the Spirit] themselves, and cried as loud as

the Spirit of God—so that from Jerusalem and all the way around to Illyricum I have fulfilled the ministry of the gospel of Christ."

222. Newell, *Life and Observations*, 273.

223. Scudder and Cummings, *American Methodism*, 89.

224. Cartwright, *Backwoods Preacher*, 104.

225. Asbury, *Journal of the Rev. Francis Asbury*, 1:23. See also Asbury, *Journal of the Rev. Francis Asbury*, 2:82.

226. Bangs, *History of the Methodist Episcopal Church*, 2:101. See also Atkinson, *Centennial History of American Methodism*, 220; Scudder and Cummings, *American Methodism*, 339; Saxton, "Holy Spirit," 633.

227. Holdich, *Life of Wilbur Fisk*, 109.

228. Cartwright, *Backwoods Preacher*, 13.

229. Holdich, *Life of Wilbur Fisk*, 225.

230. See also Cartwright, *Backwoods Preacher*, 229.

those they just before persecuted."[231] Indeed, Finley stated that, through the power "of God, [and] through the instrumentality of Methodism, a warm spiritual life was infused into these [theologically] dead forms, and awakening power roused" those present."[232]

Due to the attractiveness of supernatural presence, despite the opposition and criticism that they received from some non-Methodists and the public, Methodist revivals were "embraced [by] all classes—governor, judges, lawyers, and statesmen—old and young, rich and poor—including many of the African race."[233] The supernatural was influential in breaking down traditional barriers in gender, class, and race, joining audiences into one body in which Christ (along with his Scripture) was the head. Consequently, as early Methodism expanded, the American "social structures" were somewhat transformed and further embraced a lifestyle of scriptural holiness.[234]

Truly, the "successful" rise of Methodism was a direct result of supernatural phenomena or "the renewing and enlightening influence of the Holy Ghost."[235] As the supernatural gave birth to various revivals, the MEC achieved such tremendous expansion that it unexpectedly surpassed all other denominations. Even newspapers, such as the *Hartford Courant*, took note of how Methodism had quickly become "pretty numerous" throughout the country.[236] Similarly, the *National Standard* reported that Methodism was growing and "hundreds and thousands [had] been added to [the MEC]."[237] The *Vermont Republican and American Journal* recorded that circuit rider "gospel laboring" had ushered in such "great revival[s]" that the MEC had added "113,209" members from only 1799 to 1810.[238] *The Torch Light And Public Advertiser* confirmed the fast growth of the MEC, reporting that it expanded by "31,256" new members in 1821 alone.[239]

231. Atkinson, *Centennial History of American Methodism*, 220.

232. Finley, *Autobiography*, 382.

233. Ware, *Sketches*, 226.

234. See also CIHEC, *Church in a Changing Society*, 25.

235. Scudder and Cummings, *American Methodism*, 541.

236. "Revivals of Religion," 2.

237. "For the Columbian Patriot," 3.

238. "For the Vermont Republican," 2.

239. "Progress of Methodists," 2. See also "From Zion's Herald," 4; "Publication," 1; "Revival of Religion," 3; "Progress of Methodists," 2; "Miscellaneous," 4; Remem, "Extract of a Letter," 1.

As demonstrated in appendix B, while in 1780, there were "8,504 members,"[240] by the end of the 1830s, Methodism had reached 852,918 members.[241] Through "the presence of the Lord" in their religious meetings, though Methodists were once a "little flock," beginning with ten official preachers in 1773, they were "greatly increased," and by the early 1830s, they had become the largest denomination in America.[242] American Methodism remained the largest American denomination up until the 1860s, at which point it began to encounter numerical decline (which appears to be largely due to the absence of supernatural phenomena and evangelistic labors).[243]

Referencing these astonishing statistics, a recent article written by modern scholar Beougher summarized Methodist expansion under Asbury's leadership. Beougher explained that "the number [of Methodists] had grown from one in five thousand to one in forty of the total population of the country, largely because of camp meetings and circuit rider" evangelism, which often featured "unusual physical manifestations."[244] Wigger identified this rapid expansion as "a virtual miracle of growth."[245] Echoing this, modern scholars Finke and Starke referred to the substantial growth as "the Methodist 'miracle'"[246] because, indeed, the circuit riders "set the world on [spiritual] fire."[247] Thus, Methodism spread all over the land, with the presence of the supernatural serving as its impetus.[248] This miraculous expansion of early Methodism proved to the public and

240. Daniels and Harris, "Illustrated History of Methodism," 339.

241. GCAH, "United Methodist Membership Statistics." By 1860, Methodism grew to more than 1.6 million members. For more information, see Fuller, "Methodists," 641; Miller, Both Prayed to the Same God, 64.

242. Young, Autobiography of a Pioneer, 101. See also Fisk, "Dr. Fisk's Travels," 459; Kirby et al., Methodists, 177; Finlan, Apostle Paul, 15; Lee, Life-Study of Ephesians, 331; Leavitt, "Gifts and the Gift," 671.

243. MECS, Journal of the General Conference, 1:5; Bates, "Early Republic and Antebellum America," 641; Marsden, "Of the Methodist Doctrines," 211. Due to the successful ministry of the circuit riders, later Methodists viewed the early circuit riders, in some ways, as heroes of the faith. For more information regarding this matter, see Wakeley, Heroes of Methodism; Ayres, Methodist Heroes of Other Days; Hedding, "Bishop Hedding," 10.

244. Beougher, "Camp Meetings and Circuit Riders."

245. Wigger, "Holy, 'Knock-'Em-Down' Preachers," para. 9–11.

246. Finke and Stark, Churching of America, 113.

247. Cartwright, Backwoods Preacher, 38.

248. Marsden, "Of the Methodist Doctrines," 211; Atkinson, Centennial History of American Methodism, 121; Stevens, History of the Methodist Episcopal Church, 1:389.

their critics (as seen above and in chapter 6) that the Methodist circuit rider ministry was both divinely orchestrated and scriptural.[249]

Due to its numerical explosion, early Methodism (from the 1770s through the 1830s) is commonly considered to have been a principle protagonist that "led" and fed America's Second Great Awakening (from roughly the 1790s through the 1840s).[250] The Second Great Awakening was a period in American history when Protestantism experienced dramatic increase throughout the country.[251] This numerical surge, especially in frontier areas, directly "relied on circuit riders"[252] as, during this time, "Methodists . . . became a critical link in the Second Great Awakening."[253] Since Methodism played a vital role in fueling the Second Great Awakening, and since divine powers played a vital role in fueling Methodism, consequently, this Awakening was characterized by its many displays of various "supernatural manifestations."[254] The Second Great Awakening, which emphasized supernatural phenomena, also served as a countermovement to the prevalent influence of "rationalistic humanism and Deism," a product of the Enlightenment (discussed in chapter 2) that flowed from Europe to America.[255] Thus, as noted above, circuit riders also became a part of creating a new thought and cultural system within the Early American Republic that was more sympathetic to biblical principles.[256]

249. See also Butler et al., *Religion in American Life*, 143–44.

250. Hankins, *Second Great Awakening*, 14.

251. For an overview of the Second Great Awakening, see Hankins, *Second Great Awakening*, 1–5.

252. Nelson, "Second Great Awakening," 568.

253. Flora et al., *Companion to Southern Literature*, 483.

254. Rohde, *Viral Jesus*, 105.

255. Bloesch, *Christian Witness in a Secular Age*, 21.

256. Bilhartz, *Urban Religion and the Second Great Awakening*, 83. See also Gross, "Romance of American Methodism," 16.

Chapter 8

Concluding the Investigation

BELOW IS A SUMMARY of this book's findings along with an introduction to follow-up research, information on the continuing legacy of early Methodism, and a description of the relevance of this work within the academic, public, and Christian world. The purpose of this research was to investigate and determine the significance of the supernatural in the Methodist circuit rider ministry (regarding its impact on the circuit riders, their audiences, and their ministry's growth) from the 1770s through the 1830s. The circuit riders, who were early Methodist traveling preachers, dedicated their lives to evangelizing and ministering in America by engaging in an experiential gospel. In America, these circuit riders began their ministry (initially with ten official ministers) in the early 1770s and labored intensely up until the end of the 1830s; during that time, they expanded dramatically and became the largest American denomination.[1]

Summarizing Findings

While this work recognizes that the circuit rider ministry prospered in no small part due to the fact that the circuit riders were fully devoted to their unconventional evangelistic pursuits (while placing no value on personal comfort or gain), this is just part of the picture. Consequently, while the zealous dedication, countercultural positions, and evangelistic

---

1. Although the circuit rider ministry continued to a lesser degree beyond the 1830s (especially in the western frontier), this study focused on the height of the American circuit rider ministry (which was from the 1770s to 1830s).

strategies of the circuit riders have been noted and esteemed by scholars (who generally attributed these three factors as the primary cause of early Methodist growth),[2] this book began with the notion of investigating the apparent significance of the supernatural in the development of the circuit rider ministry—a significance that, in general, has been overlooked throughout countless scholarly works.[3] In pursuing this investigation, it became evident that the circuit riders (largely due to their spiritual dedication) were blessed with the strong power and presence of the Spirit of God that touched their personal lives, pervaded their ministry, and brought about conversions in astounding numbers. Indeed, the role that the supernatural played in the circuit rider ministry has been brought to light, specifically the role it played in the lives of the circuit riders themselves, their audiences, and, ultimately, their ministry's expansion. More specifically, the following has been illuminated:

For the circuit riders, the meaning of the term *supernatural* (antithetical to the *seen* or *natural*) was, in essence, understood to be an act, manifestation, or phenomenon that derived from the (supreme) unseen or spiritual realm and was largely attributed to God (but also included angelic or demonic beings); generally, circuit riders believed that supernatural phenomena originated from the power and presence of God's Spirit. To further delineate the concept of supernatural phenomena in the circuit rider ministry, two classes were constructed: private supernaturalism (containing spiritual experiences occurring within circuit riders' personal lives) and public supernaturalism (containing spiritual experiences occurring within circuit riders' audiences).

In order to understand the fundamental function of supernaturalism in the circuit rider ministry, this study presented a historical and theological exploration of the formation of Methodism and the circuit rider ministry. It was demonstrated that, from Wesley's *heart strangely warmed* experience, the role and theology of the supernatural in Wesley's life and ministry (as the first and ongoing model of the American circuit rider ministry) became something that he believed in, practiced,

---

2. Wigger, *Taking Heaven by Storm*, 3–9; "Fighting Bees," 94–95; Hatch, *Democratization of American Christianity*, 88–89, 139–40; O'Byrne, "How Methodists Were Made," 7–12; Hempton, *Methodism*, 5, 140, 201; Ruth, *Early Methodist Life and Spirituality*, 161–89; *Little Heaven Below*, 187–88, 208–21; Richey, *Methodism in the American Forest*, 5–8, 27, 63–64. For more information, see chapter 6.

3. See also Watson, *Class Meeting*, 21–31; Hempton, *Methodism*, 31–33; Billman, *Supernatural Thread in Methodism*, 33–34; Turner, "Redeeming the Time," 224–25.

and promoted in both his daily life and ministry. Wesley deeply relied on demonstrations of the supernatural for a productive ministry and maintained that the power of the Spirit should be a part of Methodist ministerial strategies, in England and then in America. This philosophy of supernatural ministry was continued and further developed by the circuit riders (especially Asbury) in America where it was widely practiced by American circuit riders.

The supernatural served as spiritual fuel in the lives of the circuit riders by inciting their conversions, confirming their ministerial callings, and maintaining their biblical sanctification. In general, the circuit riders were initially introduced to supernatural phenomena during their own conversions. The circuit riders were touched by God's Spirit, which caused them to be spiritually reborn; in many cases, these conversions were experienced in unusual and dramatic ways.

Even in their ministerial callings, the supernatural served as the main influence in setting circuit riders apart to preach the gospel. The circuit riders reported that they were called directly by God through various confirmations, such as personal spiritual impressions, the hearing of God's audible voice, dreams, trances, and visions. In addition, the circuit riders testified that God's Spirit was supernaturally present in their lives to equip them with various spiritual blessings so that they might have successful ministries; these blessings often included a sanctified lifestyle and the fruits and gifts of the Spirit.

Furthermore, private supernatural experiences helped shape the pragmatic evangelistic efforts and strategies of the circuit riders. Even though (initially) the circuit riders were largely uneducated, they trusted in the power and presence of God to enable them to be fruitful, preach effectively (through the power of the Spirit), and endure ministerial hardships. Their evangelistic zeal was inspired by their supernatural conversions and was a response to their divine callings. In evangelism, the circuit riders not only observed Wesley's circuit strategies but they also further developed them according to the ministerial needs of Americans, which largely revolved around the personal and practical applications of spirituality (as well as the countercultural messages). Asbury was one of the main leaders who led the circuit riders in implementing this evangelistic strategy in which the sharing of the universally accessible gospel relied on experiential or pragmatic methods.[4]

4. Hatch, *Democratization of American Christianity*, 3–5.

Thus, the circuit riders organized in groups and circuits, recruiting people to go out and preach everywhere and to everyone—to literally be spent in spreading the experiential gospel. Moreover, circuit riders practiced, ministered, and presented a gospel that was spiritually empirical; they evangelized and preached with the anticipation that their audiences would encounter God. In their ministry, it was the supernatural, derived from the power and presence of the Spirit, that served as the key to experiencing the gospel.

As it pertains to the nature and appearance of these supernatural occurrences in their evangelistic meetings, it can be argued that the circuit rider ministry looked, in essence, similar to Jesus's ministry, the Apostolic Age, and the early church wherein the gospel was spread through the demonstration of supernatural phenomena, leading to both small and large-scale conversions. It was demonstrated that, in the circuit rider ministry, God's power and presence was frequently tangible and manifested in visible forms, such as a sacred fire, a mighty wind, a heavy cloud/mist, spiritual energy, an electric shock, a radiant light, and rain. Outpourings of the Spirit caused various supernatural incidents within circuit rider audiences, as well. These incidents commonly featured the following: being slain in the Spirit, intense (and often controversial) emotional expressions of religious enthusiasm, divine dreams and visions and trances, spiritual warfare, healings, the raising of the dead, and divine weather shifts.

Largely due to the frequent visible demonstrations of the supernatural, the fame of the circuit rider ministry spread. Circuit riders also became known for the fact that, when they prayed for people, supernatural breakthrough often occurred, and members of the public began to believe that, indeed, the Methodists could work miracles. Numerous records indicate that the public often sought out the Methodists and their meetings, imploring them to pray for those who needed healing or deliverance through exorcism. Stevens confirmed this matter by declaring that the circuit riders, such as Abbott, were often "pervaded by a certain magnetic power that thrilled . . . discourses and radiated from [them], drawing, melting, and frequently prostrating the stoutest opposers . . . [They] seldom preached without visible results, and [their] prayers were overwhelming."[5]

---

5. Stevens, *History of the Methodist Episcopal Church*, 1:196.

On the other hand, as in the Apostolic Age (especially as described in Acts 2:1–41), when some witnessed these spectacular and bizarre supernatural occurrences (especially those relating to the intense emotional expressions of religious enthusiasm), they criticized the circuit rider ministry by mocking and insulting it. In these incidents, the critics had not yet been personally affected by the supernatural phenomena surrounding them (by which many others were affected) and, as a result, they could not understand them. Thus, critics often viewed Methodist religious enthusiasm as irreverent, indecent, demonic, or maddening. In short, they contested the divine origin of religious enthusiasm in the circuit rider ministry.

The circuit riders responded to criticism by either defending Methodist spiritual acts through the use of logic (endeavoring to demonstrate that such acts were scripturally sound and had derived from the Spirit of God), or they simply prayed that the Spirit would touch these critics via some similar supernatural act (which often occurred) so as to demonstrate that Methodist spirituality was truly from God. Regardless of criticism, it is evident that the circuit riders continued to evangelize with displays of the supernatural.

However, there were occasions in which a small number of circuit riders opposed certain wild enthusiastic exercises (such as shrieking and howling). While these circuit riders supported and practiced a variety of supernatural activities within their ministries (including some forms of religious enthusiasm), they feared that wild religious enthusiasm would alienate the public and, in turn, cause God's work to be criticized. Despite the caution of this small number of circuit riders, religious enthusiasm was commonly evident in circuit rider meetings, particularly camp meetings.

As circuit riders understood that their ministerial achievements were possible only through the visitations of the Spirit of God, they trusted in the power of God to make their labors fruitful. According to their faith, the circuit riders displayed a ministry in which occurrences of supernatural phenomena were present in almost every major evangelistic meeting or revival, especially camp meetings. As recorded in volume 13 of *Methodist Magazine*, within the Early Republic, supernatural acts or "miracles" performed through the circuit riders were "the proper proofs of a new religion . . . In support of their doctrine, they appealed to the law and the testimony; and [in] evidence of their mission, they pointed to the sinners truly converted by their instrumentality [of God] . . . [they had] a Divine call to their work."[6]

Thus, coupled with their evangelistic dedication and zeal, the supernatural (through the power and presence of God) in the circuit rider ministry was shown to be primarily responsible for transforming Methodism from a tiny, unknown, and insignificant movement to the largest denomination in America by the early 1830s. Indeed, regarding the significance of supernaturalism in the circuit rider ministry and its resulting membership expansion, Giles concluded that "in all this, the wisdom of God was displayed [in the circuit rider ministry]. These poor obscure men [circuit riders], [were] inspired by their Master, and endowed with supernatural power, by which they spoke with tongues, and performed miracles, completely confounded the enemies of Christ by their wonderful works [of power], and proved effectually the validity of their mission" of spreading the gospel throughout America by way of spiritual convictions and conversions (which, in turn, led to Methodist expansion).[7] Evidently, the supernatural was the primary tool of the circuit riders, used within their personal lives and throughout their evangelistic labors.

Further Research

While this study investigated the correlation between the presence of supernatural acts and the rapid growth of the early American Methodist church (from the 1770s through the 1830s), conversely, further research and analysis is needed to investigate if there is a correlation between the lack of supernatural acts and the decline in growth percentage of the American Methodist church (the 1840s onward).

Beginning in the mid-1830s and accelerating in the 1860s, there was a slow shift in Methodism wherein the supernatural (and evangelistic labors) significantly declined. This decline began because "the rising [new] generation"[8] of Methodists no longer desired to associate themselves with the supernaturalism of the old generation or with uneducated "ranting Methodists." Instead, they desired to perform things "decently and [in]

---

6. E. T., "Edification of the Church," 325.

7. Giles, *Pioneer*, 59–62.

8. Finley, *Sketches of Western Methodism*, 136.

order,"⁹ as other mainline denominations were doing (by excluding the supernaturalism of the earlier circuit riders).¹⁰ Predominantly (but not completely) due to the staggering advances of Methodist professional and educational training in which, as Cartwright observed, the Methodists multiplied "colleges, universities, seminaries, and academies . . . agencies, and editorships,"¹¹ Methodism gradually experienced a shift from simple faith in the supernatural that was "moved by the Holy Ghost"¹² to more of an intellectual or "enlightened"¹³ Christianity, which was becoming more prevalent in an increasingly urban America.

The new generation of Methodists began to proclaim and "believe that miracles ha[d] long since ceased." The main Methodist magazine of the time, *the Christian Advocate* (and its influential editor, James Buckley), reflected this notion by stating the belief that "such passages of scripture" regarding supernatural ministry available to Christians, found in Matt 17:20; 21:21; Mark 11:23; Luke 17:6; 1 Cor 12:9; 13:2 "when taken in their literal sense, [were] applicable only to those who lived in the primitive age of the church"¹⁴ or the Apostolic Age. Indeed, these supernatural promises (which only recently were believed in and practiced by the Methodists before them) were purportedly irrelevant and expired for the new generations of circuit riders and the Methodists, in general; as such, they were forgotten.¹⁵

This concept can be illustrated by an incident involving Taylor, a prominent mid-nineteenth-century circuit rider, who read of Abbott's frequent supernatural experiences in his journals and ascertained that these experiences, such as being slain in the Spirit, were what made Abbott's ministry "effective." Taylor also became aware that these phenomena were no longer present in Methodism; thus, he "prayed earnestly to God [to] use [him] in that way." Soon after, God "answered" Taylor's prayer as, during a sermon, "a man fell down in a state of insensibility." Interestingly, while such incidents were previously

9. Burritt, *Methodism in Ithaca*, 70.

10. See also Bainbridge, *Sociology*, 153; Goodrich, *Recollections of a Lifetime*, 311.

11. Cartwright, *Backwoods Preacher*, 39.

12. Lee, *Memoir*, 5.

13. Bowen, "Missionary Discourse," 105.

14. "Religious Communication," 147. See also Cartwright, *Backwoods Preacher*, 40; Beauchamp, *Letters on the Call*, 108.

15. Chase, *Recollections of the Past*, 101; Giles, *Pioneer*, 302; Boehm, *Reminiscences*, 492; Travis, *Autobiography*, 125.

common in Methodism (as demonstrated), no one there thought to associate this incident with divine power; instead, they identified it as a natural irregularity and called a doctor, although he could not wake the man from his "dead" state. Instead, the man abruptly returned to his senses and declared: "There is nothing ails me but sin." He asked to see Taylor and later "surrendered to God and received Jesus Christ." Taylor rejoiced both because of the conversion and because God had visited his ministry with "a regular knock-down case, such as [he had] been reading about." However, aside from Taylor, who continued operating under the power of the Spirit, supernatural experiences remained absent from the next generation of Methodists.[16]

Consequently, as this next generation of Methodists pursued new methods and dismissed the strategies and legacy of their Methodist fore-fathers, the MEC began to break apart and countermovements began to form, such as the Holiness movement.[17] Furthermore, it appears that as a result of the intentional distancing from supernatural experiences and evangelistic zeal (combined with the ensuing splits from the MEC, particularly the Holiness movement), the percentage of Methodist growth began to decline.[18] For example, in 1810, it was estimated that the percent of Methodist growth was 169 percent; however, in 1830, this percent of growth had reduced to 85 percent and then to 11 percent in 1870.[19] In fact, from only 1840 to 1850, American Methodism reportedly experienced a decrease of 112,102 members.[20]

Unfortunately, modern American Methodism (referring to the UMC) "has experienced a century of decline"[21] and, to this day, it remains in a state of decline, experiencing regular "membership loss by raw numbers."[22] In fact, statistics revealed that from 1968 to 2008, the UMC "dropped more than 40 percent of its membership" and it

16. Taylor, *Story of My Life*, 98–99.

17. Godbey, "Are We Losing the Sense of Sin?," 298; Burritt, *Methodism in Ithaca*, 70; Billman, *Supernatural Thread in Methodism*, 69–70; Olson, *Westminster Handbook to Evangelical Theology*, 79.

18. Calder, *Origins of Primitive Methodism*, 272.

19. Goss, *Statistical History*, 148–49; Hempton, *Methodism*, 212. For more information on these figures, see appendix B.

20. Whedon, "Methodism in the Cities of the United States," 497.

21. Stark and Finke, *Acts of Faith*, 265.

22. Scott, "Coming to Terms with Numerical Decline," para. 1. See also Fenton, "US Membership Decline Continues," lines 1–13.

shut down "more than 12,000 local Churches."[23] In 2016 alone, the denomination declined "1.6 percent,"[24] and a "net of 116,560"[25] members were lost. However, while American Methodism experiences decline, on other continents, such as Africa, which associates closely with the circuit rider ministry (especially in supernaturalism, evangelism, and scriptural holiness) and "less and less" with today's American mainline "Protestantism," Methodism reports growth. For instance, Tooley, president of the Institute on Religion & Democracy (IRD), asserted that just "between 2009 and 2012," Methodism in Africa experienced a growth of "over 662,000 members in just three years. Meanwhile, the US church lost about 280,000 members during those three years."[26]

Further research is needed to investigate, in detail, why and how the supernatural (and evangelism) decreased in later Methodism, at large. Also, since it was demonstrated that, through the supernatural (from the 1770s to the 1830s), Methodism encountered dramatic membership increase, it seems probable that Methodism's future decline might be connected to an abandonment of supernaturalism (from the 1840s); thus, research investigating the correlation between the lack of the supernatural and the gradual decline of American Methodist growth and membership is needed.

Continuing the Legacy of Early Methodism

Because both the effects and renown of the circuit rider ministry spread, early Methodism, in turn, became largely responsible for sparking the Second Great Awakening as the public flocked to their revival meetings. For this reason, this Awakening was, in many ways, a Methodist legacy (as well as Baptist and also Presbyterian to a lesser extent), which deeply altered the theological perspectives of the times and left an indelible impression that is still quite evident in even the modern American church.

However, despite the fact that Methodism's course shifted beginning in the 1840s just after the Second Great Awakening came to a close, the legacy of early Methodism (as opposed to later Methodism)

23. Ray, "United Methodist Church," 97.

24. Hahn, "Denomination's Membership," para. 16–19.

25. Scott, "Coming to Terms with Numerical Decline," para. 1. See also GCFA, "Online Directory & Statistics."

26. Tooley, "Africans May Outnumber US," lines 1–3.

continued on, and evidence of its far-reaching effects can still be seen today. Indeed, as noted previously, because the beliefs and practices of the circuit rider ministry began to fade, new movements arose out of Methodism beginning in the 1840s that protested its spiritual condition; these movements eventually separated themselves from Methodism but continued on with the circuit rider legacy in many ways. Most notably, the Holiness movement emerged, pioneered by Methodist Phoebe Palmer (1807–1874). Palmer became known as the "mother of the holiness movement" and understood that one of the strengths of early Methodism was its focus on the process of scriptural sanctification in Christian life and its connection with the Holy Spirit.[27] This movement birthed denominations such as the Wesleyan Church (1843), the Free Methodist Church (1860), and the Church of the Nazarene (1895).[28]

In addition to the Holiness movement, the Pentecostal movement (beginning in 1901) also arose through Methodism as "many of the first Pentecostal leaders were originally Methodists."[29] Pentecostalism heavily emphasized the importance of Pentecost-like supernaturalism, which was believed in and practiced by the circuit riders (and Wesley). American Pentecostalism's pioneer was the former Methodist preacher Charles Fox Parham (1873–1929). Parham, who was also inspired by the Holiness movement, eventually abandoned Methodism mainly because of Methodism's evolving hierarchal nature and its spiritual dryness, which lacked the practical supernaturalism that was present in early Methodism.[30]

While Parham continued to embrace the theology and practices of the circuit riders (and Wesley), he also began to further emphasize the individual baptism of the Holy Spirit.[31] This spiritual baptism enabled believers to live a Christian life of "empowerment" and sanctification and commonly resulted in displays of Pentecost-like supernaturalism, such as divine healing.[32] While early Methodism and Pentecostalism shared

27. Armstrong, "Phoebe Palmer." For more information on Palmer's statements regarding the role of Wesleyan holiness, see Palmer, *Way of Holiness*.

28. See also Finke and Stark, *Churching of America*, 175.

29. UMC, *Book of Resolutions*, 693. Also, Pentecostalism was largely born out of the Methodist Holiness Movement.

30. Land, *Pentecostal Spirituality*, 93; Balmer, *Encyclopedia of Evangelicalism*, 340, 521; Adewuya, *Holiness and Community*, 5; Wood, *Meaning of Pentecost in Early Methodism*, xv.

31. Fletcher, *Christian Perfection*, 25–26.

32. Fudge, *Christianity without the Cross*, 14.

many similarities, a major distinction between them was the religious enthusiastic expression of speaking in tongues.[33] Although "speaking with new tongues"[34] was present in some of the circuit rider revivals, in general, circuit riders did not focus on this phenomenon; on the other hand, in Pentecostalism, speaking in tongues became a necessary sign of having received this baptism of the Spirit.[35]

Parham became the spiritual mentor of William Joseph Seymour (1870–1922) who later initiated the three-year Azusa Street Revival that began in Los Angeles in 1906. Like the circuit rider revivals that came before it, this revival became known for its encounters with various supernatural manifestations, although it became especially known for its religious enthusiastic experience of speaking in tongues. It is commonly held that the Azusa Street Revival gave birth to global Pentecostalism, and one of the main denominations that sprang from this revival and movement was the Assemblies of God (founded in 1914).[36]

Moreover, the Charismatic movement later emerged (beginning in the 1960s). This movement occurred as parts of mainline denominations and the Roman Catholic Church began to adopt the beliefs and practices of Pentecostalism within their own traditions. Therefore, it could be said that the Charismatic movement can also be traced back to early Methodism, albeit indirectly. For this reason, the early Methodist movement and the Charismatic movement were strikingly similar in many ways. Like the early Methodists, the power and presence of God and the gifts of His

33. Anderson, *Introduction to Pentecostalism*, 23–29.

34. Finley, *Autobiography*, 297. See also Finley, *Sketches of Western Methodism*, 404.

35. Bruner, *Theology of the Holy Spirit*, 77–78. At the same time, another theological difference between Methodism and Pentecostalism that is worth noting is in regard to water baptism. Methodism followed the Anglican theology of infant baptism, although there are a number of recorded instances in which circuit riders baptized adults through immersion (i.e., believer's baptism). On the other hand, Pentecostalism practiced believer's baptism, which originated from Anabaptist theology. See also Asbury, *Journal of the Rev. Francis Asbury*, 3:85; Giles, *Pioneer*, 172; Finley, *Autobiography*, 279; Bangs and Garrettson, *Life of the Rev. Freeborn Garrettson*, 132–33; Lee, *Memoir*, 164, 176, 185–86; Newell, *Life and Observations*, 135–36; Cartwright, *Backwoods Preacher*, 204; Millet, *Shalom*, 107–9.

36. Synan, *Holiness-Pentecostal Tradition*, 155; Johnstone, *Future of the Global Church*, 125; Anderson, *Introduction to Pentecostalism*, 42.

262 THE SUPERNATURAL AND THE CIRCUIT RIDERS

Spirit were crucial to the Charismatics.[37] In fact, still today, the UMC maintains Charismatic branches within its denomination.[38]

Clearly, the notion that "the historical and doctrinal lineage of American Pentecostalism is to be found in the Wesleyan [or early Methodist] tradition" is on point.[39] Furthermore, "Pentecostalism has continued to be what Francis Asbury wanted Methodism to remain, a pliable movement more than a static institution. Whether Methodism claims it or not, Pentecostalism is an offspring and will perhaps be its greatest legacy."[40] Thus, it can essentially be argued that Pentecostalism "borrowed" the engine of early Methodism: its Pentecost-like supernaturalism. At times, the early Methodists identified this engine as "the baptism of the Spirit" or the "celestial fire" of God's Spirit, which is terminology that was later used by the Pentecostals.[41] This powerful engine blessed early Methodism through its astounding numerical increase and later enabled (and continues to enable to this day) the Pentecostal and Charismatic movement to experience global growth with "more than two billion in 2010."[42] This clearly indicates that divine supernatural manifestations are paramount to Spirit-led Christian movements and that, through them, growth will follow.

To conclude this section, the circuit rider ministry not only caused Methodism to become the largest American denomination of its time and a vital force in the Second Great Awakening, but it also became the inspiration for new movements, specifically the Holiness movement, which mirrored early Methodism's emphasis on the role of holiness or sanctification in connection with the Holy Spirit, and the Pentecostal and Charismatic movements, which mirrored early Methodism's emphasis on divine supernatural experiences.[43]

37. See also Hasset, "Charismatic Renewal," 301–6.

38. Cowan, Remnant Spirit, 60–62.

39. Synan, Holiness-Pentecostal Movement, 248.

40. UMC, Book of Resolutions, 693.

41. Fletcher, Works of the Rev. John Fletcher, 4:255. See also Hempton, Empire of the Spirit, 208–9; UMC, Book of Resolutions, 692–95; Billman, Supernatural Thread in Methodism, 69–70; Wood, Meaning of Pentecost in Early Methodism, xv.

42. Liu, "Global Christianity." See also Johnstone, Future of the Global Church, 125.

43. See also Elsbree, Rise of the Missionary Spirit in America, 30; Tennent, Theology in the Context of World Christianity, 174–75; Dayton, Theological Roots of Pentecostalism, 35–87.

The Relevance of This Work

Concerning the difference that this work hopes to make and the application of its research, this book focused on uncovering the full historical and theological reality of supernaturalism in the circuit rider ministry and the resulting early Methodist expansion from the 1770s through the 1830s. This reality has, unfortunately, been overlooked, downplayed, or disregarded by previous historians and theologians. Now scholars and the public can understand the extent of the influence that the supernatural—the work of God—had on all spheres of the circuit rider ministry and early Methodism. This perspective can now shape the way that early Methodism is viewed throughout its creation, development, and expansion: beginning from the personal lives of the circuit riders (in their convictions, conversions, callings, and the implementation of their evangelistic strategies) to their sharing of the gospel (in plain language but with tangible power from above) to, lastly, the drastic early Methodist growth.

More importantly, as a result of rigorous research, I believe that this work can now serve as a circuit rider mouthpiece. As such, I feel that their message to the present United Methodist Church, Wesleyan affiliated churches, Pentecostal and Charismatic affiliated churches, and the wider Christian world would be that, in order to have (and maintain) a successful Christian ministry (starting from personal spiritual conversion and resulting in revivalist expansion), it is essential to not only practice scriptural holiness and dedication to evangelism, but the supernatural (derived from the power and presence of God's Spirit) should be the leading influence within that ministry.

As it was in Jesus's ministry, the Apostolic Age, and the early church, the circuit riders made it clear that, without a touch of the supernatural, one cannot effectively understand Christian religion, obtain spiritual conversion, maintain scriptural holiness, or receive spiritual empowerment in sharing the gospel and igniting revival. On the other hand, however, the circuit riders assured the world that anything is possible and life is limitless through the power and presence of God's Spirit. This is also a hope for Christianity that, as American Methodism began with just ten official circuit riders who guided America into the Second Great Awakening and inspired generations of Spirit-led movements, it takes only a few dedicated Christians, equipped with divine supernatural powers, to change the world with the gospel.

Appendix A

List of Referenced Circuit Riders
from the 1770s through the 1830s

THE FOLLOWING LIST CONTAINS names, years of birth and death, and years of appointment for all circuit riders (from the 1770s through the 1830s) referenced in this study.

Name	Birth and Death	Years of Appointment
Abbott, Benjamin	1732–1796	1789–1796
Asbury, Francis	1745–1816	1767–1816
Bangs, Nathan	1778–1862	1802–1810
Bascom, Henry Bidleman	1796–1850	1813–1816
Beauchamp, William	1772–1824	1794–1824
Boardman, Richard	1738–1782	1763–1782
Boehm, Henry	1775–1875	1802–1810
Burke, William	1770–1855	1792–1834
Cartwright, Peter	1785–1872	1802–1862
Chandler, William P.	1764–1822	1797–1822
Chase, Abner	1784–1854	1810–1814
Cook, Valentine	1765–1820	1788–1800
Coke, Thomas	1747–1814	1776–1814
Collins, John	1769–1845	1806–1815
Cooper, Ezekiel	1763–1847	1787–1847
Daughaday, Thomas	1777–1810	1798–1810
Dow, Lorenzo	1777–1834	1798–1816 (Self-appointed after 1802)

Easter, John	1760s–1804	1782–1792
Embury, Philip	1729–1775	1752–1775
Emory, John	1789–1835	1810–1835
Finley, James Bradley	1781–1856	1809–1834
Finley, William P.	1785–1822	1814–1820
Fisk, Willbur	1792–1839	1818–1839
Garrettson, Freeborn	1752–1827	1776–1827
Gatch, Phillip	1751–1834	1774–1834
Giles, Charles	1783–1867	1805–1808
Granade, John A.	1763–1807	1800–1807
Gruber, Jacob	1778–1850	1802–1837
Hibbard, Billy	1771–1844	1797–1829
Hinde, Thomas S.	1785–1846	1810–1825
Hull, Hope	1763–1818	1785–1795
Ireson, Ebenezer	1800–1833	1824–1833
Jea, John	1773–18??	1789–1817
		(Self-appointed)
King, John	1746–1794	1773–1776
Lakin, Benjamin	1794–1849	1795–1800
Lee, Jesse	1758–1816	1783–1816
M'Kendree, William	1757–1835	1788–1835
Maffitt, John N.	1795–1850	1722–1838
Newell, E.F.	1775–1864	1806–1852
O'Kelly, James	1735–1826	1778–1793
Page, John	1766–1859	1792–1804
Paine, Robert	1799–1882	1818–1829
Peck, George	1797–1876	1816–1835
Pilmore, Joseph	1739–1825	1769–1774
Rankin, Thomas	1736–1810	1762–1810
Seth, Crowell	(1781–1826)	1801–1813
Shadford, George	1739–1816	1768–1816
Smith, Henry	17??–1840	1793–1814
Smith, Thomas	1776–1844	1799–1824
Snethen, Nicholas	1769–1845	1794–1814
Strawbridge, Robert	1732–1781	1756–1776
Travis, Joseph	1786–1858	1806–1825
Vasey, Thomas	1742–1826	1775–1786
Ware, Thomas	1758–1842	1784–1793
Watters, William	1751–1833	1773–1806
Webb, (Captain) Thomas	1724–1796	1767–1796
Whatcoat, Richard	1736–1806	1769–1806

Williams, Robert	1745–1775	1769–1774
Young, Dan	1783–1831	1804–1809
Young, Jacob	1776–1856	1802–1809

In addition to the above list, the below list contains all intermittently appointed Methodist preachers (along with their years of birth and death) within the early and mid-nineteenth century whose historical works were referenced in this study.

Atkinson, John (1835–1897)
Bennett, William W. (1821–1887)
Holdich, Joseph (1794 –1893)
Jones, John Griffing (1804–1888)
M'Ferrin, John B. (1807–1887)
Porter, James (1808–1888)
Scudder, Moses L. (1814–1891)
Shipp, Albert Micajah (1819–1887)
Smith, George Gilman (1836–1913)
Stevens, Abel (1815–1897)
Turner, Henry McNeal (1834–1915).[1]

1. For a comprehensive list of American Methodist preachers from the early beginnings until 1840, see Bangs, *History of the Methodist Episcopal Church*, 4:462–506.

Appendix B

American Methodist Membership Statistics from 1773 to 1840

IN ORDER TO FURTHER understand the growth of the MEC (achieved principally through the work of the circuit rider ministry), this appendix provides growth statistics, via American Methodist membership figures, from the First Annual Conference of 1773 until the year 1840. As discussed in chapter 3, there was initially only a small number of circuits and one Annual Conference; however, the number of circuits rapidly increased, and in order to manage them, new districts were created (especially beginning in the year 1800). Furthermore, as the American population continued to grow, the Methodist population grew along with it. Circuits and districts multiplied, which led to the creation of new Annual Conferences (especially beginning in the mid-1810s).

Further regarding these statistics, it is important to note that the below numbers include only those individuals who became members of Methodist societies by fulfilling Methodist membership requirements, such as participation in class meetings. Therefore, these statistics do not reflect the number of those in attendance at various Methodist meetings as these figures were never officially recorded by the MEC (although, as seen in this study, approximations were often reported by various circuit riders). As a result, exact figures in Methodist attendance cannot be quantified, although they would unquestionably be much larger than the figures presented below (which, again, count only those holding official Methodist membership).[1]

1. For more information regarding the process of becoming a Methodist member, see chapter 3.

American Methodist Membership in 1773

Circuits	Membership
Maryland	500
New Jersey	200
New York	180
Philadelphia	180
Virginia	100
Total Membership	**1,160**

American Methodist Membership in 1780

Circuits	Membership
Amelia	470
Baltimore	900
Berkley	191
Brunswick	656
Charlotte	186
Chester	90
Delaware	795
Fairfax	309
Fluvanna	300
Frederick	480
Hanover	281
James City	77
Kent	493
Mecklenburg	498
New Hope	542
New Jersey	140
Philadelphia	89
Pittsburg	500
Roanoke	470
Sussex	655
Tar River	455
Total Membership	**8,577**
Percent of Methodist Growth since 1773	**639.4**

American Methodist Membership in 1790

Circuits	Membership
Albany	267
Alleghany	395
Amelia	898
Annamessex	346
Annapolis	307
Anson	545
Baltimore C.	1,153
Baltimore Town and Point	1,043
Bath	364
Bedford	520
Berkley	856
Bertie	731
Bladen	228
Bottetourt	115
Bristol	60
Broad River	495
Brunswick	942
Burke	574
Burlington	365
Bush River	159
Calvert	1,984
Cambridge	300
Camden	803
Caroline	1,287
Caswell	513
Cecil	694
Charleston	138
Cherokee	202
Chester	326
Clarksburg	269
Columbia	382
Cumberland	282
Danville	348
Dorchester	1,183
Dover	1,125
Dutchess	410

Edisto	651
Elizabethtown	253
Fairfax	950
Fairfield	105
Flanders	329
Frederick	558
Georgetown	54
Gloucester	1,118
Great Pee Dee	317
Greenbrier	207
Greensville	1,076
Guilford	455
Hanover	897
Harford	943
Holston	464
Huntingdon	194
Kent	1,161
Lancaster	1,013
Lexington	456
Lincoln	189
Litchfield	68
Little Pee Dee	770
Little York	195
Long Island	277
Madison	220
Mecklenburg	510
Milford	1,115
Montgomery	1,110
Newburg	232
New Haven	9
New Hope	490
New River	1,511
New River	323
New Rochelle	774
New York	624
Northampton	684
Ohio	260
Orange	636
Philadelphia	229

Pittsburg	97
Portsmouth	1,642
Redstone	340
Richmond	572
Roanoke	1,247
Rockingham	330
Salem	954
Salisbury	467
Santee	427
Seleuda	255
Severn	701
Somerset	606
Surry	921
Sussex	835
Talbot	1,326
Tar River	1,320
Trenton	462
Washington	939
Williamsburg	651
Wilmington	60
Yadkin	304

| Total Membership | 57,631 |
| Percent of Methodist Growth since 1780 | 571.92 |

American Methodist Membership in 1800

Districts	Membership
Connecticut	1,571
Delaware	2,493
Georgia	1,655
Kentucky	1,741
Maryland	12,046
Massachusetts	1,577
Natchez	60
New Hampshire	171
New Jersey	3,030
New York	6,363

North Carolina	8,472
Northwestern Territory	257
Pennsylvania	3,187
Province of Maine	1,197
Rhode Island	227
South Carolina	4,682
Tennessee	743
Upper Canada	936
Vermont	1,096
Virginia	13,390
Trenton	462
Total Membership	64,894
Percent of Methodist Growth since 1790	12.6[2]

American Methodist Membership in 1810

Conferences	Membership
Baltimore	26,546
Carolinas	25,990
Genesee	10,683
New England	11,220
New York	18,514
Philadelphia	33,689
Virginia	25,034
Western	22,904
Total Membership	174,560
Percent of Methodist Growth since 1800	168.99

2. For an explanation of the decrease in the percent of growth during this decade, see chapter 7.

American Methodist Membership in 1820

Conferences	Membership
Baltimore	33,289
Carolinas	32,969
Genesee	23,947
Mississippi	2,631
Missouri	5,523
New York	23,456
Ohio	35,056
Philadelphia	34,851
Tennessee	23,164
Virginia	23,756
Total Membership	256,881
Percent of Methodist Growth since 1810	47.16

American Methodist Membership in 1830

Conferences	Membership
Baltimore	40,162
Carolinas	64,889
Genesee	15,246
Holston	20,452
Illinois	22,193
Kentucky	26,958
Maine	11,062
Mississippi	19,282
Missouri	4,386
New England	12,408
New Hampshire	11,757
New York	34,804
Ohio	36,545
Oneida	23,924
Philadelphia	45,528
Pittsburg	22,590
Tennessee	25,706

Total Membership   476,153
Percent of Methodist Growth since 1820   85.36

American Methodist Membership in 1840

Conferences	Membership
Alabama	25,312
Arkansas	14,492
Baltimore	56,693
Black River	22,359
Erie	17,910
Genesee	27,981
Georgia	38,857
Holston	28,322
Illinois	24,687
Indiana	26,080
Kentucky	37,000
Liberia	922
Maine	22,359
Memphis	14,492
Michigan	11,407
Mississippi	12,678
Missouri	13,092
New England	22,554
New Hampshire	20,084
New Jersey	23,275
New York	36,689
North Carolina	20,463
North Ohio	23,898
Ohio	54,283
Oneida	17,910
Philadelphia	43,872
Pittsburg	35,750
Rock River	11,407
South Carolina	57,426
Tennessee	26,080
Texas	1,853

Troy	24,566
Virginia	57,426
Total Membership	852,918
Percent of Methodist Growth since 1830	79.13[3]

3. MEC, *Minutes of the Annual Conferences*, 1:5, 11–12, 35–39, 89–95, 175–86, 338–53; 2:40–77, 586–660; Teir et al., *Historical Statistics of the United States*, 1152–2000; Goss, *Statistical History*, 72–79; Sprague, *Annals of the American Pulpit*, 7:31–33, 173–247. See also Wigger, *Taking Heaven by Storm*, 197–200; Powell, "Methodist Circuit Riders in America," 41–43; Hempton, *Methodism*, 212–16.

Bibliography

Abbott, Benjamin. *The Life and Labours of the Rev. Benjamin Abbott, the Revivalist.* London: Edwards & Hughes, 1844.

Abbott, Benjamin, and John Ffirth. *The Experience and Gospel Labours of the Rev. Benjamin Abbott to Which Is Annexed, a Narrative of His Life and Death.* New York: Methodist Connection in the United States, 1805.

Abraham, William J., and James E. Kirby. *The Oxford Handbook of Methodist Studies.* Oxford: Oxford University Press, 2009.

Adams, Charles Kendall, ed. *Johnson's Universal Cyclopedia: A New Edition.* Vol. 2. New York: A. J. Johnson, 1893.

Adewuya, J. Ayodeji. *Holiness and Community in 2 Cor 6:14–7:1: Paul's View of Communal Holiness in the Corinthian Correspondence.* Eugene, OR: Wipf & Stock, 2011.

Aginasare, Charles. *Power Demonstration: Understanding the Holy Spirit and His Gifts.* Bloomington, IN: Xlibris, 2012.

Ahlstrom, Sydney E. *A Religious History of the American People.* New Haven, CT: Yale University Press, 2004.

Airhart, Phyllis D., and Margaret Lamberts Bendroth, eds. *Faith Traditions and the Family.* Louisville, KY: Westminster John Knox, 1997.

Alcott, Jeanne. *Words of Power: 365 Inspirational Messages, Spiritual Powerlines, and Prayers Hear God's Heart for Your Life Every Day and Live in His Power.* Blomington, IN: WestBow, 2014.

Allen, R. W. "Walking by Faith." *The Methodist Magazine and Quarterly* 20 (1838) 198–209.

Allen, Stephen, and W. H. Pilsbury. *History of Methodism in Maine, 1793–1886.* Augusta, ME: C. E. Nash & Son, 1887.

Alvord, Clarence W., ed. *The Mississippi Valley Historical Review.* Vol. 4. Bloomington, IN: Mississippi Valley Historical Association, 1918.

Anderson, Allan H. *An Introduction to Pentecostalism: Global Charismatic Christianity.* 2nd ed. Cambridge: Cambridge University Press, 2014.

Anderson, Thurlene. "The Shaping of American Community and the Methodist Camp Meeting." Unpublished paper. Online. https://www.academia.edu/10022626/The_Shaping_of_American_Community_and_the_Methodist_Camp_Meeting.

Andrews, Dee E. *The Methodists and Revolutionary America, 1760–1800: The Shaping of an Evangelical Culture.* Princeton, NJ: Princeton University Press, 2010.

Andrews, William L. *Sisters of the Spirit: Three Black Women's Autobiographies of the Nineteenth Century*. Bloomington, IN: Indiana University Press, 1986.

Arminius, Theophilus. "Introductory Remarks to Short Sketches of Revivals of Religion, among the Methodists in the Western Country." *The Methodist Magazine* 2 (1819) 221–25.

———. "Short Sketches of Revivals of Religion among the Methodists in the Western Country." *The Methodist Magazine* 4 (1821) 28–35.

Armstrong, Chris. "Phoebe Palmer." *Christian History* 82 (2004). Online. https://www.christianitytoday.com/history/issues/issue-82/phoebe-palmer-from-editor.html.

Armstrong, James Edward. *History of the Old Baltimore Conference from the Planting of Methodism in 1773 to the Division of the Conference in 1857*. Baltimore: King Bros., 1907.

Arnett, William M. "The Role of the Holy Spirit in Entire Sanctification in the Writings of John Wesley." *Asbury Journal* 29.2 (1974) 5–23.

Asbury, Francis. "Chapter 3. The Journal and Letters of Francis Asbury—Volume 2." *Wesley Center Online*. Online. http://wesley.nnu.edu/other-theologians/francis-asbury/the-journal-and-letters-of-francis-asbury-volume-ii/francis-asbury-the-letters-vol-2-chapter-3.

———. "Chapter 13. The Journal and Letters of Francis Asbury—Volume 2." *Wesley Center Online*. Online. http://wesley.nnu.edu/other-theologians/francis-asbury/the-journal-and-letters-of-francis-asbury-volume-ii/francis-asbury-the-letters-vol-2-chapter-13.

———. *The Heart of Asbury's Journal*. Edited by Ezra Squier Tipple. New York: Eaton & Mains, 1904.

———. *The Journal of the Rev. Francis Asbury, Bishop of the Methodist Episcopal Church, From August 7, 1771, to December 7, 1815*. 3 vols. New York: N. Bangs and T. Mason, 1821.

———. "Letter CCCCX: From the Rev. Francis Asbury, to the Rev. John Wesley." *The Arminian Magazine* 9 (1785) 680–83.

———. *The Letters*. Edited by Elmer T. Clark. Vol. 3 of *The Journal and Letters of Francis Asbury*. Nashville: Abingdon, 1958.

Atkinson, John. *Centennial History of American Methodism, Inclusive of Its Ecclesiastical Organization in 1784 and Its Subsequent Development under the Superintendency of Francis Asbury: With Sketches of the Character and History of All the Preachers Known to Have Been Memebers of the Christmas Conference; Also, an Appendix, Showing the Numerical Position of the Methodist Episcopal Church as Compared with the Other Leading Evangelical Denominations in the Cities of the United States; And the Condition of the Educational Work of the Church*. New York: Phillips & Hunt, 1884.

———. *History of the Origin of the Wesleyan Movement in America: And of the Establishment Therein of Methodism*. Jersey City, NJ: Wesleyan, 1896.

———. *Memorials of Methodism in New Jersey: From the Foundation of the First Society in the State in 1770, to the Completion of the First Twenty Years of Its History. Containing Sketches of the Ministerial Laborers, Distinguished Laymen, and Prominent Societies of That Period*. Philadelphia: Perkinpine & Higgins, 1860.

Atlan, Henri. *Enlightenment to Enlightenment: Intercritique of Science and Myth*. New York: State University of New York Press, 1993.

Ayers, Philip E. *What Ever Happened to Respect?: America's Loss of Respect for Pastors.* Bloomington, IN: AuthorHouse, 2005.

Ayres, Samuel Gardiner. *Methodist Heroes of Other Days.* New York: Methodist Book Concern, 1916.

Bainbridge, William Sims. *Sociology.* Hauppauge, NY: Barron's Educational Series, 1997.

———. *The Sociology of Religious Movements.* New York: Routledge, 1997.

Baird, William. *The Days That Are Past: A Short Manual of Early Church History.* London: William Wells Gardner, 1870.

Baker, Frank. *From Wesley to Asbury: Studies in Early American Methodism.* Durham, NC: Duke University Press, 1976.

Baker, Heidi, and Rolland Baker. *Expecting Miracles: True Stories of God's Supernatural Power and How You Can Experience It.* Grand Rapids, MI: Chosen, 2007.

Baldwin, Eric. "'The Devil Begins to Roar': Opposition to Early Methodists in New England." *Church History* 75.1 (2006) 94–119.

Ballou, Eli. "A Marvelous Story." *Universalist Watchman,* August 6, 1812.

Balmer, Randall H. *Encyclopedia of Evangelicalism.* Rev. ed. Waco, TX: Baylor University Press, 2014.

Balmer, Randall H., and Mark Silk, eds. *Religion and Public Life in the Middle Atlantic Region: The Fount of Diversity.* Lanham, MD: AltaMira, 2006.

Bangs, Nathan. *A History of the Methodist Episcopal Church.* 4 vols. New York: T. Mason and G. Lane; J. Collord, 1840–1841.

Bangs, Nathan, and Freeborn Garrettson. *The Life of the Rev. Freeborn Garrettson: Compiled from His Printed and Manuscript Journals, and Other Authentic Documents.* 5th ed. New-York: Carlton & Lanahan, 1832.

Bannister, Jefferson W. "Exploring Narratives in Supernatural Healing at Grace Church of God, Brooklyn, NY." PhD diss., Drew University, 2015.

Barber, John Warner, and Henry Howe. *Our Whole Country: A Panorama and Encyclopedia of the United States, Historical, Geographical and Pictorial.* Vol. 2. Cincinnati: C. Tuttle, 1863.

Barkan, Elliott Robert, ed. *Making It in America: A Sourcebook on Eminent Ethnic Americans.* Santa Barbara, CA: ABC-CLIO Interactive, 2001.

Barker, John Marshall. *History of Ohio Methodism: A Study in Social Science.* Cincinnati: Curts & Jennings, 1898.

Barlow, Fred. *Profiles in Evangelism.* Murfreesboro, TN: Sword of the Lord Foundation, 2000.

Bartholomew, Robert, and Joe Nickell. *American Hauntings: The True Stories Behind Hollywood's Scariest Movies—From "The Exorcist" to "The Conjuring."* Santa Barbara, CA: ABC-CLIO, 2015.

Batens, Diderik, and Jean-Paul van Bendegem, eds. *Theory and Experiment: Recent Insights and New Perspectives on Their Relation.* Dordrecht: Springer Netherlands, 2012.

Battin, M. Pabst. *The Ethics of Suicide: Historical Sources.* Oxford: Oxford University Press, 2015.

Baxter, Richard. *A Christian Directory, or, a Body of Practical Divinity and Cases of Conscience: Christian Ecclesiastics (or Church Duties).* London: Richard Edwards, 1825.

Beauchamp, William. *Letters on the Call and Qualifications of Ministers of the Gospel, and on the Apostolic Character and Superior Advantages of the Itinerant Ministry.* Louisville, KY: Methodist Episcopal Church, South, 1849.

Beet, Joseph A. "Creation of Man (Wesleyan College)." *North-Western Christian Advocate* 45 (1897) 9–10.

Beiler, Samuel L. *The Worker and His Church.* Boston: Board, 1910.

Bennett, William W. *Memorials of Methodism in Virginia: From Its Introduction Into the State in the Year 1772 to the Year 1829.* Richmond: Published by the author, 1870.

Benson, Joseph. *An Apology for the People Called Methodists; Containing a Concise Account of Their Origin and Progress, Etc.* London: G. Whitefield, 1801.

Beougher, Timothy K. "Camp Meetings and Circuit Riders: Did You Know? Little Known Facts about Camp Meetings and Circuit Riders." *Christianity Today* 45 (1995). Online. https://www.christianitytoday.com/history/issues/issue-45/camp-meetings-and-circuit-riders-did-you-know.html.

Berger, Peter L. *Questions of Faith: A Skeptical Affirmation of Christianity.* Somerset, NJ: John Wiley & Sons, 2008.

Bergland, John K. *The Journeys of Robert Williams: Irish Street Preacher and Methodist Circuit Rider.* Maitland, FL: Xulon, 2010.

Berkhof, Louis. *Systematic Theology.* Grand Rapids, MI: Eerdmans, 1996.

Berkin, Carol, et al. *Making America: A History of the United States.* 7th ed. Boston: Cengage Learning, 2014.

Bernard, Frederick A. P., and Arnold Guyot, eds. *Johnson's (Revised) Universal Cyclopaedia: A Scientific and Popular Treasury of Useful Knowledge.* New York: A. J. Johnson & Co., 1890.

Beville, K. A. *Preaching Christ in a Postmodern Culture.* Newcastle upon Tyne, UK: Cambridge Scholars, 2010.

The Bible Dictionary. 2 vols. London: Cassell, Petter & Galpin, 1875.

Bilhartz, Terry D. *Urban Religion and the Second Great Awakening: Church and Society in Early National Baltimore.* Rutherford, NJ: Fairleigh Dickinson University Press, 1986.

Billman, Frank. *The Supernatural Thread in Methodism: Signs and Wonders among Methodists Then and Now.* St. Mary, FL: Creation, 2013.

Birdwell, Michael E., and W. Calvin Dickinson. *Rural Life and Culture in the Upper Cumberland.* Lexington: University Press of Kentucky, 2004.

Birx, H. James, ed. *Twenty-First-Century Anthropology: A Reference Handbook.* Vol. 1. Thousand Oaks, CA: SAGE, 2010.

Bloesch, Donald G. *The Christian Witness in a Secular Age: An Evaluation of Nine Contemporary Theologians.* Eugene, OR: Wipf & Stock, 2002.

———. *The Reform of the Church.* Eugene, OR: Wipf & Stock, 1998.

Boase, Paul H. *The Methodist Circuit Rider on the Ohio Frontier.* Vol. 1. Madison: University of Wisconsin, 1952.

Boehm, Henry. *Reminiscences, Historical and Biographical, of Sixty-Four Years in the Ministry.* Edited by J. B. Wakeley. New York: Carlton & Porter, 1866.

Boles, John B. *Religion in Antebellum Kentucky.* Lexington: University Press of Kentucky, 2015.

Bonomi, Patricia U. *Under the Cope of Heaven: Religion, Society, and Politics in Colonial America.* New York: Oxford University Press, 2003.

Botzet, Lee. *A Heart for God's Glory.* Wheaton, IL: Xulon, 2007.

Bowden, Mary Ellen, and John Kenly Smith. *American Chemical Enterprise: A Perspective on One Hundred Years of Innovation to Commemorate the Centennial of the Society of Chemical Industry (American Section)*. Philadelphia: Chemical Heritage Foundation, 1994.

Bowen, Ellias. "Missionary Discourse." *The Methodist Magazine and Quarterly Review* 22 (1840) 104–10.

Bower, Doug. *From Saddlebags to Satellites: Homilies of a Circuit Rider in the New Millennium*. Bloomington, IN: iUniverse, 2003.

Branstetter, Christopher Jon. *Purity, Power, and Pentecostal Light: The Revivalist Doctrine and Means of Aaron Merritt Hills*. Eugene, OR: Wipf & Stock, 2012.

Bratt, James, ed. *Antirevialism in Antebellum America: A Collection of Religious Voices*. New Brunswick, NJ: Rutgers University Press, 2005.

Bray, Robert. *Peter Cartwright, Legendary Frontier Preacher*. Champaign: University of Illinois Press, 2005.

Brigham, Amariah. *Observations on the Influence of Religion upon the Health and Physical Welfare of Mankind*. Boston: Marsh, Capen & Lyon, 1836.

Brown, Candy G. *Global Pentecostal and Charismatic Healing*. New York: Oxford University Press, 2011.

———. "Healing." In *The Cambridge Companion to American Methodism*, edited by Jason E. Vickers, 227–42. Cambridge: Cambridge University Press, 2013.

Brown, Kenneth O. "Camp Meeting Movement." In *Historical Dictionary of Methodism*, edited by Charles Yrigoyen Jr. and Susan E. Warrick, 62–63. 2nd ed. Historical Dictionaries of Religions, Philosophies, and Movements 57. Lanham, MD: Scarecrow, 2005.

Brown, Rebecca. *He Came to Set the Captives Free*. Chino, CA: Chick, 1986.

Brown, Richard. *Church and State in Modern Britain, 1700–1850*. London: Routledge, 2002.

Bruce, H. Addington. *Historic Ghosts and Ghost Hunters*. New York: Moffat, Yard & Co., 1908.

Bruner, Frederick D. *A Theology of the Holy Spirit: The Pentecostal Experience and the New Testament Witness*. Eugene, OR: Wipf & Stock, 1997.

Bryan, David El-Cana. *The Serpent and the Savior: A True Story of Occult-Level Spiritual Warfare*. Scotts Valley, CA: CreateSpace, 2015.

Buchanan, Claudius. "Review of Bogue & Bennett's *History of the Dissenters*." *The Wesleyan-Methodist Magazine* 35 (1811) 336–47.

Buckley, James Monroe. *Constitutional and Parliamentary History of the Methodist Episcopal Church*. New York: Eaton & Mains, 1912.

———. "Faith-Healing and Kindred Phenomena." *The Century Illustrated Monthly Magazine* 32 (1886) 221–35.

———. *A History of Methodism in the United States*. Vol. 1. New York: Harper & Brothers, 1898.

Bullen, Donald. *A Man Of One Book?: John Wesley's Interpretation and Use of the Bible*. Eugene, OR: Wipf & Stock, 2007.

Bultmann, Rudolf. *Rudolph Bultmann: Interpreting Faith for the Modern Era*. Minneapolis, MN: Fortress, 1965.

Burnett, Daniel L. *In the Shadow of Aldersgate: An Introduction to the Heritage and Faith of the Wesleyan Tradition*. Eugene, OR: Cascade, 2006.

Buroes, Joseph. "Sermon on Romans 8:16, 17." *The Methodist Magazine* 3 (1820) 401–6.

Burritt, C. D. *Methodism in Ithaca: A History*. Ithaca, NY: Andrus, Gauntlett, 1852.

Butler, Jon. *Awash in a Sea of Faith: Christianizing the American People*. Cambridge, MA: Harvard University Press, 1990.

———. "Enthusiasm Described and Decried: The Great Awakening as Interpretative Fiction." *The Journal of American History* 69.2 (1982) 305–25.

Butler, Jon, et al. *Religion in American Life: A Short History*. 2nd ed. New York: Oxford University Press, 2011.

Buy, Jean Du. "Four Types of Protestants: A Comparative Study in the Psychology of Religion." *The American Journal of Religious Psychology and Education* 3.2 (1908) 65–81.

Cairns, Earle E. *An Endless Line of Splendor: Revivals and Their Leaders from the Great Awakening to the Present*. Eugene, OR: Wipf & Stock, 2015.

Calder, Sandy. *The Origins of Primitive Methodism*. Suffolk, UK: Boydell & Brewer, 2016.

Cambridge English Dictionary (CED). Online. https://dictionary.cambridge.org.

Cameron, Euan. *Enchanted Europe: Superstition, Reason, and Religion 1250–1750*. Oxford: Oxford University Press, 2010.

Campbell, Ted. *Christian Confessions: A Historical Introduction*. Louisville, KY: Westminster John Knox, 1996.

Capers, Williams. "Recollections of Doctor Thomas Hinde." *The Methodist Magazine and Quarterly Review* 12 (1830) 121–28.

Carey, Patrick W. "Education, Theology: United States." In *Encyclopedia of Protestantism*, edited by Hans J. Hillerbrand, 208–12. New York: Facts on File, 2005.

Carroll, Bret E. *The Routledge Historical Atlas of Religion in America*. Edited by Mark C. Carnes. New York: Routledge, 2000.

Cartwright, Peter. *Autobiography of Peter Cartwright: The Backwoods Preacher*. Edited by W. P. Strickland. New York: Carlton & Porter, 1856.

———. *Backwoods Preacher: An Autobiography of Peter Cartwright, for More Than Fifty Years a Preacher in the Backwoods and Western Wilds of America*. Edited by W. P. Strickland. 31st ed. New York: Carlton & Porter, 1860.

———. *A Letter Purporting to Be from His Satanic Majesty, the Devil: With an Answer Annexed*. Cincinnati: n.p., 1859.

Cartwright, Peter, and W. S. Hooper. *Fifty Years As a Presiding Elder*. Cincinnati: Hitchcock and Walden, 1871.

Caruso, John Anthony, and John C. Inscoe. *The Appalachian Frontier America's First Surge Westward*. Knoxville: University of Tennessee Press, 2003.

Case, Jay Riley. *An Unpredictable Gospel: American Evangelicals and World Christianity, 1812–1920*. New York: Oxford University Press, 2012.

Castelo, Daniel. *Embodying Wesley's Catholic Spirit*. Eugene, OR: Wipf & Stock, 2017.

Charles, Sébastien, and Plínio J. Smith. *Scepticism in the Eighteenth Century: Enlightenment, Lumières, Aufklärung*. Dordrecht, Germany: Springer Netherlands, 2013.

Chase, Abner. *Recollections of the Past*. New York: n.p., 1848.

Cheek, H. Lee, Jr. "Original Diversity: Bishops Allen, Asbury, and Black Methodism." *Methodist History* 35.3 (1997) 188–91. Online. http://archives.gcah.org/bitstream/handle/10516/6127/MH-1997-April-Cheek.pdf?sequence=1.

Christian Work and the Evangelist. New York: Harvard Divinity School, 1903.

Clapper, Gregory Scott. *John Wesley on Religious Affections: His Views on Experience and Emotion and Their Role in the Christian Life and Theology*. Metuchen, NJ: Scarecrow, 1989.

Clark, J. C. D. *The Language of Liberty, 1660–1832: Political Discourse and Social Dynamics in the Anglo-American World*. Cambridge, UK: Cambridge University Press, 1993.

Clark, Jerome L. *1844: Religious Movements*. Vol. 1. New York: Teach Services Inc., 1968.

Clarke, Adam. *Memoirs of the Wesley Family*. London: J. Sf T. Clarke, 1823.

Clarke, Steve. "The Supernatural and the Miraculous." *Sophia* 46.3 (2007) 277–85.

Cleveland, Catharine C. *The Great Revival in the West, 1797–1805*. Chicago: University of Chicago Press, 1916.

Coke, Thomas. *Extracts of the Journals of the Late Rev. Thomas Coke, LLD: Comprising Several Visits to North America and the West-Indies, His Tour through a Part of Ireland, and His Nearly Finished Voyage to Bombay in the East-Indies: To Which Is Prefixed, a Life of a Doctor*. Dublin, Ireland: Methodist Book-Room, 1816.

———. *Extracts of the Journals of the Rev. Dr. Coke's Five Visits to America*. London: Printed by G. Paramore, 1793.

———. *The Letters of Dr. Thomas Coke*. Edited by John A. Vickers. Nashville: Abingdon, 2013.

———. "The Journal of Thomas Coke, Bishop of the Methodist-Episcopal Church." *The Arminian Magazine* 1 (1784) 286–97.

Coke, Thomas, and Francis Asbury. *Minutes of the 1784 Conference: of the Methodist Episcopal Church in America*. 1st ed. Ann Arbor, MI: Furious Studios, 2016.

Coke, Thomas, and Henry Moore. *The Life of the Rev. John Wesley, AM: Including an Account of the Great Revival of Religion in Europe and America, of Which He Was the First and Chief Instrument*. London: G. Paramore, 1792.

Collins, Kenneth J. *John Wesley: A Theological Journey*. Nashville: Abingdon, 2003.

"Commentaries: John 10:38." *Bible Hub*. Online. http://biblehub.com/commentaries/john/10-38.htm.

Commission Internationale d'Histoire Ecclésiastique Comparée (CIHEC). *The Church in a Changing Society: Conflict-Reconciliation or Adjustment? Proceedings of the CIHEC-Conference in Uppsala, August 17–21, 1977*. Uppsala: Dept. of Church History, Faculty of Theology, Uppsala University, 1978.

Compton, Stephen C. *Rekindling the Mainline: New Life Through New Churches*. Lanham, MD: Rowman & Littlefield, 2003.

Conlin, Joseph Robert. *The American Past: A Survey of American History*. Vol. 1. Boston: Wadsworth, 2013.

Coon, Lynda L., et al. *That Gentle Strength: Historical Perspectives on Women in Christianity*. Charlottesville: University Press of Virginia, 1990.

Cooper, Ezekiel. "An Account of the Work of God at Baltimore, in a Letter to [Mr. Wesley]." *The Arminian Magazine* 13 (1789) 409–12.

———. *Beams of Light on Early Methodism in America: Chiefly Drawn from the Diary, Letters, Manuscripts, Documents, and Original Tracts of the Rev. Ezekiel Cooper*. Edited by Geo. A. Phoebus. New York: Phillips & Hunt, 1887.

Corn, Kevin. "Methodism." In *Encyclopedia of Religion and Society*, edited by William H. Swatos Jr., 296–99. Walnut Creek, CA: AltaMira, 1998.

Couvares, Francis G., et al., eds. *Patterns and Perspectives through Reconstruction.* Vol. 1 of *Interpretations of American History.* 7th ed. New York: Simon and Schuster, 2000.

Cowan, Douglas E. *The Remnant Spirit: Conservative Reform in Mainline Protestantism.* Santa Barbara, CA: Greenwood, 2003.

Cowart, John. *Strangers on the Earth.* Jacksonville, FL: Bluefish, 2006.

Crawford, Geo. A. *The Centennial of New England Methodism A Full Report of the Services Held in People's Church, Boston, MA, October 21–23, 1890, with Additional Historical Material.* Boston: Crawford Brothers, 1891.

Crook, William. *Ireland and the Centenary of American Methodism. Chapters on the Palatines; Philip Embury and Mrs. Heck; and Other Irish Emigrants, Who Instrumentally Laid the Foundation of the Methodist Church in the United States of America, Canada, and Eastern British America . . . Second Thousand.* Boston: Adams & Co, 1866.

Cross, Whitney R. *The Burned-Over District: The Social and Intellectual History of Enthusiastic Religion in Western New York, 1800–1850.* 1950. Reprint, New York: Harper & Row, 1965.

Crowell, Seth. *The Journal of Seth Crowell: Containing an Account of His Travels as a Methodist Preacher, for Twelve Years.* New York: J. C. Totten, 1813.

Cruickshank, Joanna. *Pain, Passion and Faith: Revisiting the Place of Charles Wesley in Early Methodism.* Lanham, MD: Scarecrow, 2009.

Cunningham, Joseph W. *John Wesley's Pneumatology: Perceptible Inspiration.* London: Routledge, 2016.

Curti, Merle E. *The Growth of American Thought.* 3rd ed. New Brunswick, NJ: Transaction, 1957.

Daniels, W. H., and William L. Harris. *The Illustrated History of Methodism in Great Britain, America, and Australia: From the Days of the Wesleys to the Present Time.* New York: Methodist Book Concern, Phillips & Hunt, 1880.

Danielson, R. A. "Methodist Camp Meetings and Revival." *The Asbury Journal* 68.2 (2013) 160–64. Online. http://place.asburyseminary.edu/cgi/viewcontent.cgi?art icle=1206&context=asburyjournal.

Darwin, Charles. *The Origin of Species: With Introduction and Notes.* Vol. 11. Edited by Charles W. Eliot. New York: P. F. Collier & Son, 1909.

Davies, Owen. *Witchcraft, Magic and Culture: 1736–1951.* Manchester, UK: Manchester University Press, 1999.

Dayton, Donald W. *Theological Roots of Pentecostalism.* Grand Rapids, MI: Baker Academic, 1987.

DeArteaga, William L. *Quenching the Spirit: Discover the Real Spirit Behind the Charismatic Controversy.* Orlando, FL: Creation, 1996.

Deere, Jack. *Surprised by the Power of the Spirit: Discovering How God Speaks and Heals Today.* Grand Rapids, MI: Zondervan, 1993.

Denison, John H. *Christ's Idea of the Supernatural.* Boston: Houghton, 1895.

DePuy, W. H., ed. *The Methodist Year-Book: 1884. One Hundredth Year of the Separate Organization of American Methodism.* New York: Philips & Hunt, 1883.

Descartes, René. *Discourse on Method and Meditations.* Translated by Elizabeth S. Haldane and G. R. T. Ross. Mineola, NY: Dover, 2003.

———. *The Meditations, and Selections from the Principles of Philosophy, of Descartes.* Edited by John Veitch. Edinburgh: Sutherland & Knox, 1853.

DeVries, Jan. *Do Miracles Exist?* Edinburgh, UK: Random, 2011.

Dieter, Melvin E. "Revivals and Revivalism." In *Historical Dictionary of Methodism*, edited by Charles Yrigoyen Jr., 56–58. 2nd ed. Historical Dictionaries of Religions, Philosophies, and Movements. Lanham, MD: Scarecrow, 2005.

Ditchfield, G. M. *The Evangelical Revival.* London: Routledge, 2005.

Dixon, James. *Methodism in its Origin, Ecomony, and Present Position: A Sermon.* London: John Mason, 1843.

DK Eyewitness Travel Guide USA. New York: Penguin, 2017.

Dobrée, Bonamy. *John Wesley.* 1933. Reprint, Albany, OR: Books for the Ages, 1997.

Doles, Jeff. *Miracles & Manifestations of the Holy Spirit in the History of the Church.* Seffner, FL: Walking Barefoot Ministries, 2008.

Dondzila, Michael R. "Asbury, Francis (1745–1816)." In vol. 1 of *The Early Republic and Antebellum America: An Encyclopedia of Social, Political, Cultural, and Economic History*, 100–103. 4 vols. London: Routledge, 2015.

Dougherty, Jude P. *The Logic of Religion.* Washington, DC: Catholic University of America Press, 2010.

Douglas, James D. *Who's Who in Christian History.* Wheaton, IL: Tyndale, 1992.

Douglass, Frederick. *The Anti-Slavery Movement.* Rochester, NY: Lee, Mann, 1855.

Dow, Lorenzo. *History of Cosmopolite: Or, the Four Volumes of Lorenzo's Journal Concentrated in One, Containing His Experience & Travels, from Childhood to 1814. Also, Containing His Polemical Writings.* 3rd ed. Philadelphia: Joseph Rakestraw, 1816.

Dow, Lorenzo, and Peggy Dow. *The Dealings of God, Man and the Devil: As Exemplified in the Life, Experience, and Travels of Lorenzo Dow, in a Period of Over Half a Century. Together with His Polemic and Miscellaneous Writings, Complete. To Which Is Added: The Vicissitudes of Life, by Peggy Dow . . . with an Introductory Essay by the Rev. John Dowling.* New York: Nafis & Cornish, 1850.

"Dow's Preaching Appointments." *North-Carolina Star*, August 9, 1811, 3.

Drew, Samuel. *The Life of the Rev. Thomas Coke.* London: Conference-Office, 1817.

DuBose, Horace M. *Francis Asbury: A Biographical Study.* Nashville: MECS, 1916.

Duewel, Wesley L. *Heroes of the Holy Life: Biographies of Fully Devoted Followers of Christ.* Grand Rapids, MI: Zondervan, 2002.

———. *Revival Fire.* Grand Rapids, MI: Zondervan, 1996.

Duncan, Douglas S. *To Reign As Kings.* Highton, Australia: Calvary, 1988.

Duren, William Larkin. *Francis Asbury: Founder of American Methodism and Unofficial Minister of State.* New York: Macmillan, 1928.

During, Simon. *Modern Enchantments.* Cambridge, MA: Harvard University Press, 2009.

Easton, Matthew George. "Trance." *Easton's Bible Dictionary.* Online. http://www.biblestudytools.com/dictionary/trance.

Eaton, Brand W. "Jacob Gruber's 1818 Camp Meeting Sermon." *Methodist History* 37.4 (1999) 242–48. Online. http://hdl.handle.net/10516/6269.

Eayrs, George. *John Wesley: Christian Philosopher and Church Founder.* Eugene, OR: Wipf & Stock, 2010.

Edson, Gary. *Mysticism and Alchemy through the Ages: The Quest for Transformation.* McFarland, 2012.

Eke, Christopher. *The Book of Great Testimonies and Great Breakthroughs.* Scotts Valley, CA: CreateSpace, 2014.

Elliott, Stephen. "How Miracles Helped Spread the Wesleyan Revivals." *Seedbed*, July 17, 2017. Online. http://www.seedbed.com/how-miracles-helped-spread-the-wesleyan-revivals.

Elsbree, Oliver W. *The Rise of the Missionary Spirit in America, 1790–1815.* Eugene, OR: Wipf & Stock, 2013.

Emery, George. *The Methodist Church on the Prairies, 1896–1914.* Montreal: McGill-Queen's University Press, 2001.

Emory, John. *The Life of the Rev. John Emory, DD: One of the Bishops of the Methodist Episcopal Church.* Edited by Robert Emory. New York: George Lane, 1841.

Emory, Robert. *History of the Discipline of the Methodist Episcopal Church.* New York: G. Lane & C. B. Tippet, 1845.

Encyclopaedia Britannica Online (EBO). Online. https://www.britannica.com.

"Enthousiasmos." In *Brill's New Pauly,* edited by Christine F. Salazar. English ed. Online. http://dx.doi.org/10.1163/1574-9347_bnp_e12221560.

Escobar, Samuel. *The New Global Mission: The Gospel from Everywhere to Everyone.* Downers Grove, IL: InterVarsity, 2013.

Escultura, E. E. *Scientific Natural Philosophy.* Sharjah, UAE: Bentham, 2011.

Essah, Patience. *A House Divided: Slavery and Emancipation in Delaware, 1638–1865.* Charlottesville: University of Virginia Press, 1996.

The Evangelical Repository: A Quarterly Magazine of Theological Literature. Vol. 1. Seventh Series. Glasgow, UK: Thomas D. Morrison, 1879.

Evans, Christopher H. "Most Distinctive Contribution of Methodists to Christianity in the United States." In vol. 5 of *Encyclopedia of Christianity in the United States,* edited by George Thomas Kurian and Mark A. Lamport, 1495–1507. Lanham, MD: Rowman & Littlefield, 2016.

Evans, Theophilus. *The History of Modern Enthusiasm: From the Reformation to the Present Times.* London: n.p., 1757.

Ewbank, J. Robert. *John Wesley, Natural Man, and the "Isms".* Eugene, OR: Resource, 2009.

Exman, Gary W. *Get Ready—Get Set—Grow!: Church Growth for Town and Country Congregations.* Lima, OH: CSS, 1987.

"Extract of a Letter in the Weekly Miscellany." *Ipswich Journal,* February 17, 1739, 2.

Faggioli, Massimo. *A Council for the Global Church: Receiving Vatican II in History.* Minneapolis, MN: Fortress, 2015.

Fahlbusch, Erwin, and Geoffrey William Bromiley, eds. *Evangelisches Kirchenlexikon.* Vol. 3. English ed. Grand Rapids, MI: Eerdmans, 2003.

Farish, Hunter D. *The Circuit Rider Dismounts: A Social History of Southern Methodism, 1865–1900.* Boston: Da Capo, 1969.

Feinman, Peter. "Itinerant Circuit-Riding Minister: Warrior of Light in a Wilderness of Chaos." *Methodist History* 45.1 (2006) 43–53. Online. http://hdl.handle.net/10516/3218.

Fenton, Walter. "US Membership Decline Continues." *Good News,* November 20, 2015. Online. https://goodnewsmag.org/2015/11/u-s-membership-decline-continues.

Ferguson, William Martain. *Methodism in Washington, District of Columbia, Being an Account of the Rise and Early Progress of Methodism in That City, and a Succinct History of the Fourth-Street Methodist Episcopal Church; Also, Sketches of the Preachers from the Earliest Times, and an Appendix of All the Methodist Churches at Present in the City.* Baltimore: Methodist Episcopal Book Depository, 1892.

Fewier, Bishop C. H. "Appeal of the Twentieth Century Thank Offering Commission." *The Christian Advocate* 74 (1899) 88–90.

"Fighting Bees: Methodist Itinerants and the Dynamics of Methodist Growth, 1770–1820." In *Methodism and the Shaping of American Culture*, edited by Nathan O. Hatch and John H. Wigger, 87–133. Nashville: Abingdon, 2001.

Findling, John E., and Frank W. Thackeray, eds. *The Eighteenth Century.* Vol. 2 of *What Happened?: An Encyclopedia of Events That Changed America Forever.* Santa Barbara, CA: ABC-CLIO, 2011.

Finke, Roger, and Rodney Stark. *The Churching of America, 1776–1990: Winners and Losers in Our Religious Economy.* New Brunswick, NJ: Rutgers University Press, 1992.

Finlan, Stephen. *The Apostle Paul and the Pauline Tradition.* Collegeville, MN: Liturgical, 2008.

Finley, James Bradley. *Autobiography of Rev. James B. Finley, or, Pioneer Life in the West.* Edited by W. P. Strickland. Cincinnati: Methodist Book Concern, 1854.

———. *Life among the Indians; Or, Personal Reminiscences . . . Illustrative of Indian Life and Character.* Part 4. Edited by Davis Wasgatt Clark. Cincinnati: Hitchcock & Walden, 1868.

———. *Sketches of Western Methodism: Biographical, Historical, and Miscellaneous. Illustrative of Pioneer Life.* Edited by W. P. Strickland. Cincinnati: Methodist Book Concern, 1854.

Finney, Charles. *Lectures on Revivals of Religion.* 2nd ed. New York: Leavitt, Lord & Co., 1835.

———. *Memoirs of Rev. Charles G. Finney.* 1876. Reprint, Bedford, MA: Applewood, 2009.

First United Methodist Church, Cuyahoga Falls, OH (FUMC). *The History of the First United Methodist Church of Cuyahoga Falls, Ohio, 1830–1969.* Cuyahoga Falls, OH: F. W. Orth, 1968.

Fisk, Wilbur. "Dr. Fisk's Travels on the Continent of Europe." *The Methodist Magazine and Quarterly* 20–21 (1838) 443–49.

Fleming, Louise. *Excel Studies of Religion.* Glebe, Australia: Pascal, 2001.

Fletcher, John. *Christian Perfection.* Nashville: E. Stevenson & F. A. Owen, 1855.

———. *First Check to Antinomianism.* New York: B. Waugh and T. Mason, 1835.

———. *The Works of the Rev. John Fletcher: Late Vicar of Madeley.* Vol. 4. London: John Kershaw, 1836.

Flora, Joseph M., et al., ed. *The Companion to Southern Literature: Themes, Genres, Places, People, Movements, and Motifs.* Baton Rouge: Louisiana State University Press, 2002.

Foley, William E. *The Genesis of Missouri: From Wilderness Outpost to Statehood.* Columbia: University of Missouri Press, 1989.

"For the Columbian Patriot." *National Standard*, January 19, 1814.

"For the Register: Religious." *Weekly Raleigh Register*, August 29, 1817, 3.

"For the Vermont Republican." *Vermont Republican and American Journal. Windham, Windsor and Orange County Advertiser*, December 3, 1810, 2.

Forsaith, Peter, et al., ed. *The Ashgate Research Companion on World Methodism.* London: Routledge, 2016.

Forsyth, P. T. "Christianity and Society." *The Methodist Review Quarterly* 63 (1914) 3–21.

Frank, Andrew. *American Revolution: People and Perspectives*. Santa Barbara, CA: ABC-CLIO, 2008.

Frank, Thomas Edward. "Methodism's Polity: History and Contemporary Questions." In *T&T Clark Companion to Methodism*, edited by Charles Yrigoyen, 309–28. London: Bloomsbury, 2014.

———. *Polity, Practice, and the Mission of The United Methodist Church: 2006 Edition*. Nashville: Abingdon, 2006.

Freud, Sigmund. *The Future of an Illusion*. Edited by James Strachey. New York: Norton, 1961.

Frick, Philip L. "The Spirit of Methodism: Asbury at Prayer." *The Christian Advocate* 91 (1916) 351–54.

"Friday [in] Edenton." *Edenton Gazette*, July 28, 1809, 3.

"Friday, June 1 (Announcements)." *N. Carolina Chronicle*, June 2, 1827, 3.

"From the Trenton Federalists." *Post-Boy*, October 15, 1805, 1.

"From Zion's Herald." *Vermont Patriot and State Gazette*, August 15, 1826, 4.

Fry, Benjamin St. James. *The Life of Rev. William M'Kendree, One of the Bishops of the Methodist Episcopal Church*. New York: Carlton & Phillips, 1852.

Fudge, Thomas A. *Christianity without the Cross: A History of Salvation in Oneness Pentecostalism*. Irvine, CA: Universal, 2003.

Fuller, A. James. "Methodists." In *The Early Republic and Antebellum America: An Encyclopedia of Social, Political, Cultural, and Economic History*, edited by Christopher G. Bates, 640–41. London: Routledge, 2015.

Galli, Mark. "Revival at Cane Ridge." *Christianity Today* 45 (1995). Online. https://www.christianitytoday.com/history/issues/issue-45/revival-at-cane-ridge.html.

Garnett, Jane, and Colin Matthew, eds. *Revival and Religion Since 1700: Essays for John Walsh*. London: Hambledon, 1993.

Garretson, Freeborn. *The Experience and Travels of Mr. Freeborn Garrettson, Minister of the Methodist-Episcopal Church in North America*. Philadelphia: Joseph Crukshank, 1791.

———. *A Letter to the Rev. Lyman Beecher Containing Strictures and Animadversions on a Pamphlet Entitled "An Address of the Charitable Society for the Education of Indigent Pious Young Men for the Ministry of the Gospel."* New York: J. C. Totten, 1816.

———. "Union of Fear, Hope, Love, and Joy in the Believer." *The Methodist Magazine* 8 (1825) 249–57.

Garretson, [Richard]. "An Account of the Revival of the Work of God at Petersburg, in Virginia." *The Arminian Magazine* 13 (1790) 300–307.

Gatch, Philip. *Sketch of Rev. Philip Gatch*. Edited by John McLean. Cincinnati: Methodist Episcopal Church, 1854.

Gaustad, Edwin S., et al. *New Historical Atlas of Religion in America*. New York: Oxford University Press, 2001.

Gaustad, Edwin S., and Leigh Schmidt. *The Religious History of America: The Heart of the American Story from Colonial Times to Today*. New York: HarperCollins, 2002.

Gauvreau, Michael. *Evangelical Century: College and Creed in English Canada from the Great Revival to the Great Depression*. Montréal: McGill-Queen's University Press, 1991.

Geiger, Roger L., ed. *Perspectives History Higher Education*. Rutgers, NJ: Transaction, 2005.

Geisler, Norman L. *Signs and Wonders*. Eugene, OR: Wipf & Stock, 2004.

General Commission on Archives and History, UMC (GCAH). "United Methodist Membership Statistics." Online. http://www.gcah.org/history/united-methodist-membership-statistics.

General Council on Finance and Administration, UMC (GCFA). "Online Directory & Statistics." Online. http://www.umdata.org.

Giles, Charles. *Pioneer: A Narrative of the Nativity, Experience, Travels, and Ministerial Labours of Rev. Charles Giles*. New York: G. Lane & P. P. Sandford, 1844.

Gish, Dustin A., and Daniel P. Klinghard, eds. *Resistance to Tyrants, Obedience to God: Reason, Religion, and Republicanism at the American Founding*. Lanham, MD: Lexington, 2013.

Glover, Raymond F. *The Hymnal 1982 Companion*. New York: Church Hymnal, 1990.

Godard, Samuel. "Religious Intelligence: Revivals of Religion." *Vermont Journal*, July 14, 1817.

Godbey, J. E. "Are We Losing the Sense of Sin?" *The Methodist Review Quarterly* 48 (1922) 282–98.

Goetz, Stewart. "Naturally Understanding Naturalism." *Faith and Philosophy: Journal of the Society of Christian Philosophers* 27.1 (2010) 79–90.

Going, Jonathan, et al., eds. *The Christian Library: A Reprint of Standard Religious Works*. Vol. 3. New York: Thos. George, Jr., 1835.

González, Justo L. *The Story of Christianity*. Vol. 2. New York: HarperOne/HarperCollins, 2010.

Goodrich, Samuel Griswold. *Recollections of a Lifetime, Or Men and Things I Have Seen: In a Series of Familiar Letters to a Friend, Historical, Biographical, Anecdotical, and Descriptive*. Vol. 1. New York: Miller, Orton, and Mulligan, 1857.

Goodsell, Buel. "Camp Meeting on the Champlain District." *The Methodist Magazine* 8 (1825) 442–43.

Gorham, Barlow Weed. *Camp Meeting Manual: A Practical Book for the Camp Ground; in Two Parts*. Boston: H. V. Degen, 1854.

Goss, Charles C. *Statistical History of the First Century of American Methodism with a Summary of the Origin and Present Operations of Other Denominations*. New York: Carlton & Porter, 1866.

Graham, Billy. *The Secret of Happiness*. Nashville: Thomas Nelson, 2011.

Grant, Brewin, and John H. Godwin. *The Rescue of Faith; Or, a Vindication of the Cross of Christ*. London: Ward & Co., 1862.

Graves, J. R. *The Great Iron Wheel: Or, Republicanism Backwards and Christianity Reversed: In a Series of Letters Addressed to J. Soule, Senior Bishop of the ME Church, South*. Nashville: Graves and Marks, 1855.

Gray, John G. *History of the Rise and Progress of the Methodist Episcopal Church in the Wawarsing and Mamakating Valleys*. Ellenville, NY: C. F. Taylor, 1897.

Mann, Horace. *Census of Great Britain, 1851. Education: England and Wales. Report and Tables*. London: Eyre and Spottiswoode for HMSO, 1854.

Green, Michael S., and Scott L. Stabler. *Ideas and Movements That Shaped America: From the Bill of Rights to "Occupy Wall Street"*. Santa Barbara, CA: ABC-CLIO, 2015.

Green, Jay P. *Unholy Hands on the Bible: An Examination of Six Major New Versions*. Lafayette, IN: Sovereign Grace Trsut Fund, 1992.

Greengrass, Mark. *Christendom Destroyed: Europe 1517–1648*. New York: Penguin, 2015.

Gregoire, M. "History of Religious Sects." *The Quarterly Review* 28 (1823) 1–46.

Griffin, M. "Moral and Religious." *Buffalo Emporium and General Advertiser*, March 19, 1825, 1.

Gross, John O. "The Romance of American Methodism." *Methodist History*, October 1967, 14–24. Online. http://hdl.handle.net/10516/1486.

Grow, Matthew J. *From the Outside Looking In: Essays on Mormon History, Theology, and Culture*. Oxford: Oxford University Press, 2015.

Gruber, Jacob, and David Martin. *Trial of the Rev. Jacob Gruber: Minister in the Methodist Episcopal Church, at the March Term, 1819, in the Frederick County Court, for a Misdemeanor*. Fredericktown, MD: David Martin, 1819.

Grudem, Wayne A. *Systematic Theology: An Introduction to Biblical Doctrine*. Grand Rapids, MI: Zondervan, 1994.

Hahn, Heather. "Denomination's Membership Tops 12.5 Million." *United Methodist News Service*, January 29, 2018. Online. https://www.umnews.org/en/news/denominations-membership-tops-125-million.

Haines, Michael R. *A Population History of North America*. New York: Cambridge University Press, 2000.

Hall, Timothy L. *American Religious Leaders*. New York: Facts on File, 2014.

Handy, Robert T. "American Methodism and Its Historical Frontier: Interpreting Methodism on the Western Frontier: Betweeen Romanticism and Realism." *Methodist History* 23.1 (1984) 44–53. Online. http://hdl.handle.net/10516/5274.

Hankins, Barry. *The Second Great Awakening and the Transcendentalists*. Westport, CT: Greenwood, 2004.

Hardman, Keith J. *Seasons of Refreshing: Evangelism and Revivals in America*. Eugene, OR: Wipf & Stock, 2006.

Hardy, Henry. "Henry Hardy, Stationed Minister of the Methodist Episcopal Church in Richmond." *Natchez Gazette*, February 21, 1818, 3.

———. "Lorenzo Dow." *Carolina Federal Republican*, January 17, 1818, 2.

Harper, Keith. *American Denominational History: Perspectives on the Past, Prospects for the Future*. Tuscaloosa: University of Alabama Press, 2008.

Harper, Steve. *The Way to Heaven: The Gospel According to John Wesley*. Grand Rapids, MI: Zondervan, 2009.

Harrell, David Edwin, et al. *Unto a Good Land: A History of the American People*. Vol. 1. Grand Rapids, MI: Eerdmans, 2007.

Harrington, W. Frank. *First Comes Faith: Proclaiming the Gospel in the Church*. Louisville, KY: Geneva, 1998.

Harris, Antipas L. *Holy Spirit, Holy Living: Toward a Practical Theology of Holiness for Twenty-First Century Churches*. Eugene, OR: Wipf & Stock, 2013.

Hasset, Miranda K. "Charismatic Renewal." In *The Oxford Handbook of Anglican Studies*, edited by Sathianathan Clarke and Mark D. Chapman, 301–14. New York: Oxford University Press, 2016.

Hatch, Nathan O. *The Democratization of American Christianity*. Reprint ed. New Haven, CT: Yale University Press, 1991.

Hayes, Patrick J. *Miracles: An Encyclopedia of People, Places, and Supernatural Events from Antiquity to the Present*. Santa Barbara, CA: ABC-CLIO, 2016.

Hebert, Albert J. *Saints Who Raised the Dead: True Stories of Four Hundred Resurrection Miracles*. Charlotte, NC: TAN, 2012.

Hedding, Elijah. "Bishop Hedding." *The Methodist Quarterly Review* 35 (1853) 9–29.

Heitzenrater, Richard P. *Wesley and the People Called Methodists*. 2nd ed. Nashville: Abingdon, 2013.

Helland, Roger, and Leonard Hjalmarson. *Missional Spirituality: Embodying God's Love from the Inside Out*. Downers Grove, IL: InterVarsity, 2012.

Hellerman, Joseph H. *Philippians*. Edited by Andreas J. Köstenberger and Robert W. Yarbrough. Nashville: B&H, 2015.

Hempton, David. *Methodism: Empire of the Spirit*. New Haven, CT: Yale University Press, 2005.

Henkle, Moses Montgomery. *The Life of Henry Bidleman Bascom, DD, LLD: Late Bishop of the Methodist Episcopal Church, South*. Nashville: E. Stevenson and F. A. Owen, 1857.

Henry, Matthew. *Matthew Henry's Commentary on the Whole Bible*. Peabody, MA: Hendrickson, 2006.

Hervey, James, and John Wesley. *Theron and Aspasio; Or, a Series of Dialogues and Letters Upon the Most Interesting and Important Subjects; To Which Is Added, Aspasio Vindicated, in Eleven Letters from Mr. Hervey to the Rev. John Wesley*. London: Thomas Tegg and Son, 1837.

Hiatt, R. Jeffery. "John Wesley & Healing: Developing a Wesleyan Missiology." *The Asbury Theological Journal* 59.1 (2004) 89–109. Online. doi:10.7252/journal.01.2004S.07.

Hibbard, Billy. *Memoirs of the Life and Travels of B. Hibbard: Minister of the Gospel, Containing an Account of His Experience of Religion*. New York: Published by the author, 1843.

Hinde, Thomas. "Recollections of Mrs. Todd Hinde." *The Methodist Magazine and Quarterly Review* 13 (1830) 121–32.

Hinton, John H. *History of the United States of America, from the First Settlement of the Country*. Vol. 1. Boston: Samuel Walker and Company, 1875.

Hodges, Miles H. *Securing America's Covenant with God: From America's Foundations in the Early 1600s to America's Post-Civil-War Recovery in the Late 1800s*. Bloomington, IN: WestBow, 2020.

Hogarth, William. *Anecdotes of William Hogarth, Written by Himself: With Essays on His Life and Genius, and Criticisms on His Works*. London: J. B. Nichols and Son, 1833.

Holdich, Joseph. *The Life of Wilbur Fisk, DD: First President of the Wesleyan University*. New York: Harper, 1842.

Holifield, E. Brooks. "Clergy." In *The Cambridge Companion to American Methodism*, edited by Jason E. Vickers, 171–87. Cambridge: Cambridge University Press, 2013.

Hollenweger, Walter J. "An Introduction to Pentecostalisms." *Journal of Beliefs & Values* 25.2 (2004) 125–37. doi:10.1080/1361767042000251555.

————. *Pentecostalism: Origins and Developments Worldwide*. Grand Rapids, MI: Baker Academic, 2005.

Hollingdale, R. J. *Nietzsche: The Man and His Philosophy*. Cambridge: Cambridge University Press, 2001.

Holmes, D., et al. *The Methodist Preacher: Containing Twenty-Eight Sermons, on Doctrinal and Practical Subjects*. Auburn, NY: Derby and Miller, 1852.

Holmes, Isaac. *An Account of the United States of America, Derived from Actual Observation, during a Residence of Four Years in That Republic; Including Original Communications.* London: Caxton, 1823.

Hooton, Michael, and Nigel Wright. *Extended Family: Why Are There So Many Different Churches?* Eugene, OR: Resource, 2016.

Hopkins, George H. *The Circuit Rider on Foot; Or, My First Year in the Ministry.* Rockford, IL: A. F. Judd & Co, 1890.

Horton, James P. *A Narrative of the Early Life, Remarkable Conversion, and Spiritual Labours of James P. Horton: Who Has Been a Member of the Methodist Episcopal Church Upward of Forty Years.* n.p., 1839.

Hovey, Alvah. *An American Commentary on the New Testament: Issues 13–18.* Philadelphia: American Baptist Society, 1890.

Howe, Daniel W. *What Hath God Wrought: The Transformation of America, 1815–1848.* New York: Oxford University Press, 2007.

Hudson, Winthrop S. *Religion in America.* 8th ed. London: Routledge, 2016.

Hume, David. *Philosophical Essays: Concerning Human Understanding. By the Author of the Essays Moral and Political.* London: A. Millar, 1748.

Hunt, William Chamberlin. *Religious Bodies: 1906.* Vol. 2. Washington, DC: US Government Printing Office, 1910.

Hurst, Dennis G. *America on the Cusp of God's Grace: The Biblical Connection to the Stars and Stripes.* Bloomington, IN: iUniverse, 2010.

Hurst, John Fletcher. *The History of Methodism.* Vol. 4. New York: Eaton & Mains, 1903.

———. *John Wesley the Methodist: A Plain Account of His Life and Work.* New York: Eaton & Mains, 1903.

Hutson, James H., et al. "Religion in Eighteenth-Century America." *Library of Congress.* Online. https://www.loc.gov/exhibits/religion/relo2.html.

Hutton, Sarah. *British Philosophy in the Seventeenth Century.* Oxford: Oxford University Press, 2015.

Hyde, A. B. *The Story of Methodism: Tracing the Rise and Progress of That Wonderful Religious Movement, Which, like the Gulf Stream, Has Given Warmth to Wide Waters and Verdure to Many Lands; And Giving an Account of Its Various Influences and Institutions of Today.* Greenfield, MA: Willey & Company, 1887.

Imhof, Michael H. *Supernatural Testimonies.* Nappanee, IN: Evangel, 2006.

Ingersoll, Julie. *Baptist and Methodist Faiths in America.* New York: Facts on File, 2003.

Ireson, Ebenezer. *The Methodist Preacher, or, Monthly Sermons from Living Ministers.* Vols. 3–4. Boston: Kane & Co, 1833.

Iwig-O'Byrne, Liam. "How Methodists Were Made: The Arminian Magazine and Spiritual Transformation in the Transatlantic World, 1778–1803." PhD diss., University of Texas at Arlington, 2008.

Jackson, Thomas. *The Lives of Early Methodist Preachers, Chiefly Written by Themselves.* 6 vols. London: Wesleyan Conference Office, 1865–1866.

Jarratt, Devereux, and John Coleman. *The Life of the Reverend Devereux Jarratt: Rector of Bath Parish, Dinwiddie County, Virginia.* Baltimore: Warner et Hanna, 1806.

Jea, John. *The Life, History, and Unparalleled Sufferings of John Jea, the African Preacher. Compiled and Written by Himself.* Electronic ed. Chapel Hill: University of North Carolina at Chapel Hill, 2001. http://docsouth.unc.edu/neh/jeajohn/jeajohn.html.

Jefferson, Thomas. *The Jefferson Bible; The Life and Morals of Jesus of Nazareth Extracted Textually from the Gospels, Together with a Comparison of His Doctrines with Those of Others*. St. Louis, MO: N. D. Thompson, 1902.

Jennings, Daniel R. *The Supernatural Occurrences Of John Wesley*. Scotts Valley, CA: CreateSpace, 2012.

Johnson, Charles A. *The Frontier Camp Meeting: Religion's Harvest Time*. Dallas: Southern Methodist University Press, 1955.

Johnstone, Patrick J. St. G. *The Future of the Global Church: History, Trends and Possiblities*. Downers Grove, IL: InterVarsity, 2014.

Jones, G. R. "Account of the State of Religion in Scioto District, Ohio." *The Methodist Magazine* 5 (1822) 359–60.

Jones, John Griffing. *A Complete History of Methodism as Connected with the Mississippi Conference of the Methodist Episcopal Church, South*. Vol. 1. Nashville: MECS, 1908.

Jones, Scott J. *United Methodist Doctrine: The Extreme Center*. Nashville: Abingdon, 2003.

Kalas, J. Ellsworth. *Being United Methodist: What It Means, Why It Matters*. Nashville: Abingdon, 2012.

Kammen, Carol. *The Peopling of Tompkins County: A Social History*. New York: Heart of the Lakes, 1985.

Kant, Immanuel. *An Answer to the Question: "What is Enlightenment?"* Translated by H. B. Nisbet. London: Penguin, 2013.

———. "Essay on the Maladies of the Head (1764)." In *Anthropology, History, and Education*, edited by Robert B. Louden and Günter Zöller, 63–77. Cambridge Edition of the Works of Immanuel Kant. Cambridge: Cambridge University Press, 2007.

———. *Observations on the Feeling of the Beautiful and Sublime and Other Writings*. Edited by Patrick Frierson and Paul Guyer. Cambridge: Cambridge University Press, 2011.

Kapic, Kelly M., and Bruce L. McCormack. *Mapping Modern Theology: A Thematic and Historical Introduction*. Grand Rapids, MI: Baker Academic, 2012.

Kappeler, Warren A. *Communication Habits for the Pilgrim Church: Vatican Teaching on Media and Society*. New York: Peter Lang, 2009.

Keener, Craig S. *The IVP Bible Background Commentary: New Testament*. Downers Grove, IL: InterVarsity, 1993.

———. *Miracles: The Credibility of the New Testament Accounts*. Grand Rapids, MI: Baker Academic, 2011.

Kenny, Anthony. *Ancient Philosophy*. Oxford: Oxford University Press, 2006.

Kent, John. *Wesley and the Wesleyans: Religion in Eighteenth-Century Britain*. Cambridge: Cambridge University Press, 2002.

Kim, Elijah J. F. *The Rise of the Global South: The Decline of Western Christendom and the Rise of Majority World Christianity*. Eugene, OR: Wipf & Stock, 2012.

Kimbrough, S. T. *Orthodox and Wesleyan Ecclesiology*. Crestwood, NY: St. Vladimir's Seminary, 2007.

Kinghorn, Kenneth C. *The Heritage of American Methodism*. Strasbourg, France: Éditions du Signe, 1999.

————. "Richard Boardman: American Methodism's First Superintendent." *The Asbury Theological Journal* 55.2 (2000) 17–35. Online. http://place.asburyseminary.edu/cgi/viewcontent.cgi?article=1259&context=asburyjournal.

Kirby, James E., et al. *The Methodists*. Westport, CT: Greenwood, 1996.

Kirk, Harris E. "Religion, Theology, and Biblical Literature." *The Methodist Review* 66 (1917) 132–47.

Kitchin, W. C. "Thomas Webb, Lieutenant, and Local Preacher." *The Christian Advocate* 83 (1908) 542–43.

Knepper, George W. *Ohio and Its People*. Ashland, OH: Kent State University Press, 2003.

Knickerbocker, Wendy. *Bard of the Bethel: The Life and Times of Boston's Father Taylor, 1793–1871*. Newcastle, UK: Cambridge Scholars, 2014.

Knight, Henry H. *Anticipating Heaven Below: Optimism of Grace from Wesley to the Pentecostals*. Eugene, OR: Wipf & Stock, 2014.

————. *The Presence of God in the Christian Life: John Wesley and the Means of Grace*. Lanham, MD: Scarecrow, 1992.

Knox, Ronald Arbuthnott. *Enthusiasm; A Chapter in the History of Religion, with Special Reference to the XVII and XVIII Centuries*. New York: Oxford University Press, 1950.

Kostlevy, William, ed. *Historical Dictionary of the Holiness Movement*. 2nd ed. Lanham, MD: Scarecrow, 2009.

Kuiper, B. K. *The Church in History*. Grand Rapids, MI: Eerdmans, 1988.

Laborie, Lionel. *Enlightening Enthusiasm: Prophecy and Religious Experience in Early Eighteenth-Century England*. Manchester, UK: Manchester University Press, 2015.

Labron, Tim. *Bultmann Unlocked*. London: T&T Clark, 2011.

Lamport, Mark A. "John Wesley." In vol. 5 of *Encyclopedia of Christianity in the United States*, edited by George Thomas Kurian and Mark A. Lamport, 2452–55. Lanham, MA: Rowman & Littlefield, 2016.

Land, Steven J. *Pentecostal Spirituality: A Passion for the Kingdom*. London: A&C Black, 1993.

Landry, Lorraine Y. *Marx and the Postmodernism Debates: An Agenda for Critical Theory*. Wesport, CT: Praeger, 2000.

Lane, Christopher. *The Age of Doubt: Tracing the Roots of Our Religious Uncertainty*. New Haven, CT: Yale University Press, 2011.

Langford, Thomas A. *Methodist Theology*. Eugene, OR: Wipf & Stock, 2015.

Langton, Daniel R. *The Apostle Paul in the Jewish Imagination: A Study in Modern Jewish-Christian Relations*. New York: Cambridge University Press, 2010.

Lawrence, Anna M. *One Family Under God: Love, Belonging, and Authority in Early Transatlantic Methodism*. Philadelphia: University of Pennsylvania Press, 2011.

Lawson, John. *Notes on Wesley's Forty-Four Sermons*. Eugene, OR: Wipf & Stock, 2009.

Leaton, James. *History of Methodism in Illinois from 1793 to 1832*. Cincinnati: Walden and Stowe, 1883.

Leavitt, George R. "The Gifts and the Gift—1 Corinthians 12, 13." *Advance*, November 28, 1907, 671.

Lednum, John. *A History of the Rise of Methodism in America: Containing Sketches of Methodist Itinerant Preachers, from 1736 to 1785 . . . Also, a Short Account of Many Hundreds of the First Race of Lay Members, Male and Female, from New*

York to South Carolina. Together with an Account of Many of the First Societies and Chapels. Philadelphia: Published by the author, 1859.

Lee, Jarena. *Religious Experience and Journal of Mrs. Jarena Lee, Giving an Account of Her Call to Preach the Gospel.* Philadelphia: Published by the Author, 1849.

Lee, Jesse. *Memoir of the Rev. Jesse Lee: With Extracts from His Journals.* New York: N. Bangs and T. Mason, 1823.

————. *A Short History of the Methodists in the United States of America Beginning in 1766, and Continued Till 1809: To which is Prefixed a Brief Account of Their Rise in England in the Year 1729, &c.* Baltimore: Magill and Clime, 1810.

Lee, Jesse, and John Lee. *A Short Account of the Life and Death of the Rev. J. Lee: A Methodist Minister, Etc.* Baltimore: John West Butler, 1805.

Lee, Leroy M. *The Life and Times of the Rev. Jesse Lee.* Louiseville, KY: MECS, 1848.

Lee, Sidney, ed. *The Dictionary of National Biography.* Vol. 47. London: Smith, Elder, & Company, 1873.

Lee, Umphrey. *The Historical Backgrounds of Early Methodist Enthusiasm.* Eugene, OR: Wipf & Stock, 2009.

Lee, Witness. *Life-Study of Ephesians: Messages 29–63, 2.* Anaheim, CA: Living Stream Ministry, 1991.

Lee, YongBo. *Reaching Spiritual Maturity through the Teaching of Sound Doctrine of Salvation Using John Wesley as a Model.* Madison, NJ: ProQuest, 2009.

Lenton, John. *John Wesley's Preachers: A Social and Statistical Analysis of the British and Irish Preachers Who Entered the Methodist Itinerancy Before 1791.* Eugene, OR: Wipf & Stock, 2009.

Lepley, Lynne S. "Circuit Riders." In *Encyclopedia of North Carolina,* edited by William S. Powell. Chapel Hill: University of North Carolina Press, 2006. Online. http://www.ncpedia.org/circuit-riders.

Levington, John. *Power with God and with Men.* Philadelphia: Methodist Book Room, 1868.

Lindbeck, Kristen H. *Elijah and the Rabbis: Story and Theology.* New York: Columbia University Press, 2010.

Lints, Richard. *The Fabric of Theology: A Prolegomenon to Evangelical Theology.* Grand Rapids, MI: Eerdmans, 1993.

Liu, Joseph. "Global Christianity—A Report on the Size and Distribution of the World's Christian Population." *Pew Research Center,* December 19, 2011. Online. https://www.pewforum.org/2011/12/19/global-christianity-exec.

————. "Many Americans Mix Multiple Faiths." *Pew Research Center,* December 9, 2009. Online. http://www.pewforum.org/2009/12/09/many-americans-mix-multiple-faiths.

Lockwood, John P. *The Western Pioneers: Or, Memorials of the Lives and Labors of Richard Boardman and Joseph Pilmoor, the First Preachers Appointed by John Wesley to Labour in North America. With Brief Notices of Contemporary Persons and Events.* London: Wesleyan Conference Office, 1881.

Lockyer, Herbert. *All the Miracles of the Bible.* Grand Rapids, MI: Harper Collins, 1988.

"London: January 28." *Newcastle Weekly Courant,* January 28, 1744, 2.

"London: June 21." *Newcastle Weekly Courant,* June 23, 1750, 1.

Long, Zeb Bradford, and Douglas McMurry. *The Collapse of the Brass Heaven: Rebuilding Our Worldview to Embrace the Power of God.* Grand Rapids, MI: Chosen, 1994.

"Lorenzo Dow Will Deliver a Sermon." *Mississippi Free Trader,* February 14, 1816, 3.

Lovejoy, David S. *Religious Enthusiasm in the New World: Heresy to Revolution.* Cambridge, MA: Harvard University Press, 1985.

Lowery, Kevin Twain. *Salvaging Wesley's Agenda: A New Paradigm for Wesleyan Virtue Ethics.* Eugene, OR: Pickwick, 2008.

Lyerly, Cynthia Lynn. *Methodism and the Southern Mind, 1770–1810.* New York: Oxford University Press, 1998.

Lyles, Albert M. *Methodism Mocked: The Satiric Reaction to Methodism in the Eighteenth Century.* Eugene, OR: Wipf & Stock, 2015.

M., E. "On the Genius of Dr. Johnson." *The European Magazine, and London Review* 87 (1825) 426–35.

Macchia, Stephen A. *Crafting a Rule of Life: An Invitation to the Well-Ordered Way.* Downers Grove, IL: InterVarsity, 2012.

MacClenny, W. E. *The Life of Rev. James O'Kelly and the Early History of the Christian Church in the South.* Raleigh, NC: Edwards & Broughton, 1910.

MacCulloch, Diarmaid. *A History of Christianity: The First Three Thousand Years.* London: Penguin, 2010.

MacDonald, Margaret Y. *Colossians and Ephesians.* Edited by Daniel J. Harrington. Collegeville, MN: Liturgical, 2000.

MacDonald, Michael. *Sleepless Souls: Suicide in Early Modern England.* Oxford: Clarendon, 1993.

Mack, Phyllis. *Heart Religion in the British Enlightenment: Gender and Emotion in Early Methodism.* Cambridge: Cambridge University Press, 2008.

MacMullen, Ramsay. *The Early Church to the Dawn of the Reformation.* Vol. 1 of *The Story of Christianity.* New Haven, CT: Yale University Press, 1984.

Maddox, Randy L. "Reconnecting the Means to the End: A Wesleyan Prescription for the Holiness Movement." *Wesleyan Theological Journal* 33.2 (1998) 29–66. Online. https://pdfs.semanticscholar.org/66ea/d242753948acdb60bb9ff239f08ac4e3f373.pdf.

———. *Responsible Grace: John Wesley's Practical Theology.* Nashville: Kingswood, 1994.

Maffit, John Newland. "Life of John N. Maffit: The Second Whitefield." *National Gazette,* October 17, 1821, 2.

Maffitt, John Newland, et al. *Memorial of Philip Embury, The First Methodist Minister in the New World.* Cambridge, NY: Harrington & Brownell, 1888.

Mariner, Kirk. "William Penn Chandler and Revivalism in the East, 1797–1811." *Methodist History* 25.3 (1987) 135–40. Online. http://archives.gcah.org/handle/10516/5677.

Marsden, G. "Of the Methodist Doctrines." *The Methodist Magazine* 1 (1818) 209–15.

Marshall, Peter, et al. *From Sea to Shining Sea for Young Readers: 1787–1837.* Discovering God's Plan for America 2. Grand Rapids, MI: Revell, 2011.

Martin, Wade A. *Spiritual Entrepreneurialism.* Maitland, FL: Xulon, 2007.

Martindale, Don. *The Nature and Types of Sociological Theory.* New York: Routledge, 2013.

Marx, Karl, et al. *Marxism, Socialism and Religion.* Newtown, Australia: Resistance, 2001.

Masci, David, and Gregory A. Smith. "Is God Dead? No, But Belief Has Declined Slightly." *Pew Research Center,* April 7, 2016. Online. http://www.pewresearch.org/fact-tank/2016/04/07/is-god-dead-no-but-belief-has-declined-slightly.

Maser, Frederick E. "Robert Strawbridge, Founder of Methodism in Maryland." *Methodist History* 13.38 (1966) 3–21. Online. http://hdl.handle.net/10516/1426.

Matar, Anat. *Modernism and the Language of Philosophy*. London: Routledge, 2006.

Matthews, Michael R. *International Handbook of Research in History, Philosophy and Science Teaching*. New York: Springer, 2014.

Matthews, Rex Dale. *Timetables of History: For Students of Methodism*. Nashville: Abingdon, 2007.

May, Cedrick. *Evangelism and Resistance in the Black Atlantic, 1760–1835*. Athens: University of Georgia Press, 2010.

Maynard, Sampson. *The Experience of Sampson Maynard, Local Preacher of the Methodist E. Church: Written by Himself, to Which Is Prefixed, an Allegorical Address to the Christian World, Or a Thimble Full of Truth, to Blow Up the World of Error*. New York: Published by the Author, 1828.

Mazur, Eric Michael, and Kate McCarthy, eds. *God in the Details: American Religion in Popular Culture*. New York: Routledge, 2001.

M'Caine, Alexander. *The History and Mystery of Methodist Episcopacy: Or a Glance at the Institutions of the Church, as We Received Them from Our Fathers*. Baltimore: Richard J. Matchett, 1827.

———. *Letters on the Organization and Early History of the Methodist Episcopal Church*. Boston: Thomas F. Norms, 1850.

McClintock, John. *Sketches of Eminent Methodist Ministers*. New York: Carlton & Phillips, 1854.

McClymond, Michael J., and Gerald R. McDermott. *The Theology of Jonathan Edwards*. New York: Oxford University Press, 2011.

McCosh, James. *The Supernatural in Relation to the Natural*. Bedford, MA: Applewood, 2009.

McElroy, Archibald. "Deceased Preachers." *The Methodist Magazine* 10 (1827) 276–78.

McEndree, R. Duane, and Nancy L. McEndree. *The Body Temple*. New York: TEACH Services, 2010.

McGee, James. *The March of Methodism from Epworth Around the Globe: Outlines of the History, Doctrine, and Polity of the Methodist Episcopal Church*. New York: Hunt & Eaton, 1893.

McGiffert, Arthur Cushman. *A History of Christianity in the Apostolic Age*. New York: Scribner's Sons, 1897.

McGrath, Alister E., and Darren C. Marks, eds. *The Blackwell Companion to Protestantism*. New York: John Wiley & Sons, 2008.

McGuire, Franklin R. "Cane Ridge Meetinghouse." In *The Encyclopedia of the Stone-Campbell Movement*, edited by Douglas A. Foster, 163. Grand Rapids, MI: Eerdmans, 2008.

McKay, John P., et al. *From the Age of Exploration to the Present*. Vol. 2 of *Understanding Western Society: A Brief History*. Boston: Bedford, 2011.

McTyeire, Holland Nimmons. *A History of Methodism: Comprising a View of the Rise of this Revival of Spiritual Religion in the First Half of the Eighteenth Century, and of the Principal Agents by Whom it was Promoted in Europe and America; with Some Account of the Doctrine and Polity of Episcopal Methodism in the United States, and the Means and Manner of Its Extension Down to AD 1884*. Nashville: Southern Methodist, 1888.

Meredith, William Henry. *Jesse Lee: A Methodist Apostle*. New York: Eaton & Mains, 1909.

———. *The Real John Wesley*. New York: Jennings and Py, 1903.

Merritt, Timothy. "Letters on Methodism." *The Methodist Magazine and Quarterly Review* 13 (1831) 442–74.

"Methodist Camp Meeting." *Weekly Recorder 5*, October 2, 1818, 59.

Methodist Episcopal Church (MEC). *The Doctrines and Discipline of the Methodist Episcopal Church*. New York: Methodist Connection, 1808.

———. *The Doctrines and Discipline of the Methodist Episcopal Church*. Cincinnati: J. Emory and B. Waugh, 1868.

———. *The Doctrines and Discipline of the Methodist Episcopal Church in America*. Edited by Francis Asbury and Thomas Coke. 10th ed. Philadelphia: Henry Tuckniss, 1798.

———. *Journal of the General Conference of the Methodist Episcopal Church: 1848*. New York: Carlton & Porter, 1848.

———. *Journal of the General Conference of the Methodist Episcopal Church, Held in Omaha, Nebraska*. Edited by David S. Monroe. New York: Hunt & Eaton, 1892.

———. *Journals of the General Conference of the Methodist Episcopal Church: 1796–1836*. New York: Carlton & Porter, 1855.

———. *Minutes of the Annual Conferences of the Methodist Episcopal Church*. 2 vols. New York: T. Mason and G. Lane, 1840.

———. *Minutes of the Annual Conferences of the Methodist Episcopal Church*. Vol. 5. New York: Carlton & Phillips, 1852.

———. *Minutes of the Annual Conferences of the Methodist Episcopal Church, for the years 1829–1830*. Vol. 2. New York: T. Mason and G. Lane, 1840.

———. *Minutes of the Forty-Third Session of the New Jersey Annual Conference of the Methodist Episcopal Church Held at Keyport, NJ, March 12, 1879*. Philadelphia: Grant, Faires & Rodgers, 1879.

———. *Minutes of the Methodist Conferences: Annually Held in America from 1773 to 1813, Inclusive*. Vol. 1. New York: Methodist Connexion, 1813.

Methodist Episcopal Church, South (MECS). *Journal of the General Conference of the Methodist Episcopal Church, South*. Vol. 1. Virginia: MECS, 1851.

———. *Minutes of the Annual Conferences of the Methodist Episcopal Church, South*. Louisville, KY: John Early, 1853.

Methodist Error, Or, Friendly, Christian Advice: To Those Methodists Who Indulge in Extravagant Religious Emotions and Bodily Exercises. Trenton: D. & E. Fenton, 1819. https://archive.org/details/methodisterrororoowesl.

M'Ferrin, John B. *History of Methodism in Tennessee*. Vol. 1. Nashville: MECS, 1875.

Middleton, Conyers. *A New Edition of a Free Inquiry into the Miraculous Powers: Which Are Supposed to Have Subsisted in the Christian Church, from the Earliest Ages through Several Successive Centuries upon the Authority of Primitive Fathers*. London: J. and W. Boone, 1844.

Miller, Robert J. *Both Prayed to the Same God: Religion and Faith in the American Civil War*. Lanham, MD: Lexington, 2007.

Mills, Samuel. "Office of the Commissions Appointed by Act of Parliament (Under the Convention with the United States or America): General Rules." *Morning Chronicle*, May 27, 1811, 1.

Milton, Grace. *Shalom, the Spirit and Pentecostal Conversion: A Practical-Theological Study*. Leiden: Brill, 2015.

"Miscellaneous." *Newbern Sentinel*, November 30, 1822, 4.

Mode, Peter G. *The Frontier Spirit in American Christianity*. New York: Macmillan, 1923.

"Monday's Post: St. James Evening Post." *Derby Mercury*, August 16, 1739, 2.

Moore, Henry, and Mary Ann Smith. *The Life of the Rev. H. Moore . . . Including the Autobiography, and the Continuation, Written from His Own Papers, by Mrs. R. Smith*. London: T. Tegg, 1844.

Moore, Matthew H. "Methodism in War Times." *The Methodist Quarterly Review, South* 53 (1904) 687–94.

———. *Sketches of the Pioneers of Methodism in North Carolina and Virginia*. Nashville: Hardpress, 1884.

Morrell, Thomas. *The Journals of the Reverend Thomas Morrell Methodist Patriot and Preacher 1747–1838*. Edited by Michael J. McKay. New Jersey: Historical Society, Northern New Jersey Conference, UMC, 1984.

Morrow, Josiah. *The History of Warren County, Ohio: Containing a History of the County: Its Townships, Towns; General and Local Statistics; Portraits of Early Settlers and Prominent Men; History of the Northwest Territory; History of Ohio, Map of Warren County, Constitution of the United States, Miscellaneous Matters, Etc*. Chicago: W. H. Beers & Co., 1882.

Mudge, James. "A Short History of 'The People Called Methodists.'" *The Christian Advocate* 93 (1918) 11–12.

Mulder, Philip N. *A Controversial Spirit: Evangelical Awakenings in the South*. Oxford: Oxford University Press, 2002.

Munyenyembe, Rhodian G. *Christianity and Socio-Cultural Issues: The Charismatic Movement and Contextualization of the Gospel in Malawi*. Zomba, Malawi: Kachere Series, 2011.

Murphy, Timothy Francis, and Leon E. Truesdell. *Separate Denominations: Statistics, History, Doctrine, Organization, and Work*. Vol. 2 of *Census of Religious Bodies: 1926*. Washington, DC: US Government Printing Office, 1929.

Murray, Peter C. *Methodists and the Crucible of Race, 1930–1975*. Columbia: University of Missouri Press, 2004.

Murrin, John M., et al. *Liberty, Equality, Power: A History of the American People*. Enhanced Concise 4th ed. Belmont, CA: Thomson Wadsworth, 2009.

Myles, William. *A Chronological History of the People Called Methodists . . . From 1729–1812*. London: Printed at the Conference-Office, 1813.

Möllers, Christoph. *The Three Branches: A Comparative Model of Separation of Powers*. New York: Oxford University Press, 2013.

Nañez, Rick M. *Full Gospel, Fractured Minds?: A Call to Use God's Gift of the Intellect*. Grand Rapids, MI: Zondervan, 2010.

Nelson, Julie R. "Second Great Awakening." In vol. 2 of *The Historical Encyclopedia of World Slavery*, edited by Junius Rodriguez, 568–69. Santa Barbara, CA: ABC-CLIO, 1997.

New, Melvyn, and Gerard Reedy, eds. *Theology and Literature in the Age of Johnson: Resisting Secularism*. Newark: University of Delaware Press, 2014.

"New Jersey (Announcements)." *Vermont Statesman*, May 17, 1826, 1.

"News from Republic of Letters: Just Published." *Derby Mercury*, March 1, 1733, 1.

Newell, E. F. *Life and Observations of E. F. Newell . . . An Itinerant Minister in the Methodist Episcopal Church . . . Compiled from His Own Manuscripts [by C.W. Ainsworth].* Worcester, CT: Ainsworth, 1847.

Newman, John Henry, et al. *Tracts for the Times.* London: J. G. & F. Rivington, 1839.

Newman, William M., and Pater L. Halvorson. *Atlas of American Religion: The Denominational Era, 1776–1990.* Walnut Creek, CA: AltaMira, 2000.

Newton, A. Taylor. "Is Religion 'Just' Supernatural Agency, Social Support, or Meaning?" PhD diss., University of Denver, 2011.

Newton, Isaac. *The Mathematical Principles of Natural Philosophy.* Vol. 2. Translated by Andrew Motte. London: H.D. Symonds, 1803.

Nicholi, Armand M. *The Question of God: C. S. Lewis and Sigmund Freud Debate God, Love, Sex, and the Meaning of Life.* New York: Free Press, 2002.

Nockles, Peter. "Reactions to Robert Southey's Life of Wesley (1820) Reconsidered." *The Journal of Ecclesiastical History* 63.1 (2011) 61–80. doi:10.1017/s0022046910001223.

Noel, Bradley Truman. *Pentecostal and Postmodern Hermeneutics: Comparisons and Contemporary Impact.* Eugene, OR: Wipf & Stock, 2010.

Noland, S. *Will Makes Way, or, Autobiography of Rev. S. Noland of the Kentucky Conference, ME Church, South.* Nashville: Southern Methodist, 1886.

Noll, Mark A. "The Irony of the Enlightment for Presbyterians in the Early Republic." *Journal of the Early Republic* 5.2 (1985) 149. doi:10.2307/3122950.

———. *The Old Religion in a New World: The History of North American Christianity.* Grand Rapids, MI: Eerdmans, 2002.

———. *The Rise of Evangelicalism: The Age of Edwards, Whitefield and the Wesleys.* Downers Grove, IL: InterVarsity, 2010.

———. *The Work We Have to Do: A History of Protestants in America.* Oxford: Oxford University Press, 2002.

Noll, Mark A., et al. *Fides Et Historia: Conference on Faith and History.* Vols. 20–21. Ann Arbor: University of Michigan, 1988.

Norris, Clive. *The Financing of John Wesley's Methodism c. 1740–1800.* Oxford: Oxford University Press, 2017.

Northrup, Cynthia C. "Land Policies." In *Essays and Primary Source Documents*, edited by Cynthia Clark Northrup, 428–432. Vol. 2 of *The American Economy: A Historical Encyclopedia.* Santa Barbara, CA: ABC-CLIO, 2003.

Norvell, Scott J. *Terraforming For The Kingdom.* Pennsauken Township, NJ: BookBaby, 2010.

Novenson, Matthew V. *The Grammar of Messianism: An Ancient Jewish Political Idiom and Its Users.* Oxford: Oxford University Press, 2017.

O'Brien, Elmer J. "The Methodist Quarterly Review: Reflections on a Methodist Periodical." *Methodist History* 25.2 (1987) 76–90. Online. http://archives.gcah.org/bitstream/handle/10516/5610/MH-1987-January-OBrien.pdf?sequence=1&isAllowed=y.

O'Brien, Patrick K. *Atlas of World History.* New York: Oxford University Press, 2002.

O'Keefe, Joseph. *International Handbook of Catholic Education: Challenges for School Systems in the Twenty-First Century.* Edited by Gerald Grace. Berlin: Springer Science & Business Media, 2007.

O'Kelly, James. *The Author's Apology for Protesting Against the Methodist Episcopal Government.* Richmond, VA: John Dixon, 1798.

Oliverio, L. William. *Theological Hermeneutics in the Classical Pentecostal Tradition: A Typological Account*. Danvers, MA: Brill, 2012.

Olson, Roger E. *Arminian Theology: Myths and Realities*. Downers Grove, IL: IVP Academic, 2009.

———. *The Journey of Modern Theology: From Reconstruction to Deconstruction*. Downers Grove, IL: InterVarsity, 2013.

———. *The Westminster Handbook to Evangelical Theology*. Louisville, KY: Westminster John Knox, 2004.

One Hundred Thirty-One Christians Everyone Should Know. 1st ed. Holman Reference. Nashville: B&H, 2000.

Osudibia, Kizito Chike. *Religion and the Global Resurgence of Violence Connection of the Abrahamics*. Bloomington, IN: Authorhouse, 2016.

Otis, H. H. *Office of H. H. Otis, Bookseller, Publisher & Stationer. 288 Main Street, Buffalo, NY: I Have the Pleasure to Inform You That the Sixth Volume of McClintock & Strong's Cyclopedia of Biblical, Theological and Ecclesiastical Literature Is Now Ready for Delivery to Subscribers*. Buffalo, NY: H. H. Otis, 1870.

"Out in the Cold." *Harvard Health Publishing*, January 2010. Online. https://www.health.harvard.edu/staying-healthy/out-in-the-cold.

Outler, Albert Cook, ed. *John Wesley*. New York: Oxford University Press, 1980.

———. "Wesleyan Quadrilateral." In *The Wesleyan Theological Heritage: Essays of Albert C. Outler*, edited by Thomas C. Oden and Leicester R. Longden, 97–101. Grand Rapids, MI: Zondervan, 1991.

Owen, Christopher H. *The Sacred Flame of Love: Methodism and Society in Nineteenth-Century Georgia*. Athens: University of Georgia Press, 1998.

Oxford English Dictionary (OED). Online. https://en.oxforddictionaries.com.

Paine, Robert. *Life and Times of William M'Kendree: Bishop of the Methodist Episcopal Church*. 2 vols. Nashville: Southern Methodist, 1869.

Pak, Sŏng-Gyu. *Christian Spirituality in Africa: Biblical, Historical, and Cultural Perspectives from Kenya*. Eugene, OR: Wipf & Stock, 2013.

Palau, Luis, and David Sanford. *God Is Relevant: Finding Strength and Peace in Today's World*. Reprint ed. Colorado Springs, CO: Multnomah, 1998.

Palmer, Phoebe. *The Way of Holiness, with Notes by the Way; Being a Narrative of Religious Experience Resulting from a Determination to Be a Bible Christian*. New York: Piercy and Reed, 1843.

Pamphilus, Eusebius. *The Ecclesiastical History of Eusebius Pamphilus, Bishop of Caesarea in Palestine*. Translated by C. F. Cruse. London: G. Bell and Sons, 1908.

Parker, Charles A. "The Camp Meeting on the Frontier and the Methodist Religious Resort in the East—Before 1900." *Methodist History* 18.3 (1980) 179–92. Online. http://hdl.handle.net/10516/5032.

Pawlikowski, Jakub, et al. "Beliefs in Miraculous Healings, Religiosity and Meaning in Life." *Religions* 6.3 (2015) 1113–24. doi:10.3390/rel6031113.

Pease, L. "Revival of the Work of God in Brooklyn, Long Island." *The Methodist Magazine* 5 (1822) 69–72.

Peck, George. *Early Methodism within the Bounds of the Old Genesee Conference from 1788 to 1828, or, the First Forty Years of Wesleyan Evangelism in Northern Pennsylvania, Central and Western New York, and Canada: Containing Sketches of Interesting Localities, Exciting Scenes, and Prominent Actors*. New York: Carlton & Porter, 1860.

———. *The Life and Times of Rev. George Peck, DD*. New York: Nelson & Phillips, 1878.

Peirce, William. *The Ecclesiastical Principles and Polity of the Wesleyan Methodists: Comprising a Complete Compendium of Their Laws, Regulations, and General Economy; Together with a Full Account of All Their Ordinances, Institutions, Funds, and Customs, Carefully Compiled and Classified from Mr. Wesley's Journals, the Minutes of Conference, and Other Authentic Records from the Year 1774 to 1872 Inclusive*. London: Wesleyan Conference Office, 1873.

Perrin, Ruth H., and James S. Bielo. *The Bible Reading of Young Evangelicals: An Exploration of the Ordinary Hermeneutics and Faith of Generation Y*. Eugene, OR: Wipf & Stock, 2016.

Peters, John L. *Christian Perfection and American Methodism*. New York: Oxford University Press, 1956.

Peurifoy, George W. *The Tekel of Methodism: History of the Episcopal Methodism, in Which Its Claims to Being a Church of Christ Are Investigated*. Chapel Hill, NC: Gazette Office, 1858.

Phelan, Macum. *A History of the Expansion of Methodism in Texas, 1817–1866*. Nashville: Cokesbury, 1874.

Philips, Thomas E. "Coke, Thomas (1747–1814)." In *Encyclopedia of Protestantism*, edited by Hans J. Hillerbrand, 780. New York: Facts on File, 2005.

Phoebus, William. *Memoirs of the Rev. Richard Whatcoat: Late Bishop of the Methodist Episcopal Church*. New York: J. Allen, 1828.

Pickard, Samuel. *Autobiography of a Pioneer, or, the Nativity, Experience, Travels, and Ministerial Labors of Rev. Samuel Pickard, the "Converted Quaker", Containing Stirring Incidents and Practical Thoughts: With Sermons by the Author, and Some Account of the Labors of Elder Jacob Knapp*. Chicago: Church & Goodman, 1866.

Pilmore, Joseph. *The Journal of Joseph Pilmore, Methodist Itinerant, for the Years August 1, 1769, to January 2, 1774*. Edited by Frederick E. Maser and Howard T. Maag. Philadelphia: Historical Society of the Philadelphia Annual Conference of the UMC, 1969.

Plater, Ormonde. *Intercession: A Theological and Practical Guide*. Cambridge, MA: Cowley, 1995.

Platt, W. H. *The Philosophy of the Supernatural*. New York: E. P. Dutton, 1886.

Plunkett, Stephen W. "Conversion." In *Encyclopedia of Protestantism*, edited by Hans J. Hillerbrand, 850–55. New York: Facts on File, 2005.

Poewe, Karla O., ed. *Charismatic Christianity as a Global Culture*. Columbia: University of South Carolina Press, 1994.

Porter, James. *A Comprehensive History of Methodism: In One Volume, Embracing Origin, Progress, and Present Spiritual, Educational, and Benevolent Status in All Lands*. Cincinnati: Hitchcock & Walden, 1876.

Porter, Wendy, ed. *Rediscovering Worship: Past, Present, and Future*. Eugene, OR: Pickwick, 2015.

Porterfield, Amanda. *Conceived in Doubt: Religion and Politics in the New American Nation*. Chicago: University of Chicago Press, 2012.

Powell, William A., Jr. "Methodist Circuit-Riders in America, 1766–1844." MA thesis, University of Richmond, 1977.

Prentice, George, and Wilbur Fisk. *Wilbur Fisk*. Boston; New York: Houghton, 1890.

Price, Richard Nye. *Holston Methodism: From Its Origin to the Present Time*. 2 vols. Nashville: MECS, 1912.

"Progress of Methodists." *Maryland Gazette*, September 12, 1822, 2.

"Progress of Methodists." *Torch Light And Public Advertiser*, August 28, 1821, 2.

"Publication." *Gettysburg Compiler*, June 7, 1820, 1.

Puy, William H. *The People's Cyclopedia of Universal Knowledge: With Numerous Appendixes Invaluable for Reference in All Departments of Industrial Life, Brought Down to the Year 1885, with the Pronunciation and Orthography Conformed to Webster's Unabridged Dictionary*. 4th ed. New York: Philips & Hunt, 1887.

————, ed. *The Methodist Year Book: Continental Year Book 1884*. New York: Philips & Hunt, 1884.

Pyke, Richard. *Dawn of American Methodism*. Eugene, OR: Wipf & Stock, 2016.

Quantin, Jean-Louis. *The Church of England and Christian Antiquity: The Construction of a Confessional Identity in the Seventeenth Century*. Oxford: Oxford University Press, 2009.

Quayle, William A. *The Dynamite of God*. New York: Methodist Book Concern, 1918.

Rack, Henry D. "Doctors, Demons, and Early Methodist Healing." In *The Church and Healing: Papers Read at the Twentieth Summer Meeting and the Twenty-First Winter Meeting of the Ecclesiastical History Society*, edited by W. J. Sheils, 137–52. Oxford: Blackwell, 1983.

————. *Reasonable Enthusiast: John Wesley and the Rise of Methodism*. 2nd ed. Nashville: Abingdon, 1992.

Raichur, Ashish. *The Presence of God*. India: All Peoples Church, 2008.

Ramsay, William M. *Church History 101: An Introduction for Presbyterians*. Louisville, KY: Geneva, 2005.

————. *The Westminster Guide to the Books of the Bible*. Louisville, KY: Westminster John Knox, 2003.

Rawlyk, George A. "Freeborn Garrettson and Nova Scotia." *Methodist History* 30.3 (1992) 142–58. Online. http://archives.gcah.org/handle/10516/5773.

Ray, Jody Glenn. "The United Methodist Church and the Willingness to Embrace Change: Attracting Members of the Emerging Generation and a Return to Vitality." PhD diss., George Fox University, 2015. Online. http://digitalcommons.georgefox.edu/dmin/115.

Rech, Photina. *Wine and Bread*. Eugene, OR: Wipf & Stock, 2012.

Redford, A. H. *The History of Methodism in Kentucky*. Vol. 2. Nashville: Southern Methodist, 1869.

Redmile, Robert David. *The Apostolic Succession and the Catholic Episcopate in the Christian Episcopal*. Maitland, FL: Xulon, 2006.

Reeves, Russ Patrick. "Countering Revivalism and Revitalizing Protestantism: High Church, Confessional, and Romantic Critiques of Second Great Awakening Revivalism, 1835 to 1852." PhD diss., University of Iowa, 2005. Online. https://www.academia.edu/36145740/Reeves_Countering_Revivalism_and_Reviving_Protestantism_2005.

Reid, Alvin L. *Evangelism Handbook*. Nashville: B & H Academic, 2009.

Reid, Daniel G., et al., eds. *Concise Dictionary of Christianity in America*. Eugene, OR: Wipf & Stock, 2002.

"Religion." *Gallup*. Online. http://news.gallup.com/poll/1690/religion.aspx.

"Religious." *Public Opinion* 7 (1889) 436–39.

"Religious: The Methodist." *Natchez Newspaper and Public Advertiser*, May 23, 1826.

"Religious Communication: Lectures on the Shorter Catechism." *The Christian Advocate* 11 (1833) 145–55.

"Religious News: Concord." *Vermont Journal*, October 14, 1816, 3.

Remem, R. "Extract of a Letter." *Hartford Courant*, March 10, 1818, 1.

"Revival in Baltimore." *Christian Messenger*, March 4, 1818, 2.

"Revival of Religion." *Weekly Raleigh Register*, May 1, 1818, 3.

"Revivals of Religion." *Hartford Courant*, August 27, 1816.

Rhodes, Joseph W. *First United Methodist Church, Beloit, Wisconsin.* Beloit, WI: Varney, 1990.

Rhodes, Ron. *What Does the Bible Say About . . . ?: Easy-to-Understand Answers to the Tough Questions.* Eugene, OR: Harvest, 1997.

Richards, James. "Review: Lectures on the Prayer of Faith." *The Christian Advocate* 10 (1832) 501–6.

Richey, Russell E. "Early American Methodism." In *The Cambridge Companion to American Methodism*, edited by Jason E. Vickers, 44–62. Cambridge, UK: Cambridge University Press, 2013.

———. *Methodism in the American Forest.* Oxford: Oxford University Press, 2015.

Richey, Russell E., et al. *The Methodist Experience in America.* Vol. 2. Nashville: Abingdon, 2000.

———. *American Methodism: A Compact History.* Nashville: Abingdon, 2012.

Ridgeon, Lloyd V. J. *Major World Religions: From Their Origins to the Present.* London: Routledge Curzon, 2003.

Rieser, Andrew Chamberlin. *The Chautauqua Moment: Protestants, Progressives, and the Culture of Modern Liberalism, 1874–1920.* New York: Columbia University Press, 2012.

Roberts, Robert R. *The Life of the Rev. Robert R. Roberts: One of the Bishops of the Methodist Episcopal Church.* Edited by Charles Elliott. New York: G. Lane, 1844.

Robertson, C. K. *Conversations with Scripture: The Acts of the Apostles.* New York: Morehouse, 2010.

Robinson, James. *Divine Healing: The Formative Years: 1830–1880: Theological Roots in the Transatlantic World.* Eugene, OR: Wipf & Stock, 2011.

Rohde, Ross. *Viral Jesus: Recovering the Contagious Power of the Gospel.* Lake Mary, FL: Passio (Charisma), 2012.

Rorabaugh, W. J. *The Alcoholic Republic: An American Tradition.* New York: Oxford University Press, 1981.

Rosal, Nicholas Llanes. *Handbook of Miracles.* Bloomington, IN: Xlibris, 2013.

Rowe, Kenneth E., and Frederick E. Maser. "Discovery: New Light on Early Methodist Theological Education." *Methodist History* 10.1 (1971) 58–62. Online. http://hdl.handle.net/10516/1671.

Rowland, Christopher, and Christopher R. A. Morray-Jones. *The Mystery of God: Early Jewish Mysticism and the New Testament.* Leiden: Brill, 2009.

Ruddi, Thomas. "Edinburgh: August 27." *Caledonian Mercury*, August 27, 1741, 3–4.

Rühle, Otto. *Karl Marx: His Life and Work.* London: Routledge, 2011.

Ruickbie, Leo. *A Brief Guide to the Supernatural: Ghosts, Vampires and the Paranormal.* London: Robinson, 2012. Kindle ed.

Russie, Alice, ed. *The Essential Works of John Wesley.* Uhrichsville, OH: Barbour, 2011.

Ruth, Lester. "Camp Meeting." In *Encyclopedia of Protestantism*, edited by Hans J. Hillerbrand, 558–563. New York: Facts on File, 2005.

————. *Early Methodist Life and Spirituality: A Reader*. Nashville: Kingswood, 2005.

————. *A Little Heaven Below: Worship at Early Methodist Quarterly Meetings*. Nashville: Abingdon, 2000.

Samuel, Lawrence R. *Supernatural America: A Cultural History*. Santa Barbara, CA: ABC-CLIO, 2011.

Sandford, P. P. "A Discourse." *The Methodist Magazine and Quarterly Review* 17 (1835) 241–54.

————. *Memoirs of Mr. Wesley's Missionaries to America: Compiled from Authentic Sources*. New York: MEC, 1843.

Sandlin, Lee. *Wicked River: The Mississippi When It Last Ran Wild*. New York: Vintage, 2011.

Sargant, William. *Battle for the Mind: A Physiology of Conversion and Brain-Washing*. Revised ed. Baltimore, MD: Penguins, 1957.

Sargent, George Etell. *The Oxford Methodist: or The early life of John Wesley*. London: Benjamin L. Green, 1850.

Sartre, Jean-Paul. *Existentialism is a Humanism*. Edited by John Kulka. Translated by Carol Macomber. New Haven, CT: Yale University Press, 2007.

Saxton, L. "'The Holy Spirit: His Office and Work in Connexion With the Economy of Salvation, and the Means to be Employed to Secure His Influence." *The Methodist New Connexion Magazine and Evangelical Repository* 26 (1858) 625–38.

Scherck, Michael Gonder. *Pen Pictures of Early Pioneer Life in Upper Canada*. Toronto: W. Briggs, 1905.

Schivelbusch, Wolfgang. *The Railway Journey: The Industrialization of Time and Space in the Nineteenth Century*. Berkeley: University of California Press, 2014.

Schmidt, Martin F. *Kentucky Illustrated: The First Hundred Years*. Lexington: University Press of Kentucky, 2015.

Schmidt, Richard H. *God Seekers: Twenty Centuries of Christian Spiritualities*. Grand Rapids, MI: Eerdmans, 2008.

Schmookler, Andrew Bard. *The Parable of the Tribes: The Problem of Power in Social Evolution*. Albany: State University of New York Press, 1995.

Schreuder, Duco A. *Vision and Visual Perception: The Conscious Base of Seeing*. Bloomington, IN: Archway, 2014.

Scobie, Charles H. H., and John Webster Grant, eds. *The Contribution of Methodism to Atlantic Canada*. Quebec City, Canada: McGill-Queen's University Press, 1992.

Scott, David W. "Coming to Terms with Numerical Decline in the US UMC." *United Methodist Insight*, April 25, 2016. Online. https://um-insight.net/in-the-church/umc-global-nature/coming-to-terms-with-numerical-decline.

Scott, Walter. "Review of the Christian Spectator's Strictures on Dr. Adam Clarke's Discourses." *The Methodist Magazine and Quarterly Review* 12 (1830) 219–39.

Scudder, Moses Lewis, and Joseph Cummings. *American Methodism . . . with an Introduction by J. Cummings . . . Illustrated*. Bartford, CT: S. S. Scranton & Co., 1867.

Shadford, George. "A Short Account of Mr. George Shadford." *The Arminian Magazine*, 13 (1790) 180–83.

Sharp, James R. *American Politics in the Early Republic: The New Nation in Crisis*. New Haven, CT: Yale University Press, 1993.

Sheehan, Jonathan. *Enlightenment Bible: Translation, Scholarship, Culture*. Princeton, NJ: Princeton University Press, 2013.

Sherman, David. *History of the Revisions of the Discipline of the Methodist Episcopal Church.* New York: Nelson & Phillips, 1874.

Shipp, Albert Micajah. *The History of Methodism in South Carolina.* Nashville: Southern Methodist, 1884.

Shires, Preston. *Hippies of the Religious Right.* Waco, TX: Baylor University Press, 2007.

Sigsworth, John Wilkins. *World-Changers: Karl Marx and John Wesley.* Ontario, Canada: Easingwold, 1982.

Simpson, Matthew, ed. *Cyclopaedia of Methodism: Embracing Sketches of Its Rise, Progress, and Present Condition, with Biographical Notices and Numerous Illustrations.* 5th ed. Philadelphia: L. H. Everts, 1883.

Simpson, Robert. "Circuit Riders." *Archives & History, GCAH.* Online. http://www.gcah.org/history/circuit-riders.

Simpson, Robert Drew, ed. *American Methodist Pioneer: The Life and Journals of the Rev. Freeborn Garrettson, 1752–1827: Social and Religious Life in the US During the Revolutionary and Federal Periods.* Madison, NJ: Drew University Library, 1984.

Slaughter, Thomas P. *The Whiskey Rebellion: Frontier Epilogue to the American Revolution.* New York: Oxford University Press, 1988.

Smalley, Elam. *The Worcester Pulpit: With Notices Historical and Bibliographical.* Boston: Phillips, Sampson and Company, 1851.

Smith, Elias. "Address to the Public: To the Subscribers for This Paper, and to All Who May Hereafter Read Its Contents." *Herald of Gospel Liberty,* September 1, 1808, 1.

———. *The Age of Enquiry: Christian's Pocket Companion and Daily Assistant: Calculated Also for the Benefit of the Rising Generation in Leading Them Into Truth.* Exeter, NH: Abel Brown, 1825.

Smith, George Gilman. *The History of Methodism in Georgia and Florida: From 1785 to 1865.* Macon, GA: J. W. Burke & Co, 1877.

Smith, H. H. "The Religious Experience of Francis Asbury." *The Methodist Review Quarterly* 71 (1922) 563–68.

Smith, Henry. *Recollections and Reflections of an Old Itinerant: A Series of Ltters Originally Published in the Christian Advocate and Journal and the Western Christian Advocate.* Edited by George Peck. New York: Carlton & Phillips, 1854.

Smith, Roger. *American Spirit: A Story of American Individualism.* Bloomington, IN: iUniverse, 2013.

Smith, Thomas, and David Dailey. *Experience and Ministerial Labors of Rev. Thomas Smith.* Edited by George Peck. New York: Lane & Tippett, 1848.

Smith, Timothy L. *Revivalism and Social Reform: American Protestantism on the Eve of the Civil War.* New York: Harper Torchbooks, 1957.

Snethen, Nicholas. *Snethen on Lay Representation Or, Essays on Lay Representation and Church Government, Collected from the Wesleyan Repository, the Mutual Rights, and the Mutual Rights & Christian Intelligencer, from 1820 to 1829 Inclusive, and Now Republished in Chronological Order, with an Introduction.* Baltimore: J. J. Harrod, 1835.

Snider, Gordon L. *Use of the Old Testament in a Wesleyan Theology of Mission.* Cambridge: Clarke & Co., 2016.

Snyder, Howard A. *The Radical Wesley and Patterns for Church Renewal.* Eugene, OR: Wipf & Stock, 1996.

Sober, Elliott. "Intelligent Design, Irreducible Complexity, and Minds—a Reply to John Beaudoin." *Faith and Philosophy: Journal of the Society of Christian Philosophers* 25.4 (2008) 443–446. doi:10.5840/faithphil200825445.

Southwell, Charles. *An Apology for Atheism Addressed to Religious Investigators of Every Denomination by One of Its Apostles.* London: J. Watson, 1846.

Sparks, Randy J. "Religion In Mississippi." *Mississippi History Now,* November 2003. Online. http://www.mshistorynow.mdah.ms.gov/articles/96/religion-in-mississippi.

Spence-Jones, H. D. M., et al. *Christian Evidences. The Holy Spirit. The Beatitudes. The Lord's Prayer. Man, and His Traits of Character.* New York: Funk & Wagnalls, 1889.

Spielvogel, Jackson J. *Western Civilization.* 2 vols. Stamford, CT: Cengage Learning, 2014.

Spinoza, Benedictus de. *Spinoza's Short Treatise on God.* Translated by Lydia Gillingham Robinson. Chicago: Open Court, 1909.

Sprague, William B. *Annals of the American Methodist Pulpit; Or, Commemorative Notices of Distinguished Clergymen of the Methodist Denomination in the United States: From Its Commencement to the Close of the Year Eighteen Hundred and Fifty-Five with an Historical Introduction.* Vol. 7. New York: Robert Carter & Brothers, 530 Broadway, 1859.

———. *Annals of the American Pulpit; Or, Commemorative Notices of Distinguished American Clergymen of Various Denominations, from the Early Settlement of the Country to the Close of the Year Eighteen Hundred and Fifty-Five. With Historical Introductions.* Vol. 7. New York: Robert Carter & Brothers, 1861.

Sproul, R. C. *Discovering the God Who Is: His Character and Being, His Power and Personality.* Ventura, CA: Regal, 1995.

Stanford, Lee. *The Pentecostal Takeover.* Maitland, FL: Xulon, 2005.

Stanley, Brian. *Christian Missions and the Enlightenment.* New York: Routledge, 2013.

Stark, Rodney. *Exploring the Religious Life.* Baltimore: Johns Hopkins University Press, 2004.

Stark, Rodney, and Roger Finke. *Acts of Faith: Explaining the Human Side of Religion.* Berkeley, CA: University of California Press, 2000.

Staton, Knofel, and Leonard W. Thompson. *Angels.* Joplin, MO: College, 2005.

Stebbing, Henry. "This Day: Public." *Ipswich Journal,* July 21, 1739, 4.

Stevens, Abel. *History of the Methodist Episcopal Church in the United States of America.* 2 vols. New York: Carlton & Porter, 1864.

———. *The History of the Religious Movement in the Eighteenth Century, Called Methodism.* London: James Sangster & Company, 1873.

———. *The Planting and Training of American Methodism.* New York: Carlton & Porter, 1867.

Stevens, Abel, and Nathan Bangs. *Life and Times of Nathan Bangs, DD.* New York: Carlton & Porter, 1863.

Stevens, Leon G. *Circuit-Rider Days in Indiana.* Indianapolis, IN: W. K. Stewart, 1916.

———. *Men of Zeal: The Romance of American Methodist Beginnings.* Nashville: Abingdon, 1935.

———. *The Methodists: A Collection of Source Materials.* Chicago: University of Chicago Press, 1946.

———. *One Nation Under God: A Factual History of America's Religious Heritage.* Bloomington, IN: Thomas Nelson, 2012.

Stevenson, Edward, and Valentine Cook. *Biographical Sketch of the Rev. Valentine Cook . . . with an Appendix Containing His Discourse on Baptism*. Nashville: Published by the Author, 1858.

Stevenson, George John. *Methodist Worthies: Characteristic Sketches of Methodist Preachers of the Several Denominations, with Historical Sketch of Each Connexion*. Vol. 1. London: T. C. Jack, 1884.

Stinson, Charles. "The Finite Supernatural: Theological Perspectives." *Religious Studies* 9.3 (1973) 325–37. doi:10.1017/s003441250000682x.

Stock, R. D. "Enthusiasm." In *Britain in the Hanoverian Age: 1714–1837. An Encyclopedia*, edited by Jack Fruchtman et al., 253–54. New York: Garland, 1997.

Stokes, Jerry. *Changing World Religions, Cults & Occult*. Ashland, OH: Spring Study, 2007.

Stone, Barton W. *The Biography of Eld. Barton Warren Stone with Additions and Reflections*. Edited by John Rogers. Cincinnati: J. A. & U. P. James, 1847.

Storch, Robert D. *Popular Culture and Custom in Nineteenth-Century England*. London: Croom Helm, 1982.

Stormont, George. *Smith Wigglesworth: A Man Who Walked with God*. Tulsa, OK: Harrison, 2009.

Strickland, William P. *The Life of Jacob Gruber*. New York: Carlton & Porter, 1860.

Stumpf, Samuel Enoch. *Filozofia: Historia & Problemet*. Tirana, Albania: Toena, 2000.

Sutcliffe, Joseph. *The Divine Mission of the People Called Methodists: To Revive and Spread Religion: Illustrated and Defended in a Sermon [on 2 Cor. 4:1,2] Preached Before the District Meeting Assembled in Macclesfield, May 27, 1813*. London: Richard Edwards, 1814.

Sweeney, Douglas A. *The American Evangelical Story: A History of the Movement*. Grand Rapids, MI: Baker Academic, 2005.

Sweet, William Warren. *Circuit-Rider Days along the Ohio: Being the Journals of the Ohio Conference from Its Organization in 1812 to 1826*. New York: Methodist Book Concern, 1923.

Swift, Donald C. *Religion and the American Experience: A Social and Cultural History, 1765–1997*. New York: M. E. Sharpe, 1998.

Synan, Vinson. *The Century of the Holy Spirit: One Hundred Years of Pentecostal and Charismatic Renewal, 1901–2001*. Nashville: Thomas Nelson, 2001.

———. *The Holiness-Pentecostal Tradition: Charismatic Movements in the Twentieth Century*. Grand Rapids, MI: Eerdmans, 1997.

T., E. "The Edification of the Church. Promoted by a Divinely Called Minister of Diversified Talent." *The Methodist Magazine and Quarterly Review* 13 (1831) 324–50.

Taves, Ann. *Fits, Trances, and Visions: Experiencing Religion and Explaining Experience from Wesley to James*. Princeton, NJ: Princeton University Press, 1999.

Taylor, William. *Story of My Life: An Account of What I Have Thought and Said and Done in My Ministry of More Than Fifty-Three Years in Christian Lands and among the Heathen: Written by Myself*. New York: Eaton & Mains, 1896.

Teasdale, Mark R. *Methodist Evangelism, American Salvation: The Home Missions of the Methodist Episcopal Church, 1860–1920*. Eugene, OR: Wipf & Stock, 2014.

Tefft, Benjamin F. *Methodism Successful and the Internal Causes of Its Success*. New York: Derby & Jackson, 1860.

Teir, Helen E., et al., eds. *Historical Statistics of the United States: Colonial Times to 1970.* Bicentennial ed. Washington, DC: US Government Printing Office, 1975.

"Testimonies." *Freedom Ministries.* Online. https://freedom-ministries.us/testimonies.

Thacker, Joseph A. "Methodism and the Second Great Awakening." *The Asbury Seminarian* 39.3 (1984) 46–61. https://place.asburyseminary.edu/asburyjournal/vol39/iss3/5.

Thiselton, Anthony C. *The Holy Spirit: In Biblical Teaching, through the Centuries, and Today.* Grand Rapids, MI: Eerdmans, 2013.

———. *A Shorter Guide to the Holy Spirit: Bible, Doctrine, Experience.* Grand Rapids, MI: Eerdmans, 2016.

Thomas, Norman E. "Coke, Thomas (1747–1814)." In *Biographical Dictionary of Christian Missions,* edited by Gerald H. Anderson, 143. New York: Macmillan Reference USA, 1998. Online. http://www.bu.edu/missiology/missionary-biography/c-d/coke-thomas-1747-1814.

Thorsen, Donald. *The Wesleyan Quadrilateral: Scripture, Tradition, Reason, & Experience as a Model of Evangelical Theology.* Lexington, KY: Emeth, 2005.

Throness, Laurie. *A Protestant Purgatory: Theological Origins of the Penitentiary Act, 1779.* Hampshire, UK: Ashgate, 2016.

Tigert, Jno. J. *A Constitutional History of American Episcopal Methodism.* Nashville: MECS, 1908.

Tillotson, John. *Works of the Most Reverend Dr. John Tillotson, Late Lord Archbishop of Canterbury.* Vol. 2. Edinburgh: Ruddiman, 1772.

Tindal, Matthew. *Christianity as Old as the Creation: Or, the Gospel a Republication of the Religion of Nature.* Vol. 1. London: n.p., 1730.

Tinker, Elmira. "The Drama of Life." *Universalist Watchman,* August 20, 1812, 4.

Tipple, Ezra Squier. *Freeborn Garrettson.* New York: Eaton & Mains, 1910.

Tocqueville, Alexis D. *Democracy in America.* Vol. 1. Translated by Henry Reeve. London: Saunders and Otley, 1835.

Toland, John. *Christianity Not Mysterious: Or, a Treatise Showing, That There Is Nothing in the Gospel Contrary to Reason, nor above It, and That No Christian Doctrine Can Be Properly Call'd a Mystery.* 2nd ed. London: Sam Buckley, 1696.

———. *Tetradymus.* Vol. 1. London: J. Brotherton and W. Meadows in Cornhill, J. Roberts in Warwick-Lane. W. Meres without Temple-Bar, W. Chetwood in Covent-Garden, S. Chapman in Pall-Mall, and J. Graves in St. James's Street, 1720.

Tomkins, Stephen. *John Wesley: A Biography.* Brooklyn, NY: Lion, 2003.

Tooley, Mark. "Africans May Outnumber US United Methodists in Eight Years." *Juicy Ecumenism* (blog), November 18, 2013. Online. https://juicyecumenism.com/2013/11/18/africans-may-outnumber-u-s-united-methodists-in-8-years.

Towers, Frank. "African Union Methodism." In vol. 1 of *Encyclopedia of African American History, 1619–1895: From the Colonial Period to the Age of Frederick Douglass,* edited by Paul Finkelman, 44–46. 3 vols. Oxford: Oxford University Press, 2006.

Towns, Elmer L. *The Ten Most Influential Churches of the Past Century: How They Impact You Today.* Shippensburg, PA: Destiny Image, 2014.

———. *What's Right with the Church: A Manifesto of Hope.* Ventura, CA: Gospel Light, 2009.

Travis, Joseph. *Autobiography of the Rev. Joseph Travis, AM: A Member of the Memphis Annual Conference: Embracing a Succinct History of the Methodist Episcopal*

Church, South: Particularly in Part of Western Virginia, the Carolinas, Georgia, Alabama, and Mississippi: With Short Memoirs of Several Local Preachers, and an Address to His Friends. Edited by Thomas O. Summers. Nashville: MECS, 1856.

——. The Nature, Folly, Sin, and Danger of Being Righteous Over-Much; With a Particular View to the Doctrines and Practices of Certain Modern Enthusiasts. Being the Substance of Four Discourses Lately Preached in the Parish-Churches of Christ-Church, and St. Lawrence Jewry, London; and St. Martin's in the Fields, Westminster. London: S. Austen, at the Angel and Bible in St. Paul's Church-yard; L. Gilliver and J. Clarke, at Homer's-Head in Fleet-Street, 1740.

Tribble, Scott. A Colossal Hoax: The Giant from Cardiff That Fooled America. Lanham, MD: Rowman & Littlefield, 2009.

Trickler, C. Jack. A Layman's Guide To: Why Are There So Many Christian Denominations? Bloomington, IN: AuthorHouse, 2012.

Turnbull, R. D. Reviving the Heart: The Story of the Eighteenth-Century Revival. Oxford: Lion Hudson, 2012.

Turner, Henry McNeal. The Genius and Theory of Methodist Polity: Or, the Machinery of Methodism, Practically Illustrated through a Series of Questions and Answers. Philadelphia: AME Church, 1885.

Turner, John G. Brigham Young: Pioneer Prophet. Cambridge, MA: Belknap Harvard, 2012.

Turner, Michael K. "'Redeeming the Time': The Making of Early American Methodism." PhD diss., Vanderbilt University, 2009. Online. https://etd.library.vanderbilt.edu/ available/etd-03242009-143318/unrestricted/TurnerDissertation.pdf.

——. "Revivalism and Preaching." In The Cambridge Companion to American Methodism, edited by Jason E. Vickers, 119–37. Cambridge: Cambridge University Press, 2013.

Tyra, Gary. Defeating Pharisaism: Recovering Jesus' Disciple-Making Method. Downers Grove, IL: InterVarsity, 2009.

Unger, Merrill F. What Demons Can Do to Saints. Chicago: Moody, 1977.

The United Methodist Church (UMC). The Book of Discipline of The United Methodist Church 2016. Nashville: United Methodist, 2016. Kindle ed.

——. The Book of Resolutions of The United Methodist Church 2016. Nashville, TN: United Methodist, 2016.

——. "Guidelines: The UMC and the Charismatic Movement." Dec 19, 2008. Online. https://www.umc.org/en/content/guidelines-the-umc-and-the-charismatic-movement.

——. Methodist History. Vol. 35. Nashville: Commission on Archives and History, UMC, 1996.

——. Minutes of the West Michigan Annual Conference of the United Methodist Church. Vol. 36.2. Detroit: Conference, 1983.

Urban, Sylvanus, ed. The Gentleman's Magazine and Historical Chronicle. Vol. 36. London: D. Henry and E. Cave, 1766.

VanderSchel, Kevin M. Embedded Grace: Christ, History, and the Reign of God in Schleiermacher's Dogmatics. Minneapolis, MN: Fortress, 2013.

Ventrella, Francesco. "Enthusiasm." Parallax 17.2 (2011) 1–7. doi:10.1080/13534645. 2011.55935.

Vickers, Jason E. "Introduction & American Methodism: A Theological Tradition." In *The Cambridge Companion to American Methodism*, edited by Jason E. Vickers, 1–44. Cambridge: Cambridge University Press, 2013.

Vickers, John A. "British Methodism." In *Historical Dictionary of Methodism*, edited by Charles Yrigoyen and Susan E. Warrick, 56–58. 2nd ed. Historical Dictionaries of Religions, Philosophies, and Movements Series. Lanham, MD: Scarecrow, 2005.

———. *Thomas Coke: Apostle of Methodism.* Eugene, OR: Wipf & Stock, 2013.

Visala, Aku. *Naturalism, Theism and the Cognitive Study of Religion: Religion Explained?* Routledge Science and Religion Series. London: Routledge, 2016.

Volo, James M., and Dorothy D. Volo. *Family Life in Nineteenth-Century America.* Santa Barbara, CA: Greenwood, 2007.

Voltaire. *Voltaire in His Letters: Being a Selection from His Correspondence.* Translated by S. G. Tallentyre. London: Putnam's Sons, 1919.

Vu, Michelle A. "Survey: Supernatural Experiences Common Among America's Religious." *Christian Post*, September 21, 2008. Online. http://www.christianpost.com/news/survey-supernatural-experiences-common-among-america-s-religious-34406.

W., C. R. "The Dying Testimony of John Wesley on the Subject of Slavery." *Universalist Watchman*, April 22, 1813, 2.

Wakeley, J. B. *The Heroes of Methodism: Containing Sketches of Eminent Methodist Ministers, and Characteristic Anecdotes of their Personal History.* New York: Carlton & Porter, 1857.

Wakeley, J. B., and Henry Boehm. *The Patriarch of One Hundred Years: Being Reminiscences, Historical and Biographical, of Rev. Henry Boehm.* New York: Nelson & Phillips, 1875.

Walker, Aidan. *The Ecology of the Soul: A Manual of Peace, Power and Personal Growth for Real People in the Real World.* Alresford, UK: John Hunt, 2016.

Walker, Melissa, et al., eds. *Southern Women at the Millennium: A Historical Perspective.* Columbia: University of Missouri Press, 2003.

Walker, Williston. *A History of the Christian Church.* New York: Scribner's Sons, 1919.

Wallace, Adam. *The Parson of the Islands: A Biography of the Late Rev. Joshua Thomas: With Sketches of Many of His Contemporaries and an Account of the Origin of Methodism on the Islands of the Chesapeake and Eastern Shores of Maryland and Virginia.* Philadelphia: Office of the Methodist Home Journal, 1872.

Wallace, J. Warner. *Cold-Case Christianity: A Homicide Detective Investigates the Claims of the Gospels.* Colorado Springs, CO: David C. Cook, 2013.

———. *God's Crime Scene: A Cold-Case Detective Examines the Evidence for a Divinely Created Universe.* Colorado Springs, CO: David C. Cook, 2015.

Waller, Ralph. *John Wesley: A Personal Portrait.* New York: Continuum, 2003.

Ward, W. R. *The Protestant Evangelical Awakening.* Cambridge: Cambridge University Press, 2002.

Ware, Bruce A. *Father, Son, and Holy Spirit: Relationships, Roles, and Relevance.* Wheaton, IL: Crossway, 2005.

Ware, Thomas. *Sketches of the Life and Travels of Rev. Thomas Ware, Who Has Been an Itinerant Methodist Preacher for More Than Fifty Years.* New York: G. Lane & P. P. Sandford, 1842.

Warfield, Benjamin Breckinridge. *Counterfeit Miracles.* New York: Scribner's, 1918.

Warkulwiz, Victor P. *A Compendium of the Doctrines of Genesis 1–11*. Norderstedt, Germany: Books on Demand, 2012.

Warner, Laceye. *The Method of Our Mission: United Methodist Polity and Organization*. Nashville: Abingdon, 2014.

———. "Towards a Wesleyan Evangelism." *Methodist History* 40.4 (2002) 230–45. Online. http://hdl.handle.net/10516/6545.

Warrington, Keith. *Pentecostal Theology: A Theology of Encounter*. London: T&T Clark, 2008.

"Was John Wesley the Founder of American Methodism?" *The Methodist Review* 51 (1891) 609–33.

Washington, Henry A. *Letters From the Wilderness*. Maitland, FL: Xulon, 2006.

Watson, David Lowes. *The Early Methodist Class Meeting: Its Origin and Significance*. Eugene, OR: Wipf & Stock, 2002.

Watson, Kevin. *The Class Meeting: Reclaiming a Forgotten (and Essential) Small Group Experience*. Franklin, TN: Seedbed, 2013.

———. *Pursuing Social Holiness: The Band Meeting in Wesley's Thought and Popular Methodist Practice*. New York: Oxford University Press, 2015.

Watters, Dennis Alonzo. *First American Itinerant of Methodism, William Watters*. Cincinnati: Curtis & Jennings, 1898.

Watters, Philip Melancthon. *Peter Cartwright*. New York: Eaton & Mains, 1910.

Watters, William. *A Short Account of the Christian Experience and Ministereal Labours, of William Watters*. Alexandria, VA: S. Snowden, 1806.

Weatherly, Lionel A., and John N. Maskelyne. *The Supernatural?* Cambridge: Cambridge University Press, 2011.

Webber, Robert. *The Divine Embrace: Recovering the Passionate Spiritual Life*. Grand Rapids, MI: Baker, 2008.

———. *Methodism and the Miraculous: John Wesley's Idea of the Supernatural and the Identification of Methodists in the Eighteenth-Century*. Lexington, KY: Emeth, 2012.

———. "'Those Distracting Terrors of the Enemy': Demonic Possession and Exorcism in the Thought of John Wesley." *Bulletin of the John Rylands Library* 85.2 (2003) 373–85. doi:10.7227/bjrl.85.2-3.24.

"Wednesday, May 3 (Announcements)." *Nashville Whig*, May 3, 1820, 3.

Wells, Joshua. "Recollections of Mrs. Mary Todd Hinde." *The Methodist Magazine and Quarterly Review* 13 (1831) 121–31.

Wentz, Richard E. *American Religious Traditions: The Shaping of Religion in the United States with CD-ROM*. Minneapolis, MN: Fortress, 2003.

Wesley Covenant Association. *A Firm Foundation: Hope and Vision for a New Methodist Future*. Franklin, TN: Seedbed, 2017.

Wesley, John. *The Experience of Several Eminent Methodist Preachers: With an Account of Their Call to and Success in the Ministry. In a Series of Letters Written by Themselves, to the Rev. John Wesley*. New York: Mason and Lane, 1837.

———. *Explanatory Notes Upon the New Testament*. 2nd ed. London: W. Bowyer, 1757.

———. *A Farther Appeal to Men of Reason and Religion: Parts 1–3*. London: W. Strahan, 1745.

———. *John Wesley and Modern Wesleyanism*. Hayle: Banfield Brothers, 1873.

———. *Journal from September 13, 1773, to October 24, 1790*. Vol. 4 of *Works of John Wesley*. Grand Rapids, MI: Zondervan, 1872.

———. *The Journal of the Rev. John Wesley.* Vol. 1. London: J. Kershaw, 1827.

———. *The Journal of the Rev. John Wesley, AM.* Vol. 1. 1906. Reprint, New York: J. M. Dent, 1913.

———. *The Journal of the Reverend John Wesley.* Vol. 2. New York: Mason and Lane, 1837.

———. "Letter to Arthur Bedford, London, September 28, 1738." *Wesley Center Online.* Online. http://wesley.nnu.edu/john-wesley/the-letters-of-john-wesley/wesleys-letters-1738.

———. *A Letter to the Right Reverend the Lord Bishop of Gloucester: Occasioned by His Tract, On the Office and Operations of the Holy Spirit.* Bristol: William Pine, 1763.

———. *The Letters of the Rev. John Wesley.* Vol. 6. London: Epworth, 1960.

———. *Miscellaneous.* Vol. 6 of *The Works of the Rev. John Wesley, AM.* New York: Carlton & Porter, 1831.

———. *Sermons on Several Occasions.* Edited by John Emory. Vol. 1. New York: Emory and Waugh, 1829.

———. *Sermons on Several Occasions.* Edited by Thomas Jackson. London: Tegg & Son, 1832.

———. *Sermons on Several Occasions, with a Brief Memoir by Samuel Drew.* Vol. 1. London: Caxton, 1825.

———. *The Works of the Rev. John Wesley.* Vols. 1, 4, 5, 7, 13. London: John Mason; New York: J. & J. Harper; Carlton and Porter, 1826–1941.

———. *The Works of the Rev. John Wesley, AM.* Vol. 12. London: John Mason, 1830.

———. *The Works of the Reverend John Wesley, AM.* Vols. 2, 3, 5, 7. New York: Waugh and Mason, 1831–1835.

Wesley, John, and Augustine Birrell. *Letters of John Wesley.* London: Hodder and Stoughton, 1915.

Wesley, John, and Thomas Coke. *Letters of the Rev. John Wesley, MA, and the Rev. T. Coke, LLD.* 2nd ed. Baltimore: D. Brunner, 1844.

Wesleyan Methodist Connection (or Church) of America. *Discipline of the Wesleyan Methodist Connection (or Church) of America.* Syracuse, NY: W. W. Hall, Agent, 1896.

Westerkamp, Marilyn J. *Women in Early American Religion, 1600–1850.* London: Routledge, 2005.

Wheatherfield, S. S. "Rise and Progress of the Methodist Episcopal Church." *Weekly Raleigh Register,* March 21, 1811, 4.

Whedon, D. D. "Methodism in the Cities of the United States." *Methodist Quarterly Review* 59 (1877) 485–507.

Whiston, William. *A New Theory of the Earth: From Its Original, to the Consummation of All Things. Wherein the Creation of the World in Six Days, the Universal Deluge, and the General Conflagration, as Laid Down in the Holy Scriptures Are Shewn to Be Perfectly Agreeable to Reason and Philosophy. With a Large Introductory Discourse Concerning the Genuine Nature, Stile, and Extent of the Mosaick History of the Creation.* London: Printed for Sam. Tooke and Benj. Motte, at the Middle-Temple-Gate in Fleet Street, 1708.

Whitby, Daniel. "An Extract with Dr. Whitby's Discourses on the Five Points: Of Sufficient and Effectual, Common and Special Grace." *The Arminian Magazine* 10 (1787) 57–61.

White, J. "The Infortunate." *Newcastle Weekly Courant,* July 16, 1743, 3.

Whitefield, George. "Letter CCL (Sept 25, 1764; To the Rev. J. Wesley from the Rev. Mr. Whitefield)." *The Arminian Magazine* 5 (1782) 439–40.

Whitehead, John. *The Life of the Rev. John Wesley, MA: Some Time Fellow of Lincoln College, Oxford. Collected from His Private Papers and Printed Works, and Written at the Request of His Executors, to Which Is Prefixed Some Account of His Ancestors and Relations, with the Life of the Rev. Charles Wesley, Collected from His Private Journal, and Never before Published, the Whole Forming a History of Methodism, in Which the Principles and Economy of the Methodists Are Unfolded.* Auburn: J. E. Beardsley, 1793.

———. *The Life of the Rev. John Wesley, MA, to Which Is Prefixed, Some Account of His Ancestors and Relation to Which Is Subjoined an Appendix.* 2 vols. Dublin: John Jones, 1805.

Wigger, John H. *American Saint: Francis Asbury and the Methodists.* New York: Oxford University Press, 2009.

———. "Holy, 'Knock-'Em-Down' Preachers." *Christian History* 45 (1995). Online. https://www.christianitytoday.com/history/issues/issue-45/holy-knock-em-down-preachers.html.

———. *Taking Heaven by Storm: Methodism and the Rise of Popular Christianity in America.* New York: Oxford University Press, 1998.

Wildman, Wesley. "Rudolf Bultmann (1884–1976)." *Boston Collaborative Encyclopedia of Western Theology.* Online. http://people.bu.edu/wwildman/bce/mwt_themes_760_bultmann.htm.

Williams, Jarvis J. *Christ Died for Our Sins: Representation and Substitution in Romans and Their Jewish Martyrological Background.* Eugene, OR: Wipf & Stock, 2015.

Williams, Jeffrey. *Religion and Violence in Early American Methodism: Taking the Kingdom by Force.* Bloomington: Indiana University Press, 2010.

Williams, William Henry. *The Garden of American Methodism: The Delmarva Peninsula, 1769–1820.* Wilmington, DE: Scholarly Resources, 1984.

Williams, William R. "The Wesleys and Peter Bohler." *The Wesleyan-Methodist Magazine* 14 (1868) 616–24.

"Williamsburg, January 22." *Virginia Gazette,* January 22, 1767, 2. Online. https://www.newspapers.com/newspage/40443540.

Williamson, D. "Occasional Sermon." *Universalist Watchman,* October 8, 1812, 1–2.

Willimon, William H. *United Methodist Beliefs: A Brief Introduction.* Louisville, KY: Westminster John Knox, 2007.

Winslow, Forbes, ed. *Journal of Psychological Medicine and Mental Pathology* 12. London: John Churchill, 1859.

Winzeler, Robert L. *Anthropology and Religion: What We Know, Think, and Question.* Lanham, MD: AltaMira, 2008.

Withrow, William Henry. *Barbara Heck, a Tale of Early Methodism.* New York: Cranston & Curts, 1895.

Wokler, Robert. *Rousseau, the Age of Enlightenment, and Their Legacies.* Princeton, NJ: Princeton University Press, 2012.

Wood, Laurence W. *The Meaning of Pentecost in Early Methodism: Rediscovering John Fletcher as Wesley's Vindicator and Designated Successor.* Lanham, MD: Scarecrow, 2002.

Woodburn, James A., ed. *Indiana Magazine of History.* Vols. 17–18. Bloomington, IN: Department of History, Indiana University, 1921.

Wright, Richard M. *Stop the Church's Revolving Door Building Relationships with Church Members*. Bloomington, IN: West Bow, 2011.

Wuthnow, Robert. *Experimentation in American Religion: The New Mysticisms and Their Implications for the Churches*. Berkeley: University of California Press, 1978.

Yeager, Michael H. *God Still Heals: Doc's (63) Testimonies of Healings*. Scotts Valley, CA: CreateSpace, 2016.

Young, Dan. *Autobiography of Dan Young: A New England Preacher of the Olden Time*. Edited by W. P. Strickland. New York: Carlton & Porter, 1860.

Young, David. *The Origin and History of Methodism in Wales and the Borders*. London: C. H. Kelly, 1893.

Young, Jacob. *Autobiography of a Pioneer: Or, the Nativity, Experience, Travels, and Ministerial Labors of Rev. Jacob Young, with Incidents, Observations, and Reflections*. Cincinnati: L. Swormstedt & A. Poe, 1857.

Zion's Home Monthly. Salt Lake City, UT: Zion's Home Monthly, 1888.

Zucca, Lorenzo. *A Secular Europe: Law and Religion in the European Constitutional Landscape*. Oxford: Oxford University Press, 2013.

Index